Review of the Convention on Contracts for the International Sale of Goods (CISG) 2003-2004

Review of the Convention on Contracts for the International Sale of Goods (CISG) 2003-2004

edited by
Pace International Law Review

Sellier. European Law Publishers

ISBN-10 3-935808-29-1
ISBN-13 978-3-935808-29-3

Die Deutsche Bibliothek verzeichnet diese Publikation in der Deutschen Nationalbibliografie; detaillierte bibliografische Daten sind im Internet über http://dnb.ddb.de abrufbar.

Gestaltung: Sandra Sellier, München. Herstellung: Karina Hack, München. Satz: Federer & Krauß GmbH, Augsburg. Druck und Bindung: Pustet, Regensburg. Gedruckt auf säurefreiem, alterungsbeständigem Papier. Printed in Germany

Table of Contents

Part III
Case Commentaries

Part I
Articles

CISG and Mistake: Uniform Law vs. Domestic Law
The Interpretative Challenge of Mistake and the Validity Loophole

*Patrick C. Leyens**

---

* LL.M. (University of London); Research Assistant, Max Planck Institute for Foreign Private and Private International Law, Hamburg, Germany; leyens@mpipriv-hh.mpg.de. This paper was awarded a third place in the Clive M. Schmitthoff Essay Competition 2002, an annual competition jointly announced by the Institute of International Commercial Law, Pace University School of Law and the Centre for Commercial Law Studies, Queen Mary University of London; //www.cisg.law.pace.edu/cisg/text/essay.html. The paper has been slightly revised for publication. I would like to express my special thanks to Albert H. Kritzer, Michael Halberstam and Ross G. Anderson for their valuable comments. I am also indebted to Loukas A. Mistelis for valuable discussions and encouragement. Errors of fact or law are of course mine.

I. Introduction

Scholars have enthusiastically proclaimed the success of the United Nations Convention on Contracts for the International Sale of Goods, Vienna 1980 (CISG).[1] Some have gone so far as to divide the world of international trade into "Vienna and Non-Vienna" legal structures, speaking of a "bifocal world"[2] of international trade.[3] As of August 2003, 62 States have ratified the CISG –

[1] United Nations Convention on Contracts for the International Sale of Goods, April 11, 1980, S. Treaty Doc. No. 98-9 (1984), 1489 U.N.T.S. 3, *reprinted in* United Nations Conference on Contracts for the International Sale of Goods, 19 I.L.M. 668 (1980) [hereinafter CISG]. The text of the CISG is available in several languages at http://www.cisg.law.pace.edu and at http://www.unidroit.org.
The encomium that was lavished on the CISG ("quantum leap," "new legal lingua franca," "a milestone," "a triumph of co-operative legal work," "arguably the greatest legal achievement aimed at harmonizing private commercial law") is summarized by Kevin Bell, *The Sphere of Application of the Vienna Convention on Contracts for the International Sale of Goods*, 8 PACE INT'L L. REV. 237 (1996), *available at* http://www.cisg.law.pace.edu/cisg/biblio/bell.html.

including the United States and Germany.[4] The impressive development of the CISG has, at least for the time being, left behind the question whether harmonization of the law of contracts for the international sale of goods is politically desirable or economically useful.[5]

---

2 Michael G. Bridge, *The Bifocal World of International Sales: Vienna and Non-Vienna, in* MAKING COMMERCIAL LAW – ESSAYS IN HONOR OF ROY GOODE 277 (Ross Cranston, ed., 1997) [hereinafter *Bifocal World*].

3 On current trends in international trade compare the contributions by scholars from all over the world to the three-day Clive M. Schmitthoff Symposium held in London, June 2000, *reprinted in* FOUNDATIONS AND PERSPECTIVES OF INTERNATIONAL TRADE LAW (Ian Fletcher et al. eds., London 2001) [hereinafter FOUNDATIONS]. *See* COMMERCIAL AND CONSUMER LAW – NATIONAL AND INTERNATIONAL LAW (Ross Cranston & Roy Goode, eds., Oxford 1993) [hereinafter COMMERCIAL AND CONSUMER LAW]; THE UNIFICATION OF INTERNATIONAL COMMERCIAL LAW, TILBURG LECTURES, (Franco Ferrari, ed., 1998); NEW DEVELOPMENTS IN INTERNATIONAL COMMERCIAL AND CONSUMER LAW, (Ziegel & Lerner eds., 1998) [hereinafter NEW DEVELOPMENTS]. For earlier contributions see the Symposium, *United Nations Convention on Contracts for the International Sale of Goods*, 21 CORNELL INT'L L. J. 419 (1988) and INTERNATIONAL SALE OF GOODS – DUBROVNIK LECTURES (Peter Šarčević & Paul Volken eds., Oceana Publications 1986) [hereinafter DUBROVNIK LECTURES].

4 The United States in 1988; Germany in 1991. For the status of UNCITRAL Conventions and Model Laws, see *Status on UNICTRAL Convention and Model Laws – United Nations, available at* http://www.jus.uio.no/im/un.conventions.membership.status.doc (last visited Feb. 2, 2004).

5 On harmonization see Loukas Mistelis, *Is Harmonisation a Necessary Evil, The Future of Harmonisation and New Sources of International Trade Law, in* FOUNDATIONS, *supra* note 3, at 3-42 (in particular para. 1-025, at 12). For further critical remarks see Michael Joachim Bonell, *Do We Need a Global Commercial Code?*, 106 DICK. L. REV. 87 (2001), *available at* http://www.cisg.law.pace.edu/cisg/biblio/bonell1.html (last visited Jan. 25, 2004) (He argues for an interplay between an "integrated body of rules" and "more flexible instruments." *Id.* at 100); Roy Goode, *Reflections on the Harmonisation of Commercial Law, in* COMMERCIAL AND CONSUMER LAW, *supra* note 3, at 3 ("good conventions and bad conventions" *Id.* at 25); Arthur Rosett, *Unification, Harmonization, Restatement, Codification, and Reform in International Commercial Law*, 40 AM. J. COMP. L. 683, 687 (1992) ("limits of unification by codification"); Paul B. Stephan, *The Futility of Unification and Harmonization in International Commercial Law*, Working Paper No. 99-10 1 (June 1999) *available at* http://www.ssrn.com/sol3/delivery.cfm/99070752.pdf?abstractid=169209 (last visited Feb. 2, 2004) (He makes the distinction between the issues of harmonization: "Managing Legal Risk", "Improving the Law", "Developing intermediaries." *Id.* at 4. Stephan doubts that past unifications have improved the law. *Id.* at 39.).

According to *Ernst Rabel*, the "grandfather" of the CISG, the merits of an international uniform sales law must be measured by the extent to which it removes important contractual issues from the domestic and into the international realm. *Rabel's* monograph of 1936, "*Das Recht des Warenkaufs*"[6] [The law of the sale of goods],[7] is seen as the basis of today's CISG. *Rabel* was the founding director of the Max Planck Institute for Foreign Private and Private International Law in Hamburg, Germany.[8] One of his successors, *Hein Kötz*, questioned his ambitious claim – as well as the enthusiasm on the part of some scholars about the ostensible success of the CISG – and suggested that on closer inspection:

> The question appears justified (to ask) whether uniform law, in as far as it intends to simplify law, does not find itself in the position of Heracles who cut off Hydra's snake head only to be confronted with three new ones instead.[9]

This statement indicates that the development of the CISG and the preservation of its internationalist goals is an important task for courts[10] and also for commentators[11] and scholars.[12] The doctrine of mistake is one of the issues *Kötz* may have had

---

6 ERNST RABEL, DAS RECHT DES WARENKAUFS, Vol I (1936), reprint 1957, Vol. II (1988).

7 Translation by the author.

8 The Max Planck Institute [hereinafter MPI] started work on April 1, 1926 in Berlin, Germany. Since 1956 it has been seated in Hamburg. *See* Max Planck Institute for Foreign and Private International Law, *available at* http://www.mpipriv-hh.mpg.de. Prof. Rabel was director from 1926 to 1937.

9 The statement is cited from Hein Kötz, *Rechtsvereinheitlichung – Nutzen, Kosten, Methoden, Ziele*, 50 RABELSZ 1, 7 (1986). Prof. Kötz was director at the MPI from 1979 to 2000. For further critical remarks on harmonization by Prof. Kötz see the compilation by Ulrich Magnus, *General Principles of UN-Sales Law*, 3 INT'L TRADE & BUS. L. ANN. 33 (1997) *available at* http://www.cisg.law.pace.edu. For example, "The person looking at the currently effective Uniform Law from a certain distance will be surprised by its selective and fragmentary nature," and "(i)ndeed it's a scary thought that the countless current undertakings of unifying and adjusting laws develop into completed texts and that the stream of these texts could then be directed to the already overburdened mills of national legislators."

10 Twenty Years of International Sales Law Under the CISG: the UN Convention on Contracts for the International Sale of Goods: International Bibliography and Case Law Digest (1980-2000) (Will ed., The Hague 2000).

11 A 'COMMENTARY ON THE COMMENTARIES' IS PROVIDED BY ALBERT KRITZER, GUIDE TO PRACTICAL APPLICATIONS OF THE UN CONVENTION ON CONTRACTS FOR THE INTERNATIONAL SALE OF GOODS, (1989) [hereinafter Practical Applications]. The leading commentaries are in English and German:
In English: COMMENTARY ON THE INTERNATIONAL SALES LAW – THE 1980 VIENNA SALES CONVENTION (C. M. Bianca et al. eds., 1987) [hereinafter Bianca-Commentary]; Fritz

in mind when making this statement.[13] It will be shown that a case of mistake reveals a number of uncertainties, ambiguities and irregularities of the CISG.[14] The CISG is silent on the question of mistake, but its article 4(a) excludes matters of the validity of the contract from its scope. Thus, the interpretative challenge is to

---

Enderlein & Dietrich Maskow, INTERNATIONAL SALES LAW (Oceana Publications 1992), *available at* http://www.cisg.law.pace.edu; JOHN O. HONNOLD, UNIFORM LAW FOR INTERNATIONAL SALES UNDER THE 1980 UNITED NATIONS CONVENTION (Kluwer Law Int'l, 3d ed., 1999) [hereinafter Uniform Law]; JOHN O. HONNOLD, DOCUMENTARY HISTORY OF THE UNIFORM LAW FOR INTERNATIONAL SALES (1989) [hereinafter Documentary History]; COMMENTARY ON THE UN CONVENTION ON THE INTERNATIONAL SALE OF GOODS (CISG) (Peter Schlechtriem ed., Clarendon Press, 2d ed., 1998).

In German: ROLF HERBER & BEATE CZERWENKA, INTERNATIONALES KAUFRECHT (Beck 1991); KOMMENTAR ZUM UN-KAUFRECHT (Honsell ed., Springer 1997) [hereinafter HONSELL-KOMMENTAR]; Staudinger Kommentar zum Bürgerlichen Gesetzbuch mit Einführungsgesetzen und Nebengesetzen: Wiener UN-Kaufrecht (CISG) (Martinek ed., Sellier/de Gruyter 1999) [hereinafter Staudinger-Kommentar]; KOMMENTAR ZUM EINHEITLICHEN UN-KAUFRECHT – CISG (Peter Schlechtriem ed., Beck, 3d ed. 2000) (for a translation of the 2d ed. see *supra* this note) [hereinafter Schlechtriem-Kommentar]; WOLFGANG WITZ, HANNS-CHRISTIAN SALGER & MANUEL LORENZ, INTERNATIONAL EINHEITLICHES KAUFRECHT – KOMMENTAR (Verlag Recht und Wirtschaft 2000) [hereinafter Kaufrecht].

12 References to scholarly writings from all over the world are provided online by the Pace University School of Law, Institute of International Commercial Law, New York, *available at* http://www.cisg.law.pace.edu. For a selection in alphabetical order of countries see:

Africa: South Africa (not contracting): Sieg Eiselen, *Adoption of the Vienna Convention for the International Sale of Goods (the CISG) in South Africa*, 116 S. AFR. L.J., Part II, 323 (1996), *available at* http://www.cisg.law.pace.edu/cisg/biblio/eiselen.html. OHADA-States: Ulrich G. Schroeter, *Das einheitliche Kaufrecht der afrikanischen OHADA-Staaten im Vergleich zum UN-Kaufrecht*, RECHT IN AFRICA 163 (2001) (comparison to uniform sales law of the African OHADA-States).

Austria: Martin Karollus, *Judicial Interpretation and Application of the CISG in Germany 1988-1994*, CORNELL REV. OF THE CISG 51 (1995), *available at* http://www.cisg.law.pace.edu/cisg/biblio/karollus.html.

Germany: Peter Schlechtriem, *Uniform Sales Law – The Experience with Uniform Sales Laws in the Federal Republic of Germany*, *in* JURIDISK TIDSKRIFT 1 (1991-92), *available at* http://www.cisg.law.pace.edu/cisg/biblio/schlech2.html [hereinafter *The Experience*].

Italy: Franco Ferrari, *Applying the CISG in a Truly Uniform Manner: Tribunale di Vigevano*, (Italy) 12 July 2000, UNIF. L. REV. 203 (2001), *available at* http://www.cisg.law.pace.edu/cisg/biblio/ferrari4.html [hereinafter *Applying the CISG*].

United Kingdom (not contracting) (All authors cited here with critical remarks on the reluctance of the United Kingdom in not ratifying the CISG): Bridge, *Bifocal World*, *supra* note 2, at 277-296; Anette Gärtner, *Britain and the CISG: The Case for Ratification – A Comparative Analysis with Special Reference to German Law*, PACE REV. OF THE CISG 59

ascertain whether a case of mistake raises a question of validity that comes under CISG article 4(a).

Unfortunately, there is little case law on the doctrine of mistake. This is due to several reasons. First, businessmen will often be willing and able to find a friendly settlement within their contractual relationship if a mistake becomes apparent. Secondly, modern contract drafting often provides for confidential dispute resolution.[15] Thirdly, amicable settlements are often reached during the proceedings – be it in litigation or arbitration.

(2000-2001), *available at* http://www.cisg.law.pace.edu/cisg/biblio/gartner.html; A.F.M. Maniruzzaman, *Formation of International Sales Contracts: a Comparative Perspective*, 29 INT.'L BUS. LAW. 483, 489 (2001), *available at* http://www.ibanet.org; Barry Nicholas, *The United Kingdom and the Vienna Convention: Another Case of Splendid Isolation? Rome: Centro di Studi e Ricerche di Diritto Comparato e Straniero* (1993), *available at* http://soi.cnr.it/~crdcs/crdcs/nicholas.htm; Alison E. Williams, *Forecasting the Potential Impact of the Vienna Sales Convention on International Sales Law in the United Kingdom*, PACE REV. OF THE CISG 9 (2000-01), *available at* http://www.cisg.law.pace.edu/cisg/biblio/williams.html.
United States: Susanne Cook, The U.N. Convention on Contracts for the International Sale of Goods: A Mandate to Abandon Legal Ethnocentricity, 16 J.L. & COM. 257 (1997), *available at* http://www.cisg.law.pace.edu/cisg/biblio/1cook.html.

13 On mistake and the CISG: (U.S.) Helen E. Hartnell, *Rousing the Sleeping Dog: The Validity Exception to the Convention on Contracts for the International Sale of Goods*, 18 YALE J. INT'L L. 1, 72 (1993), *available at* www.cisg.law.pace.edu/cisg/biblio/hartnell.html; (U.S.) Todd Weitzmann, *Validity and Excuse in the U.N. Sales Convention*, 16 J.L. & COM. 265 (1997), *available at* http://www.cisg.law.pace.edu/cisg/biblio/1weitzm.html; (Switzerland) Christopher R. Heiz, *Validity of Contracts Under the United Nations Convention on Contracts for the International Sale of Goods, April 11, 1980, and Swiss Contract Law*, 20 VAND. J. TRANSNAT'L L., 639, at 642; (Germany) Peter Huber, *UN-Kaufrecht und Irrtumsanfechtung*, ZEuP 585 (1994); (Austria) Rudolf Lessiak, *UNCITRAL-Kaufrechtsabkommen und Irrtumsanfechtung*, ÖJBl. 487 (1989); (France) Friedrick Niggemann, *Error about a Substantial Quality of the Goods*, INT'L. BUS. L.J. 27 (1988).
A comprehensive comparative analysis of the implications of mistake is provided by Timothy Hoff, *Error in the Formation of Contracts in Lousiana: A Comparative Analysis*, 53 TUL. L. REV. 329 (1978-79). For an introduction see KONRAD ZWEIGERT & HEIN KÖTZ, INTRODUCTION TO COMPARATIVE LAW 410 (Oxford 3d ed., 1998), with further references.

14 Alejandro Garro, *Reconciliation of Legal Traditions in the U.N. Convention on CISG*, 23 INT'L LAW. 443 (1989), *available at* http://www.cisg.law.pace.edu/cisg/biblio/garro1.html, explores the irregularities and compromises between the legal systems. *See also* Weitzmann, *supra* note 13, para. III.

15 Michael R. Will, *UN-Kaufrecht und internationale Schiedsgerichtsbarkeit*, *in* RUDOLF MEYER ZUM ABSCHIED: DIALOG DEUTSCHLAND-SCHWEIZ VII, 145 (Michael R. Will ed., 1999), *available at* http://www.cisg/law.pace.edu/cisg/biblio/will4.html. Will estimates that only

The core question for a tribunal that is confronted with a case that involves a mistake, is whether domestic remedies which allow a contract to be avoided are applicable. Some have argued, perhaps simplistically, that the CISG does not govern questions of mistake, fraud, and duress and hence find that domestic remedies are applicable.[16] It is true that all three issues involve a defect of intention. But does this indicate that mistake should receive the same treatment as fraud and duress? The tension between the CISG and avoidance[17] under domestic law becomes abundantly clear in cases that involve a mistake in regard to the quality of the goods. The CISG provides a damage-based remedial scheme for cases where the seller delivers goods that do not conform with the terms of the contract. Therefore, it has been argued, it would be an undue circumvention of the CISG if the buyer could avoid the contract on the basis of a domestic remedy. In recognition of this tension between the CISG and domestic laws, the discussion about mistake has partly shifted. Today, the prevailing view seems to be that mistake, fraud and duress cannot be treated equally. A number of scholars argue that cases involving a mistake in regard to a quality of the goods do not raise issues of validity; hence, they conclude that domestic remedies are precluded.

As for a theoretical basis, the view has been put forth that we should distinguish according to the specific facts that provoked the mistake.[18] It was suggested that we ask: "mistake about what?"[19] The rule to be derived from this question would be to exclude domestic law for all those cases whose facts are addressed by the CISG. This would suggest applying the CISG exclusively to questions of non-conformity of goods, thus denying the right of the buyer in such cases to avoid the contract by

---

one seventh of the disputes arising under the CISG are settled by arbitration. He highlights though, that arbitrations regularly involve much higher amounts than cases brought before a state court.

16 *See e.g.* for example, Joseph Lookofsky, *In Dubio Pro Conventione? Some Thoughts About Opt-Outs, Computer Programs and Preemption Under the 1980 Vienna Sales Convention (CISG)*, 13 DUKE J. COMP. & INT'L L. 263, 280 (2003), *available at* http://www.law.duke.edu, who states, "Since the CISG is generally not concerned with validity, most problems which fall under this heading – like, e.g., fraud, duress, mistake or the reasonableness of contract terms – must be resolved in accordance with domestic rules of law".

17 Avoidance means "subject to nullification."

18 Michael J. Bonell & Fabio Liguori, *The U.N. Convention on the International Sale of Goods: A Critical Analysis of Current International Case Law 1997* (Part 1), UNIF. L. REV. 385 (1997), *available at* http://www.cisg.law.pace.edu/cisg/biblio/libo1.html, who give an overview of case law that illustrates that the label "validity" is vague as it allows a number of different classifications. *See also* HONNOLD, UNIFORM LAW, supra note 11, at art. 35, para. 240.

19 KRITZER, PRACTICAL APPLICATIONS, *supra* note 11, at 90 (referring to HONNOLD, UNIFORM LAW, *supra* note 11, at 97). The differentiating approach of Honnold was followed by Heiz, *supra* note 13.

claiming mistake. Such a rule would be a second step forward on the way to an internationalist interpretation of the CISG. It does, however, lead back to the question of how to correctly interpret the validity exception of CISG article 4(a). This question will be a major focus of the paper.

This paper seeks to ascertain whether the different approaches to the validity exception provide a theory consistent for cases of mistake. Section II will try to highlight the conceptual issues in the doctrine of mistake. Section III will turn to the CISG's rules of interpretation and discuss the approaches to mistake presented so far. On that basis, section IV analyses selected cases of mistake. To what extent are the questions settled by case precedent? To what extent does scholarly writing guide the decision-making by a court where case precedent has not yet settled the question? The final conclusion under section IV will evaluate whether Kötz' provoking picture of Heracles' fight against the snake-headed Hydra is justified.

II. The Doctrine of Mistake

The drafting history of the CISG impressively demonstrates a progressive attempt to achieve a meaningful unification of the law on international sales transactions.[20] The need and willingness to develop a body of universally acceptable rules involved a complicated struggle for compromise between different legal systems from all over the world. It has been argued that the finally adopted text contains a number of ambiguities and, to some extent, embodies an illusory compromise.[21] Is the CISG's failure to explicitly deal with the doctrine of mistake an example of such an illusory compromise? The discussion of selected cases of mistake (below section IV) will show that some remedies of the CISG operate on the same facts as those domestic remedies that allow the contract to be avoided on the basis of a mistake.[22] In order to provide a basis for further analysis we should examine the conceptual issues raised by a case of mistake.

---

20 The drafting history will be examined in more detail *infra*, section III (B).

21 Eörsi has described a hierarchy of compromises embodied in the text of the CISG, with "clear and recognizable compromises" on the top, and a compromise which "mask(s) continuing disagreement" on the bottom; for further discussion of Eörsi's view see Garro, *supra* note 14, at 450.

22 Garro, *supra* note 14; Gesa Baron, *Do the UNIDROIT Principles of International Commercial Contracts Form a New Lex Mercatoria?*, *available at* http://www.cisg.law. pace.edu/cisg/biblio/ baron.html.

A. The Conceptual Issues

Two different approaches can be taken to the doctrine of mistake. First, it can be argued that a key element of the contractual agreement is missing if the decision is induced by a mistake. A case of mistake therefore raises a validity question. Secondly, if the mistaken party can nullify the contract he is freed from his obligations. Hence a case of mistake also raises a question of defences for non-performance.[23] From these introductory remarks it can be concluded that mistake is either a question that concerns the stage of contract formation (is the contract valid?) or that concerns the stage of contract performance (is non-performance excused?).

B. The Search for an Internationalist Doctrine of Mistake

Lawyers from different countries each have their own understanding of the doctrine of mistake.[24] What is generally accepted is that mistake is a defect of intention (error in motive) or a defective expression of a correctly formed intention (error in expression).[25] The consequences, however, differ from country to country.

An objective of the CISG is to provide rules that are functionally equivalent to the domestic sales laws of member states from all over the world. For an internationalist understanding of the doctrine of mistake it appears most promising to follow this line and to look into the rules that are widely agreed upon and practiced within the international commercial community: the "law merchant" or the "lex mercatoria."[26]

---

23 Weitzmann, *supra* note 13, para III.

24 ZWEIGERT, *supra* note 13, at 413-430, which provides an introduction to the different legal families and undertakes to state a few common principles for the resolution of cases of mistake.

25 *Id.* at 411.

26 Uriel Procaccia, *The Case Against Lex Mercatoria*, *in* NEW DEVELOPMENTS, *supra* note 3, at 87-88, tries to "rationalise ancient ancestor's rebellion" against *lex merctoria*. *See* Baron, *supra* note 22, para. (II)(3) – (4); Klaus Peter Berger, *The relationship between the UNIDROIT Principles of International Commercial Contracts and the new lex mercatoria*, UNIF. L. REV. 153 (2000); HANS VAN HOUTTE, THE LAW OF INTERNATIONAL TRADE, para. 1.33 (1995); Roy Goode, *Usage and its Reception in Transnational Commercial Law*, *in* NEW DEVELOPMENTS, *supra* note 3.

It has been argued that the UNIDROIT Principles of International Commercial Contracts 1994[27] provide a restatement of the *lex mercatoria*.[28] It must be noted that the UNIDROIT Principles are not directly governed by the CISG unless they are incorporated into a particular contract as a body of rules supplementing the terms of the contract and supplementing the CISG as the law applicable to the contract.[29] CISG article 7(2), however, provides that matters not expressly governed by CISG are to be settled in conformity with the principles on which it is based.[30] Since both the CISG and the UNIDROIT Principles follow the same idea, the UNIDROIT Principles can be referred to as an interpretative source under CISG article 7(2).

C. The Doctrine of Mistake under the UNIDROIT Principles

Article 3.4 of the UNIDROIT Principles defines mistake as "an erroneous assumption relating to facts or to law existing when the contract was concluded."[31] This definition contains three elements. The first and very basic element is "erroneous assumption" that, by virtue of article 3.6, is explicitly broadened to include "an error occurring in the expression or transmission of a declaration."[32] It thus covers both a mistake in motive and a mistake in expression. Second, the erroneous assumption may be related "to facts or to law." Third, the element of time ("when the contract was concluded") renders irrelevant a mistake that arose before the intention is expressed. The same applies to a mistake that arises subsequent to the conclusion of the contract.[33]

---

27 *See* http://www.unilex.info [hereinafter UNIDROIT Principles].

28 *See* Jürgen Basedow, *Uniform law Conventions and the Unidroit Principles of International Commercial Contracts*, UNIF. L. REV. 129, 137 (2000), who highlights the UNIDROIT Principles as a supplementing force. MICHAEL BRIDGE, THE INTERNATIONAL SALE OF GOODS (1999), para. 2.25 suggests that "(i)n determining the meaning of validity, it may be of some assistance to turn to the UNIDROIT Principles." *See* Baron, *supra* note 22, para. (III)(3); Michael Joachim Bonell, *The UNIDROIT Principles of International Commercial Contracts and the Harmonisation of International Sales Law*, *in* FOUNDATIONS, *supra* note 3, at 309, para. 21-005. For a very detailed analysis compare FABIAN BURKART, INTERPRETATIVES ZUSAMMENWIRKEN VON CISG UND UNIDROIT PRINCIPLES, (Nomos Verlagsgesellschaft 2002).

29 *See* UNIDROIT Principles, *supra* note 27, Preamble; *see* Baron, *supra* note 22, para. (III)(1)(a).

30 BURKART, *supra* note 28, at 209.

31 UNIDROIT Principles, *supra* note 27, art. 3.4.

32 Unidroit Principles, *supra* note 27, art. 3.6.

33 In some civil law countries the irrelevance of a mistake that arises at the stage when a person forms his intention goes back to Savigny and is laid down, for example, in the German Civil Code (Bürgerliches Gesetzbuch) § 119(1). It should be remarked, that German law makes

Article 3.5(1) of the UNIDROIT Principles provides that a mistake has material effect only where it is "of such importance that a reasonable person in the same situation as the party would not have concluded the contract if the true state of affairs had been known."[34] As a consequence of a mistake that is of such importance, the mistaken party may nullify the contract by declaring it void.

The UNIDROIT Principles thus clearly reflect the approach that classifies mistake as a validity question. It is an approach reinforced by UNIDROIT Principles in article 3.7. It explicitly provides that the remedy of avoidance on grounds of mistake must not be used as an alternative remedy where the other party fails to perform.[35] By according primacy to the remedies for breach of contract in cases of conflict, the UNIDROIT Principles prevent mistake being used as a defence to non-performance.[36]

The rule in UNIDROIT Principles article 3.3 gives further support. The rules states that the validity of the contract is not affected if the performance of the obligation was impossible from the outset or if the party was not entitled to dispose of the assets to which the contract relates.[37] Thus, these typical cases of initial impossibility are expressly classified as non-validity issues. This implies that they are also removed from the scope of the provisions on mistake. A party cannot, therefore, claim

---

an exception under § 119(2) for cases where the mistake relates to a material quality of the goods or to a material characteristic of a person involved into the contract. *See* ZWEIGERT, *supra* note 13, at 413 for a comparative analysis.

34 UNIDROIT Principles, *supra* note 27, art. 3.5(1). Further requirements are set out in subparagraphs (a) and (b); but these are not relevant to the present discussion.

35 The UNIDROIT Principles and the CISG each have their own terminology. Whilst the UNIDROIT Principles regard any failure to perform as "non-performance" (UNIDROIT Principles, *supra* note 27, art. 7.1.1), under the CISG the general term is "breach of contract" (CISG, *supra* note 1, heading to Section III). Further, CISG article 49 distinguishes between "non-performance" and "any other form of breach." CISG, *supra* note 1, art. 49.

36 The Commentary on the UNIDROIT Principles, http://www.unidroit.org/english/principles/contracts/principles1994/fulltext.pdf, art. 3.7, para. 1, states:

> (t)his article is intended to resolve the conflict which may arise between the remedy of avoidance for mistake and the remedies for non-performance. In the event of such a conflict, *preference is given to the remedies for non-performance since they seem to be better suited and are more flexible than the radical solution of avoidance*.
> (emphasis added).

37 UNIDROIT Principles, *supra* note 27, art. 3.3 (initial impossibility) reads as follows:

> (1) The mere fact that at the time of the conclusion of the contract the performance of the obligation assumed was impossible does not affect the validity of the contract. (2) The mere fact that at the time of the conclusion of the contract a party was not entitled to dispose of the assets to which the contract relates does not affect the validity of the contract.

avoidance on the grounds that he was mistaken as to the ability of either party to perform.

The UNIDROIT Principles further suggest a distinct treatment of the different types of defects in intention. According to UNIDROIT Principles article 3.19, the rules on fraud and threats are mandatory while those on mistake (and initial impossibility) are not. This distinction illustrates the hierarchical order of the different defects of intention.[38] Mistake is on the bottom, fraud in the middle and duress on the top for the simple reason that at the top of this hierarchy more detailed rules are required to protect the fundamental principle of freedom of intention.[39]

In conclusion, it can be stated that the approach suggested under the UNIDROIT Principles does not rely on a single classification applicable to all cases of defective intention. Hence, support is given to those who ask "mistake about what?"[40]

III. Mistake under the CISG

The discussion of a case of mistake under CISG focuses on the so-called validity exception as set out by CISG article 4(a).

A. The Validity Exception

The provision of CISG article 4(a) gives a negative and a positive rule. The negative rule it provides is that the CISG is not concerned with "the validity of the contract or of any of its provisions or of any usage."[41] The positive rule it provides states that this applies "except as otherwise expressly provided in this Conven-

38 *See* ZWEIGERT, *supra* note 13, at 429. Note that the issues of mistake, fraud and duress are classified as defects of intention by all continental legal systems. This does not, however, imply an equal treatment nor does it imply that all cases come under the validity exception of CISG article 4(a).

39 Harry M. Flechtner, *More U.S. Decisions on the U.N. Sales Convention: Scope, Parol Evidence, "Validity" and Reduction of Price Under Article 50*, 14 J.L. & COM. 153, *available at* http://www.cisg.law.pace.edu/cisg/biblio/flechtner.html, sec.(I)(D); Heiz, *supra* note 13, at 653-654; Weitzmann, *supra* note 13, para. III; ZWEIGERT, *supra* note 13, at 424.

40 *See* the references *supra* note 19.

41 CISG, *supra* note 1, art. 4(a).

tion."[42] Hence, the scope of the negative rule is limited by the positive one. According to this structure we have to apply a twofold test if we want to find out whether the CISG applies to a case that involves a mistake: first, it has to be decided whether mistake is classified as a validity issue. If so, it secondly has to be examined whether it is governed by "expressly provided" rules of the CISG. This seems to be a simple rule. Alas, as we will see in the following sections, the simplicity is deceptive.[43]

I. The Interpretative Challenge

A case that involves a mistake is a challenge for the interpretation of the CISG. The core problem concerns the question of how to determine "validity" under CISG article 4(a) or – in other words – whether the CISG treats mistake as a validity issue.

It has correctly been argued that it would be an "analytical short-cut" to simply equate the meaning of validity with the issues listed in Chapter 3 of the UNIDROIT Principles.[44] CISG article 4(a) is a provision that promotes elasticity. As we will see in more detail below the CISG drafters did not have in mind a fixed set of validity issues. It should also be noted that the CISG was developed by UNCITRAL and not by UNIDROIT. Further, the UNIDROIT Principles were drafted long after the CISG had been adopted.

As we cannot simply look into the UNIDROIT Principles or into any other set of principles for the scope of the "validity" exception, we have only two options left; we can either argue that domestic law is responsible for the determination of validity, or we can argue for an internationalist understanding that would be based on the rules of the CISG.

If we look exclusively to domestic law for the answer of this question, we will face a problem that perhaps is best illustrated by the example of a mistake in regard to the conformity of goods. For example, Austrian law would allow avoidance of the contract if a mistake could be proven; while, under German law, a damage-based remedial scheme comparable to that of the CISG is applicable. Under Austrian law we therefore could argue that a mistake in regard to the conformity of goods is a validity issue, while under German law we could not. The consequence would be that a mistaken party in one country, for example in Austria, could nullify the contract while in another country, for example Germany, the party would be restricted to the remedies provided under the CISG. With regard to the goal of the

---

42 Id.

43 *See* Hartnell, *supra* note 13, who speaks of "rousing [a] sleeping dog."

44 *Id.* at 40.

CISG to provide a uniform remedial scheme for all contracting states, particularly in the field of breach of warranty, this result looks strange.

If we therefore look to the CISG for the determination of whether the case is one of validity, we will find that under its articles, the CISG provides a damage-based remedial scheme for cases where the goods do not conform. From this we could conclude that the issue is not one of validity. Recourse to a domestic remedy that operates on the facts of a mistake in regard to the quality of the goods would thus be precluded.

To sum up, the first interpretative challenge is to decide *how* to determine whether a case involves a validity issue; should this be characterised according to domestic law or according to an internationalist understanding? This challenge must be faced; otherwise, it will be unclear whether domestic remedies are pre-empted by the operation of the remedies of the CISG or whether they compete.[45] The question, "preemption or competition of uniform and domestic remedies?" is one of the core issues in the struggle for a correct understanding of the interplay between the CISG and domestic laws. The problem does not only arise in regard to mistake and validity issues. It also comes up in cases where the claimant tries to employ, for example, national tort remedies that go beyond what he can claim under the CISG.[46]

It should be noted that the whole problem only arises where there is a conflict between domestic law and the CISG, i.e. where domestic law provides for nullity in a case which the CISG would treat in terms of its uniform remedial scheme. The issue can be further articulated against the background of time limits set by the CISG, if one party has lost his damage based remedies under the CISG due to a failure to give timely notice (CISG article 39), he will likely try to rely on a domestic remedy whose time limits go beyond that of the CISG. As the examples show, the conflict between the uniform remedial scheme of the CISG and domestic nullification remedies can easily arise in an area very central for harmonization

[45] On preëmption/competition see Lookofsky, *supra* note 16, at 279; Ulrich Huber, *in* SCHLECHTRIEM-KOMMENTAR, *supra* note 11, art. 45, para. 46.

[46] Domestic claims in tort were held applicable by the United States Federal District Court, New York on May 10, 2002 in *Geneva Pharmaceuticals Tech. Corp. v. Barr Labs. Inc.*, 201 F. Supp. 2d 236 (S.D.N.Y. 2002), *available at* http://www.cisg.law.pace.edu/cisg/wais/db/cases2/020510u1.html, with subsequent motion proceeding on August 21, 2002, *Geneva Pharmaceuticals Tech. Corp. v. Barr Labs. Inc.*, No. 99 Civ. 3607 RWS, 2002 WL 1933881 (S.D.N.Y. 2002), *available at* http://www.cisg.law.pace.edu/cisg/wais/db/cases2/020821u1.html. On the issues of the case see Joseph Lookofsky, *CISG Case Commentary on Preemption in Geneva Pharmaceuticals*, October 2003, *at* http://www.cisg.law.pace.edu/cisg/biblio/lookofsky8.html.

effect of the CISG. Other types of mistake where a conflict rule is needed will be discussed below under the heading "selected types of mistake."

From this brief introduction into the issues of the interpretation of CISG article 4(a), in cases of mistake it is not surprising that two diametrically opposed approaches to CISG article 4(a) have developed.[47] According to the first, domestic law is exclusively responsible for the determination of validity.[48] This approach emphasizes the negative rule of CISG article 4(a) ("not concerned with"). According to the second approach, the CISG has an autonomous – if admittedly incomplete – concept of validity. The rules of CISG are seen as *leges speciales* as far as they provide functionally adequate solutions. This approach focuses on the positive rule of CISG article 4(a) ("expressly provided").[49]

2. Methods of Interpretation

Before I turn to a detailed analysis of the different approaches to CISG article 4(a), the methods of interpretation must be further explored. The CISG is a treaty that provides substantive law. In a country that adopted the CISG, a national court must apply the uniform law to all cases the state parties intended to submit to the scope of the CISG when ratifying it. Accordingly, as a first step we must interpret CISG article 4(a) in light of the drafting history.[50] This rule of interpretation is taken up

---

47 KRITZER, PRACTICAL APPLICATIONS, *supra* note 11, at 87 (Kritzer has compiled the different scholarly responses in an explanatory table).

48 *See* Franz Bydlinski, *Das allgemeine Vertragsrecht*, *in* DAS UNCITRAL-KAUFRECHT IM VERGLEICH ZUM ÖSTERREICHISCHEN RECHT 57, 85-90 (Peter Doralt ed., 1985); Hartnell, *supra* note 13, at 72; Lessiak, *supra* note 13, at 491. It should be noted that Hartnell and Lessiak, although consistent in their findings about mistake, come to different conclusions on other validity issues.

49 HONNOLD, UNIFORM LAW, *supra* note 11, art. 4, para. 65, and art. 35, para. 240; ENDERLEIN, *supra* note 11, art. 4, para. 3.1; Franco Ferrari, *in* SCHLECHTRIEM-KOMMENTAR, *supra* note 11, art. 4, para. 22, at 97; ENDERLEIN, *supra* note 11, art. 4, para. 3.1; Heiz, *supra* note 13, at 661; KRITZER, PRACTICAL APPLICATIONS, *supra* note 11, at 87; Ulrich Magnus, *in* STAUDINGER-KOMMENTAR, *supra* note 11, art. 4. para. 27; Peter Schlechtriem, *Uniform Sales Law: The UN-Convention on Contracts for the International Sale of Goods*, 32 (Manz 1986), *available at* http://www.cisg.law.pace.edu/cisg/biblio/schlechtriem.html [hereinafter *The UN-Convention*]; PETER SCHLECHTRIEM, INTERNATIONALES UN-KAUFRECHT, 42 para. 36 (1996).

50 For minor doubts see Camilla Baasch Andersen, *Reasonable Time in Article 39(1) of the CISG – Is article 39(1) Truly a Uniform Provision?*, PACE REV. OF THE CISG 63 (1999), *available at* http://www.cisg.law.pace.edu, para. I 2.1.2. She finds that the importance of the drafting

by articles 31 and 32 of the Convention on the Law of Treaties (Vienna 1969)[51] but as matter of principle also applies to the interpretation of the CISG where the Convention on the Law of Treaties has not been ratified.[52] As a second step the autonomous rules of interpretation that are embodied in CISG article 7 apply.[53]

The hierarchy between both strands of interpretation is apparent. If the analysis of the drafting history leads to the result that the state parties intended to exclude cases of mistake from the CISG there would be no room for the autonomous rules of interpretation of the CISG.[54]

B. The Drafting History of the CISG

According to the hierarchy of the two strands of interpretation the drafting history has to be examined first.

---

history is "uncertain" as some of the ratifying countries have legal systems which do not prioritize a historical interpretation.

51 Convention on the Law of Treaties, May 23, 1969, 1155 U.N.T.S. 331, 8 I.L.M. 679. HONNOLD, UNIFORM LAW, *supra* note 11, art. 7, para. 103, alluding to the interpretative rules of the Convention on the Law of Treaties (Vienna 1969), which support the suggested consultation of the *travaux préparatoires*. In article 31 the general interpretative rule is that a "treaty shall be interpreted in good faith in accordance with the ordinary meaning to be given to the terms of the treaty in their context and in the light of its object and purpose." Further, article 32 provides that:

> recourse may be had to supplementary means of interpretation including the preparatory work of the treaty and the circumstances of its conclusion, in order to confirm the meaning resulting from the application of article 31, or to determine the meaning when the interpretation according to article 31: (a) leaves the meaning ambiguous or obscure; or (b) leads to a result which is manifestly absurd or unreasonable.

Hartnell, *supra* note 13, para. III B, concludes that "by the same logic [as employed by *Honnold* the] interpretative rules should also apply to article 4(a), since this provision implies mutual obligations of the Contracting States to apply the provisions of the Convention only to cases which properly fall within its scope." *See also* Franco Ferrari, *in* SCHLECHTRIEM-KOMMENTAR, *supra* note 11, *Vorbemerkungen zu Art. 1-6 (Intro. to Arts. 1-6)*, para 29.

52 Franco Ferrari, *in* SCHLECHTRIEM-KOMMENTAR, *supra* note 11, art. 7, paras. 6, 11.

53 HONNOLD, UNIFORM LAW, *supra* note 11, art. 7, para. 103.2, at 161.

54 Hartnell, *supra* note 13, at 76, where the author states "simple logic suggests that where there is no consensus to unify, there is no unification."

I. Introduction

The drafting history of the CISG dates back to 1935 when a preliminary draft for a uniform law on international sales was issued by UNIDROIT.[55] Work was suspended during the Second World War. Parallel efforts were made to develop a uniform law exclusively on issues relating to the formation of contract. In 1964 the Diplomatic Conference finalized two conventions, the Uniform Law for the International Sales of Goods (ULIS) and the Uniform Law on the Formation of Contracts for the International Sale of Goods (ULF).[56] In 1972 both conventions came into force and were ratified by five states, mainly from Europe. Shortly after it became clear that due to their strong orientation on Western legal culture ULIS and ULF would not be attractive to countries in other parts of the world and that they would not lead to level of harmonisation that would facilitate international sales transactions.

Already in 1968, the first session of the United Nations Commission on International Trade Law (UNCITRAL) was held. In contrast to the drafting of the two conventions of 1964, the focus was not restricted to Western European legal culture. The Working Group was a cross-section of UNCITRAL's worldwide representation. Its task was to prepare a text that would facilitate "acceptance by countries of different legal, social and economic systems."[57] The decision was made to formulate a single convention governing both, sales and contract formation, which were until then divided by ULIS (sales) and by ULF (contract formation). The 1978 draft of the Convention on Contracts for the International Sale of Goods (CISG) was approved by the United Nations. Part two of the CISG on the "Formation of the Contract" is inspired by ULF. Part three of the CISG on the "Sale of Goods" – governing the rights and obligations of the parties to the contract – is based on the ULIS. In 1980 the Diplomatic Conference now representing 62 states met in Vienna and finalized the text of CISG. The subsequent ratification pace was fast, and today a total of 62 states, i.e. a number identical to the number of member states at the Diplomatic Conference, have ratified the CISG.

---

55 For details *see* Honnold, Documentary History, *supra* note 11; documents of the drafting history *available at* http://www.cisg.law.pace.edu. For brief introductions see the commentaries *supra* note 11; *See* Hartnell, *supra* note 13. A detailed analysis is provided by Ulrich Huber, *Der UNCITRAL-Entwurf eines Übereinkommens über internationale Warenkaufverträge*, 43 RabelsZ 413 (1979).

56 Uniform Law on the International Sale of Goods, July 1, 1964, 834 U.N.T.S. 107 (1972) [hereinafter ULIS], and Uniform Law on the Formation of CISG, July 1, 1964, 834 U.N.T.S. 169 (1972) [hereinafter ULF]. The texts of ULIS and ULF are *available at* http://www.lexmercatoria.org.

57 Honnold, Uniform Law, *supra* note 11, para 9, at 20.

It has been argued that for the interpretation of CISG according to its drafting history we should not only look to the actual forerunners ULIS and the ULF but also to a harmonization project called Draft Law for the Harmonization of Certain Rules Relating to the Validity of Contracts of International Sale of Goods (LUV).[58] The LUV was developed by UNIDROIT parallel to the drafting of the CISG by UNCITRAL. Issues of mistake, fraud and duress were a central focus of its rules. The drafters of the CISG discussed the rules of the LUV but finally rejected to include them. After the analysis of the role that ULIS and ULF played in the CISG, we will see what the rejection of the rules of LUV means for the interpretation of the CISG.

2. ULIS

The 1956 and 1963 ULIS drafts gave an explicit conflict rule for the application of the uniform remedial scheme where a domestic mistake-based remedy operates on the same facts: ULIS article 41 provided that if the seller does not deliver goods in conformity with the contract "the rights conferred upon the buyer (…) exclude all other remedies upon which he might otherwise have relied, and in particular those based on *mistake*."[59] The ongoing debate between internationalists and delegates who sought to preserve domestic rules finally led to a compromise. Under the 1964 ULIS, the exclusion of domestic remedies was modified and restricted to cases involving non-conforming goods. ULIS article 34 (renumbered) provided that "the rights conferred upon the buyer (…) exclude all other remedies based on lack of conformity of the goods."[60] The view prevailed that although the specific reference to mistake was deleted, domestic remedies that are applicable to cases of mistake would be precluded under the ULIS.[61] During the deliberations on the CISG the adoption of a provision resembling ULIS article 34 was discussed but finally rejected. Some argue that the mere fact of non-adoption of ULIS article 34 is sufficient to draw the conclusion that, in a case of mistake, domestic remedies are applicable alongside the CISG.[62]

This conclusion seems somewhat simplistic. This is evident from a close inspection of the drafting process of CISG. One of the main reasons for not adopting ULIS

---

58 Text *available at* http://www.lexmercatoria.org [hereinafter LUV]. *See* Hartnell, *supra* note 13, at 37.

59 Draft Uniform Law on the International Sale of Goods, U.N. Doc. V/Prep./1 (1956) and U.N. Doc. V/Prep./4 (1963)(emphasis added).

60 Uniform Law on the International Sale of Goods (1964), art. 34, *available at* http://www.jus.uio.no/lm/unidroit.ulis.convention.1964.

61 Hartnell, *supra* note 13, at 73, providing further references.

62 Lessiak, *supra* note 13, at 490; Hartnell, *supra* note 13, at 73. For opposition compare Heiz, *supra* note 13, at 649.

article 34 was that the Working Group found that its rule went too far. The drafters feared that the exclusion would also apply to remedies for mistake that are explicitly or implicitly agreed to by the parties.[63] Thus, the underlying idea of the non-inclusion of ULIS article 34 was to honor party autonomy and leave open the issue of a conflict between domestic and uniform remedies. Even more importantly, perhaps, the CISG differs from ULIS insofar as it was sought to formulate a convention reflecting a much wider range of legal systems. Further, the drafters adopted, in CISG article 7, an explicit reference to the unification purposes. The intention was to formulate a body of law that, contrary to ULIS, would be attractive to countries from all over the world and would encourage an evolution of the harmonization process.[64] The request of a Dutch delegate must also be mentioned. He explicitly addressed the issue of the parallel application of uniform and domestic remedies.[65] It is a reflection on the intentions of the drafters to formulate a law as flexible as possible so that his question was left open.[66] So far, the drafting history does not provide a compulsory rule on the applicability of domestic remedies based on mistake alongside the CISG.[67]

However, in the specific forerunner of CISG article 4(a) we find article 11 of the 1939 ULIS draft (finally renumbered article 8). It provided that ULIS "governs the obligations ...arising from a contract which is valid according to the principles of international private law."[68] From a later draft of 1956 until the version finally

---

63 *Report of the Working Group on the International Sale of Goods*, 3d Sess., [1972] III Y.B. 77, 80, U.N. Doc. A/CN.9/62, *reprinted in* HONNOLD, DOCUMENTARY HISTORY, *supra* note 11, at 97, "those remedies [would be excluded] that the parties might have agreed upon in the contract.".

64 *See* CISG art. 7 (1) which will be discussed in detail *infra*, section II(B) (3) (a).

65 *Text of Proposed Amendments, Action by First Committee*, U.N. Doc. C(5), 83, 119 [hereinafter *Text of Proposed Amendments*], *reprinted in* HONNOLD, DOCUMENTARY HISTORY, *supra* note 11, at 691. For the request of the Dutch Delegate, see *24th Meeting of the First Committee*, U.N. Doc. A/CONF.97/C.1/SR.24, *reprinted in* HONNOLD, DOCUMENTARY HISTORY, *supra* note 11, at 582.

66 Text of Proposed Amendments, supra note 65.

67 On one hand see Heiz, *supra* note 13, at 649- 651. *But cf.* Hartnell, *supra* note 13, at 75.

68 Draft of a Uniform Law on the International Sale of Corporeal Movables and Report (Revised Edition), UNIDROIT U.P.L. 1939, Draft 1(2). *See* Hartnell, *supra* note 13, at 26, noting that the validity exception dates back to 1937 when the Government of The Netherlands raised the "question of the relationship between the uniform law and issues derived from the general theory of obligations (such as mistake)." The answer was delivered by Rabel. He emphasized the need for specification of the scope of the uniform law in this field and denied that mistake was governed. Rabel also remarks that his statement has to be considered in the light of the fact that ULIS did not cover formation issues at all. Given that

adopted in 1964, the text closely resembled the current CISG article 4(a) both in structure and in wording.[69] The final version of ULIS article 8 stated that:

> the present law shall not, *except as otherwise expressly provided* therein, be concerned with the formation of the contract, nor with the effect that the contract may have on property in the goods sold, nor with the *validity* of the contract or of any of its provisions or of any usage.[70]

Since Part Two of the CISG governs formation issues, the final version of CISG article 4(a), of course, omits such matters. Otherwise, ULIS article 11 was adopted almost verbatim.[71] During the negotiations prior to adoption, the parties agreed not to deal with validity issues. There was a prevailing fear that such expansion of the discussion could endanger the harmonization project as a whole.[72]

What can we extrapolate from this lack of agreement on the complex field of validity? We have already seen that a mistake – in particular if it relates to the conformity of goods – does not necessarily imply a question of validity. The most convincing conclusion, therefore, is that as a result of a fear on the part of the drafters that since a failure to reach agreement on validity issues could endanger the entire project, it was desirable to simply refrain from providing a *comprehensive* set of rules on validity issues. It is perhaps not surprising, then, that there is no provision for cases of mistake where domestic and uniform remedies are sought to be invoked at the same time.

Numerous proposals were made to exclude ULIS article 8 (draft article 11) from the text of the CISG. One Delegate argued "it was not necessary to [negatively] state what was not covered."[73] He took the view that CISG – unlike ULIS – contained interpretative rules, which he thought, would give sufficient guidance to adjudicators.[74] The drafters finally did not follow his opinion and they adopted

a relevant mistake arises at the time of the conclusion of the contract, i.e. at a stage left out by ULIS, Rabel's statement can be understood as a mere clarification of the scope of ULIS.

69 Draft Uniform Law on the International Sale of Goods, U.N. Doc. V/Prep./1 (1956), art. 12.

70 ULIS, *supra* note 56, art. 8.

71 Franco Ferrari, *in* SCHLECHTRIEM-KOMMENTAR, *supra* note 11, art. 4, para. 1.

72 Hartnell, *supra* note 13, at 25.

73 Report of the Working Group on the International Sale of Goods, 6th Sess. [1975], VI Y.B. 49, 52, U.N. Doc. A/CN.9/100, reprinted *in* HONNOLD, DOCUMENTARY HISTORY, *supra* note 11, at 243. Further see Report of the Secretary General: Recommendations on Pending Questions, VI Y.B. 88, 93, U.N. Doc. A/CN.9/100, Annex III, reprinted *in* HONNOLD, DOCUMENTARY HISTORY, *supra* note 11, at 218: "(I)n the absence of [ULIS] article 8 there seems little likelihood that a reader would suppose that the law dealt with the formation of the contract, or the effect of the contract on the property in the goods sold."

the rule of ULIS article 8 for today's CISG article 4. It seems, however, that the main reason for the adoption was the fear that not adopting it would indicate a departure from the rule of ULIS article 8.

Further, there was a lack of debate in regard to the meaning of "validity" in CISG article 4(a). The delegates did not explore in great detail the difference between issues of validity and contract formation. When we read the authoritative report there is a strong argument that the drafters mainly had in mind mandatory rules that involve an element of public policy. The authoritative report gives the example of unfair terms in a standard form contract. This example is an indication that the drafters intended to create domestic mandatory rules which attempt to preserve an equality of bargaining positions between the parties.[75] The protection of parties with inferior bargaining power is only one example of a public policy matter and a recent decision of a U.S. Federal Court illustrates that it can raise validity issues.[76] Legal concepts might well differ from country to country although the aim of the domestic rules might be identical. Due to the differences in the approaches to matters of public policy, substantive rules on such issues are seldom included in a harmonisation instrument and often an explicit rule explains that the instrument is not applicable to them. A prominent example would be article 16 of the Rome

---

74 *Id.*

75 The Special Commission Report refers to:

> very delicate matters where the traditions of different States would have rendered difficult either the adoption of a uniform law, or, at the least, its uniform interpretation. It follows from this restriction that the [ULIS] does not in any way [affect] the imperative rules of municipal law… [I]t will be for municipal law to provide the legal rules; concerning the validity of certain clauses, as for instance *exemption or partial exemption clauses which can be found especially in standard form contracts*.

(emphasis added); *see* 1956 Special Commission Report on Draft Uniform Law on the International Sale of Goods, U.N. Doc. V/Prep./1, *reprinted in* 2 Diplomatic Conference on the Unification of Law Governing the International Sale of Goods (Documents), The Hague, 2-25 April 1964, at 235 (1966). On standard forms under CISG, see E. Allan Farnsworth, *Review of Standard Forms or Terms under the Vienna Convention*, 21 CORNELL INT.'L L. J. 439, 440-447 (1988), *available at* www.cisg.law.pace.edu/cisg/biblio/farns1.html/.edu.

76 In *Stawski Distributing Co., Inc. v. Zywiec Breweries PLC*, No. 02C8708, 2003 WL 22290412 (N.D. Ill. 2003), *available at* www.cisg.law.pace.edu/cisg/wais/db/cases2/031006u1.html, the court held that the provisions of the Illinois Beer Industry Fair Dealing Act (IBIFDA) were *not* preempted (trumped) by the arguably "conflicting" (avoidance) provisions of the CISG. The IBIFDA limits the right of foreign brewers to terminate contracts with their American buyers. According to Lookofsky, *supra* note 46, one possible rationale is that the court characterized the IBIFDA as a validity-related regime designed to protect wholesalers with arguably inferior bargaining power.

Convention of 1980. It provides that the application of a foreign law can be denied if it is "manifestly incompatible with the public policy of the forum."

The strong interrelation between the validity exception and public policy issues has been described as follows: "[I]ndeed, the purpose of [keeping] the 'validity' exception was to preserve those national rules that embod[y] important social values and which [under national law] could not be waived by the agreement of private parties," i.e., mandatory law.[77] (It should be noted, however, that the concepts of public policy and mandatory law are interrelated but not identical concepts).[78]

What does all this add to the discussion of cases of mistake under the CISG? A first observation would be that public policy concerns are less important in cases of ordinary defects of intention than in cases involving fraud or duress. In cases of fraud and duress it does not need further explanation that public policy requires the legislator to protect the defrauded party by way of mandatory law. The case of mistake is different, as the UNIDROIT Principles illustrate. Article 3.19 states "(t)he provisions of this Chapter [on the validity of the contract] are mandatory, *except insofar as they relate to the binding force of (...) mistake*."[79]

It is not indicated in the drafting history that the drafters intended to exclude a case from the scope of the CISG simply because it could also be addressed by domestic mistake-based remedies. Further, the comparison with the UNIDROIT Principles illustrates that cases of mistake do not necessarily come under a mandatory law concept. In sum, the analysis of the history of the CISG in light of its predecessor ULIS is of little assistance in understanding the interrelation between the CISG and domestic laws in cases of mistake. The only conclusion that can be drawn from the lack of debate is that the drafting history is ambiguous with respect to mistake.

3. LUV

I will now turn to the LUV developed by UNIDROIT. The LUV included a comprehensive set of validity rules, in particular on mistake, fraud and duress. Like

---

77 Harry M. Flechtner, *The Several Texts of the CISG in a Decentralized System: Observations on Translations, Reservations and other Challenges to the Uniformity Principle in article 7(1)*, 17 J.L. & Com. 187, Part II, para. B (1998), *available at* http://www.cisg.law.pace.edu/cisg/biblio/flecht1.html; *see also* Hartnell, *supra* note 13, at 54-55. Further support is given by Schlechtriem, The Experience, *supra* note 12, at 11, *available at* http://www.cisg.law.pace.edu, who states that "(d)omestic law prevails especially when contracts are considered invalid because the underlying sale is immoral or illegal and void according to domestic law."

78 Hartnell, *supra* note 13, at 54-55.

79 UNIDROIT Principles, *supra* note 27, art. 3.19.

the situation under ULIS, recourse to domestic law was precluded where the case involved a lack of conformity.[80] The CISG's Working Group decided not to include the rules of LUV on mistake, fraud and duress. It has been argued that this decision forces us to draw the conclusion that a case of mistake raises a validity issue that is outside the scope of the CISG so that the tribunal may apply the domestic law of mistake.[81]

It is argued here that the non-adoption of the provisions of LUV is not particularly relevant to the question of how to treat a case of mistake under the CISG. The drafters thought that the attempt to unify the law on mistake, fraud and duress could endanger the harmonization project and, in any case, would unduly delay it. Most importantly, they thought that the unification of the validity issues covered by the LUV was not necessary for the success of the CISG. The Secretariat General expressed this view:

> problems of validity covered by LUV rarely arise in the international sale of goods since such contracts are concluded between merchants who are – at least as compared to the average person – relatively sophisticated in matters of contracting. The problems of mistake, fraud and duress – issues at the heart of LUV – are less likely to occur between merchants than they are in transactions between merchants and consumers or between two non-merchants. Even if problems of such kind do occur, they usually [would] be handled as well under non-uniform national law as under any proposed text of uniform law.[82]

This only tells us what we already know from the analysis of the drafter's discussion of the ULIS and the ULF, they did not want to adopt a comprehensive set of rules on the validity issues of mistake, fraud and duress. The decision not to adopt the LUV's comprehensive set of rules, however, does not tell us how to analyse a case of mistake, i.e. a case that involves the lowest level (see above) of defective intention and which invokes the least public policy considerations.

---

80 LUV, *supra* note 58, art. 9 provided that "(t)he buyer shall not be entitled to avoid the contract on the ground of mistake if the circumstances on which he relies entitle him a remedy based on the non-conformity of the goods with the contract."

81 Hartnell, *supra* note 13, at 75.

82 *Secretary-General: Formation and Validity of Contracts* [1977] VIII UNICTRAL Y.B. 90, 92-93, para. 21, U.N. Doc. A/CN.9/128 Annex II, *reprinted in* 8 UNCITRAL Y.B. (1977) 90, 91, U.N. Doc. A/CN.9/SER.A/1977, and HONNOLD, DOCUMENTARY HISTORY, *supra* note 11, 256. For further analysis see Hartnell, *supra* note 13, at 37-38.

4. Summary

The drafting history is ambiguous. The conflict between a domestic and a uniform remedy, that both operate on the same facts – although the subject of much discussion – was ultimately left unresolved.[83] The determination of validity was not explored in great detail. A clear tendency towards preserving the applicability of some domestic rules is apparent; for example, the rules on fraud and duress. The exclusion of validity issues from the unification project was mainly due to the fear that the harmonization process would be endangered or unduly delayed. The adoption of the ambiguous term "validity" and the strong internationalist wording of CISG article 7 point towards the assumption that the drafters sought to balance parochial interests and internationalist unification goals by adopting a flexible and elastic concept. As regrettable as it may be, the drafting history does not tell us whether all cases of mistake come under CISG article 4(a) or whether they are subject to domestic law.

C. The CISG's Autonomous Rules of Interpretation

As the analysis of the drafting history does not provide a compulsory answer to the question of whether mistake is a validity issue, we can apply the interpretative system of the CISG. The autonomous rules of interpretation of the CISG are set out under CISG article 7 and I will start with a brief overview of the three rules contained therein. First, according to CISG article 7(1), in the interpretation of a provision of the CISG, regard is to be had to the unification purposes, the intentions underlying the CISG and to the observance of good faith.[84] Second, if a matter is governed by the CISG, but not explicitly addressed by it, the gap-filling rule of CISG article 7(2) applies. Gap-filling means that the issue is to be resolved on the basis of the general principles underlying the provisions of CISG thus bridging the missing rule.[85] Third, in cases where the preceding steps do not provide an answer, CISG

---

83 Similarly Lookofsky, *supra* note 46 (in particular footnote 8).

84 Franco Ferrari, *in* SCHLECHTRIEM-KOMMENTAR, *supra* note 11, art. 7, paras. 6-7 stating that insofar as the CISG claims observance of the origin of its rules ("international character") and the need to promote uniformity it only resembles a principle common to all international conventions. Concerning, the observance of good faith, however, it sets up a feature particular for CISG to be developed *in common* by the Contracting States.

85 The determination of such general principles can prove to be difficult in practice. *See id.*, para. 34, stating that analogous application of one provision to another is indisputably allowed. The tension, which derives from the limited harmonization intentions of the drafters, must be regarded when applying analogies in borderline issues like mistake. On analogy under CISG *see generally* Gert Brandner, *Admissibility of Analogy in Gap-filling under*

article 7(2) opens the door for the rules of private international law and allows recourse to domestic law.[86]

The interpretative system strongly indicates that it was sought to give as much power to the CISG as possible and it is widely agreed that recourse to domestic law can only be sought as an *ultima ratio*. How does this go together with the validity exception of CISG article 4(a)? Scholars from all over the world have contributed to improving the understanding of the interpretative system of CISG article 7 and its interplay with CISG article 4(a).[87] The following sections will examine the most prominent theories. It will be shown that all of them can be criticised. The important question for this paper, however, will be whether the criticism is pertinent regarding the treatment of mistake under the CISG.

---

the CISG, (Sept. 1999) (LL.M. thesis, University of Aberdeen), *available at* http://www.cisg.law.pace.edu/cisg/biblio/brandner.html.

86 Franco Ferrari, *in* SCHLECHTRIEM-KOMMENTAR, *supra* note 11, art. 7, para. 31.

87 Scholars in alphabetical order of countries: (Australia) John Felemegas, The United Nations Convention on CISG contracts for the International Sale of Goods: article 7 and Uniform Interpretation, Pace University Essay (February 2001), *available at* http://www.cisg.law.pace.edu/cisg/biblio/felemegas.html; (Colombia) Jorge Oviedo Albán, Campo de applicación y criterios de interpretacion de la Convencion de Viena para la Compraventa Internacional de Mercaderias (Comparación la legislación privada colombiana), Facultad de Ciencias Juridicas de la Pontifica Universidad Javeriana (2001), *available at* http://www.cisg.law.pace.edu/cisg/biblio/alban.html; (Croatia) Nives Povrzenic, Interpretation and Gap-Filling under the United Nations Convention on Contracts for the International Sale of Goods, *available at* http://www.cisg.law.pace.edu/cisg/biblio/gap-fill.html; (Germany) BURKART, *supra* note 28; (Germany) Brandner, *supra* note 85; (Spain) Pilar Perales Viscasillas, Una aproximación al artículo 7 de la Convención de Viena de 1980 sobre Compraventa Internacional de Mercaderías (Aplicaciones concretas en la parte II de la Convención), 16 CUADERNOS DE DERECHO Y COMERCIO 55 (1995), *available at* http://www.cisg.law.pace.edu/cisg/biblio/premio3.html; (Switzerland) Paul Volken, *The Vienna Convention: Scope, Interpretation and Gap-filling*, *in* DUBROVNIK LECTURES, *supra* note 3, 19-53, *available at* http://www.cisg.law.pace.edu/cisg/biblio/volken.html; (U.S.) Susanne Cook, *The Need for Uniform Interpretation of the 1980 United Nations Convention on Contracts for the International Sale of Goods*, 50 UNIV. PITT. L. REV. 197 (1988); (U.S.) Albert Kritzer, The Convention on Contracts for the International Sale of Goods: Scope, Interpretation and Resources, CORNELL REV. OF THE CISG 147 (1995), *available at* http://www.cisg.law.pace.edu/cisg/biblio/kritzer.html.

1. Domestic Law Approach

Those few who conclude from the drafting history that validity is determined exclusively by domestic law find that CISG article 7 is inapplicable from the outset.[88] This so-called "domestic law approach" mainly relies on the lack of debate concerning the distinction between validity and contract formation issues.

As shown above the analysis of the drafting history does not support the assumption that CISG article 7 is inapplicable. Therefore the domestic law approach only delivers an incomplete picture. It falls short of the interpretation of CISG article 4(a) in light of the unification goals embodied in CISG article 7.

It cannot be denied that, in fact, the drafters intended to provide a loophole for domestic law by including article 4(a) in the text of CISG.[89] The problem caused by the domestic law approach, however, is that it does not provide a rule that solves the conflict between domestic and uniform remedies. It thus allows parallel availability of the two remedial schemes in cases that under domestic law raise issues of validity but are also addressed by the CISG. This paper argues that such result is undesirable as it leads to unpredictability and deprives the parties of the certainty they expected from (directly or indirectly) subscribing to the uniform rules of the CISG.

The following analysis of the internationalist approaches to CISG article 4(a) will further elaborate on this finding.

2. Autonomous Interpretation

The majority of scholars favor an internationalist approach. Amongst them it is agreed that the rules of interpretation embodied by CISG article 7 do not only apply to the provisions on the formation of contract and on the sale of goods, but also to those within the sphere of the CISG and in particular to article 4(a).[90]

---

88 Bydlinski, *supra* note 48, at 85; E. Allan Farnsworth, *in* Bianca-Commentary, *supra* note 11, at 102; Gyula Eörsi, *in* Bianca-Commentary, *supra* note 11, at 140; Lessiak, *supra* note 13, at 491; Niggemann, *supra* note 13, at 408.

89 Hartnell, *supra* note 13, at 21 (stating that "[t]he drafting history undeniably suggests that the drafters intended article 4(a) to serve as a loophole which could stretch to fit the needs of each domestic legal system").

90 Main proponents: Schlechtriem, *The UN-Convention*, *supra* note 49, at 32; Schlechtriem, Internationales UN-Kaufrecht, *supra* note 49, paras. 36, 42; Honnold, Uniform Law, *supra* note 11, para. 240, at 311. *See, e.g.*, Enderlein, *supra* note 11, art. 4, para. 3.1; Ulrich Magnus, *in* Staudinger-Kommentar, *supra* note 11, art. 4, para. 27.

The mode of application differs. In essence, three different approaches can be discerned.[91] The first method has been described as an "autonomous interpretation" of the CISG.[92] The core thesis being that validity is not by itself a question of domestic law and that CISG article 7(1) calls for a detached characterisation of validity that is committed to the unification purposes of the CISG. This means that one looks first at the CISG in order to see whether it addresses the facts of the case. If the CISG provides a functionally adequate solution, the issue is a non-validity one and domestic remedies are displaced.

Critics argue that the autonomous approach is based on a circular conclusion. If all issues addressed by CISG were to be classified as non-validity issues, a question of validity would never arise under the CISG.[93] Further, if all issues addressed by the CISG were non-validity issues, the "expressly provided" exception of CISG article 4 would be redundant as none of the express provisions of the CISG would classify as an "expressly provided" rule of validity.[94]

Clearly, the most difficult task for the autonomous approach concerns the question of how to autonomously ascertain the meaning of "expressly provided" under CISG article 4(a). There is only one provision that uses the term validity. Under CISG article 55 it is provided that a "validly" concluded contract is not void for the reason that the price has not been fixed by the parties. The drafters further discussed CISG article 11 under the label of (formal) validity.[95] CISG article 11 provides that a contract does not require any formal requirements; in particular the contract need not be in writing. The finally adopted text of the CISG comprehends a number of provisions that – at least in the countries of some delegates – were and still are discussed as validity questions.[96] The interpretation of "expressly provided" as an

---

91 For a detailed overview see Hartnell, *supra* note 13, at 46; Heiz, *supra* note 13, at 647-649.

92 Schlechtriem, *The UN-Convention*, *supra* note 49, at 38.

93 Lessiak, *supra* note 13, at 492.

94 *Id.* at 493.

95 The Secretariat Commentary on the 1978 Draft, *available at* http://cisgw3.law.pace.edu/cisg/text/secomm/secomm-12.html (stating that the "expressly provided"-exception has apparent relevance only for CISG article 12 (now article 11)). This article provides that writing requirements that exist under national laws are insignificant for the (formal) validity of a contract governed by CISG.

96 In his editorial analysis of CISG article 4, Albert Kritzer identifies a minimum of six cross-references: (1) written contract requirement in some states conflicts with CISG article 11 (no form required); (2) validity rules on exclusion or modification of warranties under UCC s. 2-316 conflict with CISG article 8; (3) prohibition of interest in some Islamic states conflicts with CISG article 78 (interest allowed); (4) determinate price requirement in some states conflict with CISG article 55; (5) position of UNIDROIT Principles towards validity questions under CISG and quality of those principles as a cross-reference; (6) the common

exclusive reference to CISG article 11, however, seems a bit odd. If the drafters had intended to exclusively refer to CISG article 11 they could have explicitly referred to it.

It could be argued that "expressly" should be interpreted as a reference to the text of the CISG as a whole.[97] The problem with this interpretation is that CISG article 4 already gives a positive rule on the sphere of its application: "This Convention governs only the formation of the contract of sale..."[98] A reference to the whole text within the same article would not seem illogical but would be redundant. The most convincing reading emphasises the words "*in particular* ... not concerned."[99] It leaves the exceptions of CISG article 4 in a comparable position to regular examples of issues not included.[100]

The difficulties of the autonomous reading in defining the meaning of "expressly provided" cannot be ignored. Nevertheless, it seems somewhat technical to base the criticism of the autonomous approach on these difficulties alone. In concordance with the autonomous approach this paper argues not to analyze the provision word by word but to understand CISG article 4 according to the underlying intentions of the drafters. On one hand, they intended not to override domestic public policy and, on the other, they tried to achieve a compromise.[101]

There are further problems with the autonomous interpretation. The view taken by the autonomous approach is that an issue should be reserved to national law only if it is treated as a question of validity everywhere, i.e. in all or at least in the majority of the world's legal systems. It must be acknowledged that such comparative approach would create certainty and predictability in an ambiguous area of the

---

law doctrine of consideration which is the most prominent example. According to it a contract cannot be changed without consideration. As laid down in article 29(1), the CISG takes the position of civil law and allows contract modification by the mere agreement of the parties. Albert Kritzer, *Cross References and Editorial Analysis: Article 4*, *available at* http://www.cisg.law.pace.edu/cisg/text/cross/cross-4a.html.

97 Also the Secretariat Commentary on article 4, *available at* http://www.cisg.law.pace.edu/cisg/text/secomm/secomm-04.html, suggests a loose interpretation of "expressly provided" and argues for privileging the uniform law should a contradiction between a domestic validity rule and the uniform law come up.

98 CISG, *supra* note 1, art. 4.

99 *Id.* (emphasis added).

100 Franco Ferrari, *in* SCHLECHTRIEM-KOMMENTAR, *supra* note 11, art. 4, para. 3; Ulrich Magnus, *in* STAUDINGER-KOMMENTAR, *supra* note 11, art. 4, para. 4.

101 Warren L. H. Khoo, *in* BIANCA-COMMENTARY, *supra* note 11, at 45 (rating the inclusion of "expressly provided" to be an "abundance of caution"). With skepticism Hartnell, *supra* note 13, at 52 (speaking of a "historical accident").

CISG. The weakness of this method is that the comparative work would lead to a more or less stable list of excluded issues. Such a fixation of the issues would not be consistent with the drafters' intention to achieve flexibility that accommodate the issues of evolving public policy.[102]

The majority view approach, however, appears consistent with the unification purposes illustrated by CISG article 7(1).[103] Moreover, it corresponds to the composition of the Working Group, which was a cross section of representatives from legal systems all over the world. It also accords to the internationalist approach of the Diplomatic Conference that manifests itself in a plenary majority-voting rule. Notwithstanding such consistency it is apparent that adjudicators in practice will have difficulties to comply with the time consuming task of comparative work.[104] Particularly in complex cases that involve public policy issues, a comprehensive comparative analysis will take too much time (if it is not impossible); although, the ongoing development in informational technologies renders some of the relevant information more accessible. However, more work remains to be done.[105]

An even more important criticism against the autonomous interpretation is that its method of interpreting validity can only lead to majority views. The reliance on majority views is not in line with the idea underlying the validity exception, i.e. to preserve singular national interests particularly in regard to issues that involve public policy. According to the comparative law approach employed by the auto-

102 Hartnell, *supra* note 13, at 49.

103 For criticism see Hartnell, *supra* note 13, at 49:

However, while it is an appropriate task for comparative lawyers to strive to compile such a list [of validity issues], it is questionable whether confining article 4(a) only to those issues which are treated as valid 'in all *or at least in the majority* of the world's legal systems' is consistent with the spirit of the [CISG] as a whole, or article 4(a) in particular (emphasis added).

104 Huber, *supra* note 13, at 595. On divergences in the application of the CISG by courts see, DANIELA DE LUKOWICZ, DIVERGENZEN IN DER RECHTSPRECHUNG ZUM CISG – AUF DEM WEG ZU EINER EINHEITLICHEN AUSLEGUNG UND ANWENDUNG? (Verlag Peter Lang 2000), 36 providing empirical data from interviews of judges of the appellate court of Hamburg, Germany). For a detailed analyzis of issues, see HANNO NAUMANN, DER REGELUNGSBEREICH DES UN-KAUFRECHTS IM SPANNUNGSFELD ZWISCHEN EINHEITS-RECHT UND KOLLISIONSRECHT (Verlag Peter Lang 2000) 186.

105 Andersen, *supra* note 50, para. 2.1.3. (giving a brief overview about the accessibility to case law. She acknowledges the progress that was achieved through the availability of databases on the Internet and case law collections provided by CLOUT and UNILEX. She remarks, however, that the progress is of benefit primarily for the legal systems of the United States and Central Europe).

nomous interpretation, matters of public policy can only be taken into account if all or at least a majority of domestic laws take a similar view of them. As the autonomous interpretation does not allow recognition of such singular views – which are subject to a constant process of evolution – it lacks a methodically correct tool for reconciling the public policy changes arising only in one or a few states.[106]

To sum up, the autonomous approach is highly valuable in light of the unification goals of the CISG. The suggestion of a comparative determination of validity, however, poses major practical problems. Further, the autonomous approach is not adequate where matters of public policy are treated differently in the majority of countries.

3. Displacement Theory

According to the so-called displacement theory, domestic remedies are *always* excluded if the CISG provides a solution that operates on the same facts. Proponents speak of "cross-references" of the CISG.[107] Very much like the autonomous approach, the displacement theory employs a functional view. The test is whether the CISG addresses the operative facts that invoke the domestic validity rule. In contrast to the autonomous approach, the displacement reading determines validity from the *outside* of the CISG, i.e. by domestic law. The theory mainly relies on a wide interpretation of "expressly provided."

Support for the displacement reading derives from the drafting history.[108] Akin to the autonomous theory, the displacement reading does not stop the analysis where the label of validity is attached to a case by a domestic law. Instead it emphasises that in drafting the CISG it was sought not to use technical terms but to provide "substance rather than label(s) of law."[109] According to the displacement reading,

---

106 Hartnell, *supra* note 13, at 72-73. *See also* Lookofsky, *supra* note 46.

107 Honnold, Uniform Law, *supra* note 11, para. 69, at 117; *Id.* para. 240, at 318 (where he states that if the CISG addresses the situation in question "the uniform rules should not be displaced merely because of the labels attached to various doctrines of domestic law"). *See also* Hartnell, *supra* note 13, at 50-53; Kritzer, Practical Applications, *supra* note 11, at 91; Ulrich Magnus, *in* Staudinger-Kommentar, *supra* note 11, art. 4, para. 4.

108 The drafting history supports this statement. *See* Secretariat Commentary, Guide to CISG art. 4, para. 2, *available at* http://www.cisg.law.pace.edu/cisg/text/secomm/secomm-04.html, where it is stated:

Although there are no provisions in this Convention which expressly govern the validity of the contract or of any usage, some provisions may provide a rule which would contradict the rules on validity of contracts in a national legal system. In case of conflict the rule in this Convention would apply.

the adjudicating forum applies its own conflict of laws rules for the classification of validity issues. If it is found that under domestic law the case is one of validity, the adjudicator has to reconsider whether the domestic validity rule is displaced by a rule under the CISG that operates on the same facts. Hence, the starting point is a classification under domestic law.

The fact that the determination of validity is left to domestic law, however, "does not open a large door to escape from the uniform rules."[110] Proponents of the displacement reading argue for an extensive interpretation of the text of the CISG.[111] Compared to the autonomous approach it is apparent that the interpretative results will be similar. The method of the displacement reading, however, is much more likely to find support from practitioners than the more complex and costly comparative approach that was suggested by the autonomous reading.[112]

Opponents argue that if domestic law determines validity it is outside of the CISG. In consequence, they argue that CISG article 7(1) is not applicable and that it cannot be employed to underpin an expansive reading of "expressly provided."[113] This criticism of course also applies to the autonomous approach. Proponents of both readings argue that the idea of the "expressly provided" criterion was to close the door for any implicit displacement of national law. Under both the displacement theory and the autonomous approach there is a difficulty in differentiating between implicit and explicit displacement remains.[114] This is mainly due to the fact that the text of the CISG does not contain any rules that expressly use the term "validity." The autonomous and the displacement reading solve conflicts between the reservation embodies in CISG article 4(a) and the

---

109 Michael J. Bonell, *in* Bianca-Commentary, *supra* note 11, at 74 (stating: "(e)ven in the exceptional cases where terms or concepts were employed which are peculiar to a given national law, it was never intended to use them in their traditional meaning"). *See also* Honnold, Uniform Law, *supra* note 11, paras. 65, 240; Kritzer, Practical Applications, *supra* note 11, at 88.

110 Honnold, Uniform Law, *supra* note 11, art. 4, para. 67.

111 *Id.*

112 Andersen, *supra* note 50, para. 2.1.3, (stating that due to the fact that a centre for research and documentation in all branches of the CISG is not yet available, "practitioners will be more prone to refer to international scholars of their own nationality in their own language" to which they will find better access. She continues, "even the judge complying with his duty to apply international precedents will inadvertently apply precedents and theories which are more focused on domestic or similar practice in his interpretation of the terms of the CISG"). *See also supra* note 105.

113 Lessiak, *supra* note 13, at 493.

114 Hartnell, *supra* note 13, at 52 ("implied displacement").

unification goals by privileging the latter. It is argued here that from the wording of CISG article 7(1) this internationalist approach is justified.

Like the autonomous approach the displacement reading, however, embodies a difficult extreme as it requests tribunals to *always* replace domestic remedies where the operative facts are also addressed by the CISG.[115] Therefore, it can also be argued that the displacement reading does not fully resemble the intentions to preserve singular state interests in regard to evolving public policy.[116]

To sum up, the displacement theory accords with the internationalist approach of the CISG. In contrast to the autonomous interpretation it provides a method for the interpretation of validity that is suitable for legal practice. Unfortunately, like the autonomous approach it lacks the flexibility necessary to accommodate the interests of an individual state.

4. Balanced Approach

Some have argued that "the command in Article 7 – to have *regard* to the need to promote uniform Convention interpretation – does not warrant the conclusion that domestic remedies invariably are preempted *(trumped)*, i.e., whenever the *operative facts* of the case seem *covered* by a given CISG rule."[117] This implies that we need a certain flexibility in the interpretation of the validity exception. The problem is to find a rule that gives sufficient legal certainty.

One scholar has suggested a balanced reading of the validity exception.[118] The main objective is to duly capture "the many factors bound up in the validity exception."[119] It promises "to consider domestic validity law in light of evolving concepts of public policy and the development of jurisprudence under the CISG."[120] Hence, it is sought to avoid the main criticism raised against the approaches presented above.

The balanced approach suggests that the adjudicator should, on a case-by-case basis, "ask whether a particular domestic rule of validity meets the spirit as well as the [black] letter" of CISG article 4(a) on one hand; and, on the other, that the domestic rule should be examined "in light of the evolving international commercial context…"[121]

---

115 *See supra* note 11.

116 Hartnell, *supra* note 13, at 53.

117 Lookofsky, *supra* note 46.

118 *Hartnell, supra* note 13, at 60.

119 *Id.* at 53.

120 *Id.* at 53.

The course of decision finding can be summarised as a two-step process: first, the issue is classified under domestic conflict rules. Second, where a conflict arises between domestic and uniform remedies, the *domestic* rule[122] is re-examined in light of the unification purposes of CISG. If the domestic rule conflicts with the internationalist concept it must step back unless the issue is one of those that is left open by the CISG and cannot be bridged by gap-filling under CISG article 7(2).

The second step raises doubts.[123] It seeks to give effect to the CISG beyond its scope. In contrast to those uniform laws, which seek to harmonise rules of private international law, as, for instance, the already cited Rome Convention of 1980, the concept of CISG was to unify substantive law. Apart from setting its sphere of application, the CISG does not touch private international law or modify the domestic doctrines of characterisation of the case. It is therefore difficult to see how the CISG could provide a basis for the suggested method.[124]

D. Conclusion

To conclude, it can be stated that none of the theories are immune from criticism. It is clear that the validity exception requires adjudicators to steer a difficult path

---

121 *Id.* at 61.

122 Not the uniform rule!

123 Some support for such extensive interpretation of the unification impact of CISG can be found in scholarly writing. *See, e.g.*, Vivian Grosswald Curran, *The Interpretative Challenge to Uniformity*, 15 J.L. & COM. 175 (1995) (reviewing Claude Witz, LES PREMIÈRES APPLICATIONS JURISPRUDENTIELLES DU DROIT UNIFORME DE LA VENTE INTERNATIONALE (1995)), *available at* http://www.cisg.law.pace.edu/cisg/biblio/curran1.html, which paraphrases *Witz's* statement: "He foresees a day when the CISG will not only be well established, but will take its place as a source of juridical principles to which judges and commentators may look increasingly for instruction and inspiration on matters not limited to the *international* sales of goods." He further thinks that the CISG will be metamorphosed "into a glowing, hue-shifting, impalpable, yet permeating source of illumination." (emphasis added). *See* Ronald A. Brand & Harry M. Flechtner, *Arbitration and Contract Formation: First Interpretations of the U.N. Sales Convention*, 12 J.L. & COM. 239 para II, (1993), *available at* http://www.cisg.law.pace.edu/cisg/wais/db/articles/journal1.html, comment on *Filanto, S.p.A. v. Chilewich Int'l Corp.*, 789 F.Supp 1229 (S.D.N.Y. 1992), *appeal dismissed*, 984 F.2d 58 (2d Cir. 1993). Although the court, strictly speaking, did not apply the CISG, it "referred to CISG article 18 as an afterthought" and held that the rules of contract formation are satisfied by the correspondence of the parties.

124 Kurt Siehr, *in* HONSELL-KOMMENTAR, *supra* note 11, art. 4, para. 6, (arguing that similar results in different countries are not due to the Convention's rules but on those of domestic law).

between the reservation made by CISG article 4(a) and the unification goals that are emphasised by CISG article 7(1). The complete removal of "validity" issues from the realm of the CISG by those who advocate a domestic law approach is an extreme solution. It leads only to legal uncertainty and does not sufficiently consider the unification goals. Doubts have also been expressed in regard to the methodological consistency of the balanced approach. The autonomous approach and the displacement reading present methodically sound concepts. The main criticism against these internationalist approaches is due to their lack of flexibility in regard to matters of evolving public policy.

It is, however, highly doubtful whether public policy concerns are relevant in cases of mistake. Amongst the cases of defective intention it is mainly fraud and duress, which evoke public policy concerns. The paramount issue in cases of mistake rather points towards fairness in international trade.[125] From the viewpoint of fairness, recourse to domestic remedies would lead to a negative result. The drafters agreed on the CISG as they thought it provided a fair remedial scheme for the case it addresses. Recourse to domestic law would deprive one party of the legal certainty he expected from the CISG. Had he known about the duality of remedies, he might have preferred a choice of law.

Proponents of the autonomous or displacement reading do not argue that cases of aggravated defect of intention as those of fraud or duress are addressed by the CISG. With regard to a case involving a mistake regarding the quality of goods, one scholar pointed out that, contrary to cases of simple non-conformity, fraud involves "special circumstances above and beyond a mere lack of conformity of goods."[126] Only on this ground recourse to domestic remedies is allowed in cases of fraud and also of duress. This paper advocates that if in interpreting the CISG the hierarchy of defects of intention – mistake on the bottom, fraud in the middle and duress on the top[127] – is thoroughly observed, both internationalist approaches will lead to adequate results.

To conclude, it can be stated that both the autonomous and the displacement reading in principle meet the interpretative challenge of mistake. The "uneasy and inconclusive truce line, along which skirmishes continue"[128] will be examined with regard to specific situations of mistake in the following sections.

---

125 *See supra* sect. III(B)(2).

126 Ingeborg Schwenzer, *in* SCHLECHTRIEM-KOMMENTAR, *supra* note 11, art. 35, para. 48.

127 For references *see supra* note 19.

128 Hartnell, *supra* note 13, at 75.

IV. Selected Types of Mistake

In 1989, it was stated that the "determination of the degree to which domestic doctrines of mistake can be invoked to invalidate a contract [that is governed by the CISG] appears to be a matter whose resolution will most likely have to await the assertion of case law precedent."[129] The following sections are committed to selected situations of mistake and to the treatment by courts, arbitration tribunals and scholars.[130] A basic distinction will be made between cases of mistake that involve an unintended expression (*infra*, section A) and those that involve a defective motive (*infra*, section B).

A. Mistake in Expression

A mistake in expression can simply involve an incorrect statement, for example, a slip of the tongue.[131] Further, a mistake in expression can occur if the statement is correctly spelled out but is subject to a misunderstanding of what would reasonably be attributed to it by the other party.[132] In both cases the mistake is due to a subjective defect. It is therefore symptomatic that a third party will not identify it.

The CISG is only concerned with the formation of contract, i.e. with the question of whether "objective agreement" was reached (external consensus). That is to say, the CISG does not provide rules on subjective defects of intention (internal consensus). Independent of whether one argues for a domestic law approach or for an internationalist interpretation, it must be concluded that domestic law determines the consequences of such internal defects of intention.[133] Domestic legal concepts either consider the contract as invalid from the beginning, i.e. there is no contract (*void ab initio*), or they provide a remedy for the nullification of the contract, i.e. the contract is voidable.[134]

---

129 KRITZER, PRACTICAL APPLICATIONS *supra* note 12, at 79.

130 For a very detailed comparative analysis, see Hoff, *supra* note 13, at 329-379. *See also* ZWEIGERT, *supra* note 13, 411-30. A comparison with Swiss law is provided by Heiz, *supra* note 13, at 651.

131 ZWEIGERT, *supra* note 13, at 414.

132 *Id.*

133 Scholars are not divided on this. *See, e.g.*, Ferrari, *supra* note 100, para. 22; Huber, *supra* note 13, at 593, 601; Manuel Lorenz, *in* KAUFRECHT, *supra* note 11, art. 4, para. 24.

134 ZWEIGERT, *supra* note 13, at 412.

The decision of a German court of first instance is in line with the finding that domestic law applies to a case that involves a mistake in expression.[135] The case concerned an application for the enforcement of an arbitral award. The defendant sought to prove the lack of a valid arbitration agreement and argued that he had not intended to bind himself. The court denied that the CISG deals with the internal elements required for material validity of offer or acceptance and hold that domestic law governs.

B. Mistake in Motive

A mistake in motive concerns a defective intention on at least one side of the contract. That is to say, one of the declarations contains or lacks an element that had been intended to be included or to be excluded had the mistaken party known the real state of affairs.[136] The consequence is a lack of internal consensus.

A mistake in motive can have a number of reasons. Therefore, in examining the rules of the CISG as to the facts on which they operate, due regard must be had to the question "mistake about what?"[137] In a mistake regarding the identity of the goods or in regard to the identity of the contractual partner, the rules on contract formation can be used as a cross-reference. The concept of initial impossibility and its treatment under the CISG can be employed as a cross-reference for a mistake in regard to the existence of goods. Further, the classic example of a mistake in regard to a quality of the goods finds its cross-reference in the CISG's rules on breach of contract for non-conformity of goods. Finally, a mistake in regard to characteristics of the contractual partner will be analyzed in light of the CISG's rules on anticipatory breach that concern a lack of the creditworthiness of the other party.

I. Mistake in regard to the Identity of the Goods or the Other Party

Amongst businessmen, cases of a mistake in regard to the identity of the other party or in regard to the goods "(like ghosts and flying saucers)" are said to be "more discussed than seen."[138]

---

[135] LG Hamburg (F.R.G.), June 19, 1997, *available at* http://www.cisg.law.pace.edu/cisg/wars/db/cases2/970619g1.html.

[136] Zweigert, *supra* note 13, at 412.

[137] *See supra* note 19.

[138] Honnold, Uniform Law, *supra* note 11, para. 108.

a. Mistake in regard to the Identity of the Other Party

A mistake in regard to the identity of the person contracted with might, for example, occur if negotiations are conducted through agents. The situation might arise in which an agent who in the past ordered goods for the one company starts to work for another company. Assuming that the change of position is not expressly dealt with during negotiations, the seller might mistakenly believe that he is dealing once again with his partner of former transactions.

A case like this involves issues of contract formation. Those are governed by the CISG. In addition it involves questions of agency that, for the purpose of this paper, will be excluded from the following analysis. According to the rules of the CISG a valid contract is formed if "objective agreement" is reached between the parties.[139] Hence, it can be argued that there will simply be no contract in cases where no agreement can be found between the parties that made the declarations.[140] It has been argued that the rules provided by the CISG should be carefully explored before an "objective agreement" can be denied.[141] Under CISG article 8(2) the law provides a reasonableness-test and under article 18(1) it addresses cases where assent is given by conduct.[142]

---

139 For contract formation under the CISG, see Brand, *supra* note 123; Pilar Perales, *Recent Development Relating to CISG: Contract Conclusion under CISG*, 16 J. L. & Com. 315 (1997); Peter Winship, *Formation of International Sales Contracts under the 1980 Vienna Convention*, 17 Int.'l Law 1, 1-12 (1983), *available at* http://www.cisg.law.pace.edu/cisg/biblio/winship3.html (discussing a few model cases).

140 In practice, it seems that the system provided by the CISG is not always duly applied. *See* Curran, *supra* note 123. She is in line with Witz' critical remarks on a decision of a German court of first instance (LG Hamburg, Sept. 26, 1990, *printed in* RIW 1015 (1990), *available at* http://www.cisg.law.pace.edu/cisg/wais/db/cases2/900926g1.html). A German company contested the existence of a contract and argued that it had not intended to contract with the other company. The argument was that its agent had mistakenly assumed that he was dealing with another company. Witz emphasizes that contract formation is governed by the CISG and criticizes the judges for not applying article 8. *See also* Martin Karollus, *Judicial Interpretation and Application of the CISG in Germany 1988-1994*, *in* Cornell Rev. of the CISG 51 Sec. III, para. 3, (1995), *available at* http://www.cisg.law.pace.edu/cisg/biblio/karollus.html.

141 OGH (Austria), Mar. 20, 1997, *available at* http://www.cisg.law.pace.edu/cisg/wais/db/cases2/970320a3.html, (providing a very good example).

142 In this context, see Michael Esser [*Commercial Letters of Confirmation in International Trade: Austrian, French, German and Swiss Law and Uniform Law under the 1980 Sales Convention*] 18 Ga. J. Int'l & Comp. L. 427, 453 (1988), *available at* http://www.cisg.law.pace.edu/cisg/biblio/esser.html.

The question regarding whether the formation rules of the CISG preclude recourse to domestic nullity rules or nullification concepts only comes up where an agreement cannot be proven. Scholarly writing is focused on cases where the mistake regards the characteristics of the other party, in particular the creditworthiness of the buyer. It is also in line with the statement of *Honnold*, cited at the beginning of this section, to assume that national courts will be reluctant to find that a mistake in regard to the identity of the other party is a relevant one.[143] This is due to the fact that in commercial reality, businessmen seldom focus on the identity of the other party: a buyer wants to buy and a seller wants to sell. Hence the mistake will be held relevant only in those cases where the identity of the other party was important in deciding whether to buy or to sell. In most of the cases it is not the identity of the other person but his ability to perform that is important. Those cases of mistake in regard to the characteristics of the other party will be discussed below (section IV B 4).

The issue of an identity-based mistake has not yet been subject to detailed analysis. One scholar states "other types of representation by the seller (such as his identity and similar statements by the buyer) may not be addressed by the Convention."[144] It is true, the objective-agreement test that applies according to the rules of the CISG has as an implied condition that the party who made the declaration intended to bind himself towards the addressee of the declaration and not towards a third person. A mistake in regard to the identity of the other party therefore is outside the scope of the rules of the CISG and is a question for domestic law.[145]

b. Mistake in regard to the Identity of the Goods

With regard to the identity of the goods the same argument, as in cases of mistake as to the identity of the other party, applies: there cannot be an objective agreement according to the rules of the CISG, if, from the viewpoint of a reasonable man, one party refers to goods X and the other party to goods Y.[146]

---

143 Similar in cases of non-conformity. *See* Kurt Siehr, *in* HONSELL-KOMMENTAR, *supra* note 11, art. 4, para. 6.

144 HONNOLD, UNIFORM LAW, *supra* note 11, para. 240.

145 See, for example, the recent decision of the House of Lords in Shogun Finance Ltd. V. Hudson 3 W.L.R. 1371(H.L. 2003). The decision explores the effect of a mistake of identity (created by a fraud) upon contract formation. It was held by three to two that the contract was void (not merely voidable). The fact that the case gave rise to five separate speeches is an impressive illustration of the legal quandaries the seemingly simply problem regarding a mistake of identity can involve. For a comprehensive analysis, see Catherine McMillan, Mistake of Identity Clarified?, L.Q.R 369 (2004).

146 This was the rule in *Raffles v. Wichelhaus ("The Peerless")*, 159 ER 375 (1864). This nineteenth century English case involved a mistake of the buyer concerning the identity of

2. Mistake in regard to the Existence of the Goods

Where the goods did not exist at the time of the conclusion of the contract, or have perished before this time, it could be argued that the intention to buy or sell the goods always involves a defect, namely a mistake about the existence of the goods. On this basis, recourse to domestic nullification concepts could be had. It should be noted for clarification that if the classification of the case according to domestic law leads to a concept of initial impossibility that nullifies the contract it would be a "mistake in itself" to try to nullify the contract by the application of a mistake-based remedy.

Cases where the goods do not exist at the time of contract conclusion are mainly discussed not with a focus on mistake but with regard to the more specific domestic concepts of initial impossibility *(doctrine of res extincta)*.[147] According to a number of domestic laws, a case where the goods do not exist at the time of contract conclusion is classified as a validity issue.[148] In contrast, under the CISG it is addressed as an issue of risk allocation or as an excuse for non-performance. Under CISG article 68, it is provided that if the goods are sold in transit, the risk passes "from the *time of the conclusion of the contract*."[149] Under CISG article 79(1), a party is excused from liability for non-performance "if he proves that the failure was due to an impediment beyond his control and that he could not reasonably be expected to have taken the impediment into account at *the time of the conclusion of the*

---

the goods which was caused by the fact that goods of the same kind where stored on two different ships that both had the name Peerless. As the contract only stipulated cotton "*to arrive ex Peerless from Bombay*" it could not be made out to which of the two ships the parties had referred. Most scholars find that the rule of "*The Peerless*" is applicable under the CISG. *See, e.g.*, E. Allen Farnsworth, *in* BIANCA-COMMENTARY, *supra* note 11, art. 8, para. 3.2; Hoff, *supra* note 13, at 348; HONNOLD, UNIFORM LAW, *supra* note 11, para. 108.

147 On initial impossibility, see Ulrich Magnus, *in* STAUDINGER-KOMMENTAR, *supra* note 11, art. 4, para 48; Hartnell, *supra* note 13, at 78.

148 *See* preceeding note; Schlechtriem, *The Experience*, *supra* note 12, at 11 (alluding to domestic concepts of objective impossibility: "Under German law, as in many other legal systems stemming from Roman law and contrary to Common Law and Swedish law, a contract is void if it requires performance of something which was objectively impossible at the time of the conclusion of the contract *(impossibilium nulla est obligatio)*."); Rudolf Reischauer, *Leistungsstörungsrecht des ABGB im Vergleich zu dem des BGB mit einem Blick auf das UN-Kaufrecht*, *in* FESTSCHRIFT FÜR HANS STOLL, (Hohloch et al. eds., Tübingen 2001), 344, at 350 (alluding to the important distinction between those legal systems that see the question as one of validity (e.g., Germany) and those that see it as one of enforceability (e.g., Austria).

149 CISG, *supra* note 1, art. 68 (emphasis added).

contract ..."[150] Both rules can be interpreted as cross-references to domestic concepts that are labelled "initial impossibility."

The drafting history is ambiguous on the applicability of domestic concepts of initial impossibility alongside the CISG.[151] It seems, however, to be almost settled – at least in scholarly writing – that domestic doctrines of *res extincta* (which invalidates the contract when goods have perished before the contract has been concluded) are overruled by the CISG.[152] Only a few authors argue in favour of domestic law.[153] The majority of scholars argue for the exclusive applicability of the CISG. Their internationalist approach is in line with the view adopted by the

---

150 CISG, *supra* note 1, art. 79(1) (emphasis added).

151 Hartnell, *supra* note 13, at 78-79, who is of the opinion that the drafters of article 79 simply did not make a clear decision on the applicability of domestic validity rules in the case of this kind of mistake. On the other hand: CISG, *supra* note 1, art. 79(1) states: "A party is not liable for a failure to perform any of his obligations if he proves that the failure was due to an impediment beyond his control and that he could not reasonably be expected to have taken the impediment into account *at the time of the conclusion of the contract* or to have overcome it or its consequences" (emphasis added). When commenting on an earlier version of article 79(1) which limited the impediment to an occurrence *after* the conclusion of the contract, the Secretariat Commentary stated that "if at the time of the conclusion of the contract there was an existing impediment to performance, the national law applicable to the ... validity of the contract may provide either that no contract was concluded or that it was invalid by reason of the mistake ... of the parties ...", VII UNCITRAL Y.B. 130, para. 3, U.N. Doc. A/CN.9/SER.A/1976.
However, when the words *at the time of the conclusion of the contract* were added to article 79(1), the Secretariat Commentary was amended to state: "The impediment may have existed at the time of the conclusion of the contract. For example, goods which were unique and which were the subject of the contract may have already perished at the time of the conclusion of the contract. However, the seller would not be exempted from liability if he reasonably could have been expected to take the destruction of the goods into account at the time of the conclusion of the contract." *Secretariat Commentary on the 1978 Draft*, U.N. Doc. A/CONF/97/5, *reprinted in* HONNOLD, DOCUMENTARY HISTORY, *supra* note 11, para. 4, at 445.

152 Schlechtriem, *The Experience*, *supra* note 12, at 11, (concluding that, [U] nder Uniform Sales Law, a contract to deliver goods that have already perished at the time of the conclusion is to be regarded as valid. The impossibility of the seller to deliver is a breach of his obligation which gives the buyer the appropriate remedies, but does not make the contract void as under an applicable domestic law.) *See, e.g.*, ENDERLEIN, *supra* note 11, art. 79, para. 5.2; HONNOLD, UNIFORM LAW, *supra* note 11, art. 79, para. 425; Ulrich Huber, *in* SCHLECHTRIEM-KOMMENTAR, *supra* note 11, art. 49, para. 7; Manuel Lorenz, *in* KAUFRECHT, *supra* note 11, art. 4, para. 19; Ulrich Magnus, *in* STAUDINGER-KOMMENTAR, *supra* note 11, art. 4, para. 44; Barry Nicholas, *in* BIANCA-COMMENTARY, *supra* note 11, art. 68, para. 3.1; Hans Stoll, *in* SCHLECHTRIEM-KOMMENTAR, *supra* note 11, art. 79, para. 18.

UNIDROIT Principles. Article 3.3 provides that typical cases of impossibility (performance impossible from the outset and lack of legal title or power) are excluded from the concept of validity.[154]

To sum up, the CISG overrules domestic remedies on initial impossibility and mistake-based concepts of nullification irrespective of the classification that applies under that domestic law.

3. Mistake in regard the Quality of the Goods

A mistake in regard to the quality of goods has been mentioned above as a classical example of the problem of parallel applicability of the remedies provided under domestic law and by the CISG.

In practice, a mistaken party will prefer to rely on the damage-based remedial scheme of the CISG rather than having to endure the uncertainties caused by avoidance of the contract to the *status quo ante*.[155] The question whether a domestic concept of nullification is applicable has, however, evoked extensive discussion during the drafting process and also in subsequent scholarly writing.[156] The pivotal question is whether nullification under domestic law is precluded by the CISG's rules on breach of contract. A consequential question concerns the issue of whether uniform time-limitations as provided by CISG article 39 should apply to domestic remedies that are employed alongside the CISG.[157]

---

153 For minor doubts for example, Hartnell, *supra* note 13, at 78-79. *See* also Denis Tallon, *in* BIANCA-COMMENTARY, *supra* note 11, art. 79, para. 2.4 (finding that the rules of CISG are not exhaustive). But see Weitzmann, *supra* note 13, para. III (criticizing Tallon in that he "does not explain why a domestic law's own characterization of a 'validity' issue should be sufficient to supplant a rule contained in the Convention.").

154 *See* section II (A) (2). UNIDROIT Principles, Commentary, *supra* note 36, art. 3.3, para. 1 reads: Contrary to a number of legal systems that consider a contract of sale void if the specific goods sold have already perished at the time of conclusion of the contract, para. (1) of this article, *in conformity with the most modern trends*, states in general terms that the mere fact that at the time of the conclusion of the contract the performance of the obligation assumed was impossible *does not affect the validity of the contract*. (emphasis added).

155 Hartnell, *supra* note 13, at 77.

156 Franco Ferrari, *in* SCHLECHTRIEM-KOMMENTAR, *supra* note 11, art. 4, para. 23; KRITZER, PRACTICAL APPLICATIONS, *supra* note 11, art. 4, at 87-93; Lessiak, *supra* note 13, at 487; Manuel Lorenz, *in* KAUFRECHT, *supra* note 11, art. 4, para. 20; Ingeborg Schwenzer, *in* SCHLECHTRIEM-KOMMENTAR, *supra* note 11, art. 35, para. 45; ZWEIGERT, *supra* note 13, at 413; Ulrich Magnus, *in* STAUDINGER-KOMMENTAR, *supra* note 11, para. 48.

157 *Infra*, section IV.(B)(3)(b).

a. Conflict Rule for the Parallel Applicability of Domestic and Uniform Remedies

The need for a conflict rule arises only where the domestic sales law that is applicable according to the rules of private international law provides a choice between damage-based remedies for breach of warranty and those that allow nullification for the reason of a mistake.[158] Under, for example, German law, a buyer cannot nullify the contract on the basis of a mistake in regard to a quality of the goods but is restricted to the remedies provided for non-conformity of goods. The problem, therefore, cannot arise in Germany.[159] In contrast, the law in the United States, Switzerland and Austria, for instance, provide in principle for the remedy of rescission for mistake concurrently with claims for breach of warranty.

Concerning the CISG, scholarly writing is divided.[160] Although the position under United States domestic law would suggest concurrent application, the preponderant view seems to be that the rules of the CISG are exhaustive.[161] The same is true for Switzerland.[162] Also, in France the majority argues for an exclusion of domestic law.[163] It has already been mentioned above that the UNIDROIT Principles give precedence to the remedies for non-performance. Article 3.7 of the Principles states: "A party is not entitled to avoid the contract on the ground of mistake if the circumstances on which that party relies afford, or could have afforded, a remedy for non-performance."[164]

---

158 Ingeborg Schwenzer, *in* SCHLECHTRIEM-KOMMENTAR, *supra* note 11, art. 35, para. 45 (providing an overview of the rules applicable under several domestic laws). For a comparative analysis, see Huber, *supra* note 13, at 585 and ZWEIGERT, *supra* note 13, at 411.

159 Ingeborg Schwenzer, *in* SCHLECHTRIEM-KOMMENTAR, *supra* note 11, art. 35, para. 45.

160 KRITZER, PRACTICAL APPLICATIONS, *supra* note 11, art. 35, at 87 (compiling the views of most of the commentators in a table).

161 HONNOLD, UNIFORM LAW, *supra* note 11, art. 35, para. 240. *But see* Hartnell, *supra* note 13, at note 294, where the author advocates a balanced approach towards CISG article 4(a). She states that on application of the balanced approach "Tribunals in or applying the law of U.S. states that have adopted the provisions of the Uniform Commercial Code should consider the policies articulated by that state in cases arising under U.C.C. § 1-103, which permits state rules on mistake to supplement the U.C.C."

162 Heiz, *supra* note 13, at 651.

163 Cass. 1e Civ., 14 mai 1996, J.C.P.G. 1997, I, 4009, note Radé. *See also* Curran, *supra* note 123 (explaining Witz' view: He finds that CISG deals exhaustively with the consequences of non-conformity. Its system would be undermined if the buyer would be entitled to avoid the contract based on domestic law). According to Witz, this rule should also prevail in cases where the goods are not amenable to resale, even if the obstacle lies in a regulation or administrative ordinance. Curran is critical of this point. *See also* Niggemann, *supra* note 13, at 409.

164 UNIDROIT Principles, *supra* note 27, art. 3.7.

For an illustration of two diametrically opposed positions we can turn to German law on one hand and Austrian law on the other.[165] Amongst German scholars, the view is predominant that domestic remedies are displaced by the CISG as far as "they relate to the seller's actual (typical or atypical) obligations, in particular as it regards the quality of goods and their freedom from legal effects."[166] In contrast, Austrian scholars argue for parallel applicability of domestic and uniform remedies.[167]

In German and Austrian court practice, similar divisions are evident. A recent Austrian decision dealt with issues of contract conclusion.[168] The case concerned the question whether the buyer was entitled to avoid the contract after he had become aware that the goods did not conform to what he had (mistakenly) expected from the negotiations. The court delivered profound reasoning on the issue of contract conclusion and held the rules of the CISG applicable. With regard to mistake, it was held – without any detailed discussion of CISG article 35 – that the buyer was entitled to nullify the contract according to Austrian law.

In contrast, a German court held that the applicability of the CISG precluded recourse to domestic law regarding a mistake in regard to the quality of the goods as the matter was exhaustively covered by the CISG.[169] The facts of another German decision should be noted to support the need for the distinction between the three

---

165 Niggemann, *supra* note 13, at 398; Hartnell, *supra* note 13, at 72, notes 297-298.

166 Franco Ferrari, *in* SCHLECHTRIEM-KOMMENTAR, *supra* note 11, art. 4, para. 46; Huber, *supra* note 13, at 597; Ulrich Huber, *in* SCHLECHTRIEM-KOMMENTAR, *supra* note 11, art. 45, para. 51; Manuel Lorenz, KAUFRECHT, *supra* note 11, art. 4, para. 21; Ulrich Magnus, *in* STAUDINGER-KOMMENTAR, *supra* note 11, para. 49; SCHLECHTRIEM, INTERNATIONALES UN-KAUFRECHT, *supra* note 49, para. 261; Ingeborg Schwenzer, *in* SCHLECHTRIEM-KOMMENTAR, *supra* note 11, art. 35, para. 45; Kurt Siehr, *in* HONSELL-KOMMENTAR, *supra* note 11, art. 4, para. 6.

167 Lessiak, *supra* note 13, at 487, provides a detailed analysis. *See* Carsten Thomas Ebenroth, Internationale Vertragsgestaltung im Spannungsverhältnis zwischen ABGB, IPR-Gesetz und UN-Kaufrecht, ÖJBl 681-695, at 688 (1986); MARTIN KAROLLUS, UN-KAUFRECHT 41 (Springer 1991); Martin Karollus, UN-Kaufrecht: Hinweise für die Vertragspraxis, ÖJBl 1993, 22-33, at 31, note 49. *See also* Huber, *supra* note 13, at 599, who undertakes to rebut the domestic law approach specifically for Austria.

168 OGH (Aust.), Mar. 20, 1997, *available at* http://cisg3.law.pace.edu/cases/970320a3.html with a case note by Kritzer.

169 LG Aachen (F.R.G.), May 14, 1993, *available at* http://www.jura.uni-freiburg.de; English abstract *available at* http://cisg3.law.pace.edu/cases/930514g1.html. On this decision see Anna Kazimierska, *The Remedy of Avoidance under the Vienna Convention on the International Sale of Goods*, 1999, note 326, *at* http://www.cisg.law.pace.edu/cisg/biblio/kazimierska.html.

levels of defective intention.[170] The seller sought to annul a price reduction agreement that had been concluded between the parties after the buyer had claimed that the goods were worthless and could not be sold. It transpired that the goods could be sold and that the buyer had made a fraudulent statement in regard to their non-conformity. Although the facts of the case involved issues addressed by the CISG, based on the fraudulent statement, the court held domestic doctrines of nullification applicable.

Finally, there is an award made by a Hungarian court. It states that questions of error (and disproportionate value of the obligations) in principle are not covered by the CISG.[171] Issues involving a lack of conformity were nevertheless decided according to CISG article 36.

b. Notice Period and Cut-off Period of CISG article 39

Those who argue in favour of the parallel applicability of domestic remedies alongside the CISG must further consider whether a lack of notice in due time in accordance with CISG article 39 precludes nullification of the contract.[172] Under CISG article 39(1), notice of the "lack of conformity [must be given] within a reasonable time after [the buyer] has discovered it or ought to have discovered it" (notice period) and article 39(2) provides that "in any event, the buyer loses the right to rely on a lack of conformity of the goods if he does not give the seller notice thereof at the latest within a period of two years (...)"(cut-off period). It is evident that "[a] competing mistake-based remedy under domestic law will be most attractive to the buyer who has failed to give timely notice pursuant to [CISG] article 39 and is thus precluded from seeking the remedies provided by the Convention."[173]

The discussion of the applicability of the CISG's time limitations ranges along traditional lines. On the basis of the unification purposes of the CISG internationalists argue that domestic remedies – if available at all – are subject to the

170 OLG Hamburg (F.R.G.), Oct. 5, 1998, English abstract *available at* http://cisg3.law.pace.edu/cases/981005g1.html). *See also* Ingeborg Schwenzer, *in* SCHLECHTRIEM-KOMMENTAR, *supra* note 11, art. 35, para. 48.

171 FB Budapest (Hung.), July 1, 1997; English abstract *available at* http://cisgw3.law.pace.edu/cases/970701h1.html. The case involved a sales contract between a German seller (claimant) and a Hungarian buyer (defendant) who contested the seller's claim on three grounds: error, lack of conformity of the goods to the contract terms and disproportionate value of the obligations between the opposing parties.

172 Karollus, *supra* note 167, at 41.

173 Hartnell, *supra* note 13, at 77.

time-limitations imposed by CISG article 39.[174] In contrast, those who argue that validity-based remedies are outside the CISG conclude that the uniform rules on time-limitations are irrelevant for the exercise of domestic remedies.[175] They highlight that the issue was explicitly addressed by the Dutch Delegation during the deliberations of the Diplomatic Conference when the Delegation requested to insert a new article 48a that would have submitted domestic remedies to the uniform time-limitations of CISG article 39. The request was rejected by the majority of the delegates.[176]

This paper argues that the internationalist approach towards CISG article 39 has the better arguments. To start with, it is clear that the notice period and the cut-off period of CISG article 39 do not apply to domestic remedies that are based on facts not addressed by the CISG.[177] Cases of non-conformity of goods however *are* addressed by it and it has been argued above that accordingly the CISG also covers cases of mistake about the quality of the goods. If we would allow a buyer who has lost his remedies by operation of CISG article 39 to avoid the contract on the basis of a domestic remedy we would deprive the seller of the certainty he reasonably expected from the expiration of the period set out by CISG article 39.[178] This leads to the conclusion that domestic remedies – if we allow applicability at all – must be subject to the notice period and cut-off period of CISG article 39.

Against this background we can also explain the denial of the request to insert a new article 48a: the drafters wanted the CISG to exclusively apply to the cases whose facts are addressed. The explicit imposition of a time limit on domestic remedies that operate on the same facts must have seemed redundant.

---

[174] *See* ZWEIGERT, *supra* note 13, at 413 (stating that "a buyer, who by the operation of CISG article 39, has lost his remedies … *certainly* cannot invoke national rules on avoidance for mistake, for the rules of CISG as to the rights of the buyer when defective goods have been delivered are to be seen as a *lex specialis*" (emphasis added)). *See also* Ulrich Huber, *in* SCHLECHTRIEM-KOMMENTAR, *supra* note 11 art. 45, para. 52.

[175] Lessiak, *supra* note 13, at 495.

[176] U.N. Conf. on Contracts for the Int'l Sale of Goods, Official Records, U.N. Doc. A/CONF.97/19, U.N. Sales No. E.81.IV.3 (1981), at 362.

[177] See the doubts raised against the balanced approach, *supra*, section III (C)(5).

[178] ZWEIGERT, *supra* note 13, at 413 (stating that "a buyer, who by the operation of CISG article 39, has lost his remedies (…) *certainly* cannot invoke national rules on avoidance for mistake for the rules of CISG as to the rights of the buyer when defective goods have been delivered are to be seen as a lex specialis" (emphasis added)).

c. Summary

There is some evidence from scholarly writing of a welcome tendency to the exclude domestic mistake-based remedies that allow avoidance of the contract. It is difficult to determine the state of international practice, as there are very few court decisions and tribunal awards on the issue.

The position in Austria that argues for parallel application of domestic and uniform remedies is a logical continuation of the position under Austrian domestic law. The examples of France, Switzerland, and the United States show that an internationalist view on the CISG is possible although the position under national law in principle would allow parallel application of a domestic nullification remedy. This paper advocates the exclusion of domestic remedies in cases that involve a lack of conformity.[179]

4. Mistake in Regard to Characteristics of the Other Party

The term characteristics is used to describe those elements of a person that are important for the one party when forming the intention to enter into a transaction with the other party (i.e. *delectus personae*). As far as the buyer's intentions are concerned this means his reliance on the seller's ability to perform. From the view of the seller, this is apt to be his reliance on the creditworthiness of the buyer.

a. Remedies under the CISG

To begin with I will summarise the approach of the CISG. The basic principle of the CISG is to view avoidance of the contract as an *ultima ratio*.[180] According to the CISG's remedial scheme, embodied in CISG article 64, the contract can be avoided only in cases of fundamental breach or non-performance, the latter being subject to the expiration of an additional period of time.[181] In such cases, the CISG envisions the finality of the contractual relation so that no recourse to domestic concepts of nullification will be sought. Should the inability of the other party, however, become apparent prior to the date of performance, but after the time of contract conclusion, the remedy of avoidance is only available according to the rules of

---

179 *See also supra* section III (D).

180 In fact, it has been stated that a fundamental breach will be proven scarcely as it is subject to strict requirements; *see* HONNOLD, UNIFORM LAW, *supra* note 11, art. 25, para. 186: "last resort."

181 In cases of (final) non-delivery CISG article 49(1)(b) avoidance is subject to the expiration of an additional period of time *(Nachfrist)*.

anticipatory breach under CISG article 72 (i.e., if the anticipated breach is fundamental in the sense of CISG article 71(1)).[182] If the anticipated breach is not fundamental, only a right of suspension will be granted. The suspension can be rebutted according to CISG article 71(3) by an adequate assurance of performance. It follows that recourse to a domestic nullification remedy is attractive in cases where the breach is not fundamental. If domestic law is applicable, and a relevant mistake in regard to characteristics of the other party can be proven, the party can nullify the contract and thus evade the *favor contractus* scheme of the CISG.[183]

b. Conflict Rule for the Parallel Applicability of Domestic and Uniform Remedies

CISG article 71 addresses deficiencies in the ability to perform a substantial part of the obligations.[184] The question whether domestic remedies based on mistake are applicable, in principle, raises the same issues as discussed above for a mistake in regard to the quality of goods.[185] Again the drafting history is ambiguous.[186] Those who see the issue outside the CISG argue in favour of the availability of domestic

---

182 *See* CISG, *supra* note 1, arts. 72, 25. A failure to perform ancillary obligations does not fulfill this criterion. *See also* Hans G. Leser & Rainer Hornung, *in* SCHLECHTRIEM-KOMMENTAR, *supra* note 11, art. 71, para. 8; Peter Schlechtriem, *in* SCHLECHTRIEM-KOMMENTAR, *supra* note 11, art. 25, para. 24.

183 The implications of the *favor contractus* principle for the right to avoid are explained by Magnus, *supra* note 9, para. 9. He states: (s)everal provisions show that the CISG will allow contract avoidance only under narrow conditions and as a last resort (see Arts. 25, 34, 37, 47, 48, 49, 63, 64). If possible, an economically not feasible winding up of the sale should be avoided. Only if the gravity of the breach of contract is unacceptable, the aggrieved party has to be able to get out of the contract. This principle also applies in situations of a breach of obligations which are either not expressly regulated by the CISG or to which the parties have made the CISG applicable.

184 Hans G. Leser & Rainer Hornung, *in* SCHLECHTRIEM-KOMMENTAR, *supra* note 11, art. 71, para. 9 (stating that "(w)hat constitutes a substantial part of the obligations must be decided by considering the contract as a whole").

185 In the context of anticipatory breach, the question was raised whether the CISG provides a general right of suspension aside from the remedy of CISG article 71 or whether recourse to domestic law should be allowed. Christopher Kern, *Leistungsverweigerungsrechte im UN-Kaufrecht*, Rudolf Meyer zum Abschied: Dialog Deutschland-Schweiz VII, Faculté de droit, Université de Geneve 73 (Michael R. Will, ed., 1999), *available at* http://www.cisg.law.pace.edu/cisg/biblio/kern2.html, argues for a careful analogy to the rules of CISG. According to Hans G. Leser & Rainer Hornung, *in* SCHLECHTRIEM-KOMMENTAR, *supra* note 11, art. 71 para. 25a, any national concept of suspension is precluded.

186 Schlechtriem, *The Experience*, *supra* note 12, para. (a), at note 37.

nullification concepts.[187] In contrast internationalists who advocate an autonomous or displacement interpretation of CISG article 4(a) find that the CISG's rules are exhaustive.[188] The tension between the finality of avoidance and the merely temporary effect of a right to suspend performance is apparent;[189] yet, case law on this point is non-existent.

This paper advocates that the *favor contractus* principle, as embodied in the rules of anticipatory breach, excludes the application of domestic laws.

C. Summary

In summary, avoidance of the contract according to domestic law is possible in the following two cases: The first case is a mistake in the expression of a correctly formed intention. The second case is a mistake in regard to the identity of the other party or of the goods. The CISG does not provide a cross-reference for these cases. In contrast, recourse to domestic remedies is not open in cases where the mistake relates to the existence of the goods. This type of mistake is addressed by the CISG.

As to the remaining two cases of a mistake in motive, the positions are divided along traditional lines. It has been argued that the rules of the CISG should exclusively apply in regard to a mistake that concerns the quality of goods. The damage-based scheme for breach of contract in cases of non-conformity of goods provides a functionally adequate solution that operates on the same facts domestic remedies do.

With respect to a mistake concerning characteristics of the other party, it has been argued above that the rules on anticipatory breach strike for the exclusion of domestic remedies.

187 *See, e.g.*, Lessiak, *supra* note 13, at 488.

188 Ulrich Huber, *in* SCHLECHTRIEM-KOMMENTAR, *supra* note 11, art. 45, para. 54; HONNOLD, UNIFORM LAW, *supra* note 11, art. 35, para. 240.

189 Hans G. Leser & Rainer Hornung, *in* SCHLECHTRIEM-KOMMENTAR, *supra* note 11, art. 71, para. 17.

V. Conclusion

The analysis has shown that the issue of mistake remains unsettled in a number of respects. Throughout the above analysis, it has become apparent that the process of harmonization is challenged by the tension between the unification spirit embodied in CISG article 7 and the parochial national interests embodied in CISG article 4. A remarkable level of unification has been achieved under the CISG. This gives cause for optimism.

Tendencies towards an internationalist interpretation of the CISG can be observed in scholarly writing and has recently also been approved by U.S. courts.[190] Significant conflicts in the interpretation of the validity exception, however, has prevented a single doctrine of mistake accepted by all countries that have ratified the CISG. Much depends on the correct approach towards the issue. It is important to distinguish between the different levels of defect of intention. Mistake involves a simple defect of intention and does not necessarily come under the validity exception. It is, furthermore, important to look into the specific reason for mistake. The cases discussed above illustrate that there are only few reasons for a mistake that are not addressed under the CISG and that allow the application of a domestic remedy.

In sum, it can be said that the tenor of the picture drawn by *Kötz* that I cited at the outset of this paper applies: the CISG solves a number of problems but also creates new problems. For cases that involve a mistake, however, the analysis of the selected types of mistake has shown that the problems can be solved and it seems that the position of an adjudicator is not as difficult as that of Heracles in his fight against the snake headed Hydra.

---

190 For example see a recent decision of a U.S. court: MCC-Marble Ceramic Center v. Ceramica Nuova D'Agostino, 144 F.3d 1384 (11th Cir. 1998), *cert. denied*, 67 U.S.L.W. 3652 (1999). It was held: "Courts applying the CISG cannot, therefore, upset the parties' reliance on the Convention by substituting familiar principles of domestic law when the Convention requires a different result." *Id.* at 1389. For comments on this decision, see Rod N. Andreason, *MCC-Marble Ceramic Center: The parol evidence rule and other domestic law under the Convention on CISG*, 1999 B. Y. U. L. REV. 351 (1999); Harry M. Flechtner, *The U.N. Sales Convention (CISG) and MCC-Marble Ceramic Center Inc. v. Ceramica Nuova D'Agostino, S.p.A.: The Eleventh Circuit Weighs in on Interpretation, Subjective Intent, Procedural Limits to the Convention's Scope, and the Parol Evidence Rule*, 18 J.L. & COM. 259 (1999); Paolo Torzilli, *The Aftermath of MCC-Marble: Is this the Death Knell for the Parol Evidence Rule*, 74 ST. JOHN'S L. REV. 843 (2000); all *available at* http://www.cisg.law.pace.edu.

The Restitution of Goods on Avoidance of the Contract for Lack of Conformity within the Scope of Art. 82(2)(c) CISG: **On the Different Treatment of Defects in Quality, Third-Party Intellectual Property Rights, and Defects in Title as Elements of the Remedies for the Buyer**

*Florian Mohs**

---

* Research Assistant at the University of Basel, Switzerland. This essay has already been published in German, *see* Florian Mohs, *Die Vertragswidrigkeit im Rahmen des Art. 82 Abs. 2 lit. c CISG*, INTERNATIONALES HANDELSRECHT [hereinafter IHR] 59-66 (2002).

I. Subject Matter and Scope of Art. 82(2)(c) CISG

Under the heading "Effects of avoidance," the rules on restitution are set forth at Articles 81 through 84 of the CISG.[1] The consequences of avoidance of a contract for the international sale of goods are uniformly determined for both parties in these Articles, while the requirements of avoidance are treated separately for the buyer and seller in Article 49 CISG and Article 64 CISG, respectively.

Art. 82(1) CISG provides a bar on the exercise of the right of avoidance[2] with respect to the buyer;[3] i.e., its employment blocks the execution of this remedy and thus corresponds functionally to § 2-608(2) Uniform Commercial Code (UCC).[4] Accordingly, the buyer loses the right to declare the contract avoided or to require the seller to deliver substitute goods[5] if it is impossible[6] for the buyer to restitute the goods substantially[7] in the condition in which he received them. However,

---

1 See United Nations Convention on Contracts for the International Sale of Goods, April 11, 1980, S. Treaty Doc. No. 98-9 (1984), 1489 U.N.T.S. 3, *available at* http://www.cisg.law.pace.edu/cisg/text/treaty.html (last visited Oct. 5, 2003) [hereinafter CISG].

2 *See generally* Peter Schlechtriem, Restitution und Bereicherungsausgleich in Europa, Eine rechtsvergleichende Darstellung, 409 para. 8; 696 para. 576 (Mohr Siebeck 2000).

3 From a technical legal point of view, this bar on the exercise of the right of avoidance is not correctly classified in the Convention for two reasons: First, it is located in CISG, *supra* note 1, at Ch., V. "Provisions Common to the Obligations of the Seller and of the Buyer", despite the fact that it only bars the *buyer's* right to declare the contract avoided. Second, it is dealt with in the context of § V., "*Effects* of avoidance", although it constitutes a *requirement* of avoidance (emphasis added); *See* Markus Krebs, Die Rückabwicklung im UN-Kaufrecht, 92 n. 569 (2000).

4 § 2-608(2) UCC (2003) provides: "Revocation of acceptance must occur ... before any substantial change in condition of the goods which is not caused by their own defects."

5 Due to the fact that contract avoidance, as well as subsequent performance, lead to restitution of what had been performed, CISG, *supra* note 1, art. 82, provides a uniform approach for both situations. Though the remainder of this essay only mentions avoidance of the contract, the same applies for cases of subsequent performance.

6 Impossibility in this context means actual impediment. *See* Hans G. Leser & Rainer Hornung, *Verlust der Rechte auf Vertragsaufhebung oder Ersatzlieferung wegen Unmöglichkeit der Rückgabe im ursprünglichen Zustand*, art. 82, para. 9, *in* Kommentar zum Einheitlichen UN-Kaufrecht (CISG) (Peter Schlechtriem, ed., 3d. ed. 2000).

7 The element "*substantially*" incorporates a *de minimis* rule which prevents insubstantial changes from blocking the right of avoidance. *See id.* at art. 82, para. 11.

Art. 82(2) CISG sets out many exceptions to this general rule.[8] For instance, according to Art. 82(2)(c) CISG, the buyer does not lose the right to avoid the contract if he sells the goods in the normal course of business.[9] Yet, the buyer cannot invoke this exceptional provision if he has sold the goods, despite the fact that he discovered or ought to have discovered the *lack of conformity*.[10]

The subject matter of this essay is whether the term lack of conformity covers all cases of defective performance including defects in quality and defects in title, or whether lack of conformity includes only defects in quality. This issue has not yet been addressed by any authority in the context of Art. 82 CISG, even though this point is a contentious one with regard to other provisions[11] of the Convention. This is especially true with respect to Art. 46(2) and (3) CISG (the restrictive rules on the right to require performance as a remedy), and Art. 50 CISG (the right of price reduction).

II. The Controversy Surrounding Arts. 46(2), (3) and 50 CISG

The question of whether the buyer should unrestrictively be entitled to the remedy of substitute delivery, or a rectification of defects, or a reduction of the price is answered by the authorities in different ways. These various opinions are discussed below.

---

8 The exceptions modify the basic rule in such a fundamental way that the rule becomes the exception. *See* Hans G. Leser & Rainer Hornung, *Vorbemerkungen zu Artt. 81-84*, para. 12 and *Verlust der Rechte auf Vertragsaufhebung oder Ersatzlieferung wegen Unmöglichkeit der Rückgabe im ursprünglichen Zustand*, art. 82, para. 12, *in* KOMMENTAR ZUM EINHEITLICHEN UN-KAUFRECHT (CISG), *supra* note 6. This was also the case under the ULIS. *See generally* Convention Relating to a Uniform Law on the International Sale of Goods, 1964, 834 U.N.T.S. 109 *available at* http://www.cisg.law.pace.edu/cisg/text/ulis.html (last visited Oct. 5, 2003) [hereinafter ULIS]. See Hermann Weitnauer, *Unmöglichkeit der Rückgabe im ursprünglichen Zustand*, art. 79 EKG, para. 1, *in* KOMMENTAR ZUM EINHEITLICHEN KAUFRECHT (Hans Dölle ed., 1976) who comments that the general rule is broken by material exceptions.

9 See CISG, *supra* note 1, at art. 82(2)(c).

10 French: "*défaut de conformité*;" German: "*Vertragswidrigkeit*."

11 The term *lack of conformity* is to be found in the CISG, *supra* note 1, arts. 35(3), 36, 37, 39, 40, 46(2) and (3), 50, 51 and 82(2)(c) (The author with respect to Arts. 50 and 51 interprets "does not conform" and "do not conform" to mean "lack of conformity.").

I. Uniform Approach is De Lege Lata Impossible

According to one opinion, there are no differences in the buyer's remedies for defects in quality and defects in title.[12] Even in the case of a defect in title, the buyer, under this viewpoint, is entitled to reduce the price per Art. 50 CISG.[13] However, the buyer can only ask for substitute delivery in a case where the restrictive requirements of Art. 46(2) and (3) CISG are met.[14]

It is correct that the law of performance impairments of the CISG is based on the uniform term of violation of an obligation,[15] see Arts. 45 and 61 CISG.[16] However, in both Articles' subparagraph (a), these "connecting" rules refer to the elements of each of the remedies. Thus, their function is to maintain order.[17]

---

12 See Rolf Herber & Beate Czerwenka, Internationales Kaufrecht: Kommentar zu dem Übereinkommen der Vereinten Nationen vom 11. April 1980 über Verträge über den internationalen Warenkauf, art. 45, para. 2 (C. H. Beck 1991); Katharina Wolff, Die Rechtsmängelhaftung nach dem Uniform Commercial Code und dem UN-Kaufrecht 164 (1990) who state that regarding the remedies (Section III.) the term *conformity* includes defects in title, while with respect to the standards for liability (Section II) it only covers defects in quality.

13 *See* Herber & Czerwenka, *supra* note 12, art. 50, para. 3; Gert Reinhart, UN-Kaufrecht. Kommentar zum Übereinkommen der Vereinten Nationen vom 11. April 1980 über Verträge über den internationalen Warenkauf, art. 50, para. 2 (1991); Wolff, *supra* note 12, at 173 *et seq.*

14 *See* Herber & Czerwenka, *supra* note 12, at art. 46, paras. 6 and 9; Reinhart, *supra* note 13, at art. 46, paras. 3 *et seq.*; Wolff, *supra* note 12, at 163 *et seq.*, 166.

15 The CISG itself uses the terms "breach of contract" and "failure to perform an obligation." According to Schlechtriem, the term "violation of an obligation" (or "breach of obligation") defines more precisely the uniform element of deficiencies in a party's performance because even the CISG compares the behavior and the performance of the obligor with the schedule of obligations set out by the contract and the Convention. *See* Peter Schlechtriem, *Der Einfluß des UN-Kaufrechts auf die Entwicklung des deutschen und des internationalen Schuldrechts*, IHR 16 (2001).

16 The uniform term of violation of an obligation has been created in order to consolidate the diverse remedies into one unitary set of remedies which covers all kinds of breaches, particularly defects in title. This need was articulated in ULIS YB IV, art. 41, at 52, n. 115, U.N. Doc. A/CN.9/WG.2/WP.16 (1972) (*reprinted in* John Honnold, Documentary History of the Uniform Law for International Sales, 129 (1989) [hereinafter Honnold, Doc. History]) and carried out in ULIS, YB IV, art. 41 at 59, n. 163 (*reprinted in* Honnold, Doc. History, at 136).

17 *See* Ulrich Huber, *Rechtsbehelfe des Käufers; keine zusätzliche Frist*, art. 45, para. 1, *in* Kommentar zum Einheitlichen UN-Kaufrecht (CISG), *supra* note 6, at art. 45, para. 1;

The language used in Arts. 46(2), (3) and 50 CISG – "[I]f the goods do not conform with the contract..."[18] – could be understood as requiring a defect in quality and thus, may not be applicable to defects in title. This view is also supported by the wording of the heading of Part III, Chapter I, Section II, which reads "Conformity of the goods and third party claims."[19] This language suggests a distinction between conformity in terms of quality as opposed to defects in title.[20]

Thus, under this particular viewpoint, although a synchronism, or better, a practical congruence of the remedies for both defects in quality and defects in title,[21] would be desirable for legal policy reasons,[22] it is de lege lata impossible.[23]

Günter Hager, *Rechtsbehelfe des Verkäufers; keine zusätzliche Frist*, art. 61, paras. 1 and 3, *in* KOMMENTAR ZUM EINHEITLICHEN UN-KAUFRECHT (CISG), *supra* note 6; MATTHIAS HIRNER, DER RECHTSBEHELF DER MINDERUNG NACH DEM UN-KAUFRECHT (CISG) 199, 203 (2000). By contrast, CISG, *supra* note 1, at arts. 45(1)(b), 61(1)(b) set out the basis for claiming damages, while CISG, *supra* note 1, at art. 74, govern only the content and extent of the right to claim damages. *See* Ulrich Huber, *Rechtsbehelfe des Käufers; keine zusätzliche Frist*, art. 45, para. 1, *in* KOMMENTAR ZUM EINHEITLICHEN UN-KAUFRECHT (CISG), *supra* note 6.

18 CISG, *supra* note 1, at arts. 46(2), (3), 50.

19 CISG, *supra* note 1, at Part III, Ch. I, § II.

20 *See* Ingeborg Schwenzer, *Rechtsmängel*, art. 41, para. 20, *in* KOMMENTAR ZUM EINHEITLICHEN UN-KAUFRECHT (CISG), *supra* note 6; JOSEF LANGENECKER, UN-EINHEITSKAUFRECHT UND IMMATERIALGÜTERRECHTE, DIE RECHTSMÄNGELHAFTUNG BEI INTERNATIONALEN KAUFVERTRÄGEN NACH DEM UN-KAUFRECHTSABKOMMEN UNTER BESONDERER BERÜCKSICHTIGUNG VON IMMATERIALGÜTERRECHTEN 52, 95, 263 (Florentz 1993). But see Peter Schlechtriem, *Verjährung von Ansprüchen wegen vertragswidriger Beschaffenheit*, art. 3 VertragsG, para. 5, *in* KOMMENTAR ZUM EINHEITLICHEN UN-KAUFRECHT (CISG), *supra* note 6, according to whom defects in title are covered by the term *lack of conformity* in general because they are treated in the same section as defects in quality. According to the author's view, the second part of the heading "... *and* third party claims" has to be awarded more significance. During the drafting of the Convention the heading had been changed in order to cover defects in title as well, ULIS, YB VIII, art. 25, at 41, n. 225 (of the 1976 Sales Draft), (*reprinted in* HONNOLD, DOC. HISTORY, *supra* note 18, at 334); *see* MARTIN PRAGER, VERKÄUFERHAFTUNG UND AUSLÄNDISCHE GEWERBLICHE SCHUTZRECHTE, DIE HAFTUNG DES VERKÄUFERS BEWEGLICHER SACHEN FÜR DEREN FREIHEIT VON GEWERBLICHEN SCHUTZRECHTEN ODER URHEBERRECHTEN NACH DEM UN-KAUFRECHTSÜBEREINKOMMEN VOM 11. APRIL 1980, 135, 136, 203 (1987).

21 The differentiation between defects in quality, third-party intellectual property rights and defects in title would still lead to the following consequences: A two-year preclusive period only in the case of defects in quality pursuant to CISG, *supra* note 1, at art. 39(2); different requirements for liability and different exemptions from liability, *see* CISG, *supra* note 1, at arts. 35, 41, 42. As a consequence of these remaining differences, it would still be difficult to

2. The Prevailing View Regarding Art. 46(2) and (3) CISG

In the view of most authorities, the restrictive rules on the right to require performance in Art. 46(2) and (3) CISG only apply for defects in quality. Therefore, the buyer of goods, which are encumbered with a third-party claim, has an unrestricted entitlement to performance.[24] These authorities argue systematically that when determining the period of time by which the buyer must have required performance, paragraphs (2) and (3) of Art. 46 CISG only refer to the requirement of giving notice for defects in quality under Art. 39 CISG. However, paragraphs (2) and (3) of Art. 46 CISG do not refer to the same requirement of giving notice for defects in title under Art. 43 CISG.[25]

---

differentiate between the kinds of breaches, e.g., in the case of public-law encumbrances, despite a synchronization of the remedies.

22 *See* PETER SCHLECHTRIEM, INTERNATIONALES UN-KAUFRECHT, para. 202 (2d. ed. 2003), regarding price reduction.

23 See Ulrich Huber, *Minderung*, art. 50, para. 6, *in* KOMMENTAR ZUM EINHEITLICHEN UN-KAUFRECHT (CISG), *supra* note 8, according to whom synchronization would be possible *de lege ferenda*.

24 See STAUDINGER & MAGNUS, KOMMENTAR ZUM BÜRGERLICHEN GESETZBUCH MIT EINFÜHRUNGSGESETZ UND NEBENGESETZEN, WIENER UN-KAUFRECHT (CISG), art. 46, para. 17; art. 41, para. 23 (1999), who refers to the fact that Art. 43 CISG is not mentioned in paragraphs 2 and 3 of Art. 46 CISG. Magnus asserts that as a rule, insubstantial defects in title impede the usage or the sale of the goods. This is not convincing with respect to Art. 42 CISG because in principal goods encumbered with a third-party intellectual property right can be resold. *See also* SOERGEL/LÜDERITZ/SCHÜSSLER-LANGEHEINE, BÜRGERLICHES GESETZBUCH, VOL. 13: ÜBEREINKOMMEN DER VEREINTEN NATIONEN ÜBER VERTRÄGE ÜBER DEN INTERNATIONALEN WARENKAUF, art. 46, para. 13 (2000); WILHELM-ALBRECHT ACHILLES, KOMMENTAR ZUM UN-KAUFRECHTSÜBEREINKOMMEN (CISG), art. 46, para. 2 (2000); LANGENECKER, *supra* note 20, at 268-269; HIRNER, *supra* note 17, at 197 *et seq.*, 200 *et seq.*, 204. *But see* FRITZ ENDERLEIN, *Rights and Obligations of the Seller Under the UN Convention on Contracts for the International Sale of Goods*, *in* INTERNATIONAL SALE OF GOODS, DUBROVNIK LECTURES, 133, 190 (Petar Šarèeviè and Paul Volken eds., 1986); ENDERLEIN&MASKOW&STROHBACH, INTERNATIONALES KAUFRECHT, art. 46, n. 3 (1991).

25 *See* SCHWENZER, *supra* note 20.

3. Price Reduction Due to a Defect in Title Pursuant to Art. 50 CISG

a) Uniform Interpretation

According to the wording and the system of the Convention, and disregarding the normal use of language,[26] some authorities are of the opinion that *lack of conformity* is a technical term which only covers defects in quality. This *terminus technicus* should, under this view, be interpreted in a uniform fashion in every place it appears throughout the Convention.[27] Therefore, Art. 50 CISG should only be applied to cases of defects in quality.[28]

---

26 Under the UCC, there is no problem in designating goods with a defect in title as non-conforming to the contract. *See* UCC § 2-106(2): "Goods ... are "conforming" or conform to the contract when they are in accordance with the obligations under the contract." *But see* PRAGER, *supra* note 20, at 203, according to whom even the normal use of language covers only defects in quality; LANGENECKER, *supra* note 20, at 264. The Directive 1999/44/EC of the European Parliament and of the Council of 25 May 1999 on certain aspects of the sale of consumer goods and associated guarantees aspires only to a harmonization concerning defects in quality under the term *lack of conformity* (*see* art. 2 of the said directive).

27 *See* Ulrich Huber, *Recht des Käufers auf Erfüllung oder Nacherfüllung*, art. 46, paras. 24, 27, and 57, *in* KOMMENTAR ZUM EINHEITLICHEN UN-KAUFRECHT (CISG), *supra* note 6; HUBER, *supra* note 23; MARTIN KAROLLUS, UN-KAUFRECHT: EINE SYSTEMATISCHE DARSTELLUNG FÜR STUDIUM UND PRAXIS 115 (1991). Art. 10(2) of the Convention on the Limitation Period in the International Sale of Goods of 14 June 1974 as amended by the protocol of 11 April 1980 (The USA is a Contracting State of this Convention, *see* http://www.uncitral.org/en-index.htm last visited Oct. 5, 2003) also regards claims due to defects in title as claims due to *lack of conformity*. *See* Markus Müller-Chen, *Spezielle Regeln: Vertragsverletzung, Vertragswidrigkeit; Täuschung*, art. 10 VerjÜbk, para. 4, *in* KOMMENTAR ZUM EINHEITLICHEN UN-KAUFRECHT (CISG), *supra* note 6.

28 *See* HUBER, *supra* note 27, at para. 27; *Id.* at art. 50, para. 8; SCHLECHTRIEM, *supra* note 22, paras. 184, 202 (even though a different view would be desirable for legal policy reasons); PETER SCHLECHTRIEM, UNIFORM SALES LAW, THE UN-CONVENTION ON CONTRACTS FOR THE INTERNATIONAL SALE OF GOODS 78 (1986) *English translation of* EINHEITLICHES UN-KAUFRECHT 70 (1981), where Schlechtriem states that "the general similarity of the prejudice caused by [defects in title or third-party claims based on industrial or other intellectual property rights] with that caused by other defects ... [*generally*] ... justifies the availability of price reduction in these cases as well. *But* the formula for calculating the decrease in value due to such defects surely would have required thorough deliberations for which no time remained at the Conference." (emphasis added). Schlechtriem explicitly concluded that the right to reduce the price under Article 50 is restricted to goods which do not conform to the contract as standardized by Art. 35 CISG. *See id.* at 66, n. 248. *See also* HIRNER, *supra* note 17, at 191 *et seq.*, 214 *et seq.*; PRAGER, *supra* note 20, at 202 *et seq.*, 212,

This uniform interpretation is based on the legislative history and therefore, on the intention of the Conventions drafters, according to whom Arts. 46(2), (3) and 50 CISG should only be applied for liability due to defects in quality.[29]

Finally, it cannot be denied that due to its uniformity and clearness, this view provides for, at a minimum, a certain amount of legal certainty.[30]

b) An Interpretation that Will Yield the Desired Results

In order to allow the buyer of goods, encumbered with third-party claims, to reduce the contract price,[31] authorities argue that the scope of the provisions concerned

---

according to whom this provision could only be denoted as a failure; Anton L. Schnyder & Ralf Michael Straub, *Anspruch auf Erfüllung*, art. 46, paras. 6 and 9 and *Minderung*, art. 50, para. 11, *in* KOMMENTAR ZUM UN-KAUFRECHT (Heinrich Honsell ed., 1997); BURGHARD PILTZ, INTERNATIONALES KAUFRECHT: DAS UN-KAUFRECHT (WIENER ÜBEREINKOMMEN VON 1980) IN PRAXISORIENTIERTER DARSTELLUNG, § 5, paras. 16, 149, 154, 304 (1993); KAROLLUS, *supra* note 27, at 115, 158; Arnau Murià Tunón, *The Actio Quanti Minoris and Sales of Goods between Mexico and the U.S.: An Analysis of the Remedy of Reduction of the Price in the UN Sales Convention, CISG Art. 50 and its Civil Law Antecedents*, § 4.2.3, *available at* http://www.cisg.law.pace.edu/cisg/biblio/muria/html#minoris (last visited Oct. 5, 2003); Peter A. Piliounis, *The Remedies of Specific Performance, Price Reduction and Additional Time (Nachfrist) under the CISG: Are these worthwhile changes or additions to English Sales Law?*, § 6(a)(iii), *available at* http://www.cisg.law.pace.edu/cisg/biblio/piliounis.html#6 (last visited Oct. 5, 2003); *see* Eric E. Bergsten & Anthony J. Miller, *The Remedy of Reduction of Price* (1979) (on Art. 46 of the 1978 Draft Convention), *available at* http://www.cisg.law.pace.edu/cisg/biblio/bergsten.html (last visited Oct. 5, 2003).

29 *See* SECRETARIAT COMMENTARY ON THE 1978 DRAFT CONVENTION, O.R. 14-66, Art. 39, U.N. Doc. A/CONF.97/5 (1979), n. 7 & 8 at 36 (*reprinted in* HONNOLD, DOC. HISTORY, *supra* note 16, at 426); *Id.* at art. 40, n. 12 at 37 (*reprinted in* HONNOLD, DOC. HISTORY, *supra* note 16, at 427). Attempts to broaden the scope of application in order to also cover defects in title were unsuccessful. *See* O.R., art. 46 (of the 1978 Draft Convention), p. 118, n. 3 (motion filed by the Norwegian delegation) (*Id.* at 690); O.R., art. 46 (of the 1978 Draft Convention), pp. 360 *et seq.*, n. 68 to 76 (motion was withdrawn) (*Id.* at 581 *et seq.*).

30 *See* Ingeborg Schwenzer, *Belastung mit Schutzrechten Dritter*, art. 42, para. 26, *in* KOMMENTAR ZUM EINHEITLICHEN UN-KAUFRECHT (CISG), *supra* note 6, who in the end supports the uniform interpretation.

31 *See* STAUDINGER & MAGNUS, *supra* note 24, at art. 41, para. 26; art. 50, para. 10; *see* SOERGEL/LÜDERITZ/SCHÜSSLER-LANGEHEINE, *supra* note 24, at art. 50, para. 2, who recognize that the wording is an argument against price reduction in the case of a defect in title but in conclusion support the application of art. 50 CISG by analogy; ACHILLES, *supra* note 24, at art. 50, para. 2; ROBERT LOEWE, INTERNATIONALES KAUFRECHT, art. 50, para.

must be determined autonomously. As a systematic argument, these authorities cite the rule of Art. 44 CISG. According to this Article, the buyer is entitled to exercise his right to reduce the contract price under Art. 50 CISG if he has a reasonable excuse for his failure to give notice as required by Arts. 39 and 43 CISG.[32] Under this view, it makes little sense that a buyer should only be entitled to price reduction if he failed to give notice, but is not entitled to price reduction if he gave the required notice.[33]

Yet, this argument is neither cogent,[34] nor convincing,[35] because in accordance with its wording and rationale, which is to aid in the case of a failure to give notice, Art. 44 CISG can only be interpreted as setting forth a provision which refers to the legal grounds of other provisions. Consequently, the right of contract price reduction is only given to the buyer if all other requirements of this right to alter a legal relationship by unilateral declaration are met.[36] These other requirements are, however, not met in the case of a defect in title.[37] Moreover, the language of Art. 44 CISG does not preclude the interpretation that the buyer is only entitled to a contract price reduction in the case of a failure to give notice under Art. 39 CISG, but refers the buyer to the remedy of damages in the case of a failure to give notice under Art. 43 CISG.

---

72 (1989); Friedrich Niggemann, *Die Pflichten des Verkäufers und die Rechtsbehelfe des Käufers*, *in* DAS EINHEITLICHE WIENER KAUFRECHT 77, 106 (Hoyer/Posch eds., 1992); LANGENECKER, *supra* note 20, at 270 *et seq*.

32 *See* STAUDINGER & MAGNUS, *supra* note 24, at art. 50, para. 9; Michael Will, *Remedies for Breach of Contract by the Seller*, *in* COMMENTARY ON THE INTERNATIONAL SALES LAW: THE 1980 VIENNA SALES CONVENTION, art. 50, n. 3.4. (Bianca and Bonell eds., 1987) (doubtingly).

33 *See* ENDERLEIN&MASKOW&STROHBACH, *supra* note 24, at art. 50, n. 1; WILL, *supra* note 32, at art. 50, n. 3.4; LANGENECKER, *supra* note 20, at 264.

34 *See* SCHNYDER & STRAUB, *supra* note 28, art. 45, para. 54.

35 *See* JOHN O. HONNOLD, UNIFORM LAW FOR INTERNATIONAL SALES UNDER THE 1980 UNITED NATIONS CONVENTION, para. 313.1 (3d. ed. 1999), which states that the scope of application of the price reduction is limited to "claims for non-conformity" and refers to Arts. 74 *et seq*. CISG because they represent a more flexible and accurate basis for the assessment of damage.

36 *See* Ulrich Huber, *Entschuldigung für unterlassene Anzeige*, art. 44, para. 14, *in* KOMMENTAR ZUM EINHEITLICHEN UN-KAUFRECHT (CISG), *supra* note 6. *But see* LANGENECKER, *supra* note 20, at 264, 265.

37 *See* HUBER, *supra* note 36.

III. The Solution to the Problem Concerning Art. 82(2)(c) CISG

According to the uniform interpretation, the term *lack of conformity* in Art. 82(2)(c) CISG may be interpreted as covering only defects in quality. Under such an interpretation, the results are that the buyer would only be harmed by his bad faith in the case of a defect in quality.

Or, should this question be answered in a different way to provide a just solution in this context? Then, it follows, that the premise of the uniform interpretation would be refuted and this may bring about interpretive consequences to the other provisions of the Convention which have been thus far controverted.

In order to answer the question whether defects in quality and title should be treated in the same or under different rubrics based on Art. 82(2)(c) CISG, their substantive differences must first be recalled.

1. The Standards for Liability in Arts. 35, 41 and 42 CISG

The Convention sets out different standards of liability for defects in quality, Art. 35 CISG; liability for defects in title, Art. 41 CISG; and liability for third-party intellectual property rights, Art. 42 CISG.

When comparing these provisions, one discovers that Arts. 35(3) and 42(2)(a) CISG use the same language concerning the exemption from liability due to the buyer's knowledge of the defect.[38] According to this language, the buyer of goods, which are encumbered with a defect in quality or a third-party intellectual property right, loses his remedies if at the time of the conclusion of the contract he knew or could not have been unaware of the interference.

By contrast, in the case of a defect in title under Art. 41 CISG, even the buyer's positive knowledge of the defect does not harm him.[39] In this case, he can only lose his remedies by consenting[40] to take the goods subject to the defect.

---

38 *See* Yingxia Su, *Die Rechtsmängelhaftung des Verkäufers nach UN-Kaufrecht und im chinesischen Recht*, Praxis des internationalen Privat- und Verfahrensrechts [hereinafter IPRax] 284 *et seq.*, 287 (1997).

39 *See* Peter Schlechtriem, International Sales, Conformity of the Goods, Seller's Obligations under the United Nations Convention on Contracts for the International Sale of Goods, § 6.03, at 6-31 (Galston & Smit eds., 1984).

40 The controversy concerning the prerequisites for an acceptance of the goods despite the

2. Comparison of the standards for liability with Art. 82(2)(c) CISG

While the exemption rules in Arts. 35, 41 and 42 CISG completely exclude the liability of the seller, Art. 82(2)(c) CISG only blocks the right to declare the contract avoided pursuant to Art. 49 CISG. If Art. 82(2)(c) CISG is also considered in the comparison, a congruence appears between the cases of defects in quality and third-party intellectual property rights, whereas defects in title differ. With regard to contract avoidance, the buyer is harmed by his imputed lack of knowledge in the case of defects in quality or third-party intellectual property rights, regardless of whether these interferences had been in existence at the time of the conclusion of the contract (*see* Arts. 35 and 42 CISG) or had come to exist after that point in time (*see* Art. 82(2)(c) CISG). Contrary to this, at the time of the conclusion of the contract, the buyer of goods encumbered with a defect in title is only harmed by consenting to take the goods subject to that defect (*see* Art. 41 CISG), whereas, after that point in time his imputed lack of knowledge also serves to block the remedy of avoidance (*see* Art. 82(2)(c) CISG). This hypothetical result requires that *lack of conformity* cover every form of interference with the contract. Such an understanding would lead to the preposterous result that the buyer who obtains knowledge one minute before the time of conclusion of the contract be entitled to declare the contract avoided, but not the buyer who obtains the same knowledge one minute after the time of conclusion of the contract. In other words: a buyer does not lose his right to avoid the contract when he already had knowledge of a defect in title at the conclusion of the contract. Therefore, why should he lose that right if he obtains knowledge of a defect after the conclusion of the contract? For this reason, in cases under Art. 41 CISG, it does not make any logical sense to preclude the buyer from exercising his right to declare the contract avoided pursuant to Art. 82(2)(c) CISG.

Moreover, the opposing result would contravene the rationale of Art. 82(2)(c) CISG, which is to punish inconsistent behavior. In the case where the buyer takes over goods encumbered with a defect in title despite his knowledge of that defect, Art. 41 CISG does not take away his remedies for the sole reason that he has acted inconsistently. Actually, quite the opposite is true. Regarding the liability for title

---

defect in title known to the buyer is irrelevant because it is certain that such an acceptance requires more than mere knowledge of the defect, *see* SCHWENZER, *supra* note 20, at para. 17. Indeed, such an acceptance can be given implicitly (*see* SCHLECHTRIEM, *supra* note 39, at § 6.03, p. 6-31). However, in order for an unconditional acceptance of the goods to constitute an agreement to take the goods subject to the defect, it is necessary that, for example, the buyer pay the price directly to the third party after receiving the seller's notice of the infringed third-party trademark.

defects under Art. 41 CISG, the objection of *venire contra factum proprium*[41] is implicitly derogated.

When viewed in context with Art. 82(2)(c) CISG, it is thus justified to interpret the term *lack of conformity* as barring the remedy of avoidance for the buyer who learned, only after the conclusion of the contract, about a defect in quality or a third-party intellectual property right but resold the goods despite this knowledge. Conversely, in the case of a defect in title the buyer is never harmed by his knowledge of that defect, i.e., there is no dependence on whether he had this knowledge at the time of the contract's conclusion or afterwards.

3. History of the Convention

The drafting history of the Convention supports this author's view.[42] The relevant language of Art. 82(2)(c) CISG is based on Art. 79(2)(c) ULIS.[43] Due to the incorporation of the language, "have been sold in the normal course of business," the scope of the exceptions now covers cases of resale.[44] In addition, in order to establish an objective criterion, the language "or ought to have been discovered" was added to the element of positive knowledge.[45] Independent from these

---

41 The prohibition of *venire contra factum proprium* is a principle of the Convention, which derives from the principle of loyalty and good faith under art. 7 CISG. Moreover, it is the underlying principle of arts. 16(2) and 29(2) CISG. *See* Franco Ferrari, *Auslegung des Übereinkommens und Lückenfüllung*, art. 7, para. 50, *in* KOMMENTAR ZUM EINHEITLICHEN UN-KAUFRECHT (CISG), *supra* note 6; *see also* Franco Ferrari, *Das Verhältnis zwischen den UNIDROIT-Grundsätzen und den allgemeinen Grundsätzen internationaler Einheitsprivatrechts-konventionen*, JURISTEN ZEITUNG [hereinafter JZ] 12 (1998); Ulrich Magnus, *Die allgemeinen Grundsätze im UN-Kaufrecht*, 59 RABELS ZEITSCHRIFT FÜR AUSLÄNDISCHES UND INTERNATIONALES PRIVATRECHT [hereinafter RABELSZ] 469, 480-494 (1995).

42 *See generally* LESER & HORNUNG, *supra* note 6, at paras. 1 *et seq.*

43 *See* CISG, *supra* note 1, art. 82(2)(c) and ULIS, YB V, Art. 79(2)(c), U.N. Doc. A/CN.9/87 (1984), note 146, at 43 *reprinted in* HONNOLD, DOC. HISTORY, *supra* note 16.

44 *Working Group: Session No. 5 – Jan. 1984*, ULIS, YB V, art. 79, U.N. Doc. A/CN.9/87 (1984), n. 146, at 43 (*reprinted in* HONNOLD, DOC. HISTORY, *supra* note 16, at 189). After this decision art. 79 ULIS despite some insubstantial differences in the wording reads exactly as the present Art. 82 CISG, *see* ULIS, YB V, art. 79, U.N. Doc. A/CN.9/87(1984), note 153 at 43 (*reprinted in* HONNOLD, DOC. HISTORY, *supra* note 16, at 189).

45 *See* LESER & HORNUNG, *supra* note 6, para. 2; YANG-HO SONG, VERTRAGSAUFHEBUNG UND RÜCKABWICKLUNG NACH DEUTSCHEM UND KOREANISCHEM RECHT UND INTERNATIONALEM EINHEITSKAUFRECHT, EINE ANALYSE DER FOLGEN DES UNTERGANGS ODER EINER BEEINTRÄCHTIGUNG DER KAUFSACHE VOR ODER NACH ERKLÄRUNG DER AUFHEBUNG 237 (1999).

amendments, the exceptions of consume and transformation had already been in existence, which were also applied only to cases in which the buyer did not know of the lack of conformity, see Art. 79(2)(c) ULIS. Due to the fact that the ULIS did not contain a separate rule for liability for third-party intellectual property rights as does Art. 42 CISG, the term lack of conformity in Art. 79(2)(c) ULIS differentiated only between defects in quality and defects in title. This, for the very same reasons as was shown above with respect to the CISG, was appropriate. Article 52 ULIS was applied to cases of liability for third-party intellectual property rights because this form of liability was not expressly settled and was classified as a sort of liability for defects in title.[46] Consequently, in the case of goods encumbered with third-party intellectual property rights, the buyer was only harmed by consenting to take over the goods despite that interference.[47] Therefore, it did not make sense to block the buyer's remedies pursuant to Art. 79(2)(c) ULIS. The necessity to separate liability for third-party intellectual property rights first arose when establishing Art. 42 CISG,[48] whose content is more orientated towards liability for defects in quality than liability for defects in title.[49] The similarity in their legal conception is covered over by a technical decision in the legislative process. The liability for third-party intellectual property rights has been laid down in its own Article, subsequent and

---

46 OLG (Regional Court of Appeal) Düsseldorf, decision of 20 January 1983, *reprinted in* SCHLECHTRIEM & MAGNUS, INTERNATIONALE RECHTSPRECHUNG ZUM EKG UND EAG, Art. 76 EKG, note 4, pp. 400 *et seq.* (design patent as defect ain title) (1987); Karl H. Neumayer, *Gewährleistung für Rechtsmängel*, art. 52, para. 17, *in* KOMMENTAR ZUM EINHEITLICHEN KAUFRECHT, *supra* note 8; MERTENS & REHBINDER, INTERNATIONALES KAUFRECHT, KOMMENTAR ZU DEN EINHEITLICHEN KAUFGESETZEN, art. 52, para. 5 (1975); SOERGEL/LÜDERITZ, KOMMENTAR ZUM BÜRGERLICHEN GESETZBUCH, VOL. 3, art. 52 EKG, para. 2 (1991); Ulrich Huber, *Der UNCITRAL-Entwurf eines Übereinkommens über internationale Warenkaufverträge*, 43 RABELSZ 502 (1979); *cf.* Otto Riese, *Der Entwurf zur internationalen Vereinheitlichung des Kaufrechts*, 22 RABELSZ 16, 74 (1957), on the Rome draft; *see* HONNOLD, *supra* note 35, para. 268, who doubtingly discusses the possibility to treat an injunction as a defect in quality.

47 *Consent* was already seen in the unconditional acceptance despite the positive knowledge of the defect in title, *see* NEUMAYER, *supra* note 46, para. 12.

48 The first draft on the specific liability for third-party intellectual property rights was adopted by a working group of the tenth session of UNCITRAL and substantially accords with the present art. 42 CISG, *see UNCITRAL: Preparation of the 1977 UNCITRAL "Sales" Draft*, notes 211 *et seq* at 40 *et seq.*, YB VIII, art. 25, U.N. Doc. A/32/17 (1977) (*Reprinted in* HONNOLD, DOC. HISTORY, *supra* note 16, at 333 *et seq.*).

49 *See* SCHWENZER, *supra* note 30, para. 25; SCHLECHTRIEM, *supra* note 39, at p. 6-33; *see* SCHLECHTRIEM, *supra* note 28 (Uniform Sales Law), at 73, 74, who states: "Nevertheless, it is apparent that this case (Art. 42 CISG) is regarded as a special category of breach of contract, closer to a lack of conformity than to a defect in title." *But see* PRAGER, *supra* note 20, at 224, who assigns art. 42 CISG to the liability for defects in title under Art. 41 CISG.

consistent with the liability for defects in title, under the heading "rights and claims of a third party." This corresponds to its phenomenon as a "third-party right."[50]

4. Conclusion

As a result, the term *lack of conformity* in Art. 82(2)(c) CISG covers defects in quality as well as third-party intellectual property rights. By contrast, general defects in title are excluded.

IV. Transformation of this Interpretation on the Buyer's Remedies

This definition of *lack of conformity*, as discussed immediately above in context with Art. 82(2)(c) CISG, seems compelling because it is the only interpretation which adapts to the Convention's law of performance impairments. However, the inquiry that persists is whether this subdivision of defects in quality and third-party intellectual property rights, on the one hand, and general defects in title, on the other hand, is also sensible in the context of Arts. 46(2), (3) and 50 CISG. In other words, the question is whether the conclusions made here are applicable to the controversy which has been discussed above.

1. Application to Art. 46(2) and (3) CISG

In the context of the restrictions on the right of performance in Art. 46(2) and (3) CISG, the solution found in Art. 82(2)(c) CISG is applicable. It was clear during the drafting of the CISG, that in international trade a guarantee by the seller for worldwide protection against third-party intellectual property rights would hardly make sense due to the principle of territoriality.[51] This consideration led to limitations on the seller's liability with the effect that liability for third-party intellectual property rights is more similar to liability for defects in quality than to liability for defects in title.[52] As this structural similarity is evident with respect to the requirements for a breach of contract, it must also have a marked effect on the remedies. Otherwise, the exemption from liability would be circumvented by

---

50 CISG, *supra* note 1, art. 42.

51 *See* SECRETARIAT COMMENTARY ON THE 1978 DRAFT, *supra* note 29, para. 4 at 37 (*Reprinted in* HONNOLD, DOC. HISTORY, *supra* note 16, at 427); SCHWENZER, *supra* note 30, para. 1.

52 *See supra* note 49.

granting the buyer remedies which place too high a burden on the seller.[53] In conclusion, an application of the interpretation of lack of conformity as discussed above to Art. 46(2) and (3) CISG is sensible.

2. Application to Art. 50 CISG

The application of these conclusions to Art. 50 CISG is also sensible. First, even the authorities who agree to price reduction in the case of a "third-party right" seem to base their argument not on the premise that there is a defect in title but rather on the premise that a third party has asserted an intellectual property right.[54] Moreover, during the drafting of the Convention, the framers regarded third-party intellectual property rights as an interference with an obligation, which should naturally entitle the other party to a contract price reduction.[55] They kept the language *lack of conformity* precisely in order to delimit general defects in title.

---

53 Substitute delivery in case of fungible goods, e.g., delivery under a different brand which does not infringe a third-party trademark, or, remedying a defect by replacing the infringing component with a non-infringing component, is very incriminating to the seller in international trade, *see* SCHWENZER, *supra* note 30, para. 25. But *see* LANGENECKER, *supra* note 20, at 268, according to whom a defect in title always constitutes a fundamental breach of contract so that the additional requirement of a fundamental breach in art. 46(2) CISG is divested of any effect.

54 *See* STAUDINGER & MAGNUS, *supra* note 24, art. 50, para.10, with the following example: The goods are encumbered with a trademark so that the buyer is barred to enter the market. However, he is able and willing to use the goods in-house. If a damages claim was exceptionally excluded by virtue of art. 79 CISG, the buyer would depend on a claim for price reduction. *See also* HERBER & CZERWENKA, *supra* note 12, art. 50, para. 3, with the following example: It may be reasonable for a buyer to choose this simple remedy if his goods are only infringing a third-party intellectual property right in one region, so that he can sell the goods in other regions.

55 SCHLECHTRIEM sympathized with the intent of the Norwegian delegation's motion, which was to change the wording of art. 46 of the 1978 Draft Convention (present art. 50 CISG) in such a way that defects in title under art. 39 of the 1978 Draft Convention (present art. 41 CISG) would also entitle the remedy of contract price reduction. However, he claimed that problems would arise. First, "price reduction in the case of third-party claims might be inappropriate in certain cases. Secondly, the amendment might lead to the conclusion that in the case of Article 40 (of the 1978 Draft Convention; present art. 42 CISG) a price reduction was not permitted." SECRETARIAT COMMENTARY ON THE 1978 DRAFT, *supra* note 29, art. 46, note 74 at 360, (*Reprinted in* HONNOLD, DOC. HISTORY, *supra* note 16, at 581).

Second, the legal consequence of the *actio quanti minoris* – an adaptation of the contract through proportionate reduction of the contract price – makes no logical sense from the outset in the case of a sale of goods where the third party has legitimate title to the goods as per Art. 41 CISG because the buyer has no interest in keeping the goods but in avoiding the contract.[56] Admittedly, there are cases within the scope of Art. 41 CISG in which price reduction would offer a sensible alternative. Due to the fact that a concurring damages claim pursuant to Art. 45(1)(b) CISG in connection with Art. 74 CISG would rarely be excluded by virtue of Art. 79 CISG,[57] it would lead to the satisfaction of the buyer. Therefore, in accordance with the language of Art. 50 CISG, the buyer of goods encumbered with a defect in title is not entitled to the remedy of price reduction.[58]

However, in cases where a third party has intellectual property rights, price reduction represents a sensible alternative course of action for the buyer. In such a case, the third party has a right of exploitation and either the buyer or the seller could satisfy its business interest by paying a sum, e.g., a royalty. In return, the party who paid receives the right of use which allows the contract between the seller and the buyer to be executed as anticipated. The loss in value of the goods caused by direct payment or temporary impairment could be deducted from the contract price in the form of a price reduction. In conclusion, Art. 50 CISG should be regarded as an applicable remedy for cases involving defects in quality or third-party intellectual property rights but not to cases of defects in title.

---

56 The right to reduce the price would only be sensible if, in this case, the buyer was allowed to reduce the contract price to zero. However, it would not only be necessary to affirm that a price reduction to zero is admissible in general but also that the defective goods were objectively without any value (*see* HIRNER, *supra* note 17, at 177). The goods can only be without any value in the case of a defect in quality because this is the only case in which the seller has no interest in restitution of the goods. By contrast, in the case of a defect in title the goods are only subjectively without any value for the buyer because the property has not been transferred to him. However, the seller (and even more the proprietor) has a lawful interest in restitution of the goods which are physically unobjectionable. Thus, the goods are not objectively without any value. *But see* WOLFF, *supra* note 12, at 174, according to whom particularly in this case the goods are without any value and therefore the price reduction represents an adequate remedy. Even if it was argued in accordance with the opposing view that subjective worthlessness was sufficient, the principle of loyalty and good faith pursuant to art. 7 CISG would impose an obligation to make restitution on the buyer, *cf.* HIRNER, *supra* note 17, at 172.

57 *See* SCHWENZER, *supra* note 20, para. 21.

58 *See* CISG, *supra* note 1, art. 50.

3. Conclusion

As a result, if all other requirements are met, the buyer of goods encumbered with a defect in quality or a third-party intellectual property right is only restrictively entitled to the right to require performance and can only avoid the contract before he obtains knowledge of such a defect, but at all times, is entitled to the right of price reduction. On the other hand, the buyer of goods encumbered with a defect in title is unrestrictively entitled to the right to require performance and can avoid the contract despite his knowledge of that defect but is not entitled to price reduction in any event.

V. Compensation for Loss of Use and Damages as Correctives for Impaired Restitution

Finally, discussion is warranted regarding how to control the behavior of a buyer who has knowledge of a defect in title and resells the goods under value and possibly, with the intention of harming the seller. According to the previous view, this situation was governed by the bar created by Art. 82(1) CISG. Due to the fact that in the author's view, the buyer of goods encumbered with a defect in title is entitled to resell the goods despite his knowledge of that defect without losing his right to avoid the contract, there may be situations in which the buyer resells the goods far under value. For example, the buyer could dispose of the goods in a bargain-basement sale then avoid the contract and finally, ask the seller for reimbursement of the full contract price and interest thereon as it is permitted under Arts. 81(2)(first sentence) and 84(1) CISG.

The CISG does not follow the concept of other modern[59] laws of performance impairments,[60] which describe the problem of impaired restitution as a problem of

---

59 *See* SCHLECHTRIEM, *supra* note 22, para. 321.

60 Art. 7.3.6(1) second sentence of the UNIDROIT Principles of International Commercial Contracts: "If restitution in kind is not possible or appropriate allowance should be made in money whenever reasonable."; art. 4.305-309 of the Principles of European Contract Law, *see* Reinhard Zimmermann, *Konturen eines Europäischen Vertragsrechts*, JZ 477 *et seq.*, 485 (1995); Art.160(3) to (7) of the Gandolfi-Draft (Code Européen des Contrats), *see* Ingeborg Schwenzer, *Wandlungen des Schuldrechts, Rechtsbehelfe und Rückabwicklung im CISG, in den European und UNIDROIT Principles, im Gandolfi-Entwurf sowie im deutschen Schuldrechts-modernisierungsgesetz*, p. 46 *et seq.* (Schlechtriem ed., 2002); § 346(2) and (3) Bürgerliches Gesetzbuch (German Civil Code, *available at* http://bundesrecht.juris.de/bundesrecht/bgb/

liability and grant the seller, who does not recover the goods, a claim compensating him for the lost value of the goods.[61] This claim protects the seller from the aforementioned situation because in any case the objective value of the goods is granted to him as a minimum.

According to Art. 84(2)(b) CISG, the buyer owes the seller "all benefits which he has derived from the goods" if he is not able to make restitution of all goods.[62] The authentic French text and the (official) German translation of the Convention do not refer to the value of goods by using the language "*equivalent amount* of all benefits"[63] (emphasis added). Rather, the buyer must account for the concrete benefits which he has received.[64] Therefore, if the buyer gained only a "give-away" price, he owes only that price. While it is true that the buyer of goods encumbered with a defect in title is not harmed by his knowledge of that defect, another element of the rule of Art. 82(2)(c) CISG establishes that the buyer must resell the goods in the "normal course of business."[65] Due to the fact that bargain-basement sales are not in accordance with the ordinary course of business,[66] restitution is still barred by Art. 82(1) CISG.

However, the case of a buyer who sells the goods under value, although not at a "give-away" price, is not governed by the bar established by Art. 82(1) CISG. In any case, a resale performed with the intent to cause damage constitutes a violation of a contractual obligation to protect the other party.[67] This is not affected by

---

index.html [last visited Oct. 5, 2003]); Art. 6:265,269,271,272 of the Nieuw Burgerlijk Wetboek (Netherlands), *see* HARTKAMP, MR. C. ASSER'S HANDLEIDING TOT DE BEOEFENING VAN HET NEDERLANDS BURGERLIJK RECHT, VERBINTENISSENRECHT, PART II, note 105, para. 534 (9th ed. 1993).

61 *See* RAINER HORNUNG, DIE RÜCKABWICKLUNG GESCHEITERTER VERTRÄGE NACH FRANZÖSISCHEM, DEUTSCHEM UND NACH EINHEITSRECHT: GEMEINSAMKEITEN, UNTERSCHIEDE, WECHSELWIRKUNGEN 149 (1998), on the UNIDROIT Principles and the European Principles; KREBS, *supra* note 3, at 92 *et seq.*

62 CISG, *supra* note 1, art. 84(2)(b).

63 French: "*l'équivalent de tout profit;*" German: „*Gegenwert aller Vorteile.*"

64 *See* HORNUNG, *supra* note 61, at 152.

65 *See* CISG, *supra* note 1, art. 82(2)(c).

66 *See* SONG, *supra* note 45, at 239; *see also* OLG (Regional Court of Appeal) Düsseldorf, decision of 10 February 1994, CISG-online Case No.115, *available at* http://www.cisg-online.ch., in which the question was left open whether the exceptions of art. 82(2) CISG did not apply because of the remnant goods which had been squandered under price or because of the buyer's knowledge of the defect.

67 The basis is CISG, *supra* note 1, art. 61(1)(b).

avoidance[68] and exacts compensation for damages in accordance with Art. 74 CISG. Moreover, pursuant to Art. 86 CISG, the buyer who intends to exercise his right to reject the goods, here in the form of avoidance, has a special duty of care for the preservation of the goods.[69] A violation of the aforementioned duty of care under Art. 86 CISG also includes the consequence of damages.[70] This solution is most relevant in cases where the buyer has resold under value, but not with the intent to cause harm to the seller or, at least, where it cannot be proved that the buyer had such intent.[71] In such a situation, an exclusion of the obligor's liability pursuant to Art. 79 CISG is out of the question.

Another question is the extent to which damages can be claimed. Is it enough to compensate the seller for the value of the goods or is he also entitled to the hypothetical profit which he would have gained out of resale in the normal course of business? The value of the benefits must be objectively assessed from the view of a reasonable third person. As a rule, it will cover the initial purchase price plus net profit[72] which would have been made by a reasonable businessperson. Otherwise, the balance of restitution would be disturbed since according to Art. 84(1) CISG, the buyer can ask for interest on the full purchase price from the date payment has been made.

It has been suggested that Art. 51 CISG might assist the buyer of goods, encumbered with a defect in quality or a third-party intellectual property right, who is barred from avoiding the contract because of his knowledge of the defect. In fact, he could be entitled to avoid the contract with respect to the goods he is able to restitute.[73] In

---

68 CISG, *supra* note 1, at art. 81(1) first sentence.

69 *See* Karsten Otte, *UN-Kaufrecht: Käuferrechte bei Weiterverarbeitung der Kaufsache bzw. unterlassener Untersuchung und Mängelanzeige*, IPRAX 352 *et seq.*, 355 (1999); Klaus Bacher, *Pflicht des Käufers zur Inbesitznahme und Erhaltung der Ware*, art. 86, para. 18 and *Pflicht des Verkäufers zur Erhaltung der Ware*, art. 85, paras 12 *et seq.*, *in* KOMMENTAR ZUM EINHEITLICHEN UN-KAUFRECHT (CISG), *supra* note 6; *see also* WITZ/SALGER/LORENZ/LORENZ, INTERNATIONAL EINHEITLICHES KAUFRECHT, PRAKTIKER-KOMMENTAR UND VERTRAGSGESTALTUNG ZUM CISG, Vor arts. 85-88, para. 2 (2000), according to whom this claim could also be based on general contractual obligations of due care under art. 7(1) CISG.

70 *See* Klaus Bacher, *Vorbemerkungen zu Artt. 85-88*, para. 4, *in* KOMMENTAR ZUM EINHEITLICHEN UN-KAUFRECHT (CISG), *supra* note 8; KREBS, *supra* note 3, at 130, 131.

71 In general, the burden of proof is allocated to the party which claims facts in favor of itself. In this case, it is the seller. *See* Hans Stoll, *Umfang des Schadenersatzes*, art. 74, para. 47, *in* KOMMENTAR ZUM EINHEITLICHEN UN-KAUFRECHT (CISG), *supra* note 6.

72 Certainly, the buyer may account for costs he suffered as a consequence of the resale.

73 JAN HEILMANN, MÄNGELGEWÄHRLEISTUNG IM UN-KAUFRECHT, VORAUSSETZUNGEN UND RECHTSFOLGEN IM VERGLEICH ZUM DEUTSCHEN INTERNEN KAUFRECHT UND ZU DEN

the author's opinion such a solution is not possible because it would circumvent the buyer's obligation to restore the surrogates pursuant to Art. 84(2)(b) CISG, which represents the "price" for the buyer's possibility to avoid the contract despite his impairment in making restitution of all goods, and thereby contravene the rule of Art. 82(1) CISG.

VI. Summary

In context with the bar on the remedy of avoidance in Art. 82(2)(c) CISG, it has been shown that the term *lack of conformity* covers defects in quality as well as third-party intellectual property rights. Therefore, in the case where all other requirements are met, the buyer of goods encumbered with a defect in title, in the sense of Art. 41 CISG, is entitled to avoid the contract despite the fact that he cannot make restitution of all goods and that he had knowledge of the defect. The resulting problems of an impaired restitution due to an avoidance of a bad faith buyer can be completely solved by the general rules on compensation for loss of use and damages. Finally, with respect to the remedies of the buyer to reduce the price or to require performance, it is reasonable to distinguish between defects in quality and third-party intellectual property rights, on the one hand, and defects in title, on the other

HAAGER EINHEITLICHEN KAUFGESETZEN 486 (1994); *see* NINA FREIBURG, DAS RECHT AUF VERTRAGSAUFHEBUNG IM UN-KAUFRECHT, UNTER BESONDERER BERÜCKSICHTIGUNG DER AUSSCHLUSSGRÜNDE 264 (2001), according to whom the deprivation of the right to declare the contract avoided is restricted to the affected part of the delivery by virtue of Art. 51(1) CISG which should be applied by analogy; *see* HUBER, *supra* note 6, art. 49, para. 32, according to whom in case of unreasonable detriments resulting for the seller he might be helped with the principle of loyalty and good faith under art. 7(1) CISG. In favor of his view, Huber cites the BGH (German Federal Court of Justice) *reprinted in* NJW, 2730, 2732 (1982) and SCHNYDER & STRAUB, *supra* note 28, art. 49, para. 94. However, both citations do not concern cases of art. 82 CISG. Here is rather the problem of a buyer who is entitled to avoidance of the contract in its entirety. It is stated that in, such a case, the buyer might declare the contract avoided in part. This was in accordance with the purpose that avoidance should be the *ultima-ratio* remedy. However, avoidance of the contract in its entirety had to be admissible. Yet, under art. 82(1) CISG, which sets out a *requirement* of avoidance, the buyer is not entitled to avoid the contract in its entirety.

hand. In conclusion, the term *lack of conformity* has to be interpreted in the Convention as covering defects in quality within the parameters of Art. 35 CISG, and third-party intellectual property rights under Art. 42 CISG.[74]

---

[74] In this essay it was impossible to show in detail how the author's interpretation affects the other provisions using the term *lack of conformity* as named *supra* note 11. In the case of partial impairment of performance, the buyer is entitled to exercise his remedies only with respect to the non-conforming part according to art. 51 CISG. Only in the context with this provision, the author's differentiation is not sensible because it is possible that only a part of the goods is encumbered with a defect in title under art. 41 CISG. Therefore, in this context the term *lack of conformity* is not to be understood in its technical sense. However, with regard to all other provisions the author's interpretation leads to reasonable solutions.

Part II
Symposium Addresses

Pace University School of Law Conference on the United Nations Convention on Contracts for the International Sale of Goods (CISG), September 26, 2003

Article 7(1) of the United Nations Convention on Contracts for the Sale of Goods (CISG) states:

"In the interpretation of the Convention, regard is to be had to its international character and to the need to promote uniformity in its application and the observance of good faith in international trade."[1]

Theodore B. Olson, Solicitor General of the United States, calls attention to the fact that:

"Article 7(1)'s reference to 'the need to promote uniformity in [the Convention's] application' is not appreciably different from the rule that judicial decisions from other countries interpreting a treaty term are 'entitled to considerable weight.' *El Al Israel Airlines Ltd. v. Tsui Yuan Tseng*, U.S. 155, 176 (1999) (quoting *Air France v. Saks*, 470 U.S. 392, 404 (1985)."[2]

All countries that accord comity to treaty obligations respect this rule. The CISG is a treaty that has sixty-three sister signatories.[3]

A seminar on the Global *jurisconsultorium* and the CISG was held at the New York State Judicial Institute on September 26, 2003. The seminar was hosted by the Institute of International Commercial Law of the Pace University School of Law. It was sponsored by the International Law and Practice Section of the New York State Bar Association and the Practising Law Institute. The following were among the presentations at this seminar.

---

1 United Nations Convention on Contracts for the International Sale of Goods, April 11, 1980, S. Treaty Doc. No. 98-9 (1984), 1489 U.N.T.S. 3, *reprinted in* United Nations Conference on Contracts for the International Sale of Goods, 19 I.L.M. 668 (1980). *Available at* http://www.cisg.law.pace.edu and at http://www.unidroit.org.

2 Brief for the United States as Amicus Curiae at 10, Zapata Hermanos Sucesores, S.A v. Hearthside Baking Company, 124 S.Ct. 803 (2003). *See also at* http://cisgw3.law.pace.edu/cisg/biblio/zapata4.html

3 Current CISG status information is *available at* http://www.uncitral.org/english/status/status-e.htm. *See also*, http://www.cisg.law.pace.edu/cisg/countries/cntries.html

Keynote Address: Pace University School of Law Conference on the United Nations Convention on Contracts for the International Sale of Goods (CISG): **Of Words and Issues – Finding a Common Language for Common Issues**

Peter Schlechtriem

Your honor, distinguished colleagues, ladies and gentlemen,

It is an extraordinary honor to be invited to address you over lunch, and a great responsibility. I am not sure how to live up to it. Most of my topics have been preempted by the speakers of the morning session; to deal with the remaining issues would require me to go into details which could only be boring for you and would prevent you from enjoying your lunch.

I shall take up some very general aspects of the CISG as a chance to find a common legal language for common issues in a world of global sales transactions.

I. The Background

Legal history tells us, that when commerce and economic activities in certain regions, nations, and continents develop and grow – because borders are opened up, tariffs are abolished, new means of transportation and communication are invented – there follow increasingly calls for uniform or at least harmonized rules of law to govern this interregional, interstate or international trade.

These calls could be and were answered by different instruments: If legislators had the prerequisite competence to set uniform rules, they could enact codes – commercial codes, civil codes. The great European codifications of the nineteenth century are examples of unified laws enacted to meet the needs of territories growing together economically and to overcome the hurdles of diverging legal rules. Where such legislative competence was lacking, states could bind themselves by international conventions to enact uniform rules for certain transactions, in particular, transborder transactions.

The twentieth century brought a number of such conventions, first in the field of cheques and bills of exchange, then indispensable instruments of transborder payments. After the First World War, a number of conventions on international transport law such as carriage of goods and persons by ship, railways, airplanes and motor vehicles followed. It was about the same time – in the 1920's – that the idea was conceived not only to unify the rules for the transborder *transport* of goods, but also the transaction underlying most transports of goods, that is, the transborder *sale* of goods. This idea was promulgated in and by the Institute for the Unification of Private Law in Rome, a foundation of the League of Nations. It led to the first Uniform Laws, ULIS and ULF, the so-called Hague Sales Laws of 1964. As these laws were only ratified by nine states, UNCITRAL made a second attempt to unify the sales law for transborder sales, successfully achieved in the UN Convention on Contracts for the International Sale of Goods (CISG) of 1980.

The picture of legal instruments to overcome by unification, the obstacles to commerce caused by divergencies of local or domestic or state laws – and the obvious parallels to the development here in the USA – would be incomplete if Uniform and Model Laws or Uniform Principles such as the UNIDROIT Principles of International Commercial Contracts were not also mentioned, even if the details of their implementation and the respective competencies or their function as chosen law or law-like contract regulation cannot be explored here. And for those having to navigate the unfathomable depths of the ever-shifting laws of the European Community, its instruments to unify or harmonize the law, i.e., "regulations and directives" must be mentioned too, for here we have basically the same pattern of a region growing together and therefore trying to overcome by unification and harmonization the diversity of legal regulations that obstruct the free flow of commerce and fair competition.

Having said this, I cannot suppress a footnote that, regarding the increasing production of directives and regulations of poor quality and inconsistent contents, the CISG, in my opinion, might very well offer a safe haven in a given sales case, at least to a certain extent.

II. Reception and Acceptance of the CISG

It was already mentioned that the CISG is a success, referring to the number of ratifying states and the many cases decided by state courts and arbitration tribunals under this Convention. However, I have to retract this statement a bit and put in a reservation, for the success was not self-assured from the beginning, and resistance and aversion to the CISG and its application are still obvious in recommendations of trade associations, in-house counsels and law firms to opt out of the CISG in respective clauses. What are the reasons for the objections to submitting to the CISG in an international sale?

1. The first line of argument can be summarized as "my own sales law is much better than the CISG." It is impossible to argue with this statement, for it would require a comparison of the rules and solutions provided in the respective Civil Code, Code civile, Codice civile, Código civil, Sales of Goods Act, etc. Every solution encoded in the applicable provisions and rules of case law would have to be compared and one would also have to distinguish the situation of a seller from the situation of a buyer in regard to different types of goods. This applies, therefore, to similar rash judgments claiming that the CISG is too "buyer-friendly" or, on the contrary, too "seller-friendly." Also, there is criticism that the CISG is influenced too much by continental private law – a claim common in England, or – a fear often articulated in my home country – that it is a Trojan horse of Anglo-American law concepts such as no-fault liability in case of breach of contract.

When queried, however, for details of this or that solution and, in particular, which issues and their regulation in the CISG had to be regarded as less suited than the domestic sales law of my partner – often, the persons making this statement really did not have intimate enough knowledge of the CISG to allow such a judgment, but referred to something they had read elsewhere, not infrequently in the recommendations of trade associations, chambers of commerce or even bar associations. In fact, what they often were saying was "my own sales law is better known to me." This brings me to a tentative explanation of some of the resistance. It very often was based on the aversion to the unknown, and the legitimate preference for the relative security provided by the familiarity with one's own domestic sales law. In addition, those who had drafted standard form contracts based on a certain legal system may have a vested interest in their products, for they would have to advise their clients that these forms might have to be adjusted, requiring, again, a thorough study of the alien CISG. But the aversion against the unknown also explains why this attitude towards the CISG has begun to wane in the last ten to fifteen years in many jurisdictions.

Jurists, who have become familiar with the CISG because of the need to apply it, the increasing offerings of respective courses in law schools, or in conferences such as this, have found it less alien than expected and feared. The now known devil became less threatening than the unknown. Also, on catching up on the CISG, the loss of "imperial knowledge," deeply threatening to our self-esteem as jurists, could be made up. Even standard forms are beginning to change. And in many instances lawyers have discovered that, in a given case, the CISG may very well be more beneficial for their client. I am waiting for the day that a client sues his lawyer who ignored the CISG under which the client would have won the case.

I would like to add a personal experience as to German judges' attitudes towards the CISG: To prepare for the recent reform of our Civil Code, in particular our contract law, the German Justice Department, in the 1980s convened a commission of experts, consisting of judges, law professors, attorneys, notaries and some people from the Justice Departments of the Federal Republic and the states. I was a member, entrusted with the – so-to-speak – respresentation and infusion of foreign and International Uniform Laws. At the opening banquet, I was sitting between the president of the Court of Appeals of Hamburg and the president of the Court of Appeals of Bremen. I asked them about their practical experiences with Uniform Sales Laws, as both courts handle a lot of litigation caused by imports and exports going through the important ports of Hamburg and Bremen. The president of the Court of Appeals of Hamburg was enthusiastic. He said: "We like to apply the Uniform Sales Law – then still the Hague Sales Law ULIS – for it is much better suited to international sales than our own Civil and Commercial Code; in particular, we prefer the concept of breach of contract as influenced by Anglo-Saxon law and the notion of no-fault liability in case of breach." However, my neighbor on the other side strongly objected: "We in Bremen try to avoid the application of the Uniform Sales Laws, if we can – e.g., by advising the parties, that they can still agree on a derogation of the Uniform Sales Law in favor of a domestic law – for the Uniform Law is still not yet thoroughly analyzed, there is not sufficient case law so far, and to apply this body of law would be venturing into the unknown." Ten years later, when we submitted our report to the Minister of Justice, I sat next to this same president again during a dinner speech of a dignitary. He leaned over and whispered to me that he had become a convert and now liked to apply the CISG.

2. Nevertheless, the decisive argument *for* the applicability of the CISG does not result from a comparison of domestic sales law and the CISG, but rather from the possible necessity to choose between the alternatives of CISG and a *foreign* law, which may indeed be totally unknown and inaccessible to the jurist dealing with the case. This was the argument strongly brought forward by my great colleague John Honnold in the U.S. Senate hearings. He pointed out, that when dealing with foreign partners who have a strong bargaining position, the domestic trader may not be able to impose a choice of law clause, assuring the application of its own

domestic sales law, but rather might have to accept the other party's law or lose the contract. In this situation, it might very well be beneficial to counsel, arbitrators and judges if the "foreign" law were the CISG.

Let me give you two examples, which I have experienced in arbitration:

a) A French manufacturer of computer hardware and software sold a computer system to a Russian bank. The contract contained an arbitration clause – ICC arbitration in Paris – and a choice of law clause, choosing Russian law as the law applicable to the contract and all legal disputes arising therefrom. The seller was late in installing the software, and the purchaser had set an additional period of time, terminating the contract after the additional period had lapsed. The French seller contested the termination, arguing that under the Russian Civil Code a mere delay does not amount to a breach allowing termination.

b) A group of European investors had contracted with a Turkmen company to build a paper mill in Turkmenistan. A "Settlement of Disputes" clause provided for arbitration under ICC Rules in Paris and designated Russian law as applicable. The paper mill was never delivered. At issue were restitution of advances and damages, in particular lost profits expected from the operation of the papermill.

In both cases, to decide under Russian domestic law, which the arbitrators could not read and analyze, would have made them dependant on expert witnessess, who, being paid by the parties, gave conflicting, contrary testimonies. The tribunal in applying Russian domestic sales law would have to walk a kind of tightrope without a net and without a rope. Similarly, I assume that New York Federal courts in the cases where Italian or German law was applicable to a transborder sale, as in *St. Paul Guardian Insurance Company v. Neuromed Medical Systems & Support, GmbH,*[1] might have found it easier to apply the CISG instead of dealing with the German Civil and Commercial Code or the Italian Codice civile.[2]

---

1 *See* St.Paul Guardian Ins. Co. V. Neuromed Med. Sys. & Support, GmbH, No.00-Civ934(SHS), 92002 WL 465312 (S.D.N.Y. 2002), *available at* http://cisgw3.law.pace.edu/cases/020326u1.html. [Please note that hereinafter "WL" relates to cases currently unavailable in U.S. Federal Reporters and only accessible on the Westlaw database *at* http://www.westlaw.com.].

2 *See also* Schmitz-Werke GmbH & Co. v. Rockland Industries, Inc., 937 Fed.Appx. 687 (4th Cir. 2002), *available at* http://cisgw3.law.pace.edu/cases/020621u1.html.

III. Towards a "Lingua Franca" of Contract Law

I may overrate the CISG's success and the importance attached to the impressive number of court decisions applying it or at least referring to it (the databank at Pace Law School lists more than 1,100 judgments up-to-date, referring to CISG-Articles).[3] And having been involved in the drafting of the CISG, I am, of course, biased in favor of its merits. So I have to beg for your patience, if I dare to emphasize yet another aspect of the CISG's influence.

1. The CISG is now taught in many law schools around the world, its Articles are thoroughly commented upon in the legal literature, and cases – foreign as well as domestic cases – are frequently analyzed by students and practitioners as well. Thus, a growing familiarity with the CISG and court decisions based on it can be observed throughout the world. If one approaches – say – a French, Dutch, Danish or German jurist dealing with an international sales case and drops names of U.S. cases like *Filanto v. Chilewich Int'l Corp.*,[4] *MCC-Marble Ceramic Center, Inc., v. Ceramica Nuova d'Agostino, S.p.A.*,[5] *Delchi Carrier S.p.A. v. Rotorex Corp.*,[6] or *Calzaturificio Claudia S.n.c. v. Olivieri Footwear Ltd.*,[7] his or her eyes might light up, and after some reflection and recollection on the facts of the respective case, a lively discussion might ensue. American cases are also frequently used as teaching materials: e.g., in the post-graduate classes which I teach in Zurich and Geneva, Switzerland, we thoroughly analyze cases such as *Usinor Steel v. Leeco Steel Products, Inc.*, decided in 2002 by the U.S. District Court for the Northern District of Illinois,[8] which exceptionally deals with the intricate question of security interests under domestic law in a CISG sale. *St. Paul Guardian Insurance Co. v. Neuromed Medical Systems*, decided by a N.Y. District Court in 2002,[9] thoroughly analyzes the

---

3 *See* Pace University School of Law Database on the CISG and International Commercial Law, *at* http://cisgw3.law.pace.edu/cisg/text/casecit.html.

4 *See* Filanto, S.p.A. v. Chilewich Int'l Corp., 9789 F.Supp. 1229 (S.D.N.Y. 1992), *available at* http://cisgw3.law.pace.edu/cases/920414u1.html.

5 *See* MCC- Marble Ceramic Center, Inc. v. Ceramica Nuova D'Agostino, S.p.A., 9144 F.3d 1384 (11th Cir. 1998), *available at* http://cisgw3.law.pace.edu/cases/980629u1.html.

6 *See* Delchi Carrier, S.p.A. v. Rotorex Corp., 971 F.3d 1024 (2nd Cir. 1995), *available at* http://cisgw3.law.pace.edu/cases/951206u1.html.

7 *See* Calzaturificio Claudia S.n.c. v. Olivieri Footwear Ltd., No. 96Civ.8052(HB)(THK), (1998 WL 164824 (S.D.N.Y. 1998), *available at* http://cisgw3.law.pace.edu/cases/980406u1.html.

8 *See* Usinor Steel v. Leeco Steel Prods., Inc., 9209 F.Supp.2d 880 (N.D. Ill. 2002), *available at* http://cisgw3.law.pace.edu/cases/020328u1.html.

9 *See supra* note 1.

passing-of-risk issue under the CISG and under a CIF clause, and their relation to the passing of title question. Those two issues are so clearly distinguished by the court, that the cases merit prominent citation in textbooks on the CISG. In other words, a common language with concepts to pinpoint issues and a common understanding of the range of possible solutions is developing which facilitates communication of lawyers with entirely different backgrounds.[10]

Walking into a law office or confronting a court in, e.g., Beijing or St. Petersburg, in order to deal with the consequences of a broken down transborder sale, we can now use the same concepts to encode the problems and issues that come up in the context of a breach, to denominate the asserted remedies, and the meaning of certain words as interpreted by courts and scholars. This emerging of a "lingua franca" of international sales is further strengthened by another development. The CISG, as its predecessors, is based on a world-wide collection and comparison of domestic sales laws, striving to pick the best from the wide spectrum of possible solutions to common issues. Therefore, the CISG was and is regarded as a rather modern sales law, having gotten rid of ancient notions and rules shaped under different economic conditions and values, including rules formulated about 2000 years ago by justices of the peace for the sale of cattle and slaves in Roman markets. It is a small wonder that a number of countries which reformed their sales laws in the last twenty years, "borrowed" key concepts and solutions from the Uniform Sales Law, including, e.g., the Netherlands, Estonia and Germany. Other countries implemented the CISG more or less completely as their domestic sales law as did the Scandinavian countries[11] or Israel, and some incorporated it as their commercial sales law, as did the Czech Republic. The EC in its recent directive on consumer sales used the key concepts of "conformity versus non-conformity of goods" almost verbatim and emphasized in its so-called recitals, i.e., a preamble, that it intended to follow the CISG to a great extent as a model.

As a consequence, one finds central concepts and solutions of the Uniform Sales Law in modern domestic sales codifications as well. Accordingly, even when dealing with foreign jurists in a foreign country, one might be familiar with the law to the extent it mirrors the basic features of the CISG.

---

10 The common language or "*lingua franca*" of international sales is further facilitated by sharings of doctrinal analyses of the CISG; *see, e.g*, the archives of commentaries, monographs and texts on the CISG *at* http://cisgw3.law.pace.edu/cisg/biblio/bib2.html.

11 As to the differences in detail, *see* Jan Ramberg, *Uniform Sales Law: A Look at the Scandinavian States*, VIII UNIFORM L. REV. 201-208, 202 (2003).

IV. A "Brave New World" of Sales Law?

If I have caused the impression that the CISG lays down a set of hard and fast rules to be applied without doubt and with absolute uniformity, I must immediately correct this impression:

1. The CISG unfortunately is full of flaws, a realization which should not be supressed. First of all, it only regulates a limited sector of any sales transaction, let alone contracts going beyond mere sales of goods. A good – or better, bad – example of these restrictions and the sometimes uncertain borderline are distributorship agreements as in *Helen Kaminski Pty. Ltd. v. Marketing Australian Products, Inc.*[12] The CISG also has internal gaps, partially caused by the reluctance of the drafters to settle certain problems – an example is the notorious battle of forms issue – partially because certain problems only arose as a result of later developments and inventions such as electronic communication and commerce. This is, of course, a fate the Convention shares with codifications and it could give rise to the endless debate about the usefulness of codifying and thereby freezing legal rules.

2. Critics point out that the uniformity achieved by international instruments such as the CISG is but a verbal one, threatened and often lost by diverging interpretations. Since there is no international supreme court controlling the noble directive of Art. 7 CISG, which states that in the interpretation of the Convention "regard is to be had to its international character and to the need to promote uniformity in its application ...," and since there is no international doctrine of *stare decisis*, it is predicted that sooner or later national courts will have molded the uniform text in order to make it conform to their respective domestic legal systems to such an extent that the results will deviate greatly from the drafters' intentions and understanding.

This proposition I cannot deny, for there are indeed court decisions and scholarly interpretations which are clearly "tainted" by domestic preconceptions. A good example is the attempt to infuse into Art. 79 CISG, the provision on excuse of the obligor in case of *force majeure*, notions of negligence and fault. The German Supreme Court in a recent decision on a seller's liability for damages caused by contaminated milk powder,[13] left it to the Court of Appeal, to which the case was

---

12 *See* Helen Kaminski Pty., Ltd. v. Marketing Australian Prods., Inc., Nos. M-47(dLC), 96B46519, 97-8072A, (1997 WL 414137 (S.D.N.Y. 1997), *available at* http://cisgw3.law.pace.edu/cases/970721.html.

13 *See* Bundesgerichtshof, VIII ZR 304/00, Jan. 9, 2002, English translation *at* http://cisgw3.law.pace.edu/cases/020109g1.html.

remanded, to allow the defendant to show evidence that he could not have detected the contamination even employing the utmost care – a notion reminiscent of German domestic sales law.

I am confident, however, that these are glitches which will be overcome, and that courts will become more and more familiar with the CISG as a special set of rules, as the reading of recent Federal court decisions show. And courts will follow decisions in other jurisdictions as persuasive authority, thus developing a homogenous interpretation. Although there is no *stare decisis*, it is my conviction – and there are examples to back up this conviction – that courts will follow well-reasoned decisions of other jurisdictions, if they have sufficient information about the cases decided in other countries. Uniformity of interpretation and application hinges, to a good extent, on information, and it is in particular databases such as the one built up and entertained by Pace Law School – which deserves highest praise – where that information can be found and, thereby, further and secure the emerging case law of the CISG and its uniform understanding to an extent that is desirable. A good example of providing access to foreign court decisions and, thereby, enabling a dialogue between courts, is the case of *Medical Marketing International v. Internationale Medico Scientifica*.[14] The U.S. District Court reviewed an arbitration award to determine whether, in manifest disregard of the applicable law, it deviated from the interpretation of certain Articles of the CISG by other courts. To arrive at its holding, it thoroughly analyzed a decision of the German Supreme Court, made accessible in English by Pace's database, which dealt with the same question. The Court accepted its authority as persuasive and, distinguishing the two cases on the facts, decided contrary to the German Court (to my mind, correctly, for I regard the German leading case as stating a wrong rule).

3. Courts' analyses yielding diverging results despite common and uniform understanding of the issues encoded in the provisions of the CISG, can come up more often in the application of certain "flexible" norms, flexible by the use of open-value concepts. Another point of criticism, therefore, seems to go to the core of the endeavor to "unify" the law, namely, the frequent use of these flexible "open-value" concepts such as "fundamental" (breach), "reasonable" (period of time) and even the ominous "good faith in international trade" notion in Art. 7, para. (1). Allowing quite diverging results, these concepts seem to vitiate the very objective the drafters set out to achieve, and indeed there is already a number of decisions with diverging results in the application of such articles.

---

14 *See* Medical Mktg. Int'l v. Internationale Medico Scientifica, No. Civ.A.99-0380, 1999 WL 311945, U.S. District Court (E.D. La. 1999), *available at* http://cisgw3.law.pace.edu/cases/990517u1.html. [Please note that this case is currently unavailable in the U.S. Federal Reporter.].

Thus, while the German Supreme Court regards non-conformity, i.e., defects of goods, as a fundamental breach that justifies cancellation of the contract – avoidance of the contract, in the words of the CISG – only in the exceptional circumstances when the goods can neither be used for another purpose or resold at throw-away prices, the French Cour de Cassation, without blinking an eye, regarded red wine with too high a sugar content, violating French wine laws, as a fundamental breach.[15] This certainly reflects a special French appreciation for good wine (under the rule of the German Supreme Court, the buyer would have been expected to resell the wine to a vinegar-producer and claim damages from the seller). In *Delchi Carrier v. Rotorex*, where component parts (compressors) for air conditioners did not satisfy the agreed technical specifications (cooling capacity and power consumption), the U.S. Second Circuit Court of Appeals granted avoidance based on a fundamental breach. A German court might have questioned whether the buyer could have disposed of the units at a throw-away price and asked for damages.[16]

While some courts normally regard four weeks as a reasonable time for giving notice of non-conformity, the Austrian Supreme Court held that fourteen days are enough.[17]

The basic notion of non-conformity is not very clear in cases of implied warranties under article 35 paragraph 2 CISG, where there are different standards of public safety regulations in the seller's and in the buyer's country: While the German courts have decided that goods are in conformity with the implied quality requirements of the contract if they meet the safety standards in the seller's country, the U.S District Court for the Eastern District of Louisiana, in the case mentioned above, held that the safety standards for x-ray (mammographic) equipment in the buyer's country, i.e., the U.S.A, should determine the implied conformity standards which the seller has to meet. Good faith and fair dealing – a dangerous notion open to widely diverging interpretations and not even encoded in the CISG as a guideline for the interpretation of contracts – was invoked by an Austrian arbitration tribunal to absolve the buyer partially from his omission to give timely notice to the seller of a non-conformity of the goods, a result hardly reconcilable with the CISG regime of notice and the consequences of its omission.

---

15 *See* Sacovini/M Marrazza v. Les fils de Henri Ramel, Cass. 1e civ., Jan. 23, 1996, *available at* http://cisgw3.law.pace.edu/cases/960123f1.html.

16 Delchi Carrier, S.p.A. v. Rotorex Corp., 971 F.3d 1024 (2nd Cir. 1995), *available at* http://cisgw3.law.pace.edu/cases/951206u1.html.

17 *See* Oberster Gerichtshof (OGH), 1 Ob 223/99x, Aug. 27, 1999, English translation *available at* http://cisgw3.law.pace.edu/cases/990827a3.html.

Although the aforementioned cases are contrary to the concept of uniformity, I am less concerned about the divergencies in the results of particular cases then my first words might have indicated. The open-value concepts that allow diverging interpretations and results, although preventing uniform results, allow one to account for local, regional and national convictions and practices; they function, therefore, as a kind of safety valve. And the fact that a party was living in a country or a part of the world with certain historical traditions and convictions might well be treated as a fact allowing distinguishing and, thereby, differentiations in the interpretation and application of open value terms. We are still speaking the same language of international sales law, however, and even where our opinions do not conform, we use the same framework to express our diverging evaluations and to communicate on the same legal wavelength. I am, of course, aware of the spectre of forum shopping but, for reasons I cannot explain in detail here, I think its dangers are somewhat overrated.

4. We leave this common wavelength, however, if we succumb to another temptation, i.e., to circumvent the CISG and to apply domestic law by characterizing certain issues as non-sales law and therefore as outside the scope of the Convention. If European courts would, in case of non-delivery caused by the destruction of the goods before the conclusion of the contract, use the old Roman maxim of *impossibilium nulla est obligatio*, i.e., in case of impossibility the contract is void *ab initio* (a rule still found in some codes), and would therefore reason, that this rule applies, because questions of validity of contract are outside the scope of the Convention, this would clearly violate the Convention. The CISG is meant without doubt to cover these situations as normal breaches of contract. The same applies, if one would revert to domestic law provisions on avoiding a contract for an error or mistake, if the buyer was "mistaken" about the conformity of the goods, as proposed by some scholars. If a contract was breached, but the obligee lost its remedies under the Convention, it should not be allowed to revert to domestic unjust enrichment law to recover, e.g., an advance of the purchase price or benefits of the buyer from the goods, as was decided by a Supreme Court.[18] I also have doubts whether a buyer suffering economic loss resulting from the non-conformity of the goods delivered by a seller, could revert to a tort claim under domestic law, asserting that the delivery of non-conforming goods amounted to a tortious interference with business relations.[19] The strict rule on the validity of contracts concluded orally should not be undermined by qualifying form requirements such as the parol

---

18 *See* C. A. 20/82, Adras Construction Co. Ltd. v. Harlow & Jones GmbH, 42 P. D. 221 (1988), *available at* http://cisgw3.law.pace.ed/cases/99110215.html.

19 *See* Viva Vino Import Corp. v. Farnese Vini S.r.l., No. Civ. A.99-6384, 2000 WL 1224903 (E.D.Pa. 2000), *available at* http://cisgw3.law.pace.edu/cases/000829u1.html, where the applicability of the CISG was denied because the contract breached was a distributorship agreement.

evidence rule as a procedural rule. By way of further example, the non-recoverability of the costs of litigation should be a question of who bears the risk of certain losses under Article 74 CISG – which would very well allow the results of the "American rule" – and should not be evaded by shrugging it off as a procedural matter – Viva Zapata![20]

This, I think, is the legacy to be preserved and defended. We have here a common legal language, its concepts encoding common issues and allowing communication without the need to translate codes of another legal system, which very often might be a galaxy alien and inaccessible to our contractual partner or to ourselves, our respective lawyers, judges, arbitrators and mediators.

As a law teacher for thirty-five years, I cannot but to think that this was only the introduction to my subject, and now the real sermon has to begin.

---

20 *See* Zapata Hermanos Sucesores, S.A. v. Hearthside Baking Company, Inc., 9313 F.3d 385 (7th Cir. 2002), *available at* http://cisgw3.law.pace.edu/casesd/021119u1.html.

Address:
Pace University School of Law Conference on the United Nations Convention on Contracts for the International Sale of Goods (CISG): **Primary Differences Between the UCC and the CISG**

John P. McMahon[*]

The United Nations Convention on the Recognition and Enforcement of Foreign Arbitral Awards was the first multilateral commercial law treaty outside of the ocean shipping and international aviation fields ratified by the United States.

---

* President, McMahon & Connell, P.C., www.mcmconnpc.com. Member of the New York, North Carolina and South Carolina Bars. Chair, Committee on International Sales and Related Commercial Transactions, International Law & Practice Section, New York State Bar Association.

Such ratification represented a departure from established U.S. policy concerning adherence to multilateral private law treaties.

Traditionally, the United States did not adhere to such treaties because, in general, under our federal system, State governments and State courts, not the federal government and the federal courts, exercised lawmaking powers over commercial affairs other than those within the federal admiralty jurisdiction.

Three decades later the CISG and other private law treaties are in effect for the United States, but for most members of the Bench and Bar, treaties do not leap to mind as the source of the law governing a dispute between private parties.

In our system, traditionally, uniformity in the law governing private affairs has been achieved by the development of model uniform laws proposed for enactment by the governments of the States.

Before the CISG came into effect, forty-nine of the fifty States had adopted Article 2, Sales, of the Uniform Commercial Code. It came into effect in New York on September 27, 1964, forty-nine years ago tomorrow.

On January 1, 1988, the CISG came into effect for the United States and other nations that had adopted it. On that day it became the law of New York.

Article VI of the Constitution of the United States declares treaties to be the supreme law of the land and dictates that "the Judges in every State shall be bound thereby." It is settled law that a treaty preempts conflicting State law.

Consequently, the first thought to carry away from here today is that the CISG is the supreme law of the land and, when it applies, it supersedes familiar rules of State law.

The next and main point of this brief talk is that differences between the CISG and UCC, Article 2 matter.

The remarks that follow do not plow new ground. Professor Kritzer's *Guide to Practical Applications of the United Nations Convention on Contracts for the International Sale of Goods*, which was written some fifteen years ago, contains a detailed comparison of the provisions of the UCC and the CISG The table of contents of volume 1 of the July 2003 update of Business Laws, Inc.'s *Guide to the International Sales Convention* contains eleven section headings dealing with comparisons between the CISG and the UCC. The UCC is mentioned in the abstracts of scores of texts, articles and papers identified or published, on our host's CISG website.

Do not think that the CISG turns familiar concepts of contract law on their heads. There are many similarities between the CISG and Article 2 of the UCC and differences which are matters of nuance arising out of different terminology.

There are, however, some differences that are fundamental.

The following are my candidates for primary differences between the UCC and CISG which ought to be mentioned in a thirty-five minute talk. Differences in the rules governing offer and acceptance and proving the terms of a contract will be covered first. They will be followed by three differences in the rules governing performance.

I. UCC § 2-207 versus CISG Article 19 – The rules governing the bargaining process are very different.

The CISG undoes one of the changes the UCC made in traditional American sales contract law. Under the CISG, generally, if a communication accepting an offer contains additional or different terms, the communication operates as a rejection rather than an acceptance. This approach is quite different from that of the UCC and can create problems given the way business is most often done.

Rarely do negotiations consist of no more than an offer followed by a flat statement of acceptance. Often, the party receiving the offer will accept with certain changes or additions. Further, sellers and purchasers tend to use contract or purchase order forms containing detailed clauses favoring the side of the trade in which they are involved. The exchange of such forms as offers and acceptances or "confirmations" gives rise to what is called the "battle of the forms." These usual ways of doing business create difficulties under the rules that determine whether negotiations have ripened into a binding contract.

Under Anglo-American common law, if an acceptance of an offer contained different or additional terms, it was treated as a rejection and a counter-offer. So an "acceptance" which was not the "mirror image" of an offer did not give rise to a contract.

In section 2-207, the drafters of the UCC attempted to avoid the rigors of the common law rule and end the battle of the forms. The pertinent part of section 2-207, Additional Terms in Acceptance or Confirmation, reads as follows:

(1) A definite and seasonable expression of acceptance or a written confirmation which is sent within a reasonable time operates as an acceptance even though it states terms additional to or different from those offered or agreed upon, unless acceptance is expressly made conditional on assent to the additional or different terms.

(2) The additional terms are to be construed as proposals for addition to the contract. Between merchants such terms become part of the contract unless:

(a) the offer expressly limits acceptance to the terms of the offer;

(b) they materially alter it; or

(c) notification of objection to them has already been given or is given within a reasonable time after notice of them is received.

Thus, under the UCC, unless acceptance is stated to be conditional on the offeror's consent to additional or different terms, the expression of acceptance operates as such, with additional incidental terms becoming part of the contract unless the offeror has limited acceptance to the terms of the offer or objects to them. Absent objection, whether an additional term, e.g., a dispute resolution clause, is part of the contract depends upon whether it is considered to be "material." *See Aceros Prefabricados*, S.A. *v. Tradearbed, Inc.*, 282 F.3d 92 (2d. Cir. 2002) (Arbitration clause); and *Hugo Boss Fashions*, *Inc. v. Sam's European Tailoring*, Inc., 293 A.D.2d 296, 742 N.Y.S. 2d 1 (1st Dept. 2002)(Forum-selection).

Article 19 of the CISG contains rules of offer and acceptance that are close to the common law rule. Article 19 reads as follows:

(1) A reply to an offer which purports to be an acceptance but contains additions, limitations or other modifications is a rejection of the offer and constitutes a counter-offer.

(2) However, a reply to an offer which purports to be an acceptance but contains additional or different terms which do not materially alter the terms of the offer constitutes an acceptance, unless the offeror, without undue delay, objects orally to the discrepancy or dispatches a notice to that effect. If he does not so object, the terms of the contract are the terms of the offer with the modifications contained in the acceptance.

(3) Additional or different terms relating, among other things, to the price, payment, quality and quantity of the goods, place and time of delivery, extent

of one party's liability to the other or the settlement of disputes are considered to alter the terms of the offer materially.

Thus, under Article 19 of the CISG, additional or different terms in an acceptance prevent a contract from arising unless they are not material and the offeror does not object to them.

Under the UCC, a stipulation for arbitration in an acceptance would not keep a contract from arising. There would be a contract and an issue; does the contract contain an arbitration clause? The answer would turn on whether such a clause is "material." Under the CISG, there would be no contract.

2. UCC § 2-205 versus Article 16(2) – The CISG treats offers as irrevocable more readily than does the UCC.

Under Anglo-American common law, an offeror was free to revoke an offer, even if it had said that the offer would remain open for acceptance during a specified period of time. UCC section 2-205, Firm Offers, changed that rule. It reads:

> An offer by a merchant to buy or sell goods in a signed writing which by its terms gives assurance that it will be held open is not revocable, for lack of consideration, during the time stated or if no time is stated for a reasonable time, but in no event may such period of irrevocability exceed three months; but any such term of assurance on a form supplied by the offeree must be separately signed by the offeror.

Thus, under the UCC, the offeror's right and power to withdraw an offer is restricted only if the offer is in a signed writing which by its terms gives assurances that it will be held open and, even then, the period of irrevocability does not exceed three months.

Article 16 of the CISG deals with revocation of offers. It reads:

(1) Until a contract is concluded an offer may be revoked if the revocation reaches the offeree before he has dispatched an acceptance.

(2) However, an offer cannot be revoked:

   (a) if it indicates, whether by stating a fixed time for acceptance or otherwise, that it is irrevocable; or

(b) if it was reasonable for the offeree to rely on the offer as being irrevocable and the offeree has acted in reliance on the offer.

Under Article 16(2)(a) of the CISG, there is no writing requirement, no time limit, and an offer that states a fixed time for acceptance is regarded as irrevocable even though it does not state that it will be held open for that period.

Thus, a seller who makes an offer on the basis that it expires at the close of business on Friday may think that she is protecting herself against having to withdraw the offer to keep it from being accepted on Monday. Under the CISG, she is doing that, but she is depriving herself of the right to withdraw the offer before the close of business on Friday, too.

Further, under the CISG an offer cannot be revoked "if it was reasonable for the offeree to rely on the offer as being irrevocable and the offeree has acted in reliance on the offer."

3. UCC § 2-201 versus CISG Article 2 – No Statute of Frauds in the CISG.

There are outcome determinative differences between the CISG and UCC rules that govern the proving of contracts. Unlike the UCC, the CISG does not require that contracts for the sale of goods be in writing. Under the CISG, oral contracts of sale not evidenced by a document or combination of documents are enforceable.

Article 2 of the UCC contains a statute of frauds and a parol evidence rule. The CISG does not.

Although UCC Section 2-204 says that a contract for the sale of goods may be made in any manner sufficient to show agreement, including conduct by both parties, under section 2-201, with certain exceptions listed in section 2-201(3), a contract for the sale of goods for $500 or more is not enforceable unless there is some writing signed by or for the party against whom enforcement is sought and the writing is sufficient to indicate that a contract of sale has been made between the parties. Under the "merchants' exception," if one merchant sends a writing confirming the contract to another, if the writing is sufficient to bind the sender and if the recipient does not object in writing within ten days after receipt, the UCC's statute of frauds requirement is satisfied. But, generally, unless the existence of a contract is admitted, or there has been payment or delivery and acceptance, oral contracts for the sale of goods are not enforceable.

Article 11 of the CISG says: "A contract of sale need not be concluded in or evidenced by writing and is not subject to any other requirement as to form. It may be proved by any means, including witnesses."

GPL Treatment, Ltd. v. Louisiana-Pacific Corp., 894 P.2d 470, *aff'd* 914 P.2d 682 (Or. 1996), was a case in which the sellers sought damages for the buyer's failure to take delivery of the contract quantity of wood products.

The plaintiffs were Canadian; the defendant a Delaware corporation. The CISG had come into effect in Canada just before the contracts were made. The parties' places of business being in different Contracting States, the CISG was the governing law. The defendant asserted the UCC statute of frauds as a defense. The plaintiffs relied on the UCC's merchants' exception. Later, the plaintiffs had asserted that the CISG, not Article 2 of the UCC, applied and that the Convention's Article 11 governed, but the trial court had ruled that the attempt to raise the CISG was untimely and that the plaintiffs had waived reliance on Article 11.

The trial court held that the documents relied upon by the plaintiff were confirmations within the meaning of the UCC's merchants' exception and submitted to the jury the questions whether the confirmations were received by the defendant, whether the defendant knew their contents and whether the defendant sent written notice of objection to the plaintiffs.

On appeal from a judgment in favor of the plaintiffs, after an analysis of the merchants' exception and the documents, the Court of Appeals of Oregon affirmed. One judge disagreed with the majority's conclusion that the documents allegedly sent by the plaintiffs were sufficient to satisfy the UCC Statute of Frauds. In a footnote, the dissenting judge said he would have addressed the plaintiffs' contention that the trial court erred in ruling that the plaintiff's attempt to raise the CISG was untimely and that they had waived reliance on Article 11 of the CISG

The defendant appealed to the Supreme Court of Oregon. After a lengthy analysis of domestic law and the documents, a majority of the court affirmed. One justice wrote a concurring opinion. Another wrote a lengthy dissent in which two others joined. The CISG was not mentioned by any of the justices of the Supreme Court.

Thus, a trial court, a jury, an intermediate appellate court and the State's supreme court addressed a moot case. Because the CISG applied, as a matter of law, there was no statute of frauds defense. Article 11 of the Convention was outcome determinative.

It should be kept in mind, however, that under Article 12 of the CISG, Article 11 does not apply where a party to the contract of sale has its place of business in a Contracting State whose law requires contracts of sale to be concluded in or evidenced by a writing and which has made an Article 96 declaration that Article 11 does not apply. Some Contracting States have made this declaration or its equivalent. An important example, when you consider the source of many products sold in the United States, is the People's Republic of China.

The parties to a contract may not derogate from or vary the effect of Article 12. Consequently, if an oral contract falls under the CISG, it is necessary to determine whether Article 12 is in play. Reservations and declarations made by Contracting Parties are available in an Appendix to 15 U.S.C.A. and from the United Nations, the Department of State, UNCITRAL and our host's CISG web site.

There are equally outcome determinative differences regarding the admissibility of parol evidence to impeach the provisions of a written contract.

4. UCC § 2-202 versus CISG Article 11 – There is No Parol Evidence Rule in the CISG.

UCC Section 2-202 prohibits, subject to exceptions, contradiction of terms on which the parties' confirmations of the contract provisions agree or which are set forth in a writing intended by the parties as a final expression of their agreement by evidence of prior agreement or contemporaneous oral agreement. CISG Article 11 says a contract of sale may be proved by any means, including witnesses.

Thus, the CISG has made it possible to contradict and supersede the clear words of a signed written contract by testimony and other evidence showing that the written contract is not consistent with the real agreement between the seller and buyer.

The U.S. Court of Appeals for the eleventh circuit applied Article 11 in *MCC-Marble Ceramic Center, Inc. v. Ceramica Nuova D'Agostina*, S.p.a., 144 F.3d 1384 (11th Cir. 1998).

The parties' representatives met at a trade fair. They agreed on the price, quality, quantity, delivery and payment terms of an agreement to purchase ceramic tiles.

The buyer's representative had signed the front of the seller's standard order form on which the agreed terms had been entered. The back of the form contained clauses which, if considered to be part of the contract, would have resulted in a judgment in favor of the seller. Just beneath the line for the purchaser's signature was part of the printed form in which the buyer's representative acknowledged that he was aware of and approved of them. The acknowledgment even referred to some of the clauses relevant to the case by number.

The buyer offered evidence that the parties had intended that the clauses on the back of the form were not to be part of their agreements. The evidence included affidavits signed by a former executive of the seller who confirmed the buyer's assertion and by a translator, employed by the seller, who witnessed what had occurred. The court concluded that such evidence must be considered.

The court said that its ruling would not mean that written contracts could always be contradicted in CISG cases, because the circumstances were unusual in that two witnesses who had represented the seller in the negotiations corroborated the buyer's evidence. Nonetheless, the potential for overriding written terms by evidence of inconsistent intent exists under the Convention.

5. UCC § 2-601 versus CISG Articles. 25, 46, 49 and 51 – U.C.C Perfect Tender v. CISG Fundamental Breach.

It is generally accepted that, under the UCC, a buyer is entitled to reject a tender of delivery under a one-delivery contract of sale that fails in any respect to conform to the contract. This is the "perfect tender rule." It is not popular with some courts and commentators, but it follows from the language of UCC section 2-601 and is supported by Comment 2 to UCC section 2-106 ("It is in general intended to continue the policy of requiring exact performance by the seller of his obligations as a condition to his right to require acceptance.") A revised Article 2 of the UCC which has gone through a number drafts would retain the perfect tender rule.

Under the perfect tender rule, a buyer may reject the goods and cancel the contract even if a defect in tendered goods or documents is not serious and the buyer would receive substantially the performance and the goods for which it had bargained. (The UCC establishes a different standard for installment contracts, section 2-612, and revocation of acceptance, section 2-608. In some circumstances, its provision on cure, section 2-508, may give the seller an opportunity to remedy a non-conforming tender. Usage of trade, section 1-205, may allow some leeway. Under UCC section 1-203, every contract imposes an obligation of good faith in its performance or enforcement. In a minority of cases, the courts have viewed this obligation as limiting the right to invoke the perfect tender rule.)

The CISG imposes a much stricter standard for rejection and cancellation, which it refers to as "avoidance." Under the Convention's provisions, effectively, a buyer cannot reject defective goods and cancel unless a non-conformity substantially deprives the buyer of what it was entitled to expect under the contract and, even then, only if the seller foresaw, or a party in its position would have foreseen, such a result. This follows from Article 49(1) which permits a buyer to avoid the contract only if the seller's failure to perform amounts to a "fundamental breach," as that term is defined in Article 25. If a failure to deliver on time may or may not constitute a fundamental breach, the buyer may, by notice, establish a reasonable deadline under Article 47 and, under Article 49(1)(b), declare the contract at an end if the seller does not deliver the goods before it expires.

6. UCC § 2-609 versus CISG Article 71 – Assurance of Due Performance Doctrine Eviscerated.

Under the common law doctrine of anticipatory repudiation, the non-repudiating party was entitled to declare the contract at an end only if there was an unequivocal expression of an intent not to perform or the circumstances were such that non-performance was almost certain. A party which declared a contract at an end in other circumstances had itself repudiated the contract and was liable for breach. Consequently, under the common law, a party who had reasonable grounds to think that the other party would not perform was in a difficult position. It could not safely make substitute arrangements and had to continue its own performance.

In many common commercial situations, the common law created a difficult problem for contract parties and their lawyers. Often a purchaser has to be confident that the seller will perform, because the goods are needed to avoid a disruption of production or a breach of the purchaser's commitments to others. What could a buyer do if it learned that its seller's usual source of supply had been cut off or that its seller had delivered defective goods to others? Could a buyer safely decide that its seller was not able or willing to perform, where it received notice from the seller that the seller would have difficulty in supplying conforming goods or delivering on time or at the contract price, and requested a modification of the contract specifications, delivery date or price? On the seller's side, the problem arose when it learned of reports that its buyer had failed to take delivery under contracts with others or was having financial difficulties, that its buyer's usual bank had terminated the buyer's loan and letter of credit facility, or that a buyer had lost its contract with a major customer.

UCC section 2-609, Right to Adequate Assurance of Performance, created new sales contract law to deal with this common problem. The UCC's formulation has been followed by the American Law Institute in section 251 of the Restatement (Second) of Contracts. It has been applied by New York's highest court to a long term contract to supply electricity, which, in New York, is not subject to Article 2 *of* the UCC. *See Norcon Power Partners, L.P. v. Niagara Mohawk Power Corp.*, 92 N.Y.2d 458, 705 N.E.2d 656, 682 N.Y.S. 2d 664 (1998).

Section 2-609 of the UCC acknowledges the existence of a right to expect due performance and an obligation on each party such that the other party's right to expect due performance will not be impaired. It establishes rights to demand adequate assurance of due performance and to suspend performance until it is received.

The problem which existed under the common law of anticipatory repudiation is remedied by subsection (4) of section 2-609. It declares a failure to provide adequate assurance of due performance to be a repudiation of the contract. The words of our Court of Appeals in *Norcon* express the essence of the doctrine. "When adequate assurance is not forthcoming, repudiation is deemed confirmed, and the non–breaching party is allowed to take reasonable actions as though a repudiation had occurred." *See Norcon*, 92 N.Y.2d at 464. Without this feature, the right to demand adequate assurance fails of its essential purpose.

The CISG does not treat a failure to provide assurances as a repudiation of the contract. Article 71 merely says that the suspending party must continue with performance if the other party provides adequate assurance. Unlike section 2-609, it does not create a separate ground upon which the party suspending performance may cancel or "avoid" the contract if the other party fails to provide adequate assurance of performance. Avoidance is permitted only if it is clear that the other party will commit a "fundamental breach." (Article 72(1)). Thus, the CISG takes a buyer or seller having reasonable grounds for insecurity back to where it was under the common law.

7. UCC § 2-508 versus CISG Articles 34, 37 and 48 – Broader Seller's Right to Cure.

As we have seen, UCC section 2-601 permits a buyer to reject and cancel if the goods or the tender of delivery fail in any respect to conform to the contract, but under the CISG a buyer's rights to reject and cancel are restricted to circumstances in which it would be substantially deprived of what it is entitled to expect under the contract.

Both the UCC and CISG afford the seller a right to cure. Consistent with their fundamentally different approaches to the consequences of deficiencies in performance, the CISG's right to cure is broader than that to be found in the UCC.

Under UCC section 2-508, Cure by Seller of Improper Tender or Delivery: Replacement, when a buyer has rejected a tender or a delivery, but the time for performance has not expired, upon notice of its intention to cure, the seller may make a conforming delivery within the time fixed by the contract. In other words, the non-conforming delivery and rejection do not fix the positions of the parties, but the seller must make a conforming tender or delivery before the expiration of the delivery period fixed by the contract. Section 2-508(2) gives the seller the right to cure within a reasonable time beyond the delivery time fixed by the contract, if the seller had reasonable grounds to believe that a non-conforming tender would be acceptable to the buyer. *See* JAMES J. WHITE & ROBERT S. SUMMERS, UNIFORM COMMERCIAL CODE 334-337 (5th ed. 2000) for an analysis of the issues arising under section 2-508(2). Section 2-508 protects the seller from a surprise rejection by allowing extra time to make a conforming tender, but late delivery is not a curable breach. Neither part of Section 2-508 is restricted to circumstances in which the buyer will not be subjected to inconvenience or expense.

Under section 2-508 it is not clear whether a seller is entitled to replace a defective part instead of delivering a substitute item. In some cases, the courts have permitted the seller to repair rather than provide a substitute. In others, they have not.

Article 34 of the CISG permits a seller to remedy a tender of defective *documents* up to the time fixed for handing them over, so long as the exercise of this right does not cause the buyer unreasonable inconvenience or unreasonable expense.

Article 37 deals with deliveries of non-conforming *goods* before the delivery date fixed by the contract. In such a case, a seller has the right to replace non-conforming goods or remedy any lack of conformity in the goods delivered, so long as it does so by the delivery date and the exercise of this right does not cause the buyer unreasonable inconvenience or unreasonable expense.

Article 48 gives a seller the right to remedy "any failure to perform" its obligations after the date for delivery, if it can do so without unreasonable delay and without causing the buyer unreasonable inconvenience or uncertainty of reimbursement by the seller of expenses advanced by the buyer. This right to remedy applies to a breach by failure to deliver on time.

We have seen that under the Convention on Contracts for the International Sale of Goods:

- The rules of offer and acceptance are similar to the common law mirror image rule;
- An offer cannot be revoked if it indicates that it is irrevocable;
- Generally, there is no statute of frauds;
- The parol evidence rule does not apply;
- The perfect tender rule does not apply;
- There is no right to terminate the contract for failure to provide adequate assurance of performance;
- The seller has a broader right to cure after the time for performance has passed.

That is the mere tip of the iceberg, but concludes this short list of primary differences between Article 2 of the New York Uniform Commercial Code and the Convention on Contracts for the International Sale of Goods.

Instead of inviting questions, I would like to leave you with two, one for the judges among you; the other for the CISG experts:

> Should judges apply the CISG if counsel for the parties base their pleadings, evidence and arguments on Article 2 of the UCC? In a case involving the application of section 2-207, the United States Court of Appeals for the Seventh Circuit reiterated its view that "while a judge should never engage in advocacy from the bench, he or she has an obligation to raise legal issues that the parties have over-looked or neglected." *S. Ill. Riverboat Casino Cruises, Inc. v. Triangle Insulation & Sheet Metal Co.*, 302 F.3d 667, 677 (7th Cir. 2002).

If counsel for the parties to a dispute base their pleadings and arguments on Article 2 of the UCC, should they be regarded as excluding the application of the Convention? Under Article 8(3) "any subsequent conduct of the parties" may be considered in determining their intent.

Address:
Pace University School of Law Conference on the United Nations Convention on Contracts for the International Sale of Goods (CISG):
CISG-Advisory Council Opinion No. 1 – Electronic Communications Under the CISG

*Jan Ramberg**

Distinguished participants, I'll do my best to make this presentation in the allotted time minus 40 minutes. When the topic for this first opinion (CISG-Advisory Council Opinion No. 1 – Electronic Communications under CISG) was chosen, it was expected that the matter would be such that it would not provoke too much controversy as it covered a territory, so far, not sufficiently explored. So, the members of the Advisory Council had not yet committed themselves to opinions in their publications in a manner which could make it more difficult to reach consensus. The members of the Advisory Council are entitled to express dissenting opinions but it would perhaps weaken the recognition of the Advisory Council if its very first opinion did not represent a solid consensus. For this reason, I dared to suggest on the basis of an informal request by the International Chamber of Commerce, I will call that ICC for short in the following, electronic communication as a topic and more particularly, interpretations of various expressions in the CISG drafted with traditional means of communication in mind; expressions such as writing, reaches, notice, dispatch, oral, instantaneous communication.

As is frequently the case when somebody proposes something, he is asked to assume the responsibility for the proposal. So, our chairman Professor Peter Schlechtriem immediately proposed that I should do so. My objection that I didn't know sufficiently the technicalities of electronic communication was rejected with comforting remarks, that if I had trouble I could always ask my daughter, Professor Christina Ramberg, who has published books on the subject. In order to strengthen my willingness to go ahead, she was appointed *Rapporteur* and in that capacity did the preparatory work which resulted in the first opinion by the Advisory Council.

* Professor emeritus University of Stockholm. Professor honoris causa Riga Graduate School of Law. Vice President of the Commission on Commercial Law and Practice of the International Chamber of Commerce. Honorary Vice President of Comité Maritime International.

You will find this opinion in your files reproduced in the publication, Internationales Handelsrecht.

Now, when on this occasion, the honor to present this very first opinion has been bestowed upon me, I may nevertheless be entitled to disclaim responsibility at least with respect to the technicalities of electronic communication. Thus, I will focus on the principles expressed in the opinion. With respect to the technicalities, I may be excused for my ignorance because of my age, forcing me to rely on the expertise not only of my children, but also my grandchildren. In fact, I had to engage Christina's son, Eric, to assist me in clearing my own laptop from evil worms, effectively barring me from participating in the electronic world.

Now, first some general remarks. It is not surprising that there is a certain reluctance to replace an application of expressions and legal notions developed in the paper world with alternatives forced upon us in the world of electronic communications. Whenever there are legal requirements as to form, it becomes even more difficult to accept innovations replacing traditional procedures. Even if we could convince the traditionalists that they should not worry as the medium of expression or communication does not matter, as long as the legal function of the requirements as to form are fulfilled, there will nevertheless be objections. Suggesting to the traditionalists that an exchange be made with digital signatures just as good as a paper document with handwritten signatures, almost amounts to blasphemy. And even more difficult, I may remind you, are the efforts to get worldwide acceptance of a notion such as the electronic bill of lading as suggested by the CMI (Comite Maritime International) and supported by the ICC already in 1990. Here, indeed, in A8 of *Incoterms* 1990, and repeated in *Incoterms* 2000, it is provided that paper documents could be replaced by, I quote, "an equivalent electronic data interchange (EDI) message," provided that the parties had agreed to communicate electronically. This was later recognized in Article 17 of the 1996 UNCITRAL Model Law on electronic commerce. Nevertheless, we have to consider the problem of recognition.

ICC and CMI are both non-governmental organizations. True, UNCITRAL is a UN body, but a model law is not equivalent to statutory law and may not amount to legal recognition in the true sense. So, further steps are taken to achieve this aim such as by the Uniform Electronic Transaction Act of the United States and Directives for the Member States of the European Union to facilitate electronic communication in their respective countries. However, this may not be sufficient. Needless to say, recognition of electronic communication as an alternative to paper documentation cannot be linked to a national or even regional recognition. In this area it would be more harmful than otherwise to let the validity of an offer, or an acceptance of the offer, or of a notice, depend on the choice of law.

UNCITRAL now undertakes the colossal task to achieve an international convention dealing with this matter, and the Advisory Council had to consider to what extent and depth its opinion should be made consistent with the draft articles of the prospective convention as they presently appear. But, and this is an important but, is a convention really feasible? Is it not strange to have a convention on electronic contracting in the absence of a convention on contracting, although, perhaps in this field, Part II of the CISG plays an important role? Should not any subsequent convention be neutral to the medium of communication? After all, we never had an international convention relating to paper communication by traditional written documents, telephones, or telefaxes. And last but not the least, is there a need for such a convention? Have serious problems arisen or are they expected to arise? Could we expect a smooth development where, by and large, people including old dogs as myself will know to sit and adapt themselves in the electronic world? The efforts of the Advisory Council in its first opinion may hopefully contribute to a worldwide recognition of a possibility to replace traditional communication by electronic procedures and to remove any doubts as to the proper implementation of the guiding principals.

Now, let us address more precisely the opinion. Throughout, we must keep in mind two important principles that run through the whole opinion. First, the principle of functional equivalency, which is clearly expressed in the 1996 UNCITRAL Model Law. According to that principle, it is necessary to focus on the meaning and purpose of the respective expressions "in writing," "reaches," "notice," "dispatch," or on the situation referred to, such as "instantaneous communication." And then determine what is required in order to reach such a purpose by electronic communication as an alternative to traditional communication. Second, and this is more difficult, one has to find out whether the parties have agreed to communicate electronically. As always, merchants seldom bother to agree on means of communication. They just communicate, and as long as they do so, and no problems arise, they are happy. Nevertheless, it is our task to help them out if problems do arise. And in so doing, we have to recognize that the willingness and ability to communicate electronically may differ considerably in various situations.

Now, leaving out consumer protection, which is important enough, but as you know, outside the scope of the CISG, one has to recognize the difference between a merchant accustomed to electronic communication and a merchant still hesitant to rush wholeheartedly into the electronic world. And this difference between the respective players frequently coincides with the difference between large entities and so-called, SMEs or small and medium sized enterprises. And they, I think, deserve more or less the same protection as consumers do. Nevertheless, we cannot guarantee that there will be no misfortunes resulting from electronic communication. Neither can we guarantee certainty in traditional communication. There will always be risks and it is therefore important to achieve an appropriate allocation of these risks for messages failing to reach the addressee or to fulfill the need to preserve evidence of what has taken place. By the way, the paper bill of lading as compared with an electronic one is interesting. Is it normally possible to read signatures on a paper bill of lading? If we do know who signed, is the authority of the person signing ascertained? Can we trust the correctness of the information in the bill of lading? Do we control the disposition of the goods where they are in transit and when several originals have been issued, out of which we only have possession of one?

Now, the fact that these questions normally cannot be answered in the affirmative caused me on several occasions to shock bankers by suggesting that I do not understand why people go into banks with guns when they can go there with bills of lading, which have been said to constitute the most important tools of maritime fraud. I am not suggesting that electronic bills of lading will not entail risks. But, I am convinced that it is at least possible to apply safety measures in electronic communication which are not available for traditional communication.

It would, I think, be too ambitious to go through the opinion article by article. You can do that at home if you would like to study the opinion in more detail. Suffice it to say that there are no less than twenty-four articles of the CISG which are addressed. But the problems are much fewer and, in the opinion, reference is frequently made to the comments of a previous article when, in a later article, the same problem arises. So, let us focus on the fundamental problems. First, what does it take to constitute an electronic agreement? Second, what is equivalent to writing? Third, when does an electronic message reach the other party? Fourth, what is equivalent to an oral communication when electronic procedures are used? Fifth, when does time for acceptance start to run? When the offer is made by electronic communication – in real time or otherwise? Sixth, how should the risk for failure of a notice to reach the addressee be dealt with when we apply Article 27 of the CISG?

Now, let us first address the important matter of the electronic agreement. If there is an express agreement, everything at first sight appears to be easy. But, nevertheless, we must ascertain how far that agreement goes. Exactly what did the parties agree? To communicate by e-mail including attachments? Have they established that the software used by them is compatible? Have they understood the problem which arises when attachments cannot be opened due to the lack of an appropriate program? Have they agreed on some safety measures so that the electronic message is ineffective unless receipt is confirmed by the recipient?

Well, I'll soon revert more to these questions. But before that, I will go into a further problem. And that is that it becomes, of course, much more difficult to find an electronic agreement in the absence of an express agreement. Do we in such a case have to conclude that there is no agreement to communicate electronically or can we find that there is an agreement anyway, based upon other circumstances such as statements or conduct by a party, previous course of dealing, subsequent conduct, or custom of the trade? Now, in the comments to the opinion, reference is made in this respect, to Articles 8 and 9 of the CISG. It appears from these articles that an implied agreement may be difficult to find. Even if one party, by statement or conduct, may have expressed an intention to have his electronic communication accepted as equivalent to traditional communication, can we establish that the other party could not have been unaware of such intention? The expression "could not have been unaware," we find in Article 8 of the CISG. It comes very close to actual knowledge which, when it really matters, certainly will be denied by the prospective recipient of the electronic message.

Again, assistance from the fictitious "reasonable person of the same kind in the same circumstances," may sometimes be less helpful. Objective criteria, such as evidence showing to what extent the parties have used electronic communication previously, may give us better certainty as would evidence showing how they have behaved subsequent to the electronic communication, which is later suggested to be ineffective. In certain business transactions, it may be possible to ascertain that the merchants regularly behave in a certain fashion. And if they do, it may be possible to find an electronic agreement based upon custom of the trade using the criteria of Article 9 of the CISG. Conversely, it may be possible to establish the opposite and to negate the existence of an electronic agreement. Peter Schlechtriem told me about a case where the trader had expressly made known to prospective contracting parties that he didn't recognize the electronic messages as effective at all. In arbitration proceedings it is frequently agreed that e-mails are allowed but ineffective as statements in the proceedings unless confirmed by fax, ordinary mail, or courier mail. Now, summing up, the notion of express or implied electronic agreement with the same legal effect as traditional communication will in practice appear with many variations.

Now I turn to the expression, "in writing." Not infrequently, it is suggested that it is difficult to decide whether the requirements as to form have been met. One would have thought that it is easy to decide whether or not the parties have expressed themselves in writing, just look at the document. Well, what document? Is a copy of an original good enough? How do we know that it is a true copy of the original? And what about fax messages? Again, we cannot be sure whether the signature on a fax has been added to the text, or whether the text has been added to the signature without authorization of the person appearing to have signed. Nevertheless, exchanges of fax messages are generally recognized as equivalent to messages in writing although they result from an electronic transmission.

So, why not an electronic communication in the absence of a printout? Well, here the opinion on the interpretation of Article 13, stating that "writing" includes telegram and telex, suggests that the term "writing" also includes *any* electronic communication, that is not only telegram or telex. But when there is no paper immediately appearing, it is added that the communication should be, and now I quote, "retrievable in a perceivable form." Only then is it functionally equivalent to a telegram or telex. It has been said that the parties may, of course, agree on what should constitute "in writing" or add additional requirements for a valid communication. But, if they haven't done so, it is presumed that any electronic communication could be included in the term "in writing."

Also here, the presumption may be rebutted according to the principles of Articles 8 and 9 of the CISG. Now, since under the CISG there is no requirement as to form, the interpretation of "in writing" only becomes necessary where the parties have agreed that the validity of an offer, an acceptance, or the contract or amendments thereof requires writing. But such an agreement would usually also not deal with the interpretation of the expression "in writing." Therefore, the suggested interpretation in our opinion will be helpful in many practical situations.

A more difficult problem arises with respect to CISG-States which have made an Article 96 Reservation in order to ensure that only agreements in writing are given legal effect. Here, the question arises: according to which principles should we decide whether the requirement "in writing" has been met? And I think that Peter Schlechtriem touched upon this in his presentation. It is reasonable, I think, to assume that the test becomes stricter according to the laws of the "Reservation-States," than under the laws of other CISG-States. But what law should be applied? One view would be that regard should be had to the wish of the Reservation-States. Therefore, the decision should be based on that law only. The other, and I think better view, is based on ordinary principles of choice of law, where under the circumstances one might relax the requirements compared with the law of the Reservation-States. That would presumably be the case if they followed the interpretation in this opinion, which however does not address the issue of the applicable law.

Now, the next matter of great importance concerns the interpretation of the word, I quote, "reaches." Is an electronic mailbox equivalent to an ordinary one, and, if so, where is the electronic mailbox? Here, we must reason in terms of risk allocation. Who, of the sender or the prospective recipient, should bear the risk that the message does not penetrate the electronic network? It should not be controversial that a party should not be given the option to open his e-mail as he pleases. Therefore, the relevant time is not when he retrieves the messages from his sender and opens his e-mail. In other words, the electronic mailbox is not his own personal computer or the computer network of his company. The electronic mailbox must be somewhere else. But where?

The opinion suggests that we have to go a step back, and there we find the addressee's server from which he is able to pick up his mail. But suppose he can't? What then? It is here that we are faced with the problem of allocating the risk? And the opinion suggests that each party should bear the risk of problems relating to his server, but not to the server of the other party. So, the interpretation of Article 15, stating that the offer becomes effective when it reaches the offeree, is to the effect that "reaches" corresponds to the point in time when an electronic communication has entered the offeree's server. The risk is not that serious, as persons unaware of offers are usually not severely prejudiced. And if they expect offers to be on the way, they may always ask why they have not received them and then perhaps find out that they are stuck in their server from which the e-mail cannot be retrieved because of worms, viruses or what not. True, it would be sad, for example, for a buyer to find that the prices have doubled in the meantime, but well one might think that this is equivalent to losing in a lottery. The matter becomes more serious when we come to Article 15.2 dealing with withdrawal of an offer.

It is suggested that the offeree's server is the electronic mailbox. Now, the offeror may well assume that his offer has been adequately withdrawn and act accordingly, by making the same offer to another party and have such offer accepted. Here, the potential prejudice to the offeror is obvious and we may well feel sorry for him that he has to bear the risk for the withdrawal's failure to reach the recipient's server. But again, the prudent offeror would not gamble; he would ensure that the message of withdrawal has actually reached the offeree before he deals with other parties. It may be that the message has in fact reached the recipient's server although it has been misspelled. A dot or a letter is missing and we all know, I think, how dangerous that is. Or it has reached the addressee but it is impossible to read or understand. Therefore, some provisos are necessary. It does not follow from an electronic agreement per se, that one has agreed to receive any message of any type, in any format or to any address. Therefore, it has been added as a further prerequisite that the consent to receive electronic messages only concerns messages of the agreed type, agreed format and to the correct address.

Now, the interpretation of Article 16 dealing with revocation is to the same effect as the interpretation of Article 15. But here, the word "dispatch" also appears. Logically, when something is dispatched, the relevant mailbox becomes that of the sender. The time is up for the offeror as soon as the offeree's acceptance has left his server. Again, the risk is aggravated for the offeror when he deals with another party in the belief that the offer has been revoked. As time may be of essence, effect must be given to the rule of Article 16 shortening the time for revocation, although in the electronic world the whole period is a matter of seconds and the shortening of that time, therefore, is significant. It should be noted that the principle of "dispatch" has not been followed in the CISG with respect to the acceptance, which only becomes effective when it reaches the offeror. And that follows from Article

18.2. In Article 18.2 it is also stated that an oral offer must be accepted immediately, unless the circumstances indicate otherwise. This expression is commonly used and understood by the sophisticated reader, but may puzzle other readers who may think that they are actually compelled to accept oral offers and thus have to either stay home or apply devices to prevent the absorption of such offers.

Be that as it may, the question now arises to decide what is meant by "oral." It is suggested that it applies to any real-time communication, which may include electronically transmitted communication and other communication in real-time which would fall within the same principle as applies to oral offers. Article 20.1 helps to decide when time, in a case of an agreed upon period of time, starts to run, which is from the time when the telegram is handed in for "dispatch," or from the date shown on the letter, or the date on the envelope. How should this be interpreted? It is here suggested in the opinion that time starts to run from the time of "dispatch" of the e-mail communication, that is from the time it leaves the sender's server. This would follow from the rule relating to dispatch.

But what about so-called "passive" websites where it may be stated that offers are valid during a certain period of time? Whether they qualify as offers at all when they are directed to the world at large is a question we do not deal with. Now, the opinion does not offer a solution to this problem, but in the comments it is suggested that one has to resort to ordinary means of interpretation, observing that normally the party being unilaterally bound, that is the offeror, deserves more protection than the prospective offeree. Chatting on the internet is equivalent to an oral offer, as it is a kind of real-time communication.

Now, with respect to "notice" there is of course no reason to accept another principle than that which applies to "reaches" according to Article 24. But how should we treat "notice," dealt with in Part III of the CISG? Here, according to Article 27, the sender is relieved from further risk as soon as the "notice" has been correctly sent. Suppose the addressee's server is incapable of receiving the notice? Is it then nevertheless effective? This question is not dealt with in the opinion. My ignorance of the technicalities of electronic transmission makes it difficult to comment. Perhaps my question is totally out of place. Maybe it is now time to remind you of my disclaimer of liability as far as the computer network technicalities are concerned. Anyway, something has to be left for further discussion and valuable input in order to adequately respond to the challenges of cyberspace. Thank you for your attention.

Part III
Case Commentaries

CISG Case Commentary on Preëmption in *Geneva Pharmaceuticals* and *Stawski*

Joseph Lookofsky[1]

Article 4 of the 1980 Vienna Sales Convention (CISG)[2] helps delimit the Convention's sphere of application.[3] According to this provision, the Convention "governs only" the formation of an international sales contract (CISG Part II)[4] and the rights and obligations of the parties "arising from such a contract" (CISG Part III);[5] conversely, the Convention is "not concerned with" sales contract "validity," just as it cannot be concerned with non-contractual claims.[6]

Given this seemingly clear-cut delimitation, one might be tempted to conclude that claims relating to (e.g.) misrepresentations or other "abuses of the [sales

---

1 B.A. Lehigh University. J.D. New York University School of Law. Cand.jur. & dr.jur. University of Copenhagen. Professor of Private and Commercial Law, University of Copenhagen. Professor Lookofsky extends his thanks to Professor Albert Kritzer of Pace University for his invitation to comment upon the *Geneva* case online (in *CISGW3*) and for his subsequent "heads up" on the *Stawski* case. Professor Lookofsky also extends his thanks to Professor Harry Flechtner of the University of Pittsburgh for his comments on a prior draft of this Case Commentary and for his special contribution to note 26 *infra*.

2 *See* United Nations Convention on Contracts for the International Sale of Goods, April 11, 1980, U.N. Doc. A/CONF.97/18 (1980), 1489 U.N.T.S. 3 [hereinafter CISG].

3 The rules which define the Convention's sphere of application are set forth in Chapter I of CISG Part I (Articles 1-6).

4 E.g., questions relating to offer and acceptance, what Common lawyers sometimes refer to as the "mechanics of consent". Regarding American contract formation "mechanics" see for example, E. Allan Farnsworth, Contracts Ch. 3(C) (3d ed.).

5 *See generally* Joseph Lookofsky, Understanding the CISG in the USA §§ 2-6 & 4-6 (2d ed. 2004)[hereinafter Lookofsky-USA] regarding CISG Article 4. *See also* the corresponding sections in Herbert Bernstein & Joseph Lookofsky, Understanding the CISG in Europe (2d ed. 2002) and in Joseph Lookofsky, Understanding the CISG in Scandinavia (2d ed. 2002).

6 *See id.* Since the Convention "*governs only* ... the rights and obligations ... *arising from such a contract*" (Article 4, emphasis added), it can hardly be said to (also) "govern" rights arising from the breach of *non-contractual* obligations (tort). However, it is sometimes possible to apply CISG "general principles" to settle certain other "matters" which *are* "governed" – though not expressly "settled" – by the Convention, *see* CISG Article 7(2) and Lookofsky-USA, *supra* note 5, at § 2-11.

contract] bargaining process"[7] can only be settled by the application of domestic law rules.[8] In some such cases, however, the relationship between the Convention and domestic law is problematic.

One complicating factor which enters into the Article 4 equation relates to the fact that some domestic systems – including American (state-law) systems[9] – provide both delictual and contractual remedies for contractual "abuses" like misrepresentation,[10] just as claims grounded in tort (delict) are sometimes allowed to co-exist – and thus "compete" – with contract-based claims.[11] For these reasons, a given plaintiff might (depending on the particular jurisdiction and the particular circumstances) have access to remedial relief if she succeeds in proving the facts needed to support either claim.[12] In other systems, however, the applicability of a contractual remedy to a given set of operative facts might itself be held to "preëmpt" – and thus effectively "trump" – the assertion of a competing claim in tort.[13]

---

7 *See generally* FARNSWORTH, *supra* note 4, at § 4.1, regarding such abuse in American domestic contract law.

8 E.g., the (domestic) "law applicable by virtue of the rules of private international law" of the forum. *See* CISG Article 7(2) and LOOKOFSKY-USA, *supra* note 5, at § 2-6.

9 In the United States, questions relating to both contract and tort are usually governed by state (as opposed to federal) law. *See generally* JOSEPH LOOKOFSKY AND KETILBJORN HERTZ, TRANSNATIONAL LITIGATION AND COMMERCIAL ARBITRATION: AN ANALYSIS OF AMERICAN, EUROPEAN, AND INTERNATIONAL LAW Ch. 2.5 (2d ed. 2003).

10 *See* FARNSWORTH, *supra* note 4, at § 4.9 with note 1 (indicating the potential overlap between tort liability for misrepresentation and UCC warranty liability).

11 For a prominent example of limits to "competition" between contractual and delictual rules in a case involving the application of American federal (admiralty) law, *see* East River Steamship Corp. v. Transamerica Delaval, Inc., 476 U.S. 858 (1986).

12 Such competition between rule-sets is, for example, the starting point in the Danish law of obligations: *see* M.B. ANDERSEN & JOSEPH LOOKOFSKY, LÆREBOG I OBLIGATIONSRET Ch. 5.5.e (Copenhagen 2000).

13 In France, for example, the doctrine of *non-cumul* might well preclude the assertion of a non-contractual theory of recovery in such circumstances. *See* Peter Schlechtriem, *The Borderland of Tort and Contract – Opening a New Frontier?*, 21 CORNELL INT'L L. J. 467 (1988), *available at* http://www.cisg.law.pace.edu/cisg/biblio/sclechtriem.html. The (for many non-Americans "foreign") term *preëmption* (often spelled *preemption*, but also *pre-emption* or *preëmption*) originally referred to the policy by which first settlers ("squatters") on U.S. public lands could purchase property they had improved. Within the American legal system, where law-making powers are shared by the federal and (50) state governments, claims of preëmption sometimes arise under Article VI (the Supremacy Clause) of the United States Constitution, the test being whether there is either an "actual conflict between state and federal law," or "a congressional expression of intent to preempt." California Coastal Comm'n v. Granite Rock Co., 480 U.S. 572 (1987). With regard to "preëmption" in the

Within the international sales context this complex state of domestic affairs gives rise to two possible approaches: a court or tribunal in a particular CISG Contracting State might (a) allow a domestic theory of recovery to compete with a given plaintiff's CISG-based claim or (b) hold that the CISG preëmpts the application of such domestic remedial rules.

Assume, for example, that a seller in CISG State X negligently or even fraudulently misrepresents the quality of goods subsequently sold to a buyer in CISG State Y, and that this might give rise to delictual (tort) liability for the economic consequences of the misrepresentation under domestic (X or Y) law.[14] In this and other, arguably analogous situations,[15] the domestic remedies for misrepresentation (damages and/or "avoidance/rescission") might be seen to "overlap" with CISG remedies for breach (e.g., damages and/or "avoidance"),[16] thus raising a question of Convention interpretation: should the very fact that the plaintiff's claim "fits within" the CISG

(highly political) post-9/11 context *see, e.g.*, Seymour M. Hersh, *Lunch with the Chairman*, THE NEW YORKER MAGAZINE, April 17, 2003, *available at* http://www.newyorker.com/fact/content/?030317fa_fact.

14 *E.g.*, the domestic law otherwise applicable by virtue of private international law (conflict-of-laws rules); *see also supra* note 6. For concrete examples, *see* HERBERT BERNSTEIN & JOSEPH LOOKOFSKY, UNDERSTANDING THE CISG IN EUROPE §§ 2-6 and 4-6 (2d ed. 2002). *See also* the corresponding sections in LOOKOFSKY, *supra* note 5 and LOOKOFSKY-USA, *supra* note 5.

15 Regarding CISG cases involving (inter-parties) "product liability" claims, *see* LOOKOFSKY-USA, *supra* note 5, at § 2-6 with illustration *2e* and § 4-6 with illustration *4c*. *See also* the corresponding illustrations (2b and 4c) *in* BERNSTEIN & LOOKOFSKY, *supra* note 14.

16 Under domestic law designed to "police" contractual agreements, i.e., to guard against "abuse of the bargaining process," a seller's misrepresentation might entitle buyer to declare invalid – and "undo" – the contract, thus restoring the parties to their pre-contractual positions. Under American domestic law, for example, such "rescission" (also called "avoidance") might be allowed for a fraudulent misrepresentation without concern for its materiality (*see* FARNSWORTH, *supra* note 4, at §§ 4-10 to 4-15), whereas under CISG Article 49(1)(a) a fundamental breach is the *condicio sine qua non* for "avoidance" under the CISG (*see* Ulrich Huber, *in* COMMENTARY ON THE UN CONVENTION ON THE INTERNATIONAL SALE OF GOODS (CISG) 416 (2d ed. 1998) and in KOMMENTAR ZUM EINHEITLICHEN UN-KAUFRECHT – CISG 535 (3d ed. 2000)). Note in this connection the "conflict" between international and domestic (Common law) *terminology*, adding additional confusion to an already complex problem: whereas Common lawyers use "avoidance" (and "rescission") to describe (e.g.) a misrepresentee's right to *undo the transaction* by "avoiding" it (*see* FARNSWORTH, *supra* note 4, at § 4.9), an injured CISG party's right to "avoid" provides a *remedy for breach* (of a binding contractual obligation) under Article 49(1) or 61(1). Regarding CISG and American avoidance terminology *see also* LOOKOFSKY-USA, *supra* note 5, at § 6.2.

remedial scheme (a) *eo ipso* preëmpt domestic remedies otherwise available for abuse of the bargaining process, or should the domestic and Convention remedies (b) be allowed to serve concurrently, "side by side?"[17]

There is, I have argued, no simple answer to this complex question.[18] In some situations, courts and arbitrators will have good reason to exercise restraint before they permit domestic rules to compete with the otherwise uniform remedial solution provided by the CISG.[19] But the limited "command" in Article 7 – to have (some) "regard" to the need to promote uniform Convention interpretation[20] – hardly warrants, let alone dictates the conclusion that domestic remedies invariably are preëmpted (trumped), i.e., whenever the "operative facts" of the case seem "covered" by a given CISG rule.[21] On the contrary, in a State where

---

17 Thus leaving the plaintiff with an alternative if, in the concrete circumstances, access to (e.g.) CISG remedies is denied (*see* examples cited *supra* note 14).

18 *See* Joseph Lookofsky, *In Dubio Pro Conventione? Some Thoughts About Opt-Outs, Computer Programs and Preëmption Under the 1980 Vienna Sales Convention (CISG)*, 13 DUKE J. COMP. & INT'L L. 63 (2003), *available at* http://www.law.duke.edu/shell/cite.pl?13+Duke+J.+Comp.+&+Int%27l+L.+0263.

19 Since, for example, the exemption "safety valve" in CISG Article 79(1) provides a flexible tool for reaching fair solutions in cases involving *force majeure*-type "impediments" to performance – including certain situations which might also be subsumed under domestic headings of "impossibility" or "mistake" – the argument for preëmption of domestic remedies in such situations seems strong; *see, e.g.*, the decision of Bielloni Castello S.p.A. v. EGO S.A., Corte di Appello di Milano (Italy), Dec. 11, 1998, *available at* http://www.unilex.info/dynasite.cfm?dssid=2376&dsmid=13353&x=1. But since Article 79 was hardly designed to deal with the topic of "hardship," and since the hardship "rules" set forth in Ch. 6(2) of the UNIDROIT Principles (*see* http://www.unilex.info/dynasite.cfm?dssid=2377&dsmid=14311) do *not* "restate" generally applicable principles of international commercial law on this validity-related point (*see* Joseph Lookofsky, *The Limits of Commercial Contract Freedom: Under the UNIDROIT "Restatement" and Danish Law*, 46 AM. J. COMP. LAW 485, 500-501 (1998), *available at* http://cisgw3.law.pace.edu/cisg/biblio/lookofsky2.html), courts and arbitrators should apply applicable *domestic* law to deal with hardship and similar (validity-related) issues (*accord* Tom Southerington, *Impossibility of Performance and Other Excuses in International Trade*, *available at* http://www.cisg.law.pace.edu/cisg/biblio/southerington.html).

20 *See generally* Joseph Lookofsky, *CISG Foreign Case Law: How Much Regard Should We Have? A Commentary on the UNCITRAL Draft Digest of CISG Part I*, in BEYOND THE DRAFT UNCITRAL DIGEST: CASES, ANALYSIS AND UNRESOLVED ISSUES IN THE U.N. SALES CONVENTION (R. Brand, F. Ferrari & H. Flechtner eds., 2003).

21 *Cf.* JOHN HONNOLD, UNIFORM LAW FOR INTERNATIONAL SALES (3d ed. 1999) at 67-68; *see also* (concurring with Honnold) CLAYTON P. GILLETTE & STEVEN D. WALT, SALES LAW: DOMESTIC AND INTERNATIONAL 49 (Revised ed. 2002) (if facts trigger CISG application, domestic law triggered by same facts displaced). *Cf. also* Ulrich Huber *in* COMMENTARY ON

domestic sales law, tort law and rules of validity work to supplement each other, that State's accession to the Convention requires the substitution of domestic sales law (as such) with the CISG; it does not imply an obligation to "merge" CISG sales law with domestic tort law and/or validity-related (domestic) contractual regimes.[22]

Certain aspects of the preëmption conundrum were confronted recently by a U.S. Federal District Court in *Geneva Pharmaceuticals*,[23] a case brought against the Canadian manufacturer (S) of a chemical ingredient used in the production of an anticoagulant (blood-thinning) medication. S had supplied the American plaintiff (B) with samples of the ingredient and confirmed it would support B's application for approval by the Food and Drug Administration (FDA) as the supplier of the ingredient for the manufacture of the drug; S subsequently issued a letter to the FDA confirming it would serve as supplier to B. Two years later, after B received FDA

THE UN CONVENTION ON THE INTERNATIONAL SALE OF GOODS (CISG), *supra* note 16, at 370 and *in* KOMMENTAR ZUM EINHEITLICHEN UN-KAUFRECHT – CISG, *supra* note 16, at 476 (rejecting rule-concurrence in the absence of three "preconditions") and the decision of LG Aachen (Germany), May 14, 1993, reported in UNILEX (application of CISG precluded recourse to domestic law regarding mistake as to quality of goods). Some commentators have argued that CISG *avoidance* rules displace (some) domestic rules permitting a "mistaken" buyer to rescind: for a comparison of the widely diverging views on this point *see* Helen E. Hartnell, *Rousing the Sleeping Dog: The Validity Exception to the Convention on Contracts for the International Sale of Goods*, 18 YALE J. INT. L. 1, 72-78 (1993) and *compare, e.g.*, Peter Schlechtriem, *Uniform Sales Law – The Experience with Uniform Sales Laws in the Federal Republic of Germany*, *in* JURIDISK TIDSSKRIFT VID STOCKHOLMS UNIVERSITET 11-12 (Stockholm 1992). Regarding "hardship" and CISG Article 79, *see supra* note 19.

22 *But compare* Schlechtriem, *supra* note 13, with note 4 (legislator or court would breach obligation incurred by state in acceding to the Convention by creating or allowing remedies "inconsistent" with rules on liability under CISG). The CISG legislative history does not indicate that the CISG drafters harbored "preëmptive" intent. As regards actions in respect of non-conforming goods, the CISG drafters themselves rejected a proposal to limit recourse to competing rules of domestic law. The ULIS Convention of 1964, which preceded the CISG, expressly excluded the buyer's right of recourse to domestic law in the case of non-conforming goods (ULIS Article 34), except in cases of fraud (ULIS Article 89), whereas the Vienna drafters – hoping it would be possible to create a separate, internationally uniform set of validity rules – intentionally refrained from including a similar provision in the CISG; *see* Ulrich Huber *in* COMMENTARY ON THE UN CONVENTION ON THE INTERNATIONAL SALE OF GOODS (CISG), *supra* note 16, at, Art. 45, Rd.Nr. 46-48 with note 86, and *in* KOMMENTAR ZUM EINHEITLICHEN UN-KAUFRECHT – CISG, *supra* note 16, at Art. 45, Rd.Nr. 46-48 with note 106.

23 Geneva Pharmaceuticals Technology Corp. v. Barr Laboratories, Inc., et al., 201 F. Supp. 2d 236 (S.D.N.Y. 2002), reconsideration denied by the same court on 21 August 2002, both decisions *available at* http://cisgw3.law.pace.edu/cisg/wais/db/cases2/020510u1.html#svia.

approval, S (having incurred conflicting commitments to third parties) refused to honor a purchase order submitted by B.

In considering B's various CISG and domestic law claims against S, the *Geneva* court distinguished between intentional and negligent torts: whereas B's negligence-based (domestic law) claims were held preëmpted by the Convention, B's "business tort" claims for tortuous interference with contract and business relations were not.[24] Then, applying somewhat similar reasoning to resolve a related, equally complex problem, the *Geneva* court held that B also should be allowed to assert the (American) doctrine of promissory estoppel to support its "equitable" claim that the sales contract in question – even if not supported by "consideration"[25] – was nonetheless valid and binding under the applicable domestic (New Jersey) law.[26]

---

24 *See id.*, Parts VI(C) and VII of the *Geneva* court's discussion. Recognizing the *limited scope of CISG's preëmption* in the *Asante* case 164 F. Supp.2d 1142 (N.D. Cal. 2001), discussed in LOOKOFSKY-USA, *supra* note 5, at § 2-3 with note 11, the *Geneva* court cited Viva Vino Import Corp. v. Farnese Vini S.r.l, No. Civ. A.99-6384, 2000 WL 1224903 (E.D. Pa. 2000) for the proposition that the "CISG clearly does not preempt the claims sounding in tort," but then noted that under *New Jersey* (domestic) law, economic expectations protected by *contract* principles are *generally not* entitled to supplemental protection by *negligence* principles, i.e., even when the application of such principles is not prëmpted by the Convention. In a related statement (*id.* with note 30), the Court opined that "a tort claim which is actually a contract claim, or that bridges the gap between contract and tort law," might be preëmpted by the CISG.

25 Regarding "consideration" in the Article 29 (contract modification) context, *see* BERNSTEIN & LOOKOFSKY, *supra* note 5, at § 3-10.

26 So, as in the case of B's "business tort" claims (*see supra*, text *with* note 24), B's "equitable" claim was held *not preëmpted* by the CISG (*see* part VI.B of the opinion), even though the *Geneva* court (*Id.*, *supra* note 11) saw this as a "closer question," also notwithstanding the court's dictum that a party to a CISG contract could not employ domestic promissory estoppel doctrine to deny the existence of a CISG "firm offer" (*see id. and* BERNSTEIN & LOOKOFSKY, *supra* note 5, at § 3-6). Although the *Geneva* court first deals with consideration and its "substitutes" under the general heading of *validity* (a matter outside the Convention under Article 4; *see* part IV.A.3.b of the opinion), it proceeds to treat plaintiff's promissory estoppel (detrimental reliance) claim as an equitable cause of action separate from breach of contract (part VI.D of the opinion) – this notwithstanding the fact that promissory estoppel provides an alternative to "consideration," i.e., a sufficient reason for enforcing a promise under American law. *Compare* the court's subsequent opinion *Geneva Pharmaceuticals Technology Corp. v. Barr Laboratories, Inc.*, No. 98Civ.861RWS, 2003 WL 1345136 (S.D.N.Y. 2003) which distinguishes between promissory estoppel claims that are "contractual in nature" (since, as to these claims, detrimental reliance serves as a "consideration substitute") and promissory estoppel claims that are "independent" of contractual claims; the court found that the plaintiff's promissory estoppel claim fell into the latter category, and thus was

In yet another recent and complex illustration of the kind of "operative facts" which can trigger a preëmption-related CISG problem, a U.S. District Court held that the provisions of the Illinois Beer Industry Fair Dealing Act (IBIFDA) – which limit the right of (e.g.) Polish brewers to "terminate" contracts with their American buyers (wholesalers)[27] – were not preëmpted (trumped) by the arguably conflicting "avoidance" provisions of the CISG.[28]

Both the *Geneva* and *Stawski* decisions seem compatible with the position taken here: if the law of a given jurisdiction generally (e.g., in non-CISG contexts) permits a certain degree of rule-competition – between contract and tort, etc. – that State's adherence to the CISG (sales contract) regime does not require it to treat the

---

not required to be heard by a jury. While Article 29 makes it clear that consideration is not required to modify a CISG sales contract (*see* preceding note), that leaves open the question of whether an unmodified CISG contract requires consideration (or a consideration substitute) if U.S. law applies (under the the PIL rules of the forum), and the *Geneva* court's affirmative, but sometimes loosely-reasoned answer ought not preclude further consideration of the question. For arguments and counter-arguments, *see* Harry Flechtner, *More U.S. Decisions on the U.N. Sales Convention: Scope, Parol Evidence, "Validity," and Reduction of Price under Article 50*, 14 J.L. & Com. 153, 166-69 (1995), *available at* http://cisgw3.law.pace.edu/cisg/biblio/flechtner.html. Professor Lookofsky extends his thanks to Professor Flechtner at the University of Pittsburgh for helping shed light on the difficult consideration-related issues in *Geneva*.

27 These restrictions are deemed incorporated into *every agreement* between an Illinois wholesaler and a brewer. 815 ILCS 720/2(b). Section 3 of the IBIFDA, for example, restricts a brewer from canceling or failing to renew an agreement without proper notice, which the Act defines as a notice of cancellation in writing, sent by certified mail and containing, *inter alia*, "a complete statement of the reasons therefore, including all data and documentation necessary to fully apprise the wholesaler of the reasons for the action."

28 *See* Stawski Distributing Co., Inc. v. Zywiec Breweries PLC, No. 02C8708 2003 WL 22290412 (N.D.Ill. 2003), *available at* http://cisgw3.law.pace.edu/cisg/wais/db/cases2/031006u1.html, holding that the CISG is to be given the same weight as any other Federal statute in a case implicating issues regulated by State law in accordance with the twenty-first Amendment to the U.S. Constitution. As an alternative and/or supportive *ratio* for the holding, I would argue that the IBIFDA constitutes a *validity-related regime* (designed to protect wholesalers with arguably inferior bargaining power) containing rules which lie *outside the CISG scope* (*see* preceding note and *supra* text, corresponding with note 5), and this validity-based logic hardly seems impaired by the Court of Appeal's subsequent decision in *Stawski*, 349 F.3d 1023 (7th Cir. 2003), reversing the District Court's order which had granted Stawski's *motion to stay arbitration*; *see* 2003 WL 21209860 & 2003 WL 22595266). Regarding "avoidance" terminology in the CISG and common/American domestic law, *see supra* note 16.

Convention as a "*non-cumul*" regime.[29] In other words, domestic remedies need not be deemed preëmpted (trumped) by the Convention whenever a given set of "operative facts" (also) seems "covered" by CISG rules.[30]

To this extent the *Geneva* and *Stawski* decisions confirm that we are not likely to find simple answers to multi-faceted CISG preëmption questions.[31] When the Convention's (limited) sphere of application requires courts and arbitrators to handle "loose ends",[32] we cannot expect all decision-makers to tie the same kinds of knots.[33]

---

29 *See* text corresponding with note 13 *supra*.

30 *See generally* LOOKOFSKY-USA, *supra* note 5, at §§ 2-6 and 4-6; *accord supra* note 17. *But cf*. sources cited *supra* note 21.

31 *See* text corresponding with note 18 *supra*.

32 *See generally* Joseph Lookofsky, *Loose Ends and Contorts in International Sales: Problems in the Harmonization of Private Law Rules*, 39 AM. J. COMP. L. 403 (1991). Regarding the Convention's sphere of application *see also supra* text, corresponding with notes 4 & 5.

33 *See generally* Lookofsky, *supra* note 19.

CISG Article 78: The Endless Disagreement Among the Commentators, Much less Among the Courts

Francesco G. Mazzotta[1] (July 2004)

---

1 Dottore in Giurisprudenza, Università degli Studi di Napoli, "Federico II" (Italy), 1993; LL.M. in International & Comparative Law, University of Pittsburgh School of Law (U.S.A.), 2000; Associate of the Institute of International Commercial Law of the Pace University School of Law. I would like to thank Professor Albert Kritzer for his precious comments and Professor James Flannery for kindly editing this article. Of course, any mistake I may have made is to be attributed only to this author.

I. Introduction

Once again, an Italian court decision sets another example of clarity and thoroughness in tackling difficult issues posed by some provisions of the United Nations Convention on Contracts for the International Sale of Goods[2] (hereinafter Convention or CISG). The decision,[3] among other matters, considered the issue of interest. In dealing with it, the court, chaired by Judge Alessandro Rizzieri, who previously handed down another exemplar decision,[4] gave full application to the requirements set forth in CISG Article 7(1), acknowledging that "[i]n the interpretation of this Convention, regard is to be had to its international character and to the need to promote uniformity in its application and the observance of good faith in international trade."[5]

2 United Nations Convention on Contracts for the International Sale of Goods, Apr. 11, 1980, S. Treaty Doc. No. 98-9 (1984), 1489 U.N.T.S. 3, *reprinted in* United Nations Conference on Contracts for the International Sale of Goods, 19 I.L.M. 671(1980)[hereinafter CISG]; Preamble, U.N. Doc. A/Conf. 97/18, Annex I, English version *reprinted in* 52 Fed. Reg. 6264 (1987); 19 I.L.M. 668 (1980) [hereinafter Preamble].

3 Tribunale di Padova, [District Court] 40466 of Rig 2002, 31 Mar. 2004 (Italy), *at* http://www.cisg.law.pace.edu/cisg/wais/db/cases2/040331i3.html.

4 Tribunale di Vigevano, [District Court] 856/1997, 12 July 2000 (Italy), *at* http://www.cisg.law.pace.edu/cisg/wais/db/cases2/000712i3.html.

5 CISG, *supra* note 2, art. 7(1).

Indeed, almost twenty decisions from several jurisdictions were cited in construing the meaning of CISG Article 78. In addition, the court fully explained its reasoning, as opposed to the vast majority of cases where courts briefly, and often vaguely, state the logic supporting their decisions. The most important lesson some courts should take is that the construction of the meaning of CISG provisions should be done by giving due regard to CISG case law and, although it should be obvious, no reliance should be made to domestic cases not concerned with the CISG.

When I first started working on this introduction, I was going to compare the Italian decision with a negative example of how courts should not operate in applying the CISG. One of the most recent negative examples was an American case, *Chicago Prime Packers v. Northam Food Trading Co.*,[6] where the court disdained reference to *any* CISG Article 39 cases; instead, the *Chicago Packers* court (like some other American courts[7]) cited only American Uniform Commercial Code case law.[8] Things change, however. Gladly, I note that, on a new ruling in *Chicago Prime Packers*,[9] the court showed a different approach. The court, in fact, has cited seven foreign cases (four German, two Italian, and one Dutch), which is more than any other U.S. judge has previously cited. The new ruling of the *Chicago Packers* court must be, therefore, commended for the new approach toward foreign case law.

As it concerns the topic of this paper, I must also underscore that the court offered a very well-crafted analysis of the matter's current status. The court, in fact, after acknowledging that commentators and courts put forward several approaches in dealing with the interest rate issue, applied domestic law (private international law rules) to determine the proper rate of interest. This, I believe, is the proper method, in light of CISG case law.

---

6 Chicago Prime Packers, Inc. v. Northam Food Trading Co., 320 F. Supp. 2d 702, 2004 WL 1166628 (N.D. Ill. 2004), *at* http://www.cisg.law.pace.edu/cisg/wais/db/cases2/030529u1.html. [2003 WL 21254261, N.D. Ill., May 29, 2003].

7 *See, e.g.*, Delchi Carrier S.p.A. v. Rotorex Corp., 71 F.3d 1024, 1028 (2d Cir. 1995)(stating that "caselaw interpreting analogous provisions of Article 2 of the Uniform Commercial Code ("U.C.C.") may also inform a court where the language of the relevant CISG provisions track that of the U.C.C.").

8 For a very recent example of this kind of approach see Raw Materials, Inc. v. Manfred Forberich GmbH & Co., KG, 2004 WL 1535839 (N.D. Ill. 2004), where the District Court used the U.C.C. test for commercial impracticability to interpret CISG Article 79.

9 Chicago Prime Packers, Inc. v. Northam Food Trading Co., 320 F. Supp. 2d. 702, 2004 WL 1166628 (N.D. Ill. 2004), *available at* http://www.cisg.law.pace.edu/cisg/wais/db/cases2/040524u1.html.[Federal Court of 1st instance].

II. Article 78 background

It is well known that Article 78 is "more conspicuous for the questions it fails to answer than the questions it answers"[10] and it does not come as a surprise that interest rates are one of the most litigated and discussed topics of the Convention.[11] Because the delegates to the Vienna Convention could not reach an agreement,[12] the present version of Article 78 does not fix any rate of interest. It should be noted, however, that although considered a "headless corpse," Article 78 introduces a far-reaching principle of the general entitlement to interest,[13] which is still rather important because it makes clear that a fixed interest (even if not set by the Convention) must be applied to sums paid with delay (the "normativity" feature),[14] and that the entitlement to interest is not limited by grounds for release as provided for by CISG Article 79 (the "absoluteness" feature).[15]

---

10 *See* Jacob S. Ziegel & Claude Samson, Report to the Uniform Law Conference of Canada on Convention on Contracts for the International Sale of Goods 149 (1981), *available at* http://www.cisg.law.pace.edu/cisg/wais/db/articles/english2.html.

11 *See, e.g.*, Jeffrey S. Sutton, *Measuring Damages Under the United Nations Convention on the International Sale of Goods*, 50 OHIO ST. L.J. 737, 749-51 (1989); Phanesh Koneru, *The International Interpretation of the UN Convention on Contracts for the International Sale of Goods: An Approach Based on General Principles*, 6 MINN. J. GLOBAL TRADE 105, 123 (1997).

12 For a historical account on the issue of the rate of interest raised during the drafting period of the Vienna Sales Convention, see Pace University School of Law, Institute of International Commercial Law, Guide to CISG Article 78, *available at*, http://www.cisg.law.pace.edu/cisg/text/roadmap/intro-78.html. A bibliography of literature specifically relevant to the provisions of CISG Article 78 is *available at* http://www.cisg.law.pace.edu/cisg/text/mono78.html.

13 FRITZ ENDERLEIN & DIETRICH MASKOW, INTERNATIONAL SALES LAW, UNITED NATIONS CONVENTION ON CONTRACTS FOR THE INTERNATIONAL SALE OF GOODS – CONVENTION ON THE LIMITATION PERIOD IN THE INTERNATIONAL SALE OF GOODS 310, 311 (1992). *See also* Tribunale di Padova, *supra* note 3, *citing* Int'l Comm. Arb., award No. 7585 [1995]; Oberlandesgericht [OLG] [Provincial Court of Appeal] Koblenz 2 U 1230/91, 17 Sept. 1993 (F.R.G.), *at* http://www.cisg.law.pace.edu/cisg/wais/db/cases2/930917g1.html; Tribunale di Pavia [District Court] 29 Dec. 1999 (Italy), *at* http://www.cisg.law.pace.edu/cisg/wais/db/cases2/991229i3.html; Int'l Comm. Arb., Award No. 8908 [1998] *at* http://www.cisg.law.pace.edu/cisg/wais/db/cases2/988908i1.html; Landgericht [LG] [District Court] Landshut 54 O 644/94, 5 Apr. 1995 (F.R.G.), *at* http://www.cisg.law.pace.edu/cisg/wais/db/cases2/950405g1.html.

14 ENDERLEIN & MASKOW, *supra* note 13.

15 *Id.*

As the CISG does not directly state how to determine the applicable interest rate, Article 7(2) requires that "[q]uestions concerning matters governed by this Convention which are not expressly settled in it are to be settled in conformity with the general principles on which it is based or, in the absence of such principles, in conformity with the law applicable by virtue of the rules of private international law."[16] Our task is, therefore, to establish whether the interest rate (the actual figure and/or its method of determination) is an issue that can be settled in conformity of the general principles of the Convention and, if so, determine which principles may be useful to this end. If the interest rate cannot be determined by the CISG or through its general principles pursuant to Article 7(2), the domestic rules of private international law must determine the proper law that fixes the applicable interest rate. However, resorting to domestic law should be limited to those cases where the CISG does not apply either because the issue is explicitly excluded from the scope of the CISG (*see*, *e.g.*, Article 4) or because the CISG did not directly or indirectly settle the matter. If, however, a court deems that the matter is totally outside the CISG, the very same court can then apply its own rules to determine the proper interest. It is extremely important, therefore, to better understand the mechanics of Article 78 reviewing its history and its precedents. The reader may also find, in the appendices, a list of the cases used to prepare this article, which are arranged by country. For those decisions where an English translation and/or an abstract in English were available, the relevant phrases/sentences were reported.

III. History of Article 78

The interest issue was expressly settled by the Uniform Law on the International Sale of Goods (ULIS) (hereinafter 1964 Hague Sales Convention), Article 83, which reads:

> Where the breach of contract consists of delay in the payment of the price, the seller shall in any event be entitled to interest on such sum as is in arrears at a rate equal to the official discount rate in the country where he has his place of business or, if he has no place of business, his habitual residence, plus 1%.[17]

16 CISG, *supra* note 2, art 7(2)

17 Uniform Law on the International Sale of Goods, 1964, art. 83, 834 U.N.T.S. 109 [hereinafter ULIS].

In 1969, the United Nations Commission on International Trade Law ("UNCITRAL") set up a Working Group on the International Sale of Goods ("Working Group") with the purpose, *inter alia*, of ascertaining "which modifications of the Hague Convention of 1964 relating to Uniform Law on the International Sale of Goods might render it capable of wider acceptance by countries of different legal, social and economic systems and to elaborate a text reflecting such modification."[18] The Working Group at the fifth session (January 1974) completed its initial examination of the ULIS. The Working Group, after considering some proposals to change the current draft of ULIS Article 83,[19] decided to keep it as it was.[20]

Later, however, upon observation of the Norway delegation,[21] the Working Group decided to amend the previous draft so that the phrase "or, if he has no place of business, his habitual residence" would be deleted. The Working Group also decided to add the following phrase to the end of Article 83 with the purpose of avoiding the debtor purposefully delaying payment: "but his entitlement shall not be lower than the rate applied to unsecured short-term commercial credit in the seller's country."[22] Thus, the provision concerning interest (now Article 56), reads:

> Where the breach of contract consists of delay in the payment of price, the seller shall in any event be entitled to interest on such sum as is in arrears at a rate equal to the official discount rate in the country where he has his place of business plus one per cent but his entitlement shall not be lower than the rate applied to unsecured short-term commercial credits in the seller's country.[23]

The Working Group completed its mandate of reviewing the ULIS at its seventh session (January 1976) by approving the "Draft Convention on the International

---

18 *See Report of United Nations Commission on International Trade Law*, U.N. GAOR, 24th Sess., Supp. No. 18, U.N. Doc. A/7618 (1969).

19 *Analysis of Comments and Proposals by Representatives of State Members for Working Group Relating to Articles 71 to 101 of ULIS: Note by the Secretary General*, U.N. GAOR, Supp. No. 17, § 61, U.N. Doc. A/CN.9/WG.2/WP.17.

20 *Progress Report of the Working Group on the International Sale of Goods on the Work of its Fifth Session*, U.N. GAOR, 29th Sess., Supp. No. 87, U.N. Doc. A/CN.9/87 (1974).

21 *Comments and Proposals of Representatives on the Revised Text of a Uniform Law on the International Sale of Goods as Approved or Deferred for Further Consideration by the Working Group at its First Five Sessions*, [1975] 6 Y.B. Int'l Trade L. Comm'n 79, 82, U.N. Doc. A/CN.9/100, Annex II.

22 *See Report of the Working Group on the International Sale of Goods on the Work of its Sixth Session*, [1975] 6 Y.B. Int'l Trade L. Comm'n 17, 62, U.N. Doc. A/CN.9/100.

23 *See Revised Text of the Convention on the International Sale of Goods as Approved or Deferred for Further Consideration by the Working Group on the International Sale of Goods at its First Six Sessions*, [1975] 6 Y.B. Int'l Trade L. Comm'n 66, 68, U.N. Doc. A/CN.9/100, Annex I.

Sale of Goods" (the "1976 Draft Convention").[24] The provision pertaining interest (now Article 58) reads:

> If the breach of contract consists of delay in the payment of the price, the seller is in any event entitled to interest on such sum as is in arrears at a rate equal to the official discount rate in the country where he has his place of business, plus 1 per cent, but his entitlement is not to be lower than the rate applied to unsecured short-term commercial credits in the country where the seller has his place of business.[25]

As the commentary on this Article underscores, this

> rule of damages is an exception to the rule expressed in Article 55 that the injured party recovers 'a sum equal to the loss' in that the seller need not prove that the delay in payment caused him any loss... The interest rate formula set forth in article 58 is available to the seller 'in any event'. This makes it clear that pursuant to article 55 the seller can claim any other loss over and above the loss of interest if can prove the loss was caused him by the delay in paying the price.[26]

As required by a decision taken by UNCITRAL at its eighth session (April 1975), the text of the 1976 Draft Convention was sent to governments and international organizations for their comments. Czechoslovakia observed that

> [i]t should be considered whether it would be more appropriate for the seller to be entitled to interest charges in the country of the debtor instead of the creditor, or to combine the discount rate of interest valid in both countries in such a way (or manner) that the non-performance of the monetary obligation be advantageous for the debtor (for instance in cases when the rate of interest is higher in his country).[27]

The Federal Republic of Germany proposed that at the end of Article 58 the words "but his entitlement is not [to] be lower than the rate applied to unsecured short-

---

24 *Draft Convention on the International Sale of Goods*, Art. 58, [1975] 7 Y.B. Int'l Trade L. Comm'n 89, U.N. Doc. A/CN.9/116, Annex I (Annex 2 reproduces a Commentary on the draft Convention).

25 *Id.* at 95.

26 *See Commentary on the Draft Convention on the International Sale of Goods*, Art. 55, [1976] 7 Y.B. Int'l Trade L. Comm'n 96, 134, U.N. Doc. A/CN.9/110, Annex II.

27 *See Comments by Governments and International Organizations on the Draft Convention on the International Sale of Goods*, Art. 58, [1977] 8 Y.B. Int'l Trade L. Comm'n 2, 109, 114, U.N. Doc. A/CN.9/125/Add. 2.

term commercial credits in the country where the seller has his place of business"[28] be deleted. The German delegation was not in favor of having the seller paying such a high interest rate in any case of delay. Payment of interest should be limited to those situations where the seller had to actually borrow money. It was observed that the rate applied varies greatly depending on the customer's credit worthiness while the International Chamber of Commerce ("ICC") acknowledged that the rule fixed by Article 58 was an improvement over ULIS Article 83, and merely proposed to increase the surcharge over the official discount to 2 per cent from 1 per cent, as required by the current draft of Article 58.[29]

At its tenth session (May 23 – June 17, 1977), UNCITRAL established the Committee of the Whole to consider the 1976 Draft Convention[30] in the light of the comments and proposals submitted by governments and international organizations. On May 24, 1977, this Committee established a Drafting Group for the purpose of redrafting

> those articles of the draft Convention in respect of which modifications of substance had been agreed upon in the Committee, to consider drafting proposals submitted by Governments and international organizations in their written comments and in the course of the Committee's discussion and, generally, to examine the text of the draft Convention from the point of view of consistency of the terminology used and to ensure consistency between language versions.[31]

The discussion on the interest provision (Article 58) proved to be extremely controversial. The frustration is clear in the relevant paragraph of the report: "In view of these difficulties, coupled with the fact that the article was, in any version, inherently unacceptable to a number of representatives, particularly those of developing countries, the Committee, after considerable deliberation, decided to delete Article 58."[32]

At its eleventh session, UNCITRAL considered the question "whether the rules on formation of contracts for the international sale of goods should be the subject

---

28 *Comments by Governments and International Organizations on the Draft Convention on the International Sale of Goods*, Art. 58, [1977] 8 Y.B. Int'l Trade Law Comm'n 109, 117, U.N. Doc. A/CN.9/125/Add. 1 to 3.

29 *Id.*

30 *See supra* note 23.

31 *See Report of the United Nations Comm'n on Int'l Trade Law on the Work of its Tenth Session*, U.N. Com'n on Int'l Trade Law, 10th Sess., U.N. Doc. A/32/17 (1977), *reprinted in* 8 Y.B. UNCITRAL 11.

32 *Id.*, at para. 499.

matter of a convention separate from the Convention on the International Sale of Goods."[33] After some discussion, it decided to integrate the draft convention on the formation of contracts, which the Working Group completed at its ninth session (Geneva, September 1977),[34] with the draft Convention on the International Sale of Goods into a single text named "Draft Convention on Contracts for the International Sale of Goods" (the "1977 Draft Convention").[35]

Article 55 of the 1977 Draft Convention as well as Article 69 of the similarly worded 1978 Draft Convention[36] on Contracts for the International Sale of Goods ("1978 Draft Convention"), only provided for the seller to pay interest on the purchase price when he was under the obligation to refund the price after the avoidance of the contract (similar to CISG Article 84), but no provision similar to CISG Article 78 could be agreed upon due to irreconcilable divergences among the delegations.[37]

As the comments and proposals by governments and international organizations on the 1978 Draft Convention indicate otherwise,[38] Czechoslovakia, Finland, the Netherlands, Sweden and the ICC proposed, however, to have a provision expressly dealing with the right to receive interest. They believed that it should be clearly stated that a "buyer who does not pay the price at the time of its maturity should be obliged to pay interest on overdue payments in principle at a rate one per cent higher than the official discount rate valid in the country of the debtor."[39]

In 1980, the Diplomatic Conference held in Vienna assigned to a first committee (First Committee) the review of the various proposals to amend the 1978 Draft Convention and to a second committee the review of other draft provisions

---

33 *See Report of the United Nations Commission on International Trade Law on the Work of its Eleventh Session*, U.N. GAOR, 33rd Sess., U.N. Doc. A/33/17 (1978).

34 *Report of the Working Group on the International Sale of Goods on the Work of its Ninth Session*, U.N. GAOR, 33rd Sess., U.N. Doc. A/CN.9/142/Add.1 (1978).

35 *See* U.N. G.A.O.R., 33rd Sess., Supp. No. 17, chap. II, para. 28, U.N. Doc. A/33/17 (1978) (report of UNCITRAL in its eleventh session). *See also* The Draft Convention on the Formation of Contracts for the International Sale of Goods, prepared by the UNCITRAL Working Group (the "1977 Formation Draft") U.N. Doc. A/CN.9/142/Add 1.

36 *Id.*

37 *Id.*

38 *Secretary General, Analysis of Comments and Proposals by Governments and International Organizations on the Draft Convention on Contracts for the International Sale of Goods, and on Draft Provisions Concerning Implementation, Reservations and Other Final Clauses*, U.N. GAOR, 34th Sess., U.N. Doc. A/CONF.97/9 (1979), *available at* www.cisg.law.pace.edu/cisg/Fdraft.html.

39 *Id.* (Czechoslovakia's comments on Article 78).

concerning implementation, declarations, reservations and other final clauses of the 1978 Draft Convention.[40] A Plenary Conference would then consider the drafts submitted by the First Committee for inclusion into the CISG.[41] The First Committee considered the interest issue at its 28th meeting (March 28, 1980), 29th meeting (March 31, 1980), 34th meeting (April 3, 1980), and 37th meeting (April 7, 1980).[42] At the 29th meeting, a working group composed of the representatives of Argentina, Czechoslovakia, Ghana, Greece, India, Italy, Pakistan and Sweden was established to consider the proposals relating to Article 69 (now Article 84) and the interest issue on sums that are in arrears.[43] At the 34th meeting, the following alternatives were proposed:[44]

Alternative I:
If a party fails to pay the price or any other sum that is in arrears, the other party is entitled to interest thereon at the rate for a short-term commercial credit or at another similar appropriate rate prevailing in the main domestic financial centre of the party claiming payment.

Alternative II:
If a party fails to pay the price or any other sum that is in arrears, the other party is entitled to interest thereon at the rate for a short-term commercial credit or at another similar appropriate rate prevailing in the main domestic financial centre of the country of the party in default, or, in case the other party's actual credit costs are higher, at a rate corresponding thereto but not at a rate higher than the first said rate in his own country.

Alternative III:
If a party fails to pay the price or any other sum that is in arrears, the other party is entitled to interest thereon at the rate for a short-term commercial credit or at another similar appropriate rate prevailing in the main domestic financial centre of the party in default. However, in case the party claiming interest is not fairly

---

40 *Id.*

41 *Id.*

42 *Id.*

43 *Id.*

44 *Report of the First Committee on the Articles of the Convention on the International Sale of Goods, Prosposals; Action by First Committee*, U.N. GAOR, 97th Sess., 34th mtg., at 138, U.N. Doc. A/CONF.97/C.1/L.247 (1980) *available at* www.cisg.law.pace.edu/cisg/1stcommittee/summaries 78,84.html#b [hereinafter *First Committee Proposals*].

compensated by such rate, he may claim interest up to the first said rate in his own country.

As stated by the Swedish representative, introducing the alternatives, "[t]he proposals formulated by the working group constituted neither a package deal nor a compromise, but offered three possible solutions to the problem of interest."[45] The working group could not find a single satisfactory alternative to the United Kingdom's proposal seeking to introduce a provision of this effect: "This Convention does not affect any right of the seller or buyer to recover interest on money."[46]

Each of the alternatives formulated by the working group was composed of two parts: an introductory phrase defining the rate of interest, and a second provision dealing with the place at which interest should be calculated.[47] With respect to the second part, most members of the working group favored Alternative I, which offered the simplest solution.[48] It seemed "natural"[49] to calculate the rate of interest on the basis of the interest rate prevailing in the country of the creditor's place of business, as the creditor was the injured party who had to take steps to remedy that injury. With regard to Alternative II, all the members of the working group agreed that, if the interest rate prevailing in the country of the party in default was lower than that prevailing in the creditor's country, the latter would suffer injury; the injured party should be enabled to obtain the rate which he would have to pay for the credit in which he required.[50] On the other hand, the injured party should not be permitted to demand an excessive rate of interest. The final part of Alternative II took account of those considerations. Alternative III, which comprised a simplification of Alternative II with a slight difference of substance, did not obtain much support in the working group.[51] Although criticized by some delegations as obscure and ambiguous, Alternative II, as orally amended by the representatives of Spain,[52] was eventually adopted. The text, however, was remitted to the drafting committee to improve its wording.

---

45 *Report of the First Committee on the Articles of the Convention on the International Sale of Good, First Committee Deliberations*, U.N. GAOR, 35th Sess., 34th mtg., at 138, U.N. Doc. A/CONF.97/c.1/L.247 (1980) *available at* www.cisg.law.pace.edu/cisg/firstcommittee/Meeting34.html [hereinafter *First Committee Deliberations*].

46 *First Committee Proposals, supra* note 39.

47 *First Committee Deliberations, supra* note 45. *Report of the First Committee on the Articles of the Convention on the International Sale of Good, First Committee Deliberations*, U.N. GAOR, 35th Sess., 34th mtg., at 138, U.N. Doc. A/CONF.97/c.1/L.247 (1980).

48 *Id.*

49 *Id.*

50 *Id.*

51 *Id.*

52 The Spanish delegation proposed: "It would, however, be appropriate to clarify the rate of

The First Committee submitted to the Plenary Conference the following draft:[53]

> (1) If a party fails to pay the price or any other sum that is in arrears, the other party is entitled to interest on it at the normal rate for a short-term commercial credit prevailing in the main financial centre in the State where the party in default has his place of business or, in the absence of such a rate, at another similar appropriate rate prevailing in that centre.
> (2) However, if the other party's actual credit costs are higher, he is entitled to interest on the sum in arrears at a rate corresponding to such credit costs, but not in excess of the rate defined in the preceding paragraph prevailing in the main financial centre in the State where he has his place of business.

At the 37th meeting of the First Committee, held on April 7, 1980, at 10 a.m., due to the criticism raised by some delegations, it was decided to keep the last draft of Article 78 as proposed, with the understanding that the drafting committee would produce a clearer text.[54] In the meantime, the following amendments were proposed:[55]

(i) Denmark, Finland, Greece, Sweden proposed to add Article 73 *bis* (now CISG Article 78), to read as follows:

> If a party fails to pay the price or any other sum as is in arrears, the other party is entitled to interest thereon at the customary rate for commercial credits at his place of business.
> As a result, the title 'Section IV. Damages' should be amended to read 'Section IV. Damages and interest'[56]

(ii) Czechoslovakia proposed to add Article 60 *bis* (now CISG Article 78), to read as follows:

---

interest charged and to add, in the three texts proposed – the first three lines of which were identical – the word 'normal' before the word 'rate' in the second line since short-term commercial credit was affected by variable conditions and it was therefore important that the 'normal' rate of interest should be applied." *First Committee Deliberations*, *supra* note 44.

53 *Draft Proposals submitted to the Plenary Conference*, U.N. GAOR, 35th Sess., at 163, sec.2, U.N. Doc. A/CONF.97/11/Add.1 and 2 (1980), *available at* www.cisg.law.pace.edu/cisg/jdraft.html [hereinafter *Draft Proposals*].

54 *Report of the First Committee to the Plenary Conference*, U.N. GAOR, 35th Sess., U.N. Doc A/CONF.97/11/Add.2, p.13; A/CONF.97/L.16, L.17 and L.18, *available at* http://www.cisg.law.pace.edu/cisg/plenarycommittee/summary10.html.

55 *First Committee Proposals*, *supra* note 39, at 137-8.

56 *Id.*

> (1) If the breach of contract consists of delay in the payment of the price, the seller is in any event entitled to interest on such sum as is in arrears at a rate equal to the official discount rate prevailing in the country where the buyer has his place of business, at the time of delay increased by one per cent or, if there is no such a rate, at the rate applied to unsecured short term international commercial credits increased by one per cent.
> (2) The seller may claim damages as provided in this Convention, if the loss is not covered by interests.[57]

(iii) Japan proposed to add Article 73 *bis* (now CISG Article 78), to read as follows:

If a party has failed to pay the price or any other sum that is in arrears, the other party is presumed to have suffered damages equivalent to the amount calculated at the interest rate for [unsecured short-term commercial credits prevailing] at his place of business.[58]

(iv) The United Kingdom proposed to delete paragraph (1) of Article 69 (now CISG Article 84) and add a new article in Part I, Chapter I (sphere of application), to read as follows:

"This Convention does not affect any right of the seller or buyer to recover interest on money."[59]

However, all of the preceding proposals were later withdrawn. The United Kingdom then submitted to the Plenary Conference the following proposals and amendments (also later withdrawn, *infra*):

(i) Add, in Part I, Chapter I (sphere of application), a new article to read as follows:

"This Convention is not concerned with the payment of interest."[60]

(ii) Delete Article 73 *bis* (now CISG Article 78).[61]

At the 7th Plenary Meeting held on April 8, 1980, the main issue involving Article 78 was whether Article 45 ("Remedies for breach of contract by the seller") should also include reference to Article 78. Some representatives argued that reference to

---

57 *Id.*

58 *Id.*

59 *Id.* at 138.

60 *Draft Proposals*, *supra* note 53, at 173.

61 *Id.*

Article 78 should be made as Article 45 dealt with all remedies available to the buyer. Others, the majority, argued that the list provided under Article 45 was not exhaustive and that interest was not limited to the buyer, but also to the seller, as Article 78 expressly made reference to "any other sum."[62] The representatives took a vote on whether the scope of Article 45 should be interpreted as also including also Article 78. The result of the voting was 20 in favor, 14 against, with 12 abstentions.[63] As the required two-thirds majority had not been obtained, the interpretation had not been adopted.[64] It remained to be considered whether the Conference would adopt the contrary interpretation.

At the 8th Plenary Meeting, held on April 9, 1980, although many representatives agreed that Article 45 did not provide an exhaustive list of the remedies available to the buyer, and therefore was of no legal significance, the issue of whether reference to Article 78 should be made within Article 61 ("Remedies for breach of contract by the buyer") was tackled.[65] The representatives agreed to postpone any decision concerning Article 45 upon deciding Article 78.

At the 10th Plenary Meeting held on April 10, 1980, at 10 a.m., Mr. Nicholas (United Kingdom) announced that he was withdrawing the draft amendment in document A/CONF.97/L.18 to delete Article 78, and requested that, if Article 78 were not to be adopted, the draft amendments in documents A/CONF.97/L.16[66] and A/CONF.97/L.17[67] should be put to the vote.[68] Notwithstanding the fact that the British representatives had withdrawn their proposal to delete Article 78, some delegations (Mexico and Ghana) expressed support for it due to the strong differences among the delegations.[69] Other delegations, instead, deemed that if the Convention were not to deal with the interest issue, it would not facilitate its application.[70] Even these delegations, however, criticized the latest draft of Article

62 *Report of the First Committee to the Plenary Conference*, U.N. GAOR, 35th Sess., U.N. Doc. A/CONF.97/11 and Add. 1 and 2 (1980), *available at* http://www.cisg.law.pace.edu/cisg/plenarycommittee/summary10.html [hereinafter *Plenary Conference*].

63 *Id.*

64 *Id.*

65 *Report of the First Committee to the Plenary Conference*, U.N. GAOR, 35th Sess., U.N. Doc. A/CONF.97/11 and Add.1, 2 and 3 (1980), *available at* http://www.cisg.law.pace.edu/cisg/plenarycommittee/summary8.html.

66 *Draft Proposals*, *supra* note 52, at 173.

67 *Id.* (reading: "Delete paragraph (1) of Article 69 [now CISG Article 84]").

68 *Report of the First Committee to the Plenary Conference*, U.N. GAOR, 35th Sess., U.N. Doc A/CONF.97/11/Add.2, p.13; A/CONF.97/L.16, L.17 and L.18, *available at* http://www.cisg.law.pace.edu/cisg/plenarycommittee/summary10.html.

69 *Id.*

70 *Id.*

73 *bis*.[71] In particular, the Belgian representative noted that both paragraphs of Article 73 *bis* were unclear, although the first paragraph was less troublesome.[72] Therefore, they proposed to take a separate vote on the two paragraphs composing Article 73 *bis*. However, the proposal was quickly criticized by some delegations. The Swedish representative, particularly, noted that the latest draft of Article 73 *bis* "struck a balance between the views of delegations which wished the rate prevailing where the debtor had his place of business to be taken into account in the calculation of interest, and those of delegations which preferred that the rate where the creditor had his place of business should be taken into account. To adopt only one of the two paragraphs of the article would be to upset that compromise."[73] The majority of the Conference rejected (35 votes to 4, with 7 abstentions) the proposal to take a separate vote on the two paragraphs of Article 73 *bis*.[74] The Egyptian delegation unsuccessfully renewed the proposal to have the Convention providing explicitly for the possibility of making reservation to Article 73 *bis*.[75]

A vote on Article 73 *bis* was then taken. There were 24 votes in favor, 17 against and 10 abstentions.[76] Having failed to obtain the required two-thirds majority, Article 73 *bis* was not adopted.[77] The Swedish representative noted that, although Article 73 *bis* had not obtained the required two-thirds majority, a substantial majority had pronounced in its favor. Given such a favorable attitude, the Swedish representative argued that it would be "indispensable to set up a working group in an attempt to remove the outstanding uncertainties in the text of paragraph 2."[78] The Swedish proposal was adopted by 16 votes to 12, with 16 abstentions.[79] The Working Group set up to prepare a new text for Article 73 *bis* included Canada, Egypt, Singapore, Sweden, the United Kingdom and the Union of Soviet Socialist Republics.[80]

At the 11th Plenary Meeting, held on April 10, 1980, at 3 p.m., the Working Group set up at the previous meeting submitted the following proposals to the Conference:

---

71 *Id.*

72 *Id.*

73 *Records of the Plenary Meeting on the Articles of the Convention on the International Sale of Goods*, U.N. GAOR, 35th Sess., U.N. Doc. A/CONF.97/11/Add.2 (1980), *available at* http://www.cisg.law.pace.edu/cisg/plenarycommittee/summary10.html [hereinafter *Plenary Meeting*].

74 *Id.*

75 *Id.*

76 *Id.*

77 *Id.*

78 *Id.*

79 *Plenary Meeting*, U.N. Doc. A/CONF.97/11/Add.2

80 *Id.*

1. The words "and interest" should be deleted from the title of Section II, so that it would read (**only**): "Damages."

2. There should be a *new* section II *bis* entitled "*Interest*," consisting **solely** of article 73 *bis*;

3. Article 73 *bis* should read:
   "If a party fails to pay the price or any other sum that is in arrears, the other party is entitled to interest on it, without prejudice to any claim for damages recoverable under article 70 [became CISG Article 74]."

Here it is, in the words of the drafters of the Convention the explanation of the current wording of Article 78:

> Mr. KHOO (Singapore), speaking as the Chairman of the working group set up at the previous meeting, said that it had initially tried to work on the basis of the text of Article 73 *bis*, as it appeared in document A/CONF.97/11/Add.2, *but had finally come to the conclusion that fundamental differences in the approach of different national legal systems to the question of interest rendered that task too difficult. A further difficulty arose from the attempt to treat damages and interest under the same heading.* The working group had decided to recommend a provision based, as it were, on the highest common factor, so that *the Convention might at least contain a clear statement on the question of interest*. The text of Article 73 *bis* [became CISG Article 78] just read out by the Secretary represented such a solution. *The first part of the article established that a party which failed to pay the price or any other sum in due time was under obligation to pay interest on that sum to the other party. The second part of the article, intended to accommodate legal regulations under which interest was considered to be part of the damages recoverable in default situations, referred to the right of the second party to claim damages under article 70* [became CISG article 74].[81]

Article 73 *bis* as proposed by the Working Group was adopted by 30 votes to 2, with 12 abstentions.[82] The title of Chapter V, Section II *bis*, proposed by the Working Group, "Section II *bis*: Interest", was adopted by 35 votes to 1, with 3 abstentions. The title of Chapter V, Section II, as amended by the Working Group ("Section II: Damages") was adopted by 42 votes to none.[83]

---

81 *Plenary Meeting*, *supra* note 73, 11th Plenary mtg. at 226, *available at* http://www.cisg.law.pace.edu/cisg/plenarycommittee/summary11.html (emphasis added).

82 *Report of the First Committee to the Plenary Conference*, U.N. GAOR, 35th Sess., U.N. Doc A/CONF.97/11/Add.2, p.13, *available at* http://www.cisg.law.pace.edu/cisg/plenarycommittee/summary11.html

83 *Id.*

IV. Operation of Article 78

Article 78 reads as follows, "If a party fails to pay the price or any other sum that is in arrears, the other party is entitled to interest on it, without prejudice to any claim for damages recoverable under Article 74." If, however, the seller must return the purchase price after the contract has been avoided, Article 84 applies.

Failure to pay the price or any other sum that is in arrears is the only condition to be satisfied under Article 78.[84] Failure refers to a failure to comply with the obligation to pay the price by a specific time, whether the time is set by contract[85] or by the CISG (Article 58).[86] Interest is due regardless of proof of any losses[87] and it is independent of any claim for damages.[88] While there are no problems in deter-

---

84 *See, e.g.*, Kantonsgericht [KG] [District Court] A3 2001 34, 12 Dec. 2002 (Switz.), *at* http://www.cisg.law.pace.edu/cisg/wais/db/cases2/021212s1.html; Amtsgericht [AG] [Petty District Court] Koblenz 16 C 1056/96, 12 Nov. 1996 (F.R.G.), *at* http://www.cisg.law.pace.edu/cisg/wais/db/cases2/961112g1.html; Oberlandesgericht [OLG] [Provincial Court of Appeal] Rostock 1 U 247/94, 27 July 1995 (F.R.G.), *at* http://www.cisg.law.pace.edu/cisg/wais/db/cases2/950727g1.html.

85 Handelsgericht [HG] [Commercial Court], OR.97.00056, 19 Dec. 1997 (Switz.), *at* http://www.cisg.law.pace.edu/cisg/wais/db/cases2/971219s1.html.

86 *See* Landgericht [LG] [District Court] Stendal 22 S 234/94, 12 Oct. 2000 (F.R.G.), *at* http://www.cisg.law.pace.edu/cisg/wais/db/cases2/001012g1.html; Oberlandesgericht [OLG] [Provincial Court of Appeal] Frankfurt am Main 5 U 15/93, 18 Jan. 1994 (F.R.G.), *at* http://www.cisg.law.pace.edu/cisg/wais/db/cases2/940118g1.html; Oberlandesgericht [OLG] [Provincial Court of Appeal] Frankfurt am Main 5 U 261/90, 13 June 1991 (F.R.G.), *at* http://www.cisg.law.pace.edu/cisg/wais/db/cases2/910613g1.html.

87 *See* OLG Frankfurt am Main, 5 U 15/93, *supra* note 55; Landgericht [LG] [District Court] Hamburg 5 O 543/88, 26 Sept. 1990 (F.R.G.), *at* http://www.cisg.law.pace.edu/cisg/wais/db/cases2/900926g1.html; Amtsgericht [AG] [Petty District Court] Oldenburg in Holstein 5 C 73/89, 24 Apr. 1990 (F.R.G.), *at* http://www.cisg.law.pace.edu/cisg/wais/db/cases2/900424g1.html.

88 *See, e.g.*, Bundesgericht [BG] [Supreme Court] 4C.179/1998/odi, 28 Oct. 1998 (Switz.), *at* http://www.cisg.law.pace.edu/cisg/wais/db/cases2/981028s1.html; Handelsgericht [HG] [Commercial Court] HG 930476, 21 Sept. 1995 (Switz.), *at* http://www.cisg.law.pace.edu/cisg/wais/db/cases2/950921s1.html; OLG 5 U 15/93, *supra* note 86; Oberlandesgericht [OLG] [Provincial Court of Appeal] Düsseldorf, 17 U 146/93, 14 Jan. 1994 (F.R.G.), *at* http://www.cisg.law.pace.edu/cisg/wais/db/cases2/940114g1.html; OLG 2 U 1230/91, *supra* note 12; ICC Int'l Comm. Arb., Award No. 7197 [1992], *available at* http://www.cisg.law.pace.edu/cisg/wais/db/cases2/927197i1.html; AG Oldenburg in Holstein 5 C 73/89, *supra* note 87. *See also, e.g.*, Enderlein & Maskow, *supra* note 12, at 311; Rolf Herber & Beate

mining the time when the buyer is bound to pay the price (as said, it will be governed either by the agreement between the parties or, as a default rule, by the CISG, Article 58);[89] however, there are no default rules with respect to the time of performance of "other sums". In this case, in the absence of any other indication, it must be assumed that interest is to be paid from the day the other sum is due.[90] It is

---

CZERWENKA, INTERNATIONALES KAUFRECHT 348 (1991); Hans Stoll, *Internationalprivatrechtliche Fragen bei der landesrechtlichen Ergänzung des einheitlichen Kaufrechts*, *in* FESTSCHRIFT FÜR MURAD FERID 495, 509-10 (Andreas Heldrich ed., 1988). *But see* F.J.A. van der Velden, *Het Weense Koopverdrag 1980 en zijn Rechtsmiddelen* 405 (1988), who sustains that interest is part of damages. According to this view, payment of interest could be exempted on the grounds of impediments.

89 *See* Hans H. Eberstein & Klaus Bacher, *Annotations 1-36 on Article 78*, *in* COMMENTARY ON THE UN CONVENTION ON THE INTERNATIONAL SALE OF GOODS 591-99, 593 (Peter Schlechtriem ed., 1998) [hereinafter Eberstein & Bacher, *Annotations*]; ENDERLEIN & MASKOW, *supra* note 12, at 313. *See also* Oberlandesgericht [OLG] [Provincial Court of Appeal] Rostock 6 U 126/00, 25 Sept. 2002 (F.R.G.), *at* http://www.cisg.law.pace.edu/cisg/wais/db/cases2/020925g1.html; Amtsgericht [AG] [Petty District Court] Viechtach 1 C 419/01, 11 Apr. 2002 (F.R.G.), *at* http://www.cisg.law.pace.edu/cisg/wais/db/cases2/020411g1.html; Handelsgericht [HG] [Commercial Court] 930634/O, 30 Nov. 1998 (Switz.), *at* http://www.cisg.law.pace.edu/cisg/wais/db/cases2/981130s1.html; HG OR.97.00056, *supra* note 85; Amtsgericht [AG] [Petty District Court] Kehl 3 C 925/93, 6 Oct. 1995 (F.R.G.), *at* http://cisgw3.law.pace.edu/cases/951006g1.html. There are, however, several cases whereby the "due date" is determined pursuant to other factors: Landgericht [LG] [District Court] München 12 HKO 5593/01, 30 Aug. 2001(F.R.G.), *at* http://www.cisg.law.pace.edu/cisg/wais/db/cases2/010830g1.html (interest due as of the day as the request from the attorney); Landgericht [LG] [District Court] München 12 HKO 3804/00, 16 Nov. 2000 (F.R.G.), *at* http://www.cisg.law.pace.edu/cisg/wais/db/cases2/001116g1.html (receipt of invoice); Tribunal Cantonal [Canton Appellate Court] 01 93 1061 [163/96/BA and 164/96/BA], 11 Mar. 1996 (Switz.), *at* http://www.cisg.law.pace.edu/cisg/wais/db/cases2/960311s2.html (by domestic law); Société Cámara Agraria Provincial de Gipuzcoa v. André Margaron, Cour d'appel [CA] [Appeal Court] Grenoble 93/2821, 29 Mar. 1995 (Fr.), *at* http://www.cisg.law.pace.edu/cisg/wais/db/cases2/950329f1.html (from the date of the interest pleading); Int'l Comm. Arb., Award No. 7531 [1994], *at* http://www.cisg.law.pace.edu/cisg/wais/db/cases2/947531i1.html (from the date when buyer communicated the amount of its claim to seller).

90 Eberstein & Bacher, *Annotations*, *supra* note 89. *See also* HERBER & CZERWENKA, *supra* note 88; ULRICH MAGNUS, UN-KAUFRECHT (1995) (separate volume of Staudingers KOMMENTAR ZUM BÜRGERLICHEN GESETZBUCH (13th ed. 1994)); HERBERT BERNSTEIN & JOSEPH LOOKOFSKY, UNDERSTANDING THE CISG IN EUROPE 149 (2d ed. 2003).

not required to satisfy any additional requirements under domestic law (*e.g.*, the issue of a formal prior warning).[91]

As noted in the previous sections, due to irreconcilable differences among the delegations participating in the Vienna Convention with regard to the appropriate method for fixing the interest rate, the drafters left the issue unanswered in the text of Article 78.[92] Notwithstanding the fact that the interest rate method was not

---

91 Tribunale di Padova, *supra* note 3; KG A3 2001 34, *supra* note 84; AG Viechtach 1 C 419/01, *supra* note 89; Tribunal de commerce [District Court] Namur 985/01, 15 Jan. 2002 (Belg.), *at* http://www.cisg.law.pace.edu/cisg/wais/db/cases2/020115b1.html; Rechtbank van Koophandel [District Court] Kortrijk A.R. 04576/00, 4 Apr. 2001 (Belg.), *at* http://www.cisg.law.pace.edu/cisg/wais/db/cases2/010404b1.html; Rechtbank van Koophandel [District Court] Kortrijk A.R. 3669/2000, 3 Oct. 2001 (Belg.), *at* http://www.cisg.law.pace.edu/cisg/wais/db/cases2/011003b1.html; LG Stendal 22 S 234/94, *supra* note 86; Landgericht [LG] [District Court] Flensburg, 2 O 291/98, 24 Mar. 1999 (F.R.G.), *at* http://www.cisg.law.pace.edu/cisg/wais/db/cases2/990324g2.html; Handelsgericht [HG] [Commercial Court], OR.96.0-0013, 26 Sept. 1997 (Switz.), *at* http://www.cisg.law.pace.edu/cisg/wais/db/cases2/970926s1.html; Amtsgericht [AG] [Petty District Court] Nordhorn 3 C 75/94, 14 June 1994 (F.R.G.), *at* http://www.cisg.law.pace.edu/cisg/wais/db/cases2/940614g1.html; Tribunale d'Appello [Appellate Court] 12.95.00300, 12 Feb. 1996 (Switz.), *at* http://www.cisg.law.pace.edu/cisg/wais/db/cases2/960212s1.html; Schiedsgericht der Handelskammer [Arbitral Tribunal] Hamburg, 21 Mar. 1996 (F.R.G.), *at* http://www.cisg.law.pace.edu/cisg/wais/db/cases2/960321g1.html; Tribunal Cantonal [Canton Appellate Court] 01 93 0661, 11 Mar. 1996 (Switz.), *at* http://www.cisg.law.pace.edu/cisg/wais/db/cases2/960311s1.html; Landgericht [LG] [District Court] Aachen 41 O 111/95, 20 July 1995 (F.R.G.), *at* http://www.cisg.law.pace.edu/cisg/wais/cases2/950720g1; M. Marques Roque Joachim v. La Sarl Holding Manin Rivière, Cour d'appel [CA] [Appeal Court] 93/4879, 26 Apr. 1995 (Fr.), *at* http://www.cisg.law.pace.edu/cisg/wais/db/cases2/950426f2.html; Landgericht [LG] [District Court] München 10 HKO 23750/94, 20 Mar. 1995 (F.R.G.), *at* http://cisg.law.pace.edu/cases/950320g1.html; Int'l Comm. of Arb., Award No. 7585 [1992], *at* http://www.cisg.law.pace.edu/cisg/wais/db/cases2/927585i1.html; Amtsgericht [AG] [Petty District Court] Zweibrücken 1 C 216/92, 14 Oct. 1992 (F.R.G.), *at* http://www.cisg.law.pace.edu/cisg/wais/db/cases2/921014g1.html; Pretore [District Court] 15/91, 16 Dec. 1991 (Switz.), *at* http://www.cisg.law.pace.edu/cisg/wais/db/cases2/911216s1.html. *But see*, [Court of Appeal] Turku, (docket number unavailable) 12 Apr. 2002, (Fin.); *at* http://www.cisg.law.pace.edu/cisg/wais/db/cases/020412f5.html Landgericht [LG] [District Court] Zwickau 3 HK O 67/98, 19 Mar. 1999 (F.R.G.), *at* http://www.cisg.law.pace.edu/cisg/wais/db/cases2/990319g1.html; Bulgarska turgosko-promishlena palata [Bulgarian Chamber of Commerce and Industry] 11/1996, 12 Feb. 1998 (Bulg.), *at* http://www.cisg.law.pace.edu/cisg/wais/db/cases2/980212bu.html; Int'l Comm. Arb., Award No. 7331 [1994], *at* http://www.cisg.law.pace.edu/cisg/wais/db/cases2/947331i1.html.

92 *See Plenary Meeting*, *supra* note 73 and accompanying text.

fixed, the delegations wanted to make sure that a general entitlement to interest arises in certain circumstances and that such a right is not subject to any limitations otherwise applicable to claims of damages.[93]

As to the relationship between Article 78 (concerning interest) and Article 74 (concerning damages), there are several cases tackling the matter. It is well-settled that the aggrieved party is entitled, in addition to interest, to damages under Article 74 if it proves them.[94] Such a possibility may be particularly relevant in those situations where the applicable interest rate is lower than the one applied in the country where the creditor may have to borrow money.[95] On the other hand, given that interest under Article 78 should be awarded without furnishing any evidence of actual damages and that the limitations under Article 79 do not apply to interest, a claim under Article 78 may be the fastest and the cheapest way to get the award.

Other relevant topics to be considered include the following:

---

93 *Id.*

94 *See*, *e.g.*, Tribunale di Padova, *supra* note 3; KG A3 2001 34, *supra* note 84; SA AZ I v. Entreprise Em de su In, Cour d'appel, [CA][Appeal Court] Grenoble (docket number unavailable) 28 Nov. 2002 (Fr.), *at* http://www.cisg.law.pace.edu/cisg/wais/db/cases2/021128f2.html; Oberlandesgericht [OLG] [Provincial Court of Appeal] Schleswig 11 U 40/01, 22 Aug. 2002 (F.R.G.), *at* http://www.cisg.law.pace.edu/cisg/wais/db/cases2/020822g2.html; Landgericht [LG] [District Court] Darmstadt 10 O 72/00, 9 May 2000 (F.R.G.), *at* http://www.cisg.law.pace.edu/cisg/wais/db/cases2/000509g1.html; Amtsgericht [AG] [Petty District Court] Duisburg 49 C 502/00, 13 Apr. 2000 (F.R.G.), *at* http://www.cisg.law.pace.edu/cisg/wais/db/cases2/000413g1.html; Landgericht [LG] [District Court] München 12 HKO 4174/99, 6 Apr. 2000 (F.R.G.), *at* http://www.cisg.law.pace.edu/cisg/wais/db/cases2/000406g1.html; LG 2 O 291/98, *supra* note 91; BG 4C.179/1998/odi, *supra* note 88: Handelsgericht [HG] [Commercial Court], 95 0347, 5 Feb. 1997 (Switz.), *at* http://www.cisg.law.pace.edu/cisg/wais/db/cases2/970205s1.html; Pretura di Torino [District Court] (docket number unavailable) 30 Jan. 1997 (Italy), *at* http://www.cisg.law.pace.edu/cisg/wais/db/cases2/970130i3.html; AG 16 C 1056/96, *supra* note 84; Amtsgericht [AG] [Petty District Court] Bottrop 12 C 177/96, 25 June 1996 (F.R.G.), *at* http://www.cisg.law.pace.edu/cisg/wais/db/cases2/960625g2.html; Landgericht [LG] [District Court] Düsseldorf 36 O 178/95, 5 Mar. 1996 (F.R.G.), *at* http://www.cisg.law.pace.edu/cisg/wais/db/cases2/960305g1.html; HG 930476, *supra* note 88; Oberlandesgericht [OLG] [Provincial Court of Appeal] Hamm 11 U 206/93, 8 Feb. 1995 (F.R.G.), *at* http://www.cisg.law.pace.edu/cisg/wais/db/cases2/950208g3.html; Int'l Comm. Arb., Award No. 7197, *supra* note 88.

95 *See*, *e.g.*, KG A3 2001 34, *supra* note 84; OLG 11 U 40/01, *supra* note 94; AG 16 C 1056/96, *supra* note 53; Landgericht [LG] [District Court] Flensburg 4 O 369/99, 19 Jan. 2001 (F.R.G.), *at* http://www.cisg.law.pace.edu/cisg/wais/db/cases2/010119g1.html. Klaus Peter Berger, INTERNATIONAL ECONOMIC ARBITRATION 626 (1993). *See also* UNIDROIT Principles of International Commercial Contracts, Art. 7.4.9.

1. Compound interest

As to the compound interest issue, CISG, Article 78 does not expressly deal with it. Although controversial, compound interest cannot be claimed.[96]

2. The meaning of "sums" under Article 78

As to the meaning of the word 'sums,' interest should accrue with regard to any sum which is due, even if it is not "liquidated" (*i.e.*, made certain).[97]

3. Whether interest can be also awarded on the "other sums"

While there are no issues on the obligation to pay interest on the primary contractual obligation (price), it is not totally clear whether the interest is owed on secondary monetary obligations, such as damages.[98] It has been also suggested that the otherwise applicable law should define the term "sums."[99]

---

96 *See* Eberstein & Bacher, *Annotations*, *supra* note 89, at 599; ENDERLEIN & MASKOW, *supra* note 12, at 315. *But see* JOHN O. HONNOLD, UNIFORM LAW FOR INTERNATIONAL SALES UNDER THE 1980 INTERNATIONAL SALE LAW 469 (3d ed. 1999) [hereinafter HONNOLD]. *See also* Int'l Comm. Arb., Award No. 8908, *supra* note 12; Int'l Comm. Arb., Award No. 8611/HV/JK [1997], *at* http://www.cisg.law.pace.edu/cisg/wais/db/cases2/978611i1.html; *See also* PRINCIPLES OF EUROPEAN CONTRACT LAW, Art. 9:508 [hereinafter PECL]. *But see*, Schiedsgericht der Börse für Landwirtschaftliche Produkte [Arbitral Tribunal], Wien S 2/97, 10 Dec. 1997 (Aus.), *at* http://www.cisg.law.pace.edu/cisg/wais/db/cases2/971210a3.html.

97 *See* Eberstein & Bacher, *Annotations*, *supra* note 84, at 593 (stating "[t]he wording of Article 78 ... hardly provides for such an assumption. Nor are there any substantive grounds discernible for such a restriction on the obligation to pay interest. Interest is therefore payable also in respect of periods during which the claim had arisen, even though the precise amount of the claim had not yet been made certain"). *But see* BARRY NICHOLAS, COMMENTARY ON THE INTERNATIONAL SALES LAW, THE 1980 VIENNA SALES CONVENTION 568, 571 (Massimo C. Bianca & Michael Joachim Bonell eds., 1987); HONNOLD, *supra* note 96, at 468-9.

98 Any "other sum" on which courts awarded payment of interest. *See* Ginza Pte. Ltd. v. Vista Corp. Pty. Ltd., Supreme Court of Western Australia, WASC 11 CIV 1647, 12 May 2000 *at* http://www.cisg.law.pace.edu/cisg/wais/db/cases2/030117a2.html: ("[Buyer] is also entitled to interest on such damages [breach of contract] at the rate of 6 per cent per annum, pursuant to s 32 [section 32] of the *Supreme Court Act 1935* (WA), calculated from 10 Dec. 1997 (when formal demand for damages was made following the third recall of the goods in question)

4. Interest and public policy limitations

Interest should be awarded even though it may be unlawful pursuant to the applicable domestic law.[100] In those countries, if a court deems that the CISG (an international treaty) prevails over domestic rules, lacking any domestic interest provision, the court should determine the applicable rate pursuant to the reasonableness principle, which would lead to the standard interest rate applied in international transactions of that kind.[101] If a court, on the other hand, cannot directly award interest due to validity concerns of domestic law, it may still circumvent such prohibition by awarding interest under a different heading (damages).[102]

---

until judgment"); Helsingin hoviokeus [Helsinki Court of Appeals] S 00/82, 26 Oct. 2000 (Fin.), *at* http://www.cisg.law.pace.edu/cisg/wais/db/cases2/001026f5.html (legal expenses): "[Seller] will be made to pay for [buyer's] legal expenses accrued in the Court of First Instance in the amount of *Fmk* [...]. The sum is subject to interest on arrears as defined in the Finnish Law of Interest starting from one month after the issuance of judgment onwards"); Kantonsgericht Zug [LG II District Court] Zug A3 1997 61, 21 Oct. 1999 (Switz.), *at* http://www.cisg.law.pace.edu/cisg/wais/db/cases2/991021s1.html ("Interest accrues from the due date for claims of damages as well, i.e., from the original date of breach"); Int'l Comm. Arb. Award No. 9187 [1999], *available at* http://cisgw3.law.pace.edu/cases/999187i1.html ("damages interest calculated from the date of occurrence of the damage"); Landgericht, 54 O 644/94, *supra* note 12 ("According to the prevailing opinion, Art. 78 CISG also applies to claims for damages (*cf.* von Caemmerer/Schlechtriem – Eberstein/Bacher, Kommentar zum einheitlichen UN-Kaufrecht, Art. 78, Annotation 15). The claim comes into existence with the occurrence of the loss."). *See also* UNIDROIT Principles of International Commercial Contracts, Art. 7.4.10: "Unless otherwise agreed, interest on damages for non-performance of non-monetary obligations accrues as from the time of non-performance." *But see* PECL, *supra* note 96, art. 9:508.

99 *Id. See also* Nicholas, *supra* note 97.

100 Enderlein & Maskow, *supra* note 12, at 312; Franco Ferrari, *Specific Topics of the CISG in the Light of Judicial and Scholarly Writing* 15 J. L. & Com. 1, 125 (1995) [hereinafter Ferrari, *Specific Topics*]. As to case law, see Internationales Schiedsgericht der Bundeskammer der gewerblichen Wirtschaft, Wien, SCH-4366, 15 June 1994 (Aus.), *at* http://www.cisg.law.pace.edu/cisg/wais/db/cases2/940615a3.html) [hereinafter Int'l Arbitral Tribunal Vienna, SCH-4366]; Internationales Schiedsgericht der Bundeskammer der gewerblichen Wirtschaft, Wien, SCH-4318, 15 June 1994 (Aus.), *at* http://www.cisg.law.pace.edu/cisg/wais/db/cases2/940615a4.html [hereinafter Int'l Arbitral Tribunal Vienna, SCH-4318].

101 Franco Ferrari, Fondamenti Della Vendita Internazionale 132 (1998) [hereinafter Ferrari, Fondamenti].

102 Fatima Akaddaf, *Application of the United Nations Convention on Contracts for the International Sale of Goods (CISG) to Arab Islamic Countries: Is the CISG Compatible with Islamic Law Principles*, 13 Pace Int'l L. Rev. 1, 53 (2001).

The main reasons in support of the approach herein suggested may be summarized as follows: (i) the CISG expressly entitles the creditor to a general right to collect interest; (ii) there is no CISG provision whereby a signing country may make a reservation to Article 78; (iii) the issue of providing a reservation to Article 78 was proposed by some countries but never adopted;[103] (iv) parties to a contract who believe that an interest provision may invalidate a contract or part thereof may partially opt out pursuant to CISG Article 6; and (v) the current trend in Islamic countries with regard to charge of interest seems to suggest that interest may be awarded.[104] It would not be surprising, however, if domestic courts decide not to award interest due to public policy considerations.[105] However, the downside of this approach is that it negates the express mandate of Article 78.[106]

---

103 *See Plenary Meeting*, *supra* note 73 and accompanying text.

104 Akaddaf, *supra* note 102, at 55; T.S. Twibell, *Implementation of the United Nations Convention on Contracts for the International Sale of Goods (CISG) under Shari'a Law: Will Article 78 of the CISG Be Enforced When the Forum Is an Islamic State?* 9 INT'L LEGAL PERSP. 25-92, 75-89 (1997); John Yukio Gotanda, *Awarding Interest in International Arbitration*, 90 AM. J. INT'L L. 40 (1996). In general, see Daniel Klein, *The Islamic and Jewish Laws of Usury: A Bridge to Commercial Growth and Peace in the Middle East*, 23 DENV. J. INT'L L. & POL'Y 535 (1995).

105 *See* PETER SCHLECHTRIEM, UNIFORM SALES LAW – THE UN CONVENTION ON CONTRACTS FOR THE INTERNATIONAL SALE OF GOODS 99-100 (Peter Oralt & Helmut H. Haschek eds., 1986) [hereinafter SCHLECHTRIEM, UNIFORM SALES LAW]. *See also* Joseph M. Lookofsky, *The 1980 United Nations Convention on Contracts for the International Sale of Goods*, *in* INTERNATIONAL ENCYCLOPEDIA OF LAWS 1, 158, n. 3 (H. Herbots & Roger Blanpain eds., 1993 & Supp. 2000) (stating the validity of a contractual claim to interest remains a national concern "[i]n those countries where interest is forbidden, the mere mention of interest in the agreement will render it invalid"); Peter Schlechtriem, *From Hague to Vienna–Progress in Unification of the Law of International Sale Contracts? in* THE TRANSNATIONAL LAW OF INTERNATIONAL COMMERCIAL TRANSACTIONS 132, n. 21 (Horn & Schmittoff eds. 1982) (stating "[I]nsofar as a national law does not allow interest – for religious reasons, for example – [Article 78] has no effect"). *See also* Kantonsgericht [KG] [District Court] Berlin 2 U 7418/92, 24 Jan. 1994 (F.R.G.), *at* http://www.cisg.law.pace.edu/cisg/wais/db/cases2/940124g1.html, (noting that "[t]he interest rate is determined by the national Italian law and its prerequisites").

106 FERRARI, FONDAMENTI, *supra* note 101. It should also be noted that there is no language on the interest issue that recognizes and/or tries to compromise the differences among different legal systems similar to the provisions set forth by CISG Article 28, according to which, where under domestic law in a similar case specific performance would not be granted, a court is allowed not to grant specific performance.

5. Interest pursuant Article 78 and Article 84

It should be noted that interest as described under Article 78 is different from interest under Article 84(1). Interest under Article 84(1) is intended to compensate the creditor (buyer) for the fruits (interest) of not having benefited the money owed by the debtor (seller) due to the avoidance of the contract. In other words, interest under Article 84(1) is based on the principle that money produces fruits, but is owed only when, as a result of the avoidance of the contract, the price must be refunded to the buyer. Moreover, interest under CISG Article 84(1), as opposed to Article 78, must be paid from the date on which the price was paid[107] and there is no reference to any "arrears" requirement.

A. Whether the interest rate and/or its method of calculation is expressly settled in the Convention

As mentioned, Article 78 does not fix any specific interest rate. There is a disagreement with regard to how to determine the appropriate rate of interest under the Convention,[108] which looks unjustified if one reviews the case law on this matter. The overwhelming majority of the courts, as well as some arbital tribunals, determine interest pursuant to the law otherwise applicable to the contract.[109] Although, in the majority of the cases considered for the purpose of this paper, it is

---

[107] *See*, Int'l Comm. Arb., Award No. 6653 [1993], *at* http://www.cisg.law.pace.edu/cisg/wais/db/cases2/936653i1.html.

[108] *See generally* Volker Behr, *The Sales Convention in Europe: From Problems in Drafting to Problems in Practice*, 17 J.L. & Com. 263 (1998). *See also* Christian Thiele, *Interest on Damages and Rate of Interest Under Article 78 of the U.N. Convention on Contracts for the International Sale of Goods*, 2 Vindobona J. Int'l Com. L. & Arb. 3 (1998) *at* http://www.cisg.law.pace.edu/cisg/biblio/thiele.html; Karin Kizery, *Minding the gap: Determining interest rates under the UN Convention for the International Sale of Goods*, 65 U. Chic. L. Rev. 1279 (1998). For a list of the various approaches applied by the courts to determine the rate of interest, *see, e.g.*, Int'l Comm. Arb., Award No. 7585, *supra* note 91.

[109] It is not feasible to mention all cases decided "pursuant to the law otherwise applicable." For the most recent cases adopting such an approach, *see, e.g.*, OLG 11 U 40/01, *supra* note 94; Int'l Comm. Arb., Award No. 9448 [1999], *at* http://www.cisg.law.pace.edu/cisg/wais/db/cases2/999448i1.html; Gerechtshof [Hof] [District Appeal Court] Arnhem 95/570, 15 Apr. 1997 (Neth.), *at* http://www.cisg.law.pace.edu/cisg/wais/db/cases2/970415n1.html; KG Zug A3 1997 61, *supra* note 98; SA AZ I v. Entreprise Em de su In, Cour d'appel, [CA][Appeal Court] Grenoble (docket number unavailable) 28 Nov. 2002 (Fr.), *supra* note 94; Arb. Ct. of the Chamber of Comm. & Indus. of Budapest VB 96074, 10 Dec. 1996 (Hung.), *at* http://www.cisg.law.pace.edu/cisg/wais/db/cases2/961210h1.html; Tribunale di Pavia, *supra* note

not clear where the courts position the interest issue, whether within the CISG or outside the CISG. There are many cases where the law of the creditor's country has been applied without making any reference to rules of private international law.[110]

The law of the debtor's country has also been applied by courts[111] or suggested by commentators.[112] There are also cases in which the law of the country of the legal tender to be used was applied (*lex monetae*),[113] as well as cases in which the law of the country where the price must be paid.[114] Finally, some courts have applied the rate of interest as determined by the UNIDROIT Principles of International Commercial Contracts (Art. 7.4.9)[115] and usage.[116]

12; Trib. Int'l Comm. Arb. at the Russian Fed'n Chamber of Comm. & Industry 196/1997, 22 Oct. 1998, *at* http://www.cisg.law.pace.edu/cisg/wais/db/cases2/981022r1.html.

110 *See, e.g.*, AG, 49 C 502/00, *supra* note 94; Bezirksgericht [BG] [District Court] 341/1994, 9 Dec. 1994 (Switz.), *at* http://www.cisg.law.pace.edu/cisg/wais/db/cases2/941209s1.html; Landgericht [LG] [District Court] Frankfurt 3/11 O 3/91, 16 Sept. 1991 (F.R.G.), *at* http://www.cisg.law.pace.edu/cisg/wais/db/cases2/910916g1.html; Landgericht [LG] [District Court] Stuttgart 3 KfH O 97/89, 31 Aug. 1989 (F.R.G.), *at* http://www.cisg.law.pace.edu/cisg/wais/db/cases2/890831g1.html.

111 *See, e.g.*, AG 49 C 502/00, *supra* note 111; Tribunal Cantonal Vaud, 01 93 1061, *supra* note 89.

112 *See* STOLL, *supra* note 88.

113 *See* Handelsgericht [HG] [Commercial Court] OR.2001.00029, 5 Nov. 2002 (Switz.), *at* http://www.cisg.law.pace.edu/cisg/wais/db/cases2/021105s1.html; OLG, 6 U 126/00, *supra* note 89; Arb. Ct. of the Chamber of Comm. & Indus. of Budapest VB 94131, 5 Dec. 1995 (Hung.), *at* http://www.cisg.law.pace.edu/cisg/wais/db/cases2/951205h1.html; Arb. Ct. of the Chamber of Comm. & Ind. of Budapest VB 94124, 17 Nov. 1995 (Hung.), *at* http://www.cisg.law.pace.edu/cisg/wais/db/cases2/951117h1.html. *See also* Wolfang Grunsky, *Anwendbares Recht und gesetzlicher Zinssatz*, *in* FESTSCHRIFT FÜR FRANZ MERZ 147, 147-157 (Walter Gerhard et al. eds., 1992).

114 *See* HG 95 0347, *supra* note 94; Arrondissementsrechtbank [Rb] [District Court] Almelo 4367, 9 Aug. 1995 (Neth.), *at* http://www.cisg.law.pace.edu/cisg/wais/db/cases2/950809n1.html; Int'l Comm. Arb., Award No. 7331, *supra* note 91; Int'l Comm. Arb., Award No. 5460 [1987], *at* http://www.cisg.law.pace.edu/cisg/wais/db/cases2/875460n1.html.

115 Int'l Comm. Arb., Award No. 9333 [1998], *at* http://www.cisg.law.pace.edu/cisg/wais/db/cases2/989333i1.html; Int'l Comm. Arb., Award No. 8128 [1995] *at* http://www.cisg.law.pace.edu/cisg/wais/db/cases2/958128i1.html; Société Thyssen Stahlunion GmbH v. Maaden General Foreign Trade Organisation for Metal and Building Materials, Cour d'appel [CA] Paris [Appeal Court] (docket number unavailable), 6 Apr. 1995 (Fr.), *at* http://www.cisg.law.pace.edu/cisg/wais/db/cases2/950406f1.html. *See also* Int'l Arbitral Tribunal Vienna SCH-4366, *supra* note 100, Int'l Arbitral Tribunal Vienna SCH-4318, *supra* note 100 expressly mentions the UNIDROIT Principles.

As mentioned, however, the majority of authors and courts have clearly stated that the interest is to be governed by the law of the country as determined by the rules of conflict of laws of the forum state (*lex contractus*).[117] For example, if the contract is between European Community nationals, according to Article 4(2) of the EEC

---

116 *See* Landgericht [LG] [District Court] Saarbrücken 8 O 68/02, 25 Nov. 2002 (F.R.G.), *at* http://www.cisg.law.pace.edu/cisg/wais/db/cases2/021125g1.html (although usage was not actually used to determine the applicable interest); Juzgado Nacional de Primera Instancia en lo Comercial No. 10 [National Commercial Court of First Instance] 56.179, 6 Oct. 1994 (Arg.), *at* http://www.cisg.law.pace.edu/cisg/wais/db/cases2/941006a1.html; Juzgado Nacional de Primera Instancia en lo Comercial No. 10 [National Commercial Court of First Instance], 23 Oct. 1991, *at* http://www.cisg.law.pace.edu/cisg/wais/db/cases2/911023a1.html.

117 *See, e.g.*, Nicholas, *supra* note 97, at 570; SCHLECHTRIEM, UNIFORM SALES LAW, *supra* note 105; LEIF SEVÓN, INTERNATIONAL SALES OF GOODS: DUBROVNIK LECTURES 229 (Petar Šarčević & Paul Volken eds., 1986); ENDERLEIN & MASKOW, *supra* note 12, at 311; HERBER & CZERWENKA, *supra* note 88, at 349; Ulrich Magnus, *Währungsfragen im Einheitlichen Kaufrecht: Zugleich ein Beitrag zu Seiner Lückenfüllung und Auslegung*, *in* 53 RABELS ZEITSCHRIFT FÜR AUSLÄNDISCHES UND INTERNATIONALES PRIVATRECHT 116 (1989); BURGHARD PILTZ, INTERNATIONALES KAUFRECHT 280 (1993); Martin Karollus, *Judicial Interpretation and Application of the CISG in Germany 1988-1994*, CORNELL REV. OF THE CISG 51 (1995); Leif Sevón, *Obligations of the Buyer under the Vienna Convention on the International Sale of Goods*, 126 SUOMALAINEN LAKIMIESTEN YHDISTYS – TIDSKRIFT UTGIVEN AV JURIDISKA FÖRENINGEN I FINLAND [Finnish Law Society] 327, 340 (1990). For case law, *see* LG 5 O 543/88, *supra* note 87; OLG 5 U 261/90, *supra* note 86; Pretore della Giurisdizione di Locarno-Campagna 15/91, *supra* note 91; Fovárosi Biróság [FB] [Metropolitan Court] 12.G.41.471/1991/21, 24 Mar. 1992 (Hung.), *at* http://www.cisg.law.pace.edu/cisg/wais/db/cases2/920324h1.html; Zivilgericht [ZG] [Civil Court] P4 1991/238, 21 Dec. 1992 (Switz.), *at* http://www.cisg.law.pace.edu/cisg/wais/db/cases2/921221s1.html; Int'l Comm. Arb., Award No. 7153 [1992], *at* http://www.cisg.law.pace.edu/cisg/wais/db/cases2/927153i1.html; Handelsgericht [HG] [Commercial Court] HG 930138.U/HG93, 9 Sept. 1993 (Switz.), *at* http://www.cisg.law.pace.edu/cisg/wais/db/cases2/930909s1.html; OLG 2 U 1230/91, *supra* note 12; Arrondissementsrechtbank [District Court] Arnhem 1992/1251, 30 Dec. 1993 (Neth.), *at* http://www.cisg.law.pace.edu/cisg/wais/db/cases2/931230n1.html; Int'l Comm. Arb., Award No. 6653, *supra* note 101; OLG 5 U 15/93, *supra* note 86; Oberlandesgericht [OLG] [Provincial Court of Appeal] Düsseldorf 6 U 152/95, 11 July 1996 (F.R.G.), *at* http://www.cisg.law.pace.edu/cisg/wais/db/cases2/960711g1.html; Oberlandesgericht [OLG] [Provincial Court of Appeal] München 7 U 4419/93, 2 Mar. 1994 (F.R.G.), *at* http://www.cisg.law.pace.edu/cisg/wais/db/cases2/940302g1.html; Oberlandesgericht [OLG] [Provincial Court of Appeal] Hamm 7 U 1720/94, 8 Feb. 1995 (F.R.G.), *at* http://www.cisg.law.pace.edu/cisg/wais/db/cases2/950208g1.html; Tribunal Cantonal [Canton Appellate Court] Valais C1 97 167, 28 Oct. 1997 (Switz.), *at* http://www.cisg.law.pace.edu/cisg/wais/db/cases2/971028s1.html; Oberlandesgericht [OLG][Pro-

Convention on Law Applicable to Contractual Obligations, the law of the country in which the seller has his principal place of business will be applied, absent a choice of law.[118]

B. Whether the interest rate and/or its method of calculation is within the Convention[119]

The question of the interest rate calculation raises several other issues. As noted, the interest rate issue is not expressly settled in the Convention. Is it, however, governed by the CISG although not expressly settled (*lacuna praeter legem*)?[120] Or, is this a matter excluded from the sphere of CISG application(*lacuna intra legem*)?[121] If it is a matter that must be solved according to the principles of the Convention,

---

vincial Court of Appeal] Koblenz 2 U 31/96, 31 Jan. 1997 (F.R.G.), *at* http://www.cisg.law.pace.edu/cisg/wais/db/cases2/970131g1.html; BG, 4C.179/1998/odi, *supra* note 88; LG 2 O 291/98, *supra* note 91; Oberlandesgericht [OLG] [Provincial Court of Appeal] Stuttgart 5 U 118/99, 28 Feb. 2000 (F.R.G.), *at* http://www.cisg.law.pace.edu/cisg/wais/db/cases2/000228g1.html; LG 22 S 234/94, *supra* note 86.

118 *See* EEC Convention on the Law Applicable to Contractual Obligations of June 19, 1980, 1980 O.J. (L 266), a treaty which may be converted into a EU Community instrument: *See* COM/2002/0654 final. *See* SCHLECHTRIEM, *Uniform Sales Law, supra* note 105, at 100; Behr, *supra* note 108, at 288; KG, A3 1997 61, *supra* note 98. Note, however, that the Hague Convention of June 15, 1955 on the law applicable to international sales of goods may come into play when the forum is located within a contracting state of the Hague Convention. *See* Corte di Cassazione [Supreme Court], Sezioni Unite, 448, 10 Mar. 2000 (Italy), *at* http://www.cisg.law.pace.edu/cisg/wais/db/cases2/000310i3.html; Tribunal Cantonal Valais, [Canton Appellate Court] C 323/94, 20 Dec. 1994 (Italy), *at* http://www.cisg.law.pace.edu/cisg/wais/edu/cases2/941220s1.html. However, recourse to the Hague Convention may not be the correct approach, as underlined, among other courts, by Tribunale di Padova, *supra* note 3.

119 Some cases whereby the issue of whether or not the interest rate is within the Convention is clearly posed. *See, e.g.*, Tribunale di Padova, *supra* note 3; HG OR.2001.00029, *supra* note 113; Tribunale di Pavia, *supra* note 12; Amtsgericht [AG] [Petty District Court] Alsfeld 31 C 534/94, 12 May 1995 (F.R.G.), *at* http://www.cisg.law.pace.edu/cisg/wais/db/cases2/950512g1.html; LG 41 O 111/95, *supra* note 91; Int'l Comm. Arb., Award No. 7565 [1994], *at* http://www.cisg.law.pace.edu/cisg/wais/db/cases2/947565i1.html.

120 *Id. See also* Franco Ferrari, *Uniform Application and Interest Rates Under the 1980 Vienna Sales Convention*, 24 GA. J. INT'L & COMP. L. 467, 477 (1995) [hereinafter Ferrari, *Uniform Application*]; Ferrari, *Specific Topics*, *supra* note 100, at 120; Behr, *supra* note 108, at 295.

121 *Id. See also* Ferrari, *Uniform Application*, *supra* note 120.

what are the principles on this issue?[122] On the other hand, if the issue is not within the CISG, how should a court determine the proper interest rate?

The current application of Article 78, as well as the way it is construed by commentators, suggests that there are two broad ways of understanding Article 78. The majority of the commentators believe that the interest rate issue is not governed by the Convention, and therefore they suggest that domestic rules of private international law should fix the proper interest rate. Similarly, some courts clearly state the issue is not within the CISG,[123] even though the majority of the courts resort to its own domestic law regarding private international law without even saying whether the gap is *praeter* or *intra legem*. The minority, on the other hand, believes the interest rate issue is within the scope of the Convention and struggles to find a general principle able to discipline the issue. At the very same time, they are attempting to avoid any deference to domestic rules. These authors suggest that although the mechanism for determining the rate of interest is not

---

122 *See* HONNOLD, *supra* note 96, stating that the issue is within the CISG because "[t]he mandate of Article 7(1) to construe the Convention to promote 'uniformity in its application' requires us to seek a principle governing the scope of Article 78 that can be considered as a basis for uniform application of the Convention"; *see also* Koneru, *supra* note 10; Joanne M. Darkey, *A U.S. Court's Interpretation of Damage Provisions Under the U.N. Convention On Contracts for the International Sale of Goods: A Preliminary Step toward an International Jurisprudence of CISG or a Missed Opportunity?*, 15 J.L. & COM. 139, 149 (1995); Dominique Hascher, *Commentary on Journal of Law and Commerce Case III: International Court of Arbitration, Matter No. 7153 in 1992*, 14 J.L. & COM. 220, 224 (1995); James J. Callagan, *U.N. Convention On Contracts for the International Sale of Goods: Examining the Gap-Filling Role of CISG in Two French Decisions*, 14 J. L. & COM. 183, 200 (1995); Alan Zoccolillo, *Determination of the Interest Rate Under the 1980 United Nations Convention on Contracts for the International Sale of Goods: General Principles vs. National Law*, 1 VINDOBONA J. INT'L COM. L. & ARB. 30 (1997); John Felemegas, *The Award of Counsel's Fees Under Article 74 CISG, in Zapata Hermanos Sucesores v. Hearthside Baking Co.*, 6 VINDOBONA J. INT'L COM. L. & ARB. 40 (2002); Arthur B. Colligan Jr., *Applying the General Principles of the United Nations Convention on Contracts for the International Sale of Goods to fill the Article 78 interest rate gap in Zapata Hermanos Sucesores v. Hearthside Baking Co.*, 6 VINDOBONA J. INT'L COM. L. & ARB. 40 (2002). As to case law, *see* Zapata Hermanos Sucesores v. Hearthside Baking Co., 155 F. Supp. 2d 969 (N.D. Ill. 2001), *at* http://www.cisg.law.pace.edu/cisg/wais/db/cases2/010822u1.html; Juzgado Nacional de Primera Instancia en lo Comercial n. 10, 56.179, *supra* note 116; Juzgado Nacional de Primera Instancia en lo Comercial n. 10, Argentina, 23 Oct. 1991, *supra* note 116; Internationales Schiedsgericht der Bundeskammmer der gewerblichen Wirtschaft – Wien; SCH-4366, *supra* note 100; Internationales Schiedsgericht der Bundeskammmer der gewerblichen Wirtschaft – Wien; SCH-4318, *supra* note 100.

123 *See* Tribunale di Pavia, *supra* note 12.

expressly settled by the Convention, the general principles of the Convention resolve the matter. However, it must be said, however, that even within this view it is not clear which general principle best fits the problem.[124]

I believe, for the reasons stated below, that the interest issue is within the sphere of CISG application (as the CISG does establish a general entitlement to interest[125]). However, the actual figure would not be determined through the Convention or its general principles, but by resorting to the domestic law that otherwise applies to the contract.[126]

It is not disputed that when a matter is not directly solved by the Convention, its general principles be the first guide. However, the Convention also expressly states that when its general principles do not give any help, the domestic law should be applied. Determining the actual interest rate is one of those cases where the general principles of the Convention (if there are any in the matter of interest) cannot be applied. Besides, even if there are general principles that may give some guidance on this matter, as abundantly shown by those cases where they were actually applied, they are not helpful in terms of assuring either certainty or uniformity. As further evidence of the uncertainty governing the matter, one should consider that commentators cannot even agree on which, if any, general principle should govern the matter. Given that, how can it be expected that a domestic court, overwhelmed by thousands of cases, would be willing to figure out the meaning of Article 78 in

---

124 Int'l Comm. Arb., Award No. 7565, *supra* note 119. *See also* André Corterier, *A New Approach to Solving the Problem of the Interest Rate Under Article 78 CISG*, 5 INT'L TRADE & BUS. L. ANN. 33, 39 (2000).

125 *See supra* note 81.

126 *See* Richteramt [RA] [District Court] Laufen des Kantons Berne, 7 May 1993 (Switz.), *at* http://www.cisg.law.pace.edu/cisg/wais/db/cases2/930507s1.html: "Only in regard to the determination of the interest in arrears does the national law gain significance, since Art. 78 CISG only constitutes the obligation to pay interest, however, without determining the rate of interest … Nevertheless, it is all in all clear that the present case, regarding the matters disputed, is solely governed by the scope of application of the CISG; in other words, on the merits of the case, the CISG is relevant and has to be referred to for the solution of the matter of dispute, and not any pure national Finnish law. Finnish law is presently significant only for the determination of the rate of interest." *See also* Franco Ferrari, *Tasso degli interessi ed applicazione uniforme della Convenzione di Vienna sui contratti di vendita internazionale* (hereinafter *Tasso degli interessi*), RIVISTA DI DIRITTO CIVILE II 277 (1995); ULRICH MAGNUS, *Stand und Entwicklungen des UN-Kaufrechts*, ZEITSCHRIFT FÜR EUROPÄISCHES PRIVATRECHT 202 (1995). *See also* AG 31 C 534/94, *supra* note 119; Int'l Comm. Arb., Award No. 7660 [1994], *at* http://www.cisg.law.pace.edu/cisg/wais/db/cases2/947660i1.html; Bezirksgericht der Saane (Zivilgericht) [District Court] T 171/95, 20 Feb. 1997 (Switz.), *at* http://www.cisg.law.pace.edu/cisg/wais/db/cases2/970220s1.html.

light of the general principles of the CISG, particularly since its inception more than 20 years ago, no solution (even on the general principles) has been agreed upon? Regardless of some confusion among the commentators, the vast majority of courts and arbitral tribunals have spoken. The rate of interest must be determined according to the law that would otherwise govern the contract.[127]

C. Uncertainty deriving from solutions based on the general principles of the Convention

Although, solutions calling for the application of the general principles deserve some credit, they both defy the express text of the Convention and have failed to produce either uniformity or certainty. Indeed, in those very limited instances where the courts resorted to the general principles of the Convention, two arbitral awards ended up applying the interest rate commonly practiced in the creditor's country with respect to the currency of payment (based on full compensation),[128] while other courts applied LIBOR rates.[129] In a very recent case tried in the U.S., the actual interest rate was to be determined by the jury based on reasonableness.[130]

Full compensation and reasonableness principles may not be used mainly because: (i) they fail to consider the core function of interest as defined by Article 78, (ii) reliance on them has been clearly excluded in the final written text of the

---

127 Out of 220 cases reviewed (only those for which an English translation/abstract was available), at least 94 *clearly* made reference to this approach. I believe, however, that the actual number of cases relying on it is much higher (emphasis added).

128 *See* Int'l Arbitral Tribunal Vienna SCH-4366, *supra* note 100; Int'l Arbitral Tribunal Vienna SCH-4318, *supra* note 100.

129 Int'l Comm. Arb., Award No. 8128, *supra* note 115; Int'l Comm. Arb., Award No. 8769 [1996], *at* http://www.cisg.law.pace.edu/cisg/wais/db/cases2/968769i1.html. With regard to issues arising from using LIBOR, *see infra* comments on UNIDROIT and PECL. *See also* Franco Ferrari, *Interpretation of the Convention and Gap-filling: Article 7*, *in* THE DRAFT UNCITRAL DIGEST AND BEYOND: CASES, ANALYSIS AND UNRESOLVED ISSUES IN THE U.N. SALES CONVENTION, 138, 170 (Franco Ferrari et al. eds., 2004) [hereinafter Ferrari, *Interpretation*], who sustains that "Article 7(2) CISG clearly refers to 'the general principles on *which it* [the CISG] *is based*.' Thus, recourse to external principles, such as the UNIDROIT Principles and the Principles of European Contract Law, appears to be excluded [footnote omitted]. This does not mean, however, that the UNIDROIT Principles and the Principles of European Contract Law are meaningless with respect to a contract governed by the CISG. These principles can be useful, for instance, to corroborate a solution reached through the application of the CISG's rules, as evidenced not only by several arbitral awards [footnote omitted], but also by one state court decision."

130 *See* Zapata Hermanos Sucesores, 115 F. Supp. 2d 969, *supra* note 116.

provision, and (iii) the legislative history of Article 78. In particular, pursuant to the full compensation approach, the obligation of paying interest on the sums due is aimed at fully compensating the aggrieved party for the benefit of the bargain. Accordingly, this view applies Article 74 of the Convention in determining the interest rate. This view, however, results from a misunderstanding of the nature of the interest as defined by Article 78, the express wording of Article 78 and its legislative history.

Article 78 draws a clear, distinct line between damages and interest, as defined under Article 74 and Article 78 respectively.[131] Under Article 78, interest is not meant to fully compensate the creditor for the benefit of the bargain. A party is generally entitled to interest, but it may not be entitled to damages. Article 78 expressly excludes interest linked to damages, since interest is due even when damages are excluded under Article 79 (a party is entitled to interest "without prejudice to any claim for damages recoverable under article 74").[132] Interest under Article 78 is based on the general principle that the party who benefited from property belonging to another must remunerate the latter. This remuneration is based on the assumption that money automatically produces interest. Interest is due as a result of failure to pay according to the terms of the contract or the applicable default rules. It is not a kind of damage, as it is not measured by damages that may have actually occurred, but pursuant to pre-existing fixed rules. As interest is not intended to cover damages, the aggrieved party may be entitled to both damages and interest.

It should also be considered that the interest rate provision belongs to Section III (Interest), which is completely separate from the section dealing with damages (Section II. Damages).[133] The legislative history of Article 78 tells us that the

---

131 *See* Behr, *supra* note 108, at 286.

132 *Id.*

133 *See* Nicholas, *supra* note 97, at 570; SCHLECHTRIEM, UNIFORM SALES LAW, *supra* note 105; Behr, *supra* note 108, at 286; Dionysios P. Flambouras, *The Doctrines of Impossibility of Performance and clausula rebus sic stantibus in the 1980 Vienna Convention on Contracts for the International Sale of Goods and the Principles of European Contract Law: A Comparative Analysis*, 13 PACE INT'L L. REV. 261, 281 (2001). *See also* UNIDROIT Principles of International Commercial Contracts, Art. 7.4.9; Official Comment of Art. 9:508 of PECL: "*Interest is not a species of ordinary damages. Therefore the general rules on damages do not apply* (emphasis added). Interest is owed whether or not non-payment is excused under Article 8:108. Also, the aggrieved party is entitled to it without regard to any question whether it has taken reasonable steps to mitigate its loss." (emphasis added). Consider also that ULIS, Art. 83, which provides for interest under the damages provisions, was clearly rejected by the drafters of the CISG. For case law, *ex plurimis*, Int'l Comm. Arb., Award No. 7585, *supra* note 91; Tribunale di Pavia, *supra* note 12.

choice of keeping the two concepts distinct and separate was an informed decision.[134] Thus, those provisions normally used to calculate damages (Article 74) cannot be used to calculate the interest rate under Article 78.

With the exceptions referred to below, resorting to reasonableness principles for purposes of determining the appropriate interest rate raises even more concerns. Lacking any guidance from the Convention, and lacking any international common understanding of what might be the reasonable interest that is applicable to a certain transaction, uncertainty and unpredictability reign. Furthermore, international businesses should not need to take chances on these legal aspects of a transaction.[135]

I am not implying that reasonableness is not to be used at all. I am only saying that reasonableness should not be used as the only guiding principle in order to determine the proper interest rate. In fact, while the reasonableness principle may not be used to accomplish those tasks mentioned in Article 7(2), it may still play a role pursuant to the requirements set forth by Article 7(1), which provides for courts to promote, *inter alia*, good faith and the international character of the Convention. While courts may not seek uniformity in this matter (as noted, there is no uniformity requirement in this context), good faith and international character requirements prevent a party from deliberately delaying payment to take advantage of more favorable interest rates or to take advantage of unforeseeable (and excessive) fluctuations of the applicable interest rate resulting in an unjustified impoverishment of one party over the other.

Seller and buyer know that interest is going to be charged in certain circumstances.

---

134 *See* Summary Records of the Plenary Meetings, 11th Plenary Meeting, Apr. 10, 1980, *at* http://www.cisg.law.pace.edu/cisg/plenarycommittee/summary11.html, and compare to the amendment proposed by Denmark, Finland, Greece, Sweden (U.N. Doc. No. A/CONF.97/C.1/L.216) (seeking to have an interest and damages under the same section), which was later withdrawn. *See also* SCHLECHTRIEM, UNIFORM SALES LAW, *supra* note 105, at 99-100, where he states: "The goal of the delegations that believed that a special interest provision was necessary was precisely to prevent interest from being considered as damages and thereby to maintain the obligation to pay interest in case of exemptions under Article 79."

135 Reasonableness, although one of the most important principles sustaining the Convention, is not capable of setting a method of calculating interest which complies with the express wording of Article 78 and its legislative history. Moreover, it is not capable to warrant uniformity. Reasonableness must be determined on a case-by-case basis, which, by its terms, contradicts the concept of uniformity. As to the meaning of the concept of reasonableness, *see* Professor Albert H. Kritzer's Commentary *at* http://www.cisg.law.pace.edu/cisg/text/reason.html.

Business people, even when they have not specifically considered choice of law, forum and rules of private international law, can easily foresee that the interest rate is going to be something close to the current or foreseeable applicable rates in one of the countries involved in the transaction. However, if due to unforeseeable conditions, that rate has gone beyond any foreseeable expectation, good faith in the contract relationship should prevent any unreasonable enrichment. So, while interest must be paid, excessive interest (windfall) must not. Moreover, while domestic sellers and buyers may have a better knowledge of major domestic political and economic events, such knowledge may be lacking in an international context. Even though contracting with a foreign party may be more risky, a party to a contract may not be charged with the results of unforeseeable political and economic changes. Parties to a contract, however, are well aware that some interest will be charged as a result of delays. Similarly, when the debtor deliberately delays payment with the intent of taking advantage of the more favorable rates of the applicable interest, a court should prevent such party from harming the other party. It is, of course, very difficult to show that a party purposefully delayed payment.

Therefore, although reasonableness is not a general principle directly applicable pursuant to Article 7(2) (in other words, although it may not prevent recourse to the rules of private international law rules for the purposes of determining the proper rate), it may play a role in the context of excessive unforeseeable interest rate, which unreasonably impoverishes one party over the other, and in the context of lack of good faith by the debtor. In such circumstances, interest is to be limited to what is reasonable in the context of the transaction. Any other additional claim in connection with interest actually paid should be allowed only to the extent that the requirements of CISG, Article 74 are met.

As mentioned earlier, a court should also resort to general principles of reasonableness when dealing with domestic laws that do no not provide for interest at all. In those circumstances, given that the CISG does entitle the creditor to interest, the proper rate should be what is reasonable in international transactions of that kind.[136]

D. Other general principles: UNIDROIT and Principles of European Contract Law[137]

As mentioned, interest under Article 78 is based on the general principle that the party who unreasonably benefited of property belonging to another must remunerate

---

[136] *See supra* note 100 and accompanying text.

[137] Int'l Comm. Arb., Award No. 8128, *supra* note 84, noting that UNIDROIT and PECL principles must be considered general principles on which CISG is based Art. 7(2) CISG. *But see* Ferrari, *Interpretation*, *supra* note 129.

the latter including the payment of interest. These concepts are embodied in the texts of the UNIDROIT Principles of International Commercial Law and Principles of European Contract Law (hereinafter PECL). However, we must be careful in referring to the rules and principles set forth by them. While we may take into consideration the UNIDROIT Principles and PECL in order to better understand the nature of interest and its relationship to damages, we may not, in the context of a CISG dispute, rely on their methods for determining the proper interest rate.[138]

UNIDROIT

Article 7.4.9[139] reads:

(1) If a party does not pay a sum of money when it falls due the aggrieved party is entitled to interest upon that sum from the time when payment is due to the time of payment whether or not the non-payment is excused.

(2) The rate of interest shall be the average bank short-term lending rate to prime borrowers prevailing for the currency of payment at the place for payment, or where no such rate exists at that place, then the same rate in the State of the currency of payment. In the absence of such a rate at either place the rate of interest shall be the appropriate rate fixed by the law of the State of the currency of payment.

(3) The aggrieved party is entitled to additional damages if the non-payment caused it a greater harm."[140]

UNIDROIT reaffirms the rule requiring the non-performing party to pay interest on an unpaid sum, which also includes damages.[141] Interest accrues from the time when payment of the money was due to the time of actual payment. Interest is payable simply as a result of the delay in payment, without any need for the aggrieved party to give formal notice of the default. If the delay in the payment is due to *force majeure*, "interest will still be due not as damages but as compensation for the enrichment of the debtor as a result of the non-payment as the debtor continues to receive interest on the sum which it is prevented from paying."[142] UNIDROIT fixes

---

138 Ferrari, *Interpretation*, *supra* note 129.

139 For a match-up of CISG Article 78 with counterpart provisions of UNIDROIT Principles visit http://www.cisg.law.pace.edu/cisg/principles/uni78.html.

140 *See* UNIDROIT art. 7.4.9.

141 UNIDROIT art. 7.4.10.

142 *See* Official Comments on Art. 7.4.9 of the UNIDROIT Principles *at* http://cisgw3.law.pace.edu/cisg/principles/uni78.html.

the rate of interest at the average bank short-term lending rate to prime borrowers.[143] The rate in question is the rate at which the aggrieved party will normally borrow at the place of payment for the currency of payment.[144] If no such rate exists, reference is made in the first instance to the average prime rate in the State of the currency of payment.[145] In the absence of such a rate at either place, the rate of interest will be the "appropriate" rate fixed by the law of the State of the currency of payment.[146] In most cases this will be the legal rate of interest and, as there may be more than one, the most appropriate for international transactions should be applied.[147] If there is no legal rate of interest, the rate will be the most appropriate bank rate.[148]

Although it may not seem clear from reading the comment to Article 7.4.9,[149] one may argue that interest is not a kind of damage, even under UNIDROIT. In fact, the comment to the Article states that, "the aggrieved party may not prove that it could have invested the sum due at a higher rate of interest or the non-performing party that the aggrieved party would have obtained interest at a rate lower than the average lending rate referred to in paragraph 2."[150] Interest, therefore, is to be determined solely pursuant to paragraph 2 of Article 7.4.9. Thus, interest is a lump sum due to the aggrieved party as a result of a delay in the payment. Such lump sum must be determined not in consideration of the damage actually suffered (the full compensation principle does not apply for the determination of the interest rate), but by resorting to preexisting parameters, as set forth by the applicable law. Similar to Article 78, should the delay in the payment cause additional harm, UNIDROIT provides that the aggrieved party, if it can prove the existence and the foreseeability of such harm, can also seek damages.[151]

UNIDROIT, therefore, similar to the CISG, reaffirms the existence of a right to interest on unpaid sums, even in case of *force majeure*. However, under UNIDROIT, interest is a kind of damage, and both actual damages and interest are meant to fully compensate the aggrieved party the benefit of the agreement. On the other hand, under the CISG the two concepts are kept clearly separate. Due to substantial and conceptual differences, therefore UNDROIT principles may not be taken into consideration in construing CISG, Article 78.

---

143 *See* UNIDROIT art. 7.4.9(1).

144 *See* UNIDROIT art. 7.4.9(2).

145 *Id.*

146 *Id.*

147 Official Comments on Art. 7.4.9 of the UNIDROIT Principles, *supra* note 142.

148 Official Comments on Art. 7.4.9 of the UNIDROIT Principles, *supra* note 142.

149 Also consider that UNIDROIT art. 7.4.9 falls within sec. 4 "Damages."

150 Official Comments on Art. 7.4.9 of the UNIDROIT Principles, *supra* note 142.

151 Official Comments on Art. 7.4.9 of the UNIDROIT Principles, *supra* note 111.

PECL

Article 9:508(1) of PECL simply states that "[i]f a payment of a sum is delayed, the aggrieved party is entitled to interest on that sum."[152] Interest is owed from the date payment is due.[153] Moreover, interest is owed regardless of whether or not payment may be excused under Article 8:108.[154] The aggrieved party is entitled to it regardless of whether it has taken reasonable steps to mitigate its loss. The rate of interest is fixed by reference to the average commercial bank short-term lending rate applicable to prime borrowers prevailing for the contractual currency of payment[155] at the place of payment.[156] It should be noted that a right to interest arises only on primary contractual obligations to pay; the provision does not cover interest on secondary monetary obligations, such as damages or interest. Finally, interest is *not* a species of ordinary damages. Thus, the general rules on damages *do not* apply.

PECL gives a definition of the nature of interest similar to the definition herein contended.[157] Indeed, the commentary to PECL, Article 9:508 clearly states that interest is not a damage and that it cannot be determined by resorting to the rules for calculating damages.[158] Clearly, under PECL, interest is meant to remunerate one party for having conferred a benefit on another; it does not have a compensatory goal (in other words, it is not a species of ordinary damages), and, therefore, general rules on damages do not apply. In fact, the aggrieved party is entitled to it regardless of whether it has taken reasonable steps to mitigate its loss.

Similar to Article 78, PECL, Article 9:508 (2) provides that, "[t]he aggrieved party may in addition recover damages for any further loss so far as these are recoverable under this Section."[159] Therefore, both CISG, Article 78 and PECL, Article 9:508

---

152 *See* PECL, *supra* note 96 Art. 9:508 *at* http://www.cisg.law.pace.edu/cisg/text/textef.html#a 9508.

153 PECL, *supra* note 96 Art 9:508 *at* http://www.cisg.law.pace.edu/cisg/text/textef.html#a7102.

154 PECL, *supra* note 96 Art. 8:108 *at* http://www.cisg.law.pace.edu/cisg/text/textef.html#a 8108.

155 PECL, *supra* note 96 Art. 7:108 *at* http://www.cisg.law.pace.edu/cisg/text/textef.html#a 7108 for the definition of "Currency of Payment" under the PECL.

156 PECL, *supra* note 96, Art. 7:101 *at* http://www.cisg.law.pace.edu/cisg/text/textef.html#a 7101 for the definition of "Place of Performance" under the PECL.

157 *See* PECL, *supra* note 96, Art. 9:508 *at* http://www.cisg.law.pace.edu/cisg/text/textef.html#a 9508.

158 Guide to CISG Article 78 & 84(1), Comment and Notes on PECL 9:508 *at* http://cisgw3.law.pace.edu/cisg/text/peclcomp78.html.

159 *See* PECL, *supra* note 96, Art. 9:508 *at* http://www.cisg.law.pace.edu/cisg/text/textef.html#a 9508.

allow the damaged party to recover additional damages as long as the requirements for recovery of damages (CISG, Article 74) are met. PECL, Article 9:508 is very useful to understand the nature of the interest and its relationship to damage provisions. It has, however, limited relevance as a tool for construing the meaning of CISG, Article 78 with regard to the method of calculating the interest rate.

E. Resorting to the domestic rules of private international law

The main difference between the UNIDROIT Principles and PECL, on the one hand, and CISG, on the other, relates to the method of computing interest. While CISG, Article 78 expressly leaves the issue out of the Convention, UNIDROIT and PECL set a precise method for computing interest. Methods like those set by UNIDROIT and PECL may be useful and may encourage uniformity, however, they cannot be used under the CISG.[160] The CISG does not set a method because states' delegations could not reach any agreement on the issue.[161] This means that there was not a uniform and commonly accepted rate of interest that could be applied in all transactions falling within the scope of the Convention. This is still true today. The majority of courts clearly prefer the domestic law solution.[162] Allowing courts to use the UNIDROIT, PECL, or any other single method,[163] would go against the spirit of the Convention and the will of the majority of member States.[164]

It must be acknowledged that the proposal to include express reference to the domestic rules of conflicts (within Article 78) was not accepted either. Some commentators have drawn the conclusion that the "drafters saw the question at issue not outside the scope of the Convention but rather wanted it to be governed by Article 7(2)."[165] I believe that had the drafters wanted to have the interest rate issue

---

[160] *Id.* Kritzer, *supra* note 135, noting "[T]he weight of all current judicial authority is to the effect that it is inappropriate to use the UNIDROIT Principles as an aid to the interpretation of CISG Article 78." *See also* Ferrari, *Interpretation*, *supra* note 129.

[161] *See infra* note 165

[162] *See supra* note 78

[163] Int'l Comm. Arb., Award No. 6653, *supra* note 101.

[164] *See* UNITED NATIONS CONFERENCE ON CONTRACTS FOR THE INTERNATIONAL SALE OF GOODS, 137-8, U.N. Doc. A/CONF.97/19, U.N. Sales No. E.81.IV.3 (1980). *See* Eberstein & Bacher, *Annotations*, *supra* note 89, at 596, stating "[i]f the Conference was unable to solve that task [determining an uniform interest rate], *any solutions proposed by legal writers and courts will need to be treated with particular caution.*" (emphasis added). *See* Behr, *supra* note 108, at 290.

[165] *See* Thiele, *supra* note 108. The English delegation sought to introduce a provision such that the Convention would not be "concerned with the payment of interest." However, it was later withdrawn due to lack of support. The delegations, although unable to reach any

dealt with by the Convention, there would have been no better place to do it (*Ubi lex voluit. Dixit. Ubi noluit. Tacuit.*). Although resorting to domestic rules of private international law is not, of course, the best solution, it is, however, the only possible correct way to apply Article 78. Rules of private international law, although not expressly indicated as the applicable method under Article 78, nonetheless should be applied *ex* Article 7(2).[166] Thus, absent any general CISG principle for the determination of the appropriate interest, solving the issue according to the applicable domestic law is expressly provided for by the Convention as a default rule, while resorting to any other method is expressly outside the scheme of the Convention. As mentioned earlier, however, recourse to the domestic rules of private international law should be subject to the good faith and international character requirements set forth by Article 7(1) of the Convention.[167]

V. Conclusion

Once we acknowledge that the interest rate is not expressly settled in the Convention, that the general principles of the CISG do not answer the issue either, and that the CISG requires resorting to the domestic rules of private international law, it is clear that any other method cannot be of any help. By allowing courts to apply any *ad hoc* and *ex post* method is a clear violation of the Convention. Thus, UNIDROIT, PECL as well as any other formula, although they state a clear method for calculating the interest rate in a way that may be acceptable in many countries, is not of any help in the construction of the current text of Article 78 of the CISG. However, when a new Article 78 is drafted, and if an interest rate method is ever to

agreement on the method of calculating interest, nonetheless, wanted to make clear that the aggrieved party does have a right to interest, which is owed regardless of any damage claim. By no means, however, should one also draw the further conclusion that the drafters wanted to have the Convention also governing the method of calculating the interest rate. *See* Summary Records of the Plenary Meetings, 11th Plenary Meeting, Apr. 10, 1980, *at* http://www.cisg.law.pace.edu/cisg/firstcommittee/Meeting37.html. *See also* SCHLECHTRIEM, UNIFORM SALES LAW, *supra* note 105, at 99, where he states: "The goal of the delegations that believed that a special interest provision was necessary was precisely to prevent interest from being considered as damages and thereby to maintain the obligation to pay interest in case of exemptions under Article 79."

166 Ferrari, *supra* note 94. *See also* AG, 31 C 534/94, *supra* note 119. Therefore, it seems very difficult to see how "by applying national law to fill the interest rate gap, national courts and arbitral tribunals may contravene the intent of the Convention and further promote discontinuity." *See* Zoccolillo, *supra* note 122.

167 *See supra* note 104 and accompanying text.

be embodied in the text of an international agreement, those methods may be a very good starting point in a *de jure condendum* analysis.

In order to avoid arbitrary results,[168] taking into consideration the transaction between the parties (the contract), and without aiming at any uniformity in calculating the rate which is neither sought nor required by Article 78 of the Convention,[169] the interest rate must be determined according to the law otherwise applicable as result of the application of the rules of the private international law rules of the forum state (as required by CISG Article 7(2)). Notwithstanding any contrary domestic provision proscribing payment of interest, the express text of the CISG requires award of it.[170] In light of the good faith and international character requirements, excessive unforeseeable interest resulting in an unreasonable enrichment of one party over the others may not be awarded. In these cases, the applicable interest rate should be determined pursuant to reasonableness principles.

The view based on the rules of private international law rules accomplishes much more certainty than any other approach. Certainty in the case of Article 78 is given by the fact that the vast majority of the courts clearly prefer such approach,[171] although,

> [t]his result in different outcomes based on different regulations in non-unified private international law [footnote omitted]. While this might be considered deplorable, in no respect are these differences a violation of the principle of uniformity in application of the Convention. The lack of uniformity actually conforms to the standards of the Convention. Uniformity in the outcome of the case would be obviously be preferable. This deficiency in the Convention must be accepted.[172]

---

168 Tribunale di Padova, *supra* note 3.

169 Int'l Comm. Arb., Award No. 7331, *supra* note 91: "Regarding the precise rate of interest to be applied, there is no single internationally accepted rate of interest. This is reflected in the Vienna Convention, which only generally provides that parties are entitled to interest without specifying any particular rate of interest." *See also* Behr, *supra* note 108, at 296.

170 *But see*, *supra* note 108 and accompanying text.

171 *See* Tribunale di Padova, *supra* note 3, (recent example considered in drafting this article).

172 Behr, *supra* note 77, at 296-97. As Professor Flechtner made clear: "The uniformity principle is only of several interpretative principles that co-exist in Article 7(1) ... [T]he uniformity principle of Article 7(1), while fundamental to the purposes of the Convention, is neither a rigid nor a simple mandate ... [A]ttempts to apply the uniformity principle in a rigid or absolutist fashion not only are unjustified by the Convention, but also could undermine the substantive purposes and the political underpinnings of the CISG." *See* Harry M. Flechtner, *The Several Texts of the CISG in a Decentralized System: Observations on Translations, Reservations and other Challenges to the Uniformity Principle in Article 7(1)*, 17 J.L. & Com. 187, 188 (1998).

Appendix I
Argentina, Australia, Bulgaria and Canada

ARGENTINA

Courts

Juzgado Nacional de Primera Instancia en lo Comercial	National Commercial Court of First Instance

1. Juzgado Nacional de Primera Instancia en lo Comercial No. 7 [National Commercial Court of First Instance] n. 50.272, 20 May 1991 (Arg.), *at* http://cisgw3.law.pace.edu/cases/910520a1.html.

   Original language: Spanish
   Translation: Available

   Court (translation):
   "However, there is no express norm of the Convention which can indicate the source or origin of [the amount of] of interest when payment was agreed to at a fixed period of time. Payment of interest on such transactions is a widely spread and accepted practice in international commerce (art. [9(2)] 1980 Vienna Convention)."

2. Juzgado Nacional de Primera Instancia en lo Comercial No. 10 [National Commercial Court of First Instance] 23 Oct. 1991 (Arg.), *at* http://cisgw3.law.pace.edu/cases/911023a1.html.

   Original language: Spanish
   Translation: Available

   Court (translation):
   "The payment of interest on a debt in dollars at an internationally recognized and used rate, such as the prime rate, is an accepted usage in international trade, even if it is not found to have been expressly agreed by the parties."

   Unilex abstract:
   "In order to ascertain whether the buyer was obliged to pay interest, the Court expressly referred to the international trade usages on the basis of Art. 9 CISG. In this respect the Court held that payment of interest, 'at an internationally known and used rate such as the Prime Rate', constitutes 'an accepted usage in in-

ternational trade, even when it is not expressly agreed between the parties', then granting the seller recognizance for its credit for interest 'at the Prime Rate … as required by the creditor', without specifying which Prime Rate it was, and applying a rate of 10%. In the same decision, the Court also entitled another US seller, on the same grounds, to recover interest at the Prime Rate plus a spread of 2%, as provided in the contract."

3. Juzgado Nacional de Primera Instancia en lo Comercial No. 10 [National Commercial Court of First Instance] n. 56.179, 6 Oct. 1994 (Arg.), *at* http://cisgw3.law.pace.edu/cases/941006a1.html.

   Original language: Spanish
   Translation: Available

   Unilex abstract:
   "With respect to interest accruing on the credit deriving from the performance of the first sales contract, the Court gave recognizance to the credit for interest at the rate of 24%, that is corresponding to the rate agreed upon by the parties. The Court held this on the ground that CISG, as envisaged by its Art. 6, grants the parties with the widest possibility of determining the contents of their contract. With respect to interest accruing on the credit deriving from the performance of the second sales contract, the Court determined interest at the rate of 12%, as a rate generally recognized in international trade. In the Court reasoning, since CISG does not determine the interest rate, reference should be made to international trade usages 'which are assigned by CISG itself a hierarchical position higher than the very same CISG provisions (Art. 9 CISG)'."

4. Cámara Nacional de Apelaciones en lo Comercial de Buenos Aires [Second Instance Court of Appeal] (docket # unavail), 21 July 2002 (Arg.), *at* http://cisgw3.law.pace.edu/cases/020721a1.html.

   Original language: Spanish
   Translation: Unavailable

Summary

Cases involving Article 78: 4

Cases for which an English translation is available: 3

Cases for which only an abstract was available: 0

Cases for which neither translation nor abstract was available: 1

AUSTRALIA

1. Supreme Court of Queensland, 17 Nov. 2000 (Austl.), *at* http://cisgw3.law.pace.edu/cases/001117a2.html.

   Original language: English

2. Supreme Court of Western Australia, n. Civ 1647, 17 Jan. 2003 (Austl.), *at* http://cisgw3.law.pace.edu/cases/030117a2.html.

   Original language: English

   Court:
   "[Buyer] is entitled to damages for breach of contract and in negligence in the total sum of $AUD307,998.44. Vista is also entitled to interest on such damages at the rate of 6 per cent per annum, pursuant to s 32 [section 32] of the *Supreme Court Act 1935* (WA), calculated from 10 December 1997 (when formal demand for damages was made following the third recall of the goods in question) until judgment."

Summary

Cases involving Article 78: 2

Cases for which an English translation is available: 2

Cases for which only an abstract was available: 0

Cases for which neither translation nor abstract was available: 0

BULGARIA

1. Bulgarska turgosko-promishlena palata [Bulgarian Chamber of Commerce and Industry] n. 56/1995, 24 Apr. 1996 (Bulg.), *at* http://cisgw3.law.pace.edu/cases/960424bu.html.

   Original language: Bulgarian
   Translation: Available (English, German)

2. Bulgarska turgosko-promishlena palata [Bulgarian Chamber of Commerce and Industry] n.11/1996, 12 Feb. 1998 (Bulg.), *at* http://cisgw3.law.pace.edu/cases/980212bu.html.

   Original language: Bulgarian
   Translation: Available (English, German)

   Court (translation):
   "According to Article 78 CISG, if a party fails to pay the price or any other sum that is in arrears, the other party is entitled to interest on it. The Convention only defines the principle that the party in arrears owes interest, without determining the amount of that interest. First, a debtor is in arrears when his liability becomes subject to execution. Second, the creditor must invite the debtor to fulfill its liability voluntarily. The [seller] did not claim for interest in his complaint. He only declares that a separate suit will be brought against the [buyer] for interest calculated according to the quarterly LIBOR. There is no evidence proving that the [seller] invited the [buyer] to satisfy its debt and pay the interest upon it voluntarily. Consequently, there is no evidence proving that the [buyer] is in arrears. With the addition to the complaint received by the Arbitral Tribunal on 3 December 1997, the [seller] claims interest. The Arbitral Tribunal allowed this addition to the complaint with its ruling of 15 December 1997. After this act of the Arbitral Tribunal, the [buyer] is in arrears and owes the interest. The Arbitral Tribunal accepts that the [buyer] is in arrears from the date when the lawsuit was brought (3 December 1997), but not for the period before that date. With its addition to the complaint from 3 December 1997, the [seller] [creditor] cannot put in arrears the [buyer] [debtor] for a period preceding that date. This becomes clearer if we take into consideration the fact that according to the Convention, the amount of the interest is not defined and has to be determined by the contracting parties themselves or by other means. The innocent party cannot be in arrears for the period before an invitation is made to voluntarily pay."

3. Bulgarska turgosko-promishlena palata [Bulgarian Chamber of Commerce and Industry] n. 33/98, 12 Mar. 2001 (Bulg.), *at* http://cisgw3.law.pace.edu/cases/010312bu.html.

   Original language: Bulgarian
   Translation: Available (English)

   Court (translation):
   "The legal basis for the interest claim is article 78 of CISG, according to which if a party fails to pay the price that is in arrears, the other party is entitled to interest on it. According to article 59 of the CISG, the buyer must pay the price on the date fixed by or determinable from the contract and the CISG. The CISG does not define the amount of the interest in arrears. Considering that in this particular case the contracting parties did not stipulate the applicable law, the Arbitral Tribunal accepts that the substantive law of the plaintiff's country must be applied, because he owes the characterizing contractual obligation. According to Government Decree N 72/94 for the determination of the amount of the interest, quarter LIBOR for the US dollar is used plus 10 points. Considering the above, the Arbitral Tribunal finds the claim for the interest reasonable. The defendant is directed to pay to the plaintiff the interest over the main amount calculated until the date when the claim was brought to trial. The claim for the legal interest over the main amount, calculated from the day when the claim was brought to trial until its final payment, is also reasonable.

4. Bulgarska turgosko-promishlena palata [Bulgarian Chamber of Commerce and Industry] n. 26/99, 28 Feb. 2002 (Bulg.), *at* http://cisgw3.law.pace.edu/cases/020228bu.html.

   Original language: Bulgarian
   Translation: Available (English)

Summary

Cases involving Article 78: 4

Cases for which an English translation is available: 4

Cases for which only an abstract was available: 0

Cases for which neither translation nor abstract was available: 0

CANADA

1. Ontario Superior Court of Justice, n. 98-CV-14293CM, 31 Aug. 1999 (Can.), *at* http://cisgw3.law.pace.edu/cases/990831c4.html.

   Original language: English

   Court:
   "There shall be pre-judgment interest in accordance with s. 128 of the *Courts of Justice Act* from the date the cause of action arose, which I find to be from the date of the final invoice of April 16, 1996, as well as post-judgment interest."

2. Supreme Court of British Columbia, n. C993594 21 Aug. 2003 (Can.), *at* http://cisgw3.law.pace.edu/cases/030821c4.html.

   Original language: English

   Court:
   "[Buyer] claims the sum of $12,331 in extra interest payments it made to its banker as a result of the interest rates on its operating and term loans being increased. The rate on the operating loan was increased from the bank's prime rate plus 0.875% to prime rate plus 1.375% in March 1999. The rate on the term loan was increased from prime plus 1.250% to prime plus 1.5% in November 2000.

   There is no evidence as to why [Buyer] 's banker increased the interest rates. The interest rates charged on the two types of loans were changed at different times and they were not lowered after [Buyer] had a very profitable year in fiscal 2000. There is insufficient evidence for me to conclude that the interest rates were increased as a result of Kurtz's breaches of its contract with [Buyer].

   I hold that [Buyer] has not proved a loss under this head of damages attributable to [Seller]'s breaches.

   [...]

   [Buyer] is also entitled to pre-judgment interest on its past losses. If the parties are unable to agree on the amount of pre-judgment interest, I direct that there be an accounting in respect of the interest before the registrar, who is to prepare a report and recommendation."

Summary

Cases involving Article 78: 2

Cases for which an English translation is available: 2

Cases for which only an abstract was available: 0

Cases for which neither translation nor abstract was available: 0

Cases applying domestic law to determine the applicable rate: 2

Appendix 2
AUSTRIA

Court

Oberlandesgericht	Court of Appeals

1. Internationales Schiedsgericht der Bundeskammer der gewerblichen Wirtschaft [Arbitral Tribunal] n.SCH-4318 15 June 1994 (Aus.), *at* http://cisgw3.law.pace.edu/cases/940615a4.html.

   Original language: German
   Translation: Available

   Court (translation):
   "Article 78 of the CISG, while granting the right to interest, is silent on the question of the applicable rate. In international writings and case law to date it is disputed whether the question is outside the scope of the Convention – with the result that the interest rate is to be determined according to the domestic law applicable on the basis of the relevant conflict-of-laws rules (in this sense see, among others, HERBER/CZERWENKA, loc. cit., 1991, 347; Oberlandesgericht Frankfurt, 13 June 1991, Recht der Internationalen Wirtschaft 1991, 591) – or whether there is a true gap in the Convention within the meaning of Article 7(2) so that the applicable interest rate should possibly be determined autonomously in conformity with the general principles underlying the Convention (see in this sense, for example, J.O. HONNOLD, Uniform Sales Law, 2nd edition, Deventer, Boston 1991, 525-526; ICC Arbitral Award No. 6653 (1993), Clunet 1993, 1040). This second view is to be preferred, not least because the immediate recourse to a particular domestic law may lead to results which are incompatible with the principle embodied in Art. 78 of the CISG, at least in the cases where the law in question expressly prohibits the payment of interest. One of the general principles underlying the CISG is that of "full compensation" of the loss caused (cf. Art. 74 of the CISG). It follows that, in the event of failure by the debtor to pay a monetary debt, the creditor, who as a business person must be expected to resort to bank credit as a result of the delay in payment, should therefore be entitled to interest at the rate commonly practised in its country with respect to the currency of payment, i.e. the currency agreed upon by the parties (cf. Art. 7.4.9 of the Principles of International Commercial Contracts prepared by the International Institute of the Unification of Private Law (UNIDROIT), on which see M.J. BONELL, An International Restatement of

Contract Law. The UNIDROIT Principles of International Commercial Contracts, Transnational Juris Publications, Irvington – N.Y., 1994, 114-115). The information received from the Deutsche Bundesbank is that the average "prime borrowing rate" for US dollars in Germany in the period in question was 6.25%. The interest due from the [seller] should be calculated at that rate."

2. Internationales Schiedsgericht der Bundeskammer der gewerblichen Wirtschaft [Arbitral Tribunal] n.Sch-4366 15 June 1994 (Aus.), *at* http://cisgw3.law.pace.edu/cases/940615a3.html.

   Original language: German
   Translation: Available

   Court (translation):
   "5.2. In accordance with Art. 78 of the CISG, the seller is entitled to interest in the event of arrears in payment of the price by the buyer.

   5.2.1. The interest is payable from the effective date of the obligation for payment of the purchase price. According to Art. 58(1) of the CISG, this time is primarily determined by the agreements between the parties themselves; only in the absence of such a special agreement is it the time when the seller places the goods at the buyer's disposal in accordance with the contract. In the present case, the parties had derogated from the payment modalities and time-limits originally laid down in the contract by subsequently agreeing that the [buyer] could take delivery of and pay for the goods in partial consignments according to its possibilities of resale, provides that it bore the storage costs incurred thereby [...]. Accordingly, the invoices in question here stipulate "Payment: immediately upon receipt of the invoice". It was therefore at that time, and not earlier, that the [buyer] was under the obligation to pay the amount invoiced at the time, and it is only from that time that the [seller] was entitled to interest [...].

   5.2.2. Article 78 of the CISG, while granting the right to interest, says nothing about the level of the interest rate payable. In international legal writings and case law to date it is disputed whether the question is outside the scope of the Convention – with the result that the interest rate is to be determined according to the domestic law applicable on the basis of the relevant conflict-of-laws rules (see inter alia HERBER/CZERWENKA, Internationales Kaufrechts, 1991, 347; Oberlandesgericht Frankfurt, 13 June 1991 in Recht der Internationalen Wirtschaft 1991, 591) – or whether there is a true gap in the Convention within the meaning of Article 7(2) so that the applicable interest rate should possibly be determined autonomously in conformity with the general principles underlying the Convention (see in this sense, for example, J.O. HONNOLD, Uniform Sales Law, 2nd edition, Deventer, Boston 1991, 525-526; ICC arbitral award No. 6653 (1993), Clunet 1993, 1040). This second view is to be preferred, not least because the immediate recourse to a particular domestic law may lead to results which are incompatible with the principle embodied in Art. 78 of the CISG, at least in the cases where the law in question expressly prohibits the payment of interest. One of the general legal principles underlying the CISG is the requirement of "full compensation" of the loss caused (cf. Art. 74 of the CISG). It follows that, in the event of failure to pay a monetary debt, the creditor, who as a business person must be expected to resort to bank credit as a result of the delay in payment, should therefore be entitled to interest at the rate commonly practiced in its country with respect to the currency of payment, i.e. the currency of the creditor's country or any other foreign currency agreed upon by the parties (cf. Art. 7.4.9 of the Principles of International Commercial Contracts prepared by the International Institute for the Unification of Private Law (UNIDROIT), on which see M.J. BONELL, An International Restatement of Contract Law. The UNIDROIT Principles of International Commercial Contracts, Transnational Juris Publications, Irvington – N.Y., 1994, 114-115). The information received from the leading Austrian banks is that the average "prime borrowing rates" for US dollars and DM in Austria in the period in question were 4.5% and 8%, respectively. The interest due from the [buyer] should be calculated at those rates."

3. Oberlandesgericht [OLG] [Provincial Court of Appeal Linz] n.11R24/95-27, 5 Oct. 1995 (Aus.), *at* http://cisgw3.law.pace.edu/cases/951005a3.html.

Original language: German
Translation: Unavailable

4. Schiedsgericht der Börse für Landwirtschaftliche Produkte [Arbitral Tribunal], n.S 2/97, 10 Dec. 1997 (Aus.), *at* http://cisgw3.law.pace.edu/cases/971210a3.html.

Original language: German
Translation: Unavailable

Unilex abstract:
"The seller was further awarded damages for lost profits according to the rules of the market for farm products in Vienna expressly referred to by the parties – and interest on the sums due as damages (Arts. 78 and 74 CISG) at the rate fixed by the seller's standard terms."

Summary

Cases involving Article 78: 4

Cases for which an English translation is available: 2

Cases for which only an abstract was available: 1

Cases for which neither translation nor abstract was available: 1

There are only four cases dealing with Article 78. Among them, two very well-known decisions were drafted by Professor Bonell in two arbitration proceedings. He basically says: Although Article 78 does not expressly determine the rate of interest, nonetheless this gap is to be filled with general principles of the CISG. One of the general legal principles underlying the CISG is the requirement of "full compensation" of the loss caused (*cf.* Art. 74 of the CISG). It follows that, in the event of failure to pay a monetary debt, the creditor, who as a business person must be expected to resort to bank credit as a result of the delay in payment, should therefore be entitled to interest at the rate commonly practiced in its country with respect to the currency of payment, i.e. the currency of the creditor's country or any other foreign currency agreed upon by the parties.

Appendix 3
Belgium

Courts

Rechtbank van Koophandel	District Court
Tribunal de Commerce	Commercial Court
Hof van Beroep	Appellate Court

1. Tribunal de Commerce Bruxelles n.A.R. [District Court] 2700/90; R.G. 4.825.91, 13 Nov. 1992 (Belg.), *at* http://www.cisg.law.pace.edu/cisg/wais/db/cases2/921113b1.html.

   Original language: French
   Translation: Unavailable

   Unilex abstract:
   "In addition, the Court granted the seller the right to interest at the Italian statutory rate, accruing from the date when payment was due."

2. Rechtbank van Koophandel Hasselt n.A.R. [District Court] 722/94, 23 Feb. 1994 (Belg.), *at* http://www.cisg.law.pace.edu/cisg/wais/db/cases2/940223b1.html.

   Original language: Dutch
   Translation: Unavailable

   Unilex abstract:
   "The seller was granted payment and the right to interest on the sums due, at the rate determined by the applicable national law (German law)."

3. Rechtbank van Koophandel Hasselt [District Court], 16 Mar. 1994 (Belg.), *at* http://www.cisg.law.pace.edu/cisg/wais/db/casesw/940316b1.html.

   Original language: Dutch
   Translation: Unavailable

Unilex abstract:
"The seller was granted payment and the right to interest on the sums due, at the rate determined by the applicable national law (Dutch law)."

4. Tribunal de Commerce Bruxelles n.R.G. [Commercial Court] 1.205/93, 5 Oct. 1994 (Belg.), *at* http://www.cisg.law.pace.edu/cisg/wais/db/cases2/941005b1.html.

Original language:	French
Translation:	Available

Unilex abstract:
"In addition, the Court granted the seller the right to interest at the rate of 14.5% per year, as requested by the seller, without further specifying the reason for such interest rate and without making any reference to Art. 78 CISG."

5. Rechtbank van Koophandel Hasselt n.A.R. [District Court] 3641/94, 1 Mar. 1995 (Belg.), *at* http://www.cisg.law.pace.edu/cisg/wais/db/cases2/950301b1.html.

Original language:	Dutch
Translation:	Unavailable

Unilex abstract:
"The seller was further awarded damages and interest on the sums due. Without referring to CISG the Court applied the interest rate determined by the standard practice of the same Court."

6. Rechtbank van Koophandel Hasselt n.A.R. [District Court] 1849/94, 4205/94 2 May 1995 (Belg.), *at* http://www.cisg.law.pace.edu/cisg/wais/db/cases2/950502b1.html.

Original language:	Dutch
Translation:	Unavailable

7. Rechtbank van Koophandel Hasselt, [District Court] 18 Oct. 1995 (Belg.), *at* http://www.cisg.law.pace.edu/cisg/wais/db/cases2/951018b1.html.

Original language:	Dutch
Translation:	Unavailable

Unilex abstract:
"In the Court's opinion the interest rate and the penalty clauses contained in the seller's invoices were unilateral and could not bind the buyer. Therefore Arts. 74

and 78 CISG were not derogated from. The Court assessed damages ex aequo et bono."

8. Rechtbank van Koophandel Hasselt [District Court], 8 Oct. 1996 (Belg.), *at* http://www.cisg.law.pace.edu/cisg/wias/db/cases2/961008b1.html.

   Original language: Dutch
   Translation: Unavailable

9. Rechtbank van Koophandel Hasselt n.A.R. [District Court] 2012/96, 9 Oct. 1996 (Belg.), *at* http://www.cisg.law.pace.edu/cisg/wais/db/cases2/961009b1.html.

   Original language: Dutch
   Translation: Unavailable

   Unilex abstract:
   "The seller was awarded interest according to Art. 78 CISG. As CISG does not determine the interest rate, the Court applied the average bank lending rate in the creditor's country (the seller's), because the creditor would have received interest on the sums due in that country had the debtor paid on time. No formal request was considered necessary under CISG."

10. Rechtbank van Koophandel Hasselt n.A.R. [District Court] 1970/95, 8 Nov. 1995 (Belg.), *at* http://www.cisg.law.pace.edu/cisg/wais/db/cases2/951108b1.html.

    Original language: Dutch
    Translation: Unavailable

    Unilex abstract:
    "The seller was awarded the rest of the purchase price and interests according to Art. 78 CISG. As CISG does not determine the interest rate, the Court applied the average bank lending rate in the creditor's country (the seller's), because the creditor would have received interest on the sums due in that country had the debtor paid on time. No formal request for payment was considered necessary under CISG."

11. Rechtbank van Koophandel Kortrijk n.A.R. [District Court] 4328/93, 16 Dec. 1996 (Belg.), *at* http://www.cisg.law.pace.edu/cisg/wais/db/cases2/961216b1.html.

Original language: Dutch
Translation: Unavailable

Unilex abstract:
"The Court awarded the seller payment of the price as well as interest under Art. 78 CISG. As CISG does not specify the rate of interest payable, the Court, considering the circumstances of the case, decided to award interest at the Belgian statutory rate. Furthermore the Court, though observing that CISG does not require a formal request for payment, decided that under the circumstances of the case interest accrued from the date of the seller's formal request for payment."

12. Rechtbank van Koophandel Hasselt n.A.R. [District Court] 1972/96, 21 Jan. 1997 (Belg.), *at* http://www.cisg.law.pace.edu/cisg/wais/db/cases2/970121b1.html.

    Original language: Dutch
    Translation: Unavailable

    Unilex abstract:
    "The seller was further awarded interests on the sums due. As CISG does not determine the interest rate (Art. 78 CISG) the Court held that the rate had to be determined in accordance with that provided for in the seller's standard terms if lower than the one required by the domestic law otherwise applicable to the contract."

13. Rechtbank van Koophandel Kotrijk n.A.R. [District Court] 4143/96, 6 Oct. 1997 (Belg.), *at* http://www.cisg.law.pace.edu/cisg/wais/db/cases2/971006b1.html.

    Original language: Dutch
    Translation: Available

14. Rechtbank van Koophandel Hasselt n.A.R. [District Court] 1639/95, 17 June 1998 (Belg.), *at* http://www.cisg.law.pace.edu/cisg/wais/db/cases2/980617b1.html.

    Original language: Dutch
    Translation: Unavailable

15. Hof van Beroep Antwerpen [Appellate Court] n.1995/AR/1558, 4 Nov. 1998 (Belg.), *at* http://www.cisg.law.pace.edu/cisg/wais/db/cases2/981104b1.html.

Original language: Dutch
Translation: Unavailable

16. Rechtbank van Koophandel Hasselt, [District Court] 17 June 1998 (Belg.), *at* http://www.cisg.law.pace.edu/cisg/wais/db/cases2/981202b1.html.

    Original language: Dutch
    Translation: Unavailable

17. Hof van Beroep Antwerpen n.A.R. [Appellate Court] 3312/96, 18 May 1999 (Belg.), *at* http://www.cisg.law.pace.edu/cisg/wais/db/cases2/990518b1.html.

    Original language: Dutch
    Translation: Unavailable

18. Rechtbank van Koophandel Hasselt n.A.R. [District Court] 1079/99, 2 June 1999 (Belg.), *at* http://www.cisg.law.pace.edu/cisg/wais/db/cases2/990602b1.html.

    Original language: Dutch
    Translation: Unavailable

19. Rechtbank van Koophandel Hasselt, [District Court], 17 Feb. 2000 (Belg.), *at* http://www.cisg.law.pace.edu/cisg/wais/db/cases2/000217b1.html.

    Original language: Dutch
    Translation: Unavailable

20. Rechtbank van Koophandel Ieper, [District Court] 29 Jan. 2001 (Belg.), *at* http://www.cisg.law.pace.edu/cisg/wais/db/cases2/010129b1.html.

    Original language: Dutch
    Translation: Unavailable

21. Rechtbank van Koophandel Kortrijk n.A.R. [District Court] 04576/00, 4 Apr. 2001 (Belg.), *at* http://www.cisg.law.pace.edu/cisg/wais/db/cases2/010404b1.html.

    Original language: Dutch
    Translation: Unavailable

22. Rechtbank van Koophandel Veurne [District Court] n.A/00/00665, 25 Apr. 2001 (Belg.), *at* http://www.cisg.law.pace.edu/cisg/wais/db/cases2/010425b1.html.

Original language:	Dutch
Translation:	Available

Court (translation):
"The [seller] is entitled to a claim for interest because of the late payment, under Article 78 CISG. Whereas the CISG does not itself determine the interest rate in the case of late payment, this interest rate is determined according to the law of the currency of payment (*cf*. H. Van Houtte, "Het Weens Koopverdrag in het Belgish recht", T.B.H., 1998, p. 344 e.v., inz. No. 33, pp. 352-353); in this case, the Belgian legal interest."

23. Hof van Beroep Gent [Appellate Court] n.1999/A/2160, 23 May 2001 (Belg.), *at* http://www.cisg.law.pace.edu/cisg/wais/db/cases2/010523b1.html

Original language:	Dutch
Translation:	Available

Court (translation):
"From the evidence, and more specifically "the standard purchase and sales clauses" ("*Algemeine Einkaufs- und Verkaufsbedingungen*", item no. 33, [seller]'s file), it is not evident that a contractual interest rate of 10% had been agreed upon. No other piece of evidence that could provide the contractual basis for such an interest rate has been presented. In these circumstances, interest is awarded equal to the legal Belgian interest rate from the date of the first proven default, being 2 July 1996. An interest award from an earlier date cannot be justified, because [buyer] has lawfully requested a deduction for a part of [seller]'s claim, being *Bf* 278,499."

24. Rechtbank van Koophandel Kortrijk n.A.R. [District Court] 3669/2000, 3 Oct. 2001 (Belg.), *at* http://www.cisg.law.pace.edu/cisg/wais/db/cases2/011003b1.html.

Original language:	Dutch
Translation:	Unavailable

25. Rechtbank van Koophandel Namur n.R.G. [District Court] no. 985/01, 15 Jan. 2002 (Belg.), *at* http://www.cisg.law.pace.edu/cisg/wais/db/cases2/020115b1.html.

Original language: French
Translation: Available

Court (translation):
"That invoice relates to some performances regarding the regulation of the machine; those performances are connected to the sale in such a way that the interest on the unpaid invoiced sum is owed notwithstanding the absence of a warning notice pursuant to Article 78 of the CISG. The calculation of interest is not contested as such."

26. Rechtbank van Koophandel Ieper n.A.R. [District Court] 318/00, 18 Feb. 2002 (Belg.), *at* http://www.cisg.law.pace.edu/cisg/wais/db/cases2/020218b1.html.

Original language: Dutch
Translation: Unavailable

27. Rechtbank van Koophandel Hasselt n.A.R. [District Court] 2671/01, 6 Mar. 2002 (Belg.), *at* http://www.cisg.law.pace.edu/cisg/wais/db/cases2/020306b1.html.

Original language: Dutch
Translation: Unavailable

28. Rechtbank van Koophandel Hasselt n.A.R. [District Court] 01/1710, 22 May 2002 (Belg.), *at* http://www.cisg.law.pace.edu/cisg/wais/db/cases2/020522b1.html.

Original language: Dutch
Translation: Unavailable

29. Hof van Beroep Gent [Appellate Court] n.2001/AR/677, 17 Oct. 2002 (Belg.), *at* http://www.cisg.law.pace.edu/cisg/wais/db/cases2/021017b1.html.

Original language: Dutch
Translation: Unavailable

30. Rechtbank van Koophandel Veurne [District Court] n.A/02/00430, 15 Jan. 2003 (Belg.), *at* http://www.cisg.law.pace.edu/cisg/wais/db/cases2/030115b1.html.

Original language: Dutch
Translation: Unavailable

31. Hof van Beroep Gent [Appellate Court] n.1998/AR/2649, 3 Mar. 2003 (Belg.), *at* http://www.cisg.law.pace.edu/cisg/wais/db/cases2/030303b1.html.

Original language: Dutch
Translation: Unavailable

32. Rechtbank van Koophandel Veurne [District Court] n.A/01/00392, 19 Mar. 2003 (Belg.), *at* http://www.cisg.law.pace.edu/cisg/wais/db/cases2/030319b1.html.

Original language: Dutch
Translation: Unavailable

33. Hof van Beroep Gent [Appellate Court] n.2000/AR/1957, 12 May 2003 (Belg.), *at* http://www.cisg.law.pace.edu/cisg/wais/db/cases2/030512b1.html.

Original language: Dutch
Translation: Unavailable

34. Hof van Beroep Gent [Appellate Court] n.2002/AR/1184, 8 Oct. 2003 (Belg.), *at* http://www.cisg.law.pace.edu/cisg/wais/db/cases2/031008b1.html.

Original language: Dutch
Translation: Unavailable

35. Rechtbank van Koophandel Hasselt n.AR [District Court] 04/79, 25 Feb. 2004 (Belg.), *at* http://www.cisg.law.pace.edu/cisg/wais/db/cases2/040225b1.html.

Original language: Dutch
Translation: Available

Court (translation):
"Articles 74 and 78 of the Vienna Sales Convention provide for the principle of damages and interest charged on sums in arrears without determining the applicable interest rate. In this regard, the [Seller] can rely on the *lex contractus* for the determination of this rate. The [Seller] was to perform the most characteristic performance and the parties have not agreed on the applicable law. One can therefore assume that the applicable law is Belgian law, which implies that the [Seller] justly invokes the Act of 2 August 2002, specifically addressing arrears of payment in commercial transactions.

Nevertheless, the [Seller] unjustly claims on the basis of this Act interest at 10.5% on the amounts of the invoices which were issued during the first half of

2003, as the interest rate is set to be 10% for that period according to article 5(2) of the Act of 2 August 2003 (B.S., 14 February 2003). The debates are reopened to allow the [Seller] to calculate the total amount of interest on the sums in arrears.

[…]

FOR THESE REASONS,

The court holds, after deliberations, by default that the claim is admissible and partially allowed.

- The court hereby orders the [Buyer] to pay the [Seller] € 356,118.76 and declares that the [Seller] is also entitled to default interest from the due date of the invoices until the date of the writ of summons according to article 5 of the Act of 2 August 2002 specifically addressing arrears of payment in commercial transactions; for the first half of 2003 at 10% and from then at 9.5%. It also reopens the proceedings to allow the [Seller] to calculate the total amount of arrears interest and orders a hearing on 7 April 2004 at 9.30h.
- The court also orders the [Buyer] to pay judicial interest determined by article 5 of the Act of 2 August 2002 specifically addressing arrears of payment in commercial transactions (at this moment 9.5%) on € 353,618.76.
- The court also holds that the [Seller] is not entitled to compensation for legal costs, and declares the judgment to have immediate effect."

36. Rechtbank van Koophandel Hasselt n.AR [District Court] 04/601, 25 Feb. 2004 (Belg.), *at* http://www.cisg.law.pace.edu/cisg/wais/db/cases2/040225b2.html.

Original language: Dutch
Translation: Available

Court (translation):
"The Vienna Sales Convention addresses the issues of damages and interest charged on sums in arrears in articles 74 and 78 respectively, but does not determine the applicable interest rate.

The [Seller] can only invoke the Belgian Act of 2 August 2002 on arrears of payment in commercial transactions, and the provisions on damages and interest laid down therein to the extent that the Belgian Act is the *lex contractus*. This is apparently not the case here.

Futhermore, in that case the [Seller] would not be entitled to compensation for legal costs.

The claim of the [Seller] can be allowed, but on the basis of articles 74 and 78 of the Vienna Sales Convention.

Summary

Cases involving Article 78: 36

Cases for which an English translation is available: 5

Cases for which only an abstract was available: 10

Cases for which neither translation nor abstract was available: 21

- Courts, apparently, apply the forum law to determine the proper rate of interest. However, it is difficult from reading only abstracts to understand how courts reach such a determination.
- Courts, though observing that CISG does not require a formal request for payment, decided, at least in one case, that under the circumstances of the case interest accrued from the date of the seller's formal request for payment.

Appendix 4
China

Courts

CIETAC	China International Economic and Trade Arbitration Commission

1. U.S. v. P.R.C., CISG/1991/02 (CIETAC 1991), *at* http://www.cisg.law.pace.edu/cisg/wais/db/cases2/910419c1.html.

   Original language: Chinese
   Translation: Available

   Court (translation):
   "[Seller] should compensate $56,000 for Claimant [buyer's] loss (calculated at $200/t) plus interest on it in the amount of $5,226.70 (from November 1990 to December 1991, calculated at an annual rate of 8%): a total payment of $61,226.70."

2. P.R.C. v. U.S., CISG/1991/04 (CIETAC 1991), *at* http://www.cisg.law.pace.edu/cisg/wais/db/cases2/911030c1.html.

   Original language: Chinese
   Translation: Available

3. Lian Zhong v. Xiamen Trade (Xiamen Intermediate People's Court, Dec. 31, 1992), *at* http://www.cisg.law.pace.edu/cisg/wais/db/cases2/921231c1.html.

   Original language: Chinese
   Translation: Unavailable

   Unilex abstract:
   "Finally, the seller was awarded interest on the sums the buyer owed (Art. 78 CISG)."

4. Zhanjiang Textiles v. Xian Da Fashion (Guandong Higher People's Court, 7 Mar. 1994), *at* http://www.cisg.law.pace.edu/cisg/wais/db/cases2/940307c1.html.

Original language: Chinese
Translation: Unavailable

5. (U.S. v. P.R.C.), CISG/1995/01 (CIETAC 1995), *at* http://www.cisg.law.pace.edu/cisg/wais/db/cases2/950000c1.html.

   Original language: Chinese
   Translation: Unavailable

6. You Li v. Gold Star, 166 (Fujian Higher People's Court, 31 Dec. 1996), *at* http://www.cisg.law.pace.edu/cisg/wais/db/cases2/961231c1.html.

   Original language: Chinese
   Translation: Unavailable

7. Sino-Add (Singapore) PTE. Ltd. v. Karawasha Resources Ltd., (2001) Haishangchuzi No.119 (Guangxi Beihai Maritime, 5 Mar. 2002), *at* http://www.cisg.law.pace.edu/cisg/wais/db/cases2/020305c1.html.

   Original language: Chinese
   Translation: Available

   Court (translation):
   "The two parties did not choose the applicable law and the destination of the transportation contract is located in the jurisdiction of the court. Therefore, pursuant to Article 269 of the Maritime Law of the People's republic of China, which stipulates that 'where the parties do not choose the applicable law, the law of the nation holding the closest connection with the contract shall be applied', the Maritime Law of the People's Republic of China, the Contract Law of the People's Republic of China and the relevant international conventions shall be applied to this case

   [...]

   However, [Buyer]'s claim for the interest counted at the London Interbank Offered Rate was not proper. To be fair, the interest shall be counted at the contemporary lending rate of the liquid capital promulgated by the People's Bank of China."

Summary

Cases involving Article 78: 7

Cases for which an English translation is available: 2

Cases for which only an abstract was available: 1

Cases for which neither translation nor abstract was available: 4

Appendix 5
Finland

Courts

Käräjäoikeus	District court
Hovioikeus	Court of Appeal

1. Käräjäoikeus of Kuopio [District Court], n. 95/3214, 5 Nov. 1996 (Fin.), *at* http://cisgw3.law.pace.edu/cases/961105f5.html.

   Original language: Finnish
   Translation: Available

   Court (translation):
   "According to CISG Article 74, [buyer] is entitled to damages for breach of contract consisting of a sum equal to the loss, including loss of profit suffered by [buyer] as a consequence of the breach. Such damages may not exceed the loss which the party in breach foresaw or ought to have foreseen at the time of the conclusion of the contract, in the light of facts and matters of which he then knew or ought to have known, as a possible consequence of the breach of contract.

   The defendants have denied their duty to pay damages for interest loss caused to [buyer]. According to his own statement, K [CEO of the seller] has known that [buyer] will take credit to finance the advance payment. Consequently, K may have anticipated that interest loss might be caused to [buyer] if, for some reason, the sale would not go through. On these grounds, damages include compensation of interest loss.

   It has not been shown that K knew the interest rates in Lithuania, namely 7% per month and 0.5% per day interest on arrears, which essentially differs from interest rates in Western Europe. One could not even assume that he should have known it. It is the estimate of the Court, that K should have pre-estimated that the interest loss resulting from not fulfilling the contractual obligations could be about 10% of the sale price, meaning U.S. $8,000. The amount of lost profit announced by the seller, namely 20%, the Court sees as reasonable. The butter consignment bought by the buyer has had a buyer."

2. Hoviokeus of Helsinki [Court of Appeal], n. S 00/82, 26 Oct. 2000 (Fin.), *at* http://cisgw3.law.pace.edu/cases/001026f5.html.

Original language: Finnish
Translation: Available

Court of First Instance (translation):
"[Seller] will pay [buyer] a sum total of *Sf* 70,000 or an equal amount of *Fmk* at the exchange rate of the date of payment. The sum will be added with interest as defined in the Finnish Law on interest (section 4) starting from one month after the notification of summons onwards, 28 October 1997.

Court of Appeals:
"[Seller] will be made to pay for [buyer's] legal expenses accrued in the Court of First Instance in the amount of *Fmk* 235,000. The sum is subject to interest on arrears as defined in the Finnish Law of Interest starting from one month after the issuance of judgment onwards."

3. Hovioikeus of Turku [District Court], 12 Apr. 2002 (Fin.), *at* http://cisgw3.law.pace.edu/cases/020412f5.html.

Original language: Finnish
Translation: Available

Court (translation):
"Additionally, CISG is not applicable in terms of evaluating the reasonableness of the contract or the interest rate, because it has no article dealing with enhancing the reasonableness of the contract as does Finnish law, or articles to evaluate the interest rate except article 78. According to the section 4 of the Finnish law defining the applicable law in international sale of goods, the law of the seller's place of business applies, unless the parties to the contract have agreed on the applicable law. According to section 6, a foreign law that contravenes the principles of Finnish law is not to be applied by the Finnish Courts. As a consequence of the fact that the parties have not agreed on the applicable law, it is decided that, according to the above mentioned principles, when evaluating the conclusion of the contract, its fairness, possible mediation and the interest rate, Finnish law is applicable.

[...]

[Buyer] has demanded interest for the return payment. Because of the fact that the claim is based on a mistaken payment and the benefit derived from such a payment, according to the Finnish law on interest, interest accrues only after one month from the presentation of the claim onwards. Therefore, [buyer] is entitled to legal interest from 17 March 1997 onwards – one month after [seller] was served with summons."

Summary

Cases involving Article 78: 3

Cases for which an English translation is available: 3

Cases for which only an abstract was available: 0

Cases for which neither translation nor abstract was available: 0

Appendix 6
France

1. Cour d'appel Grenoble [Appeal Court] n. 93/2821, 29 Mar. 1995 (Fr.), *at* http://cisgw3.law.pace.edu/cases/950329f1.html.

Original language: French
Translation: Available

Court (translation):
"Whereas, as to the interest, that Article 78 CISG provides that the interest on overdue payments is owed when the debtor is in arrears; That, unlike French law, a formal request is not necessary; That it is proper to hold that the interest runs from the day after the date when [buyer] should have paid the corresponding invoice; Whereas, as to the compounding of the interest, it is proper to grant the demand, to be calculated from the date of the pleadings seeking it [interest claim] (2 May 1994), until one full year shall have run.

[...]

For these reasons, the Appellate Court:

[...]

- Orders [buyer] to pay [seller] *f* 101,825.50 in principal, plus interest on the overdue payments as of right, to be calculated from the day after the invoices should have been paid;
- Decides that the interest will be compounded from 2 May 1994, until one full year shall have run."

2. Cour d'appel Paris [Appeal Court], 6 Apr. 1995 (Fr.), *at* http://cisgw3.law.pace.edu/cases/950406f1.html.

Original language: French
Translation: Available

Court (translation):

"Considering that:

- That the Arbitral Court decided on a matter which was not pleaded, ordering the [seller] to pay, besides the principal amount, interest on this amount calculated from the date on which the purchase price of the goods was paid;
- That [the Arbitral Court] violated the *principe de la contradiction* [right to be heard fully on a matter of fact or law], the parties being deprived of any opportunity to be heard on the issue, either on the law or on the modality of the award itself.
- The arbitral mission consists of the determination of a legal dispute according to limits established by the parties;
- The *principe de la contradiction* implies that the Arbitral Court cannot raise any plea on fact or law if the parties have not been invited to reply on it.

Considering that:

- The Arbitral Court answered in the affirmative the question whether the designated interest in Article 84 of the CISG, which constitutes the French law of international sale of goods, was obligatory rather than merely a "formal claim." The CISG specifies that if the seller is bound to refund the price, he "must" (and not "may") also pay interest on the price calculated from the date on which the price was paid, and the French law of obligations provides in Article 1153-1 of the Civil Code that interest is obligatory in all matters, "even if this was not pleaded;"
- The CISG does not expressly settle the mode of determination of interest rate; [the Arbitral Court] offered as a solution "the most logical one, from an economic point of view," acknowledging the LIBOR [*] rate for "one year;"
- [The Arbitral Court] resolved the questions under discussion without hearing the parties, pointing out that the international trade usage invoked by [buyer] does not provide a method for determining the interest rate;
- On this question, [the Arbitral Court] did not respect the *principe de la contradiction*, the relevant part of [the arbitral award] on interest, divisible from other dispositions, has to be quashed;

On these grounds, the Court of Appeal:

Quashes the arbitral award delivered on 26 March 1993, in Paris, in ICC case no. 6653/ES/FMS between [buyer] and [seller], in which [the Arbitral Court] had ordered [seller] to pay, in addition to the principal payment, interest calculated at the LIBOR rate for one year, accruing from the date on which the price was paid."

3. Cour d'appel Grenoble [Appeal Court] n. 93/4879, 26 Apr. 1995 (Fr.), *at* http://cisgw3.law.pace.edu/cases/950426f2.html.

Original language: French
Translation: Available

Court (translation):
"On the demands for interest and the compounding of the interest, Article 78 of the CISG provides that any delay in payment gives rise to the payment of interest, without a legal demand being necessary. The interest thus will run, on 130,000 F, from …, the date on which the damaged girders were held available for [buyer], after being repaired. The interest will be compounded until one full year will have lapsed, counting from the pleadings of …, which made the demand for the first time."

4. Cour d'appel Grenoble [Appeal Court], 28 Nov. 2002 (Fr.), *at* http://cisgw3.law.pace.edu/cases/021128f2.html.

Original language: French
Translation: Unavailable

Unilex abstract:
"The Court of Appeal furthermore confirmed the lower Court's decision concerning the payment of the price, granting however the seller in addition interest on the unpaid sum, as provided by art. 78 CISG. As to the rate of interest, the Court applied the statutory rate of the domestic law otherwise applicable (Cuban law) and, for the period of time with respect to which it was not possible to establish the Cuban statutory rate, the French statutory rate. As to the damages, the Court of Appeal held that, even if according to art. 74 the aggrieved party may claim damages, it is up to that party to provide the necessary evidence of the loss suffered. In the case at hand the seller had only proved the non-payment of the price by the seller, with the consequence that no further damages in addition to the interest can be awarded for its benefit."

Summary

Cases involving Article 78: 4

Cases for which an English translation is available: 3

Cases for which only an abstract was available: 1

Cases for which neither translation nor abstract was available: 0

- French courts do award interest to delayed payments due as of the day the payment is due. No formal request for interest, contrary to the French law requirements. French courts also award compounded interest. However, the party entitled to interest must formally request payment of interest at the trial.
- The CISG does not expressly settle the mode of determination of interest rate; international trade usage does not provide a method for determining the interest rate; resorting to LIBOR may not be the right answer.

Appendix 7
Germany

Courts

AG	*Amtsgericht*	Petty District Court
LG	*Landgericht*	District Court
OLG	*Oberlandesgericht*	Provincial Court
KG	*Kammergericht*	Upper Court Berlin

Codes

EGBGB	*Einführungsgesetzbuch zum Bürgerlichen Gesetzbuche*	German code on the conflict of laws
HGB	*Handelsgesetzbuch*	German commercial code
BGB	*Bürgerliches Gesetzbuch*	German civil code
ZPO	*Zivilprozeßordnung*	German code on civil procedure
CC	Codice Civile	Italian civil code

Law reviews

JL&C	Journal of Law and Commerce
NJW-RR	*Neue Juristische Wochenschrift Rechtsprechungs-Report*
IPRax	*Praxis des internationalen Privat- und Verfahrensrecht*

1. Landgericht [LG] [District Court] Stuttgart n. 3 KfH O 97/89, 31 Aug. 1989 (F.R.G.), *at* http://www.cisg.law.pace.edu/cisg/wais/db/cases2/890831g1.html.

   Original language: German
   Translation: Available

   Court (translation):
   "The CISG does not fix the rate of interest. This is a controversial subject. It is advisable to fall back on the national law of the creditor because the consequences of the debtor's non-fulfillment of his payment obligation take effect there and payment was due in Italian currency. Therefore, the debtor must

carry the risk of paying the monetary debt in the foreign currency according to the rate of interest there (References: Stoll in Schlechtriem, Einheitliches Kaufrecht und nationals Obligationenrecht, 1987, §§ 279/280, 291; Schlechtriem, Einheitliches UN-Kaufrecht, 1981, §§ 93/94)."

2. Landgericht [LG] [District Court] Aachen n. 41 O 198/89, 3 Apr. 1990 (F.R.G.), *at* http://www.cisg.law.pace.edu/cisg/wais/db/cases2/900403g1.html.

Original language:	German
Translation:	Unavailable

Unilex abstract:
"The court awarded interest rate of 12% for the period of delayed payment as average bank lending rate at the seller's place of business (Arts. 61(1)(b), 74 and 78 CISG)."

3. Amtsgericht [AG] [Petty District Court] Oldenburg in Holstein n. 5 C 73/89, 24 Apr. 1990 (F.R.G.), *at* http://www.cisg.law.pace.edu/cisg/wais/db/cases2/900424g1.html.

Original language:	German
Translation:	Unavailable

Unilex abstract:
"Further the court held that the seller was entitled to interest accruing from when the payment was due (Arts. 59 and 78 CISG) at the statutory rate of interest in force in the seller's country (Italy). The court awarded additional interest as damages (Arts. 78 and 74 CISG)."

Journal of Law and Commerce abstract:
"The interest claim [in this case] is well-founded under CISG, Articles 59, 78, 74 ... Because of its rights under CISG, Article 78, [the seller] is entitled to interest at the legal rate of 5% pursuant to Article 1274(1) Codice Civile. The higher interest claim asserted by the [seller] is also well-founded. This follows from CISG, Article 78 [which preserves the right to damages under Article 74]. According to this provision the seller can assert larger interest claims resulting from the fact that the seller could not invest the purchase price or had to borrow funds."

4. Landgericht [LG] [District Court] Frankfurt n. 3/13 O 125/89, 2 May 1990 (F.R.G.), *at* http://www.cisg.law.pace.edu/cisg/wais/db/cases2/900502g1.html.

Original language: German
Translation: Unavailable

5. Landgericht [LG] [District Court] Hildesheim n. 11 O 116/89, 20 July 1990 (F.R.G.), *at* http://www.cisg.law.pace.edu/cisg/wais/db/cases2/900720g1.html.

Original language: German
Translation: Unavailable

6. Landgericht [LG] [District Court] Hamburg n. 5 O 543/88, 26 Sept. 1990 (F.R.G.), *at* http://www.cisg.law.pace.edu/cisg/wais/db/cases2/900926g1.html.

Original language: German
Translation: Unavailable

Unilex abstract:
"The court awarded the seller the purchase price plus interest accruing from the maturity date of the bill of exchange. As CISG does not expressly specify the rate of interest payable, the court in order to determine the rate referred to Italian law as the law of the creditor's place of business. Although the Italian statutory rate was 5%, the court awarded additional damages to the seller and the interest finally awarded was 13%, being the Italian discount rate."

CLOUT abstract:
"[I]nterest was awarded under article 78 CISG at the statutory Italian rate plus additional interest as damages under article 74 CISG assessed on the basis of the Italian discount rate."

Journal of Law and Commerce abstract:
"The amount of the interest claim under CISG, Article 78 is to be obtained from Article 1284(1) Codice Civile. According to this [provision] the Italian legal rate is 5%. Article 1284(1) Codice Civile is applicable, since the question of the amount of interest, which was intentionally left open in CISG, Article 78, has to be determined according to the applicable national as determined by the rules of conflict of laws. To the extent that the interest claim exceeds the rate of 5% awardable under CISG, Article 78, it is based on CISG, Article 74."

7. Landgericht [LG] [District Court] Bielefeld n. 15 O 201/90, 18 Jan. 1991 (F.R.G.), *at* http://www.cisg.law.pace.edu/cisg/wais/db/cases2/910118g1.html.

Original language: German
Translation: Unavailable

8. Oberlandesgericht [OLG] [Provincial Court] Frankfurt n. 5 U 261/90, 13 June 1991 (F.R.G.), *at* http://www.cisg.law.pace.edu/cisg/wais/db/cases2/910613g1.html.

Original language: German
Translation: Unavailable

CLOUT abstract:
"As regard the rate of interest, the court referred to the widely prevailing view that the law of the country of the seller (the creditor) applied, but mentioned the opposite view according to which the debtor's law should apply. The court did not take a final stand on that controversy since in the case at hand the statutory rates of interest in both laws were identical."

Journal of Law and Commerce abstract:
"Since the rate of interest was not stipulated under CISG, Article 78, according to German international private law the rate of interest on the claim for the purchase price is governed by French Law. Referring to the predominant legal opinion, the legal rate applicable to money claims at the seller's domicile determines the interest rate pursuant to CISG, Article 78... A deviating opinion is given by [the commentator] Stoll, according to whom the amount of interest has to be determined under the domestic law of the debtor. He argues that the duty to pay interest aims at preventing the debtor from deriving advantage by withholding sums due and investing the money [rather than paying the amount owed]; on the other hand, [others argue] that interest is given as compensation to the creditor, in the amount proper under the domestic law of the seller's country. The court, however, need not decide [which law determines the interest rate] because it does not affect the outcome of the case."

9. Landgericht [LG] [District Court] Frankfurt n. 3/11 O 3/91, 16 Sept. 1991 (F.R.G.), *at* http://www.cisg.law.pace.edu/cisg/wais/db/cases2/910916g1.html.

Original language: German
Translation: Available

Court (translation):
"The [seller] is the holder of a claim for payment of 5% accrued interest since 16 May 1990 and 10% accrued interest since 16 December 1991. According to Art. 78 CISG, one party can claim payment of accrued interest if the other party does not meet his obligation to pay the due and payable purchase price. It is sufficient enough that such a mature claim has not been paid at the agreed payment day. Further, it is worth noting that there is no need for a default under German law (*see* Eberstein, in: Schlechtriem, Art. 78 No. 11 CISG)... The level

of the interest rate has not been set forth in Art. 78 CISG. Consequently, the relevant obligor is to pay the interest rate which is due and payable pursuant to the relevant national substantive law of the creditor (*see* LG Stuttgart, *op. cit.*, p. 985 providing further literature references; Asam/Kindler, Indemnification of any interest and/or money devaluation damages under the CISG, RIW 1989, p. 842; Eberstein, in: Schlechtriem, Art. 78 No. 11 CISG). The [seller] does not have the right to claim any further interest under Art. 74 CISG. The [seller] has not provided evidence for his disputed assertion that he borrows money continuously at an interest rate of 15% *per annum*. It is hereby irrelevant that the [seller] demonstrated that the discount interest rate was 12.5%, respectively 13.5% in Italy. Furthermore, any agreement to a higher interest rate than what is legally owed would require a document complying with the written form (Art. 1284 Par. 3 Cc). In this case, however, the [buyer] has not provided such a document."

10. Landgericht [LG] [District Court] Baden-Baden n. 4 O 63/91, 13 Jan. 1992 (F.R.G.), *at* http://www.cisg.law.pace.edu/cisg/wais/db/cases2/920113g1.html.

    Original language: German
    Translation: Unavailable

11. Landgericht [LG] [District Court] Saarbrücken n. 9 O 4084/89, 23 Mar. 1992 (F.R.G.), *at* http://www.cisg.law.pace.edu/cisg/wais/db/cases2/920323g1.html.

    Original language: German
    Translation: Unavailable

12. Landgericht [LG] [District Court] Mönchengladbach n. 7 O 80/91, 22 May 1992 (F.R.G.), *at* http://www.cisg.law.pace.edu/cisg/wais/db/cases2/920522g1.html.

    Original language: German
    Translation: Unavailable

13. Landgericht [LG] [District Court] Heidelberg n. O 42/92 KfH I, 3 July 1992 (F.R.G.), *at* http://cisg.law.pace.edu/cisg/wais/db/cases2/920703g1.html.

    Original language: German
    Translation: Unavailable

    Unilex abstract:
    "In addition, the Court granted the seller the right to interest (Art. 78 CISG). The interest rate was determined in accordance with the law applicable by

virtue of German private international law rules. The interest accrued from the expiration of the additional period of time fixed by the seller for performance."

14. Oberlandsgericht [OLG] [Provincial Court] Hamm n. 19 U 97/91, 22 Sept.1992 (F.R.G.), *at* http://www.cisg.law.pace.edu/cisg/wais/db/cases2/920922g1.html.

    Original language: German
    Translation: Unavailable

    Unilex abstract:
    "[T]he court held that the seller was entitled to interest on the unpaid price (Art. 78 CISG). The rate of interest was determined by applying German private international law rules."

15. Landgericht [LG] [District Court] Berlin n. 99 O 123/92, 30 Sept. 1992 (F.R.G.), *at* http://www.cisg.law.pace.edu/cisg/wais/db/cases2/920930g1.html.

    Original language: German
    Translation: Unavailable

    Unilex abstract:
    "The seller recovered further damages arising from the buyer's breach of contract, including legal fees and interest paid for loans (Arts. 74 and 78 CISG)."

16. Amtsgericht [Petty District Court] Zweibrücken n. 1 C 216/92 14 Oct. 1992 (F.R.G.), *at* http://www.cisg.law.pace.edu/cisg/wais/db/cases2/921014g1.html.

    Original language: German
    Translation: Unavailable

    Unilex abstract:
    "In addition, the Court awarded the seller interest (Art. 78 CISG) and observed that under CISG the duty to pay interest for delay in payment for the price is not conditional upon formal request. The interest rate was determined in accordance with the law applicable by virtue of German private international rules."

17. Landgericht [LG] [District Court] Göttingen n. 30 100/92, 19 Nov. 1992 (F.R.G.), *at* http://www.cisg.law.pace.edu/cisg/wais/db/cases2/921119g1.html.

    Original language: German
    Translation: Unavailable

18. Landgericht [LG] [District Court] Krefeld n. 12 O 153/92, 24 Nov. 1992 (F.R.G.), *at* http://www.cisg.law.pace.edu/cisg/wais/db/cases2/921124g1.html.

Original language: German
Translation: Unavailable

19. Landgericht [LG] [District Court] Verden n. 9 O 85/92, 8 Feb. 1993 (F.R.G.), *at* http://www.cisg.law.pace.edu/cisg/wais/db/cases2/930208g1.html.

Original language: German
Translation: Unavailable

Unilex abstract:
"The Court awarded the assignee the purchase price with interest accruing from the date when payment was due (Art. 78 CISG) ... The interest rate was determined in accordance with the law applicable by virtue of German private international law rules (Italian law as the law of the seller's country)."

20. Amtsgericht [AG] [Petty District Court] Cloppenburg n. 2 C 425/92, 14 Apr. 1993, (F.R.G.), *at* http://www.cisg.law.pace.edu/cisg/wais/db/cases2/930414g1.html.

Original language: German
Translation: Unavailable

21. Landgericht [LG] [District Court] Krefeld n. 11 O 210/92, 28 Apr. 1993 (F.R.G.), *at* http://www.cisg.law.pace.edu/cisg/wais/db/cases2/930428g1.html.

Original language: German
Translation: Unavailable

22. Landgericht [LG] [District Court] München n. 15 HKO 19978/91, 24 May 1993 (F.R.G.), *at* http://www.cisg.law.pace.edu/cisg/wais/db/cases2/930524g1.html.

Original language: German
Translation: Unavailable

23. Landgericht [LG] [District Court] Aachen n. 42 O 68/93, 28 July 1993 (F.R.G.), *at* http://www.cisg.law.pace.edu/cisg/wais/db/cases2/930728g1.html.

Original language: German
Translation: Unavailable

24. Oberlandesgericht [OLG] [Provincial Court] Koblenz n. 2 U 1230/91, 17 Sept. 1993 (F.R.G.), *at* http://www.cisg.law.pace.edu/cisg/wais/db/cases2/930917g1.html.

Original language: German
Translation: Unavailable

Unilex abstract:
"The court finally found that the seller was entitled on the unpaid price (Art. 78 CISG) and that the interest rate had to be determined by applying German private international law rules which led to the application of French law as the law chosen by the parties. French statutory interest rate was held applicable. According to the court additional damages could be recovered under Art. 74 CISG."

25. Landgericht [LG] [District Court] Hamburg n. 404 O 175/92, 5 Nov. 1993 (F.R.G.), *at* http://www.cisg.law.pace.edu/cisg/wais/db/cases2/931105g1.html.

Original language: German
Translation: Unavailable

26. Landgericht [LG] [District Court] Köln n. 86 O 119/93, 11 Nov. 1993 (F.R.G.), *at* http://www.cisg.law.pace.edu/cisg/wais/db/cases2/931111g1.html.

Original language: German
Translation: Unavailable

27. Landgericht [LG] [District Court] Memmingen n. 2 H O 1434/92,1 Dec. 1993 (F.R.G.), *at* http://www.cisg.law.pace.edu/cisg/wais/db/cases2/931201g2.html.

Original language: German
Translation: Unavailable

Unilex abstract:
"Finally, the Court held that the seller was entitled to interest and to further damages according to Arts. 78 and 74 CISG. The Court left open the question of the determination of the applicable interest rate but awarded interest at the rate reported on a bank certificate submitted by the seller."

28. Oberlandesgericht [OLG] [Provincial Court] Düsseldorf n. 17 U 146/93, 14 Jan. 1994 (F.R.G.), *at* http://www.cisg.law.pace.edu/cisg/wais/db/cases2/940114g1.html.

Original language: German
Translation: Available

29. Oberlandesgericht [OLG] [Provincial Court] Frankfurt n. 5 U 15/93, 18 Jan. 1994 (F.R.G.), *at* http://www.cisg.law.pace.edu/cisg/wais/db/cases2/940118g1.html.

Original language: German
Translation: Available

Court (translation):
"The interest claim is well-founded only to the extent of 10%. The claim is justified on grounds of CISG, Article 78. Pursuant to this article, the contracting party in default either as to payment of the purchase price or any other amount due has to pay interest rates for the sum owing (von Caemmerer-Eberstein, Article 78, Rn. 9, 10; Herber/Czerwenka, Article 78, Rn. 3; Asam RIW1989, 942, 945)... Since the amount of recoverable interest has been left unregulated in CISG, Article 78 (as opposed to EKG [ULIS] Article 83), according to the predominant legal opinion, pursuant to German international private law, the domestic German Law is applicable (see comments in Senat, Urt. v. 13. Juni 1991 – 5 U 261/90 – NJW 1991, 3102). In the case before the court, pursuant to Article 28(2) EGBGB, Italian law is applicable to the claim for the purchase price and it also governs the accompanying interest claim. According to the isolated deviating opinion by Stoll (Festschrift für Ferid, 1988, 495, 509f.; similar: von Caemmerer-Leser, Article 84, Rn. 13 on the obligation to pay interest under CISG Article 84(1)), the legal rate [of interest] has to be determined by the domestic sales law of the debtor. Whether or not Stoll's opinion has to be followed did not have to be decided in the [previous] ruling of this court rendered on June 13, 1991, because in that case the [seller] at the very beginning limited her interest claim to 5%, a rate that is justified both under German and under French Law. In this case, however, the court has to decide according to the prevailing legal opinion. Since the amount of interest intentionally is not prescribed in the Convention, the answer can only be taken from the rules of international private law. Absent any point of reference, no principle can be derived from the Convention such as saying that the domicile of the debtor would be decisive, because the duty to pay interest was aimed at preventing the withholding of money from being advantageous to the debtor (Stoll as referred to above [Festschrift für Ferid, *supra*]) who still has the possibility to use or invest the funds as compared to payment. Furthermore, this argument is not persuasive, since it is not guaranteed that the domestic legal rate [of interest] fully compensates for (see § 352 HGB) the advantage of non-payment and any other calculation of interest would erase the dividing line [between interest and] damages. The

practical disadvantage of eventually being obliged to investigate foreign law to calculate the interest has to be accepted because of the partial incompleteness of the Convention arising from unsettled disputes during the negotiation process (Herber/Czerwenka, Article 78, Rn. 1). Besides, disadvantage can be diminished by the availability of adequate charts (Piltz, § 5, Rn.415)... The [seller's] claim for default interest at an amount of 13.5% could not be awarded. CISG, Article 78 does not bar a claim for damages under CISG, Article 74 to recover additional loss resulting from finance charges (Herber/Czerwenka, Article 78, Rn. 8). However, the [seller] has no shown evidence of any further loss caused by using credit (as to the burden of proof: von Caemmerer-Stoll, Article 74, Rn. 41). The submitted certificates issued by the Banca d'ltalia only refer to the discount [rate] fluctuations."

30. Kammergericht [KG] [Upper Court Berlin] n. 2 U 7418/92, 24 Jan. 1994 (F.R.G.), *at* http://www.cisg.law.pace.edu/cisg/wais/db/cases2/940124g1.html.

Original language: German
Translation: Available

Court (translation):
"To the extent stated in the decision's tenor, the [seller]'s assignee may claim interest on the purchase price as compensation under Arts. 78 and 74 CISG, from the time payment was due according to Art. 58 CISG. A payment notice was not necessary for this claim to arise. According to the parties' agreement, the purchase price was due sixty days after the date on which the invoice was issued. The interest rate is determined by the national law and its prerequisites (*cf.* v.Caemmerer/Schlechtriem/Eberstein, Art. 78 n. 111 and Asam/Kindler, *op. cit.*). It follows from the bank certificate that [seller]'s assignee had to pay interest on the amount stated in the decision."

31. Landgericht [LG] [District Court] Düsseldorf n. 6 U 32/93' 10 Feb. 1994 (F.R.G.), *at* http://www.cisg.law.pace.edu/cisg/wais/db/cases2/940210g1.html.

Original language: German
Translation: Available

Court (translation):
"Within the scope of the main claim, to which the [seller] is entitled, it is at any rate entitled, under CISG Art. 78, to interest for the asserted period of time. In this regard, the interest rate is calculated under French law, which, according to the contract and EGBGB Arts. 28(1) and (2), applies to the contract at issue."

32. Landgericht [LG] [District Court] Düsseldorf n. 6 U 119/93, 10 Feb 1994 (F.R.G.), *at* http://www.cisg.law.pace.edu/cisg/wais/db/cases2/940210g2.html.

Original language: German
Translation: Available

Court (translation):
"The interest granted by the District Court at a rate of 5% from 27 November 1992 (date of service of the claim), the amount of which is not disputed by the [buyer], is founded under Art. 78 CISG in connection with § 352 HGB and § 291 BGB. Under Art. 78 CISG, if the buyer fails to pay the purchase price, the seller is entitled to interest on it. The interest rate is not provided for in the Convention, but is to be settled in conformity with the law applicable by virtue of the rules of private international law (*cf.* v.Caemmerer/Schlechtriem, CISG-Kommentar, Munich 1990, Art. 78 n. 3). As both parties rely on German law for the legal dispute, they have formed an implicit agreement on the applicability of German law (Art. 27(1) sent. 2 EGBGB). The [buyer] is therefore obliged to render the commercial interest rate of 5% from the time of the service of the claim (§ 352 HGB, § 291 BGB). The result would not be any different if – due to a lack of choice of law – Italian law was to apply to the sales contract following Art. 28(1) and (2) EGBGB. According to Art. 1282, 1284(1) CC the legal interest rate for sums in arrears is also 5%."

33. Oberlandesgericht [OLG] [Provincial Court] München n. 7 U 4419/93, 2 Mar. 1994 (F.R.G.), *at* http://www.cisg.law.pace.edu/cisg/wais/db/cases2/940302g1.html.

Original language: German
Translation: Available

Court (translation):
"The claim for interest is based on Art. 78 CISG, since the [buyer] failed to pay the purchase price due under Art. 58 CISG. Following Art. 28(2) sent. 1 EGBGB, the rate of interest is determined by Swedish law, as the [seller]'s obligation is the one characteristic of a sales contract. Under Swedish law, the [seller] is entitled to interest at a rate of 8% on top of the discount rate of the Swedish State bank, par. 6 Räntelag (1975: 635) (*cf.* Högland, Sveriges Rikes Lag, date: 1 January 1991, p. 530/531). There, a surcharge ("*tillägg*", *cf.* Parsenow, Fachwörterbuch für Recht und Wirtschaft Schwedisch/Deutsch Deutsch/Schwedish, 2nd ed., p. 168) of 8% ("*atta*", *cf.* Kornitzky, Taschen-wörterbuch Schwedisch/Deutsch, 1958, p. 521) is fixed. Therefore, the lower interest rate referred to in the literature (*cf.* Fischler/Vogel, Schwedisches

Handels- und Wirtschaftsrecht mit Verfahrensrecht, 3rd ed. 1978, p. 94) is incorrect."

34. Oberlandesgericht [OLG] [Provincial Court] Frankfurt n. 13 U 51/93, 20 Apr. 1994 (F.R.G.), *at* http://www.cisg.law.pace.edu/cisg/wais/db/cases2/940420g1.html.

Original language:	German
Translation:	Unavailable

CLOUT abstract:
"The appellate court ordered the [buyer] to pay the purchase price (CISG 78) and interest at the rate of 5%, which is the statutory interest rate under both German and Swiss law."

35. Landgericht [LG] [District Court] Giessen n. 6 O 85/93, 5 July 1994 (F.R.G.), *at* http://www.cisg.law.pace.edu/cisg/wais/db/cases2/940705g1.html.

Original language:	German
Translation:	Unavailable

Unilex abstract:
"In addition, the seller was entitled to interest, according to Art. 78 CISG. The rate of interest was determined by applying German private international law rules, which led to the Italian statutory interest rate."

36. Amtsgericht [AG] [Petty District Court] Nordhorn n. 3 C 75/94, 14 June 1994 (F.R.G.), *at* http://www.cisg.law.pace.edu/cisg/wais/db/cases2/940614g1.html.

Original language:	German
Translation:	Available

Court (translation):
"The [seller]'s claim for interest is justified under Art. 78 CISG. According to that provision, interest is due from the time the claim was mature; a reminder of payment is not necessary. Consequently, it would have been up to the [buyer] to submit that the parties reached a different agreement regarding the payment of interest. As the [buyer] failed to make an according submission, the interest was granted according to the [seller]'s request. The legal interest rate in Italy is 10% pursuant to Art. 1284 Codice civile."

37. Landgericht [LG] [District Court] Kassel n. 11 O 4279/94, 14 July 1994 (F.R.G.), *at* http://www.cisg.law.pace.edu/cisg/wais/db/cases2/940714g1.html.

Original language: German
Translation: Unavailable

38. Landgericht [LG] [District Court] Düsseldorf n. 31 O 27/92, 25 Aug. 1994 (F.R.G.), *at* http://www.cisg.law.pace.edu/cisg/wais/db/cases2/940825g1.html.

Original language: German
Translation: Unavailable

Unilex abstract:
"The Court stated that the seller was entitled to interest on the price. As CISG does not determine the rate of interest the Court held that the rate was to be determined in accordance with the law otherwise applicable to the contract."

39. Amtsgericht [AG] [Petty District Court] Riedlingen n. 2 C 395/93, 21 Oct. 1994 (F.R.G.), *at* =http://www.cisg.law.pace.edu/cisg/wais/db/cases2/941021 g1.html.

Original language: German
Translation: Available

Court (translation):
"The claim for interest is based on Art. 78 CISG in connection with Art. 1284 I Codice Civile (Italian Civil Code). The higher rate of interest requested by the [seller] has been disputed by the [buyer], and the [seller] did not render any proof of the higher rate of interest."

40. Landgericht [LG] [District Court] Darmstadt n. 18 O 848/92, 25 Oct. 1994 (F.R.G.), *at* http://www.cisg.law.pace.edu/cisg/wais/db/cases2/941025g1.html.

Original language: German
Translation: Unavailable

Unilex abstract:
"As to the interest the court held that the seller was entitled to interests. Since CISG does not determine the rate of interest the court stated that the rate was to be determined in accordance with the domestic law applicable in the seller's country."

41. Landgericht [LG] [District Court] Oldenburg n. 12 O 674/93, 9 Nov. 1994 (F.R.G.), *at* http://www.cisg.law.pace.edu/cisg/wais/db/cases2/941109g1.html.

Original language: German
Translation: Available

Court (translation):
"The [seller] is entitled to interest under Art. 78 CISG. As the CISG does not regulate the interest rate, reference is to be made to the national law to be determined by the EGBGB (OLG Frankfurt, NJW 94, 1013; *Schwenzer*, NJW 90, 602, 606 *et seq.*). In this case, with an Italian seller, Italian law applies… The [seller] has not shown that it suffered losses higher than the legal interest rate of 10% that applies in this case."

42. Oberlandesgericht [OLG] [Provincial Court] Hamm n. 11 U 206/93, 8 Feb. 1995 (F.R.G.), *at* http://www.cisg.law.pace.edu/cisg/wais/db/cases2/950208g3.html.

Original language: German
Translation: Unavailable

CLOUT abstract:
"The court also awarded 10% interest on the sum to be paid by the [buyer] (art. 78 CISG). As the CISG does not provide for a specific interest rate, the court took recourse to the governing contract law … The requested interest at the rate of 14% could have been recovered under article 74 CISG only if the [seller's assignee] had not failed to prove the higher interest damage."

Unilex abstract:
"The Court held that the bank was entitled to recover interest on price, according to Art. 78 CISG. The Court further held that, as CISG does not determine the interest rate, the bank was entitled, according to German rules of private international law."

43. Landgericht [LG] [District Court] München n. 8 HKO 24667/93, 8 Feb. 1995 (F.R.G.), *at* http://www.cisg.law.pace.edu/cisg/wais/db/cases2/950208g4.html.

Original language: German
Translation: Available

Court (translation):
"The [seller's] claim is admissible and successful. The adjudicated main amount is owed to the [seller] as the contractually agreed upon price for the sale and use of the *Graphiplus* software programme. Additionally, the [seller] is entitled to the requested interest on the amount after the date of maturity (Art. 78 CISG, § 352 HGB)."

44. Landgericht [LG] [District Court] Oldenburg n. VIII ZR 18/94, 15 Feb. 1995 (F.R.G.), *at* http://www.cisg.law.pace.edu/cisg/wais/db/cases2/950215g1.html.

Original language:	German
Translation:	Unavailable

Unilex abstract:
"The Court finally awarded interest to the seller pursuant to Art. 78 CISG. As CISG does not indicate the interest rate, the Court referred to German private international law rules to ascertain the applicable law for the determination of the interest rate."

45. Amtsgericht [AG] [Petty District Court] Wangen n. 2 C 600/94, 8 Mar. 1995 (F.R.G.), *at* http://www.cisg.law.pace.edu/cisg/wais/db/cases2/950308g2.html.

Original language:	German
Translation:	Unavailable

Unilex abstract:
"The Court argued that ... interest was payable according to Art. 78 CISG. In determining the applicable rate of interest the Court awarded a rate of 10% as the statutory rate usually adopted in the seller's country for unsecured bank loans. According to the Court, the seller was not entitled to the higher interest rate of 16,5 as further damages, since it should have applied for obtaining a bank loan at the average market rate."

46. Landgericht [LG] [District Court] München n. 10 HKO 23750/94, 20 Mar. 1995 (F.R.G.), *at* http://www.cisg.law.pace.edu/cisg/wais/db/cases2/950320g1.html.

Original language:	German
Translation:	Available

Court (translation):
"The [seller] is entitled to interest for the mature claims for payment of the purchase price without having to send a reminder of payment, Art. 78 CISG. Since the [seller] did not prove the (contested) rate of interest by submitting a confirmation of his bank, [seller] is only granted 10% interest under Art. 1284(1) C.c. Italian law must also be applied in this respect to fill a gap in the Convention."

47. Landgericht [LG] [District Court] Landshut n. 54 O 644/94, 5 Apr. 1995 (F.R.G.), *at* http://www.cisg.law.pace.edu/cisg/wais/db/cases2/950405g1.html.

Original language: German
Translation: Available

Court (translation):
"The [buyer's] claim for interest is based on Art. 84(1) CISG. The purchase price was paid in the year 1993; therefore, the claim for interest exists since 25 January 1994. The rate of interest is not regulated by Art. 84 CISG. Also, in Art. 78 CISG no mention is made of the rate of interest. According to the prevailing opinion, the rate of interest within the scope of Art. 78 CISG is governed by the applicable national law, which is determined by the rules of private international law. This notion is also applicable to Art. 84 CISG. Thus, the applicable law of the contract needs to be is determined in accordance with Art. 27 *et seq*. EGBGB. According to Arts. 32(1) no. 3 and 27(1) EGBGB, the parties can choose the applicable law. By both parties pleading the provisions of the BGB from the beginning, they have chosen German law. This contract regarding the choice of law has been validly concluded under Art. 27(4) EGBGB. Thus, the provisions of the German law apply. The rate of 11.5% interest was disputed. As the [buyer] has not proven [the interest rate], the legal provisions apply. According to § 352 I HGB, the legal interest rate is 5% for mutual commercial transactions. Both [buyer] and [seller] are merchants in accordance with § 1 II no. 1 HGB. The conclusion of the sales contract at issue is part of the commercial business of both parties, § 343 HGB. Thus, the rate of interest is 5%... The [buyer's] claim for interest is provided basically by Art. 78 CISG. According to the prevailing opinion, Art. 78 CISG also applies to claims for damages (*cf*. von Caemmerer/Schlechtriem – Eberstein/Bacher, Kommentar zum einheitlichen UN-Kaufrecht, Art. 78, Annotation 15). The claim comes into existence with the occurrence of the loss. On 25 January 1994, the asserted loss had already occurred. The interest rate of 5% is applicable, as already stated above, from § 352 I, sentence 1, HGB."

48. Amtsgericht [AG] [Petty District Court] Bayreuth n. 8 C 348/95, 2 May 1995 (F.R.G.), *at* http://www.cisg.law.pace.edu/cisg/wais/db/cases2/950502g3.html.

Original language: German
Translation: Unavailable

49. Amtsgericht [AG] [Petty District Court] Alsfeld n. 31 C 534/94, 12 May 1995 (F.R.G.), *at* http://www.cisg.law.pace.edu/cisg/wais/db/cases2/950512g1.html.

Original language: German
Translation: Unavailable

Unilex abstract:
"The seller was awarded interest on the price (Art. 78 CISG). As to the applicable interest rate, the Court considered this to be a question governed by the CISG but not expressly settled in it (Art. 7(2) CISG). According to German private international law rules it applied the Italian statutory rate, being Italian law otherwise applicable to the contract. A higher interest rate as further damages was not awarded since the seller did not provide sufficient evidence of recourse to bank loans."

50. Landgericht [LG] [District Court] München n. 21 O 23363/94, 29 May 1995 (F.R.G.), *at* http://www.cisg.law.pace.edu/cisg/wais/db/cases2/950529g1.html.

Original language: German
Translation: Unavailable

51. Landgericht [LG] [District Court] Kassel n. 8 O 2391/93, 22 June 1995 (F.R.G.), *at* http://www.cisg.law.pace.edu/cisg/wais/db/cases2/950622g1.html.

Original language: German
Translation: Unavailable

Unilex abstract:
"The Court finally held that interest was payable according to Art. 78 CISG. Absent an express provision in CISG, the Court held that the interest rate was to be determined in accordance with the law otherwise applicable to the contract and not with the law of the creditor's country."

52. Oberlandesgericht [OLG] [Provincial Court] München n. 27 U 798/94, 28 June 1995 (F.R.G.), *at* http://www.cisg.law.pace.edu/cisg/wais/db/cases2/950628g1.html.

Original language: German
Translation: Unavailable

53. Oberlandesgericht [OLG] [Provincial Court] Frankfurt n. 9 U 81/94, 5 July 1995 (F.R.G.), *at* http://www.cisg.law.pace.edu/cisg/wais/db/cases2/950705g1.html.

Original language: German
Translation: Available

Court (translation):
"The decision on interest falls under Art. 78 CISG; other issues fall under §§ 97, 708 No. 10, 713, 546(2) ZPO old version"

54. Landgericht [LG] [District Court] Aachen n. 41 O 111/95, 20 July 1995 (F.R.G.), *at* http://www.cisg.law.pace.edu/cisg/wais/db/cases2/950720g1.html.

Original language: German
Translation: Available

Court (translation):
"In Art. 78 CISG there is a regulation for interest. This provision is applicable in principle, as Art. 4, sentence 1, CISG stipulates that the Convention governs all rights and obligations of the seller and the buyer arising from the contract of sale. This provision [Art. 78 CISG] provides only for an obligation to pay interest. This norm does not say anything about the interest rate to be paid. Thus there is a gap in the law; there is dispute about how to fill it. It has been argued that the interest rate must be determined by having recourse to the general principles of the CISG in order to achieve an internationally uniform regulation (*cf.* Eberstein/Bacher in von Caemmerer/Schlechtriem, Kommentar zum einheitlichen UN-Kaufrecht, 2nd ed., Art. 78, Annotation 21, Footnote 30). Against this, it has been argued that a uniform solution could not be achieved at the conferences for the drafting of the CISG, as the different opinions about the interest obligation were irreconcilable (*cf. op. cit.*, Annotation 2). Preferable is the opinion that the interest rate is to be taken from the applicable national law supplementing the CISG, which in turn is to be determined in accordance with the conflict of laws rules of the forum State (*cf. op. cit.*, Annotation 21, Footnote 31). According to German private international law, the interest rate is determined – even though this is not undisputed (*cf.* Palandt/Heldrich, BGB, 54th ed., Art. 32 EGBGB, Annotation 5) – according to the law governing of the contract; thus, according to the law which would be applicable to the sales contract if the contract were not subject to the Convention. According to Art. 28 EGBGB, the law of the State which has had the closest connection with the contract would have to be applied (Art. 28 I 1 EGBGB). Thereby one has to look to the characteristic performances under the contract (*cf.* Art. 28 II 1 EGBGB, respectively Art. 4 II EVU). With contracts of sales, therefore, the law of the State where the seller has its main place of business is applicable (*cf.* Palandt-Heldrich, *op. cit.*, Art. 28 EGBGB, Annotation 8). Thus, Italian law applies to the interest rate. In Italian law – insofar equivalent to the German regulation – there is a distinction between the legal interest rate and an interest rate based on damages caused by delay. Since under Art. 1284 I Codice Civile (Italian Civil Code) the legal interest rate is already 10%, there is no objection to the requested interest rate in the present case. The point in time from which interest is owed is derived from Art. 78 CISG. According to this provision, the maturity of the obligation to pay the price or any other sum in arrears is sufficient for the right to request interest. A default must not be present (*cf.* Eberstein/Bacher, *op. cit.*, Annotation 9 to Art. 78). The pre-trial costs have

to be reimbursed under Art. 78 CISG in connection with Arts. 74, 61(1)(b) CISG."

55. Oberlandesgericht [OLG] [Provincial Court] Rostock n. 1 U 247/94, 27 July 1995 (F.R.G.), *at* http://www.cisg.law.pace.edu/cisg/wais/db/cases2/950727g1.html.

Original language: German
Translation: Available

Court (translation):
"In accordance with Art. 78 CISG, the [seller] can request from the [buyer] the payment of 7% interest on the purchase price debt since 1 December 1992. The only prerequisite for the obligation to pay interest is that the purchase price is due (*cf.* von Caemmerer/Schlechtriem/Eberstein/Bacher, op. cit., Art. 78, Annotation 9). According to Art. 58(1) CISG, the purchase price in the amount of DM 10,146.99 became due not later than 1 December 1992. Due to the absence of a different regulation in the CISG, the interest rate is regulated by the national law to which the rules of the private international law refer (*cf.* von Caemmerer/Schlechtriem/Eberstein/Bacher, op. cit., Art. 78, Annotations 26, 27). According to Art. 32(1) (No. 3) EGBGB, Danish law has to be applied. Under this law, the interest rate while in default amounts to 6% p.a. above the respective discount rate of the Danish National Bank (§§ 3, 5 Renteloven [Law on Interest]). The [seller] has not stated how high the discount rate of the Danish National Bank has been since 1 December 1992. The [seller] also did not prove that the claimed default damage of 12% occurred. The Court estimates that the discount rate of the Danish National Bank was at least 1%, so that a unified interest rate of 7%."

56. Landgericht [LG] [District Court] Kassel n. 11 O 4261/94, 21 Sept. 1995 (F.R.G.), *at* http://www.cisg.law.pace.edu/cisg/wais/db/cases2/950921g1.html.

Original language: German
Translation: Unavailable

57. Amtsgericht [AG] [Petty District Court] Kehl n. 3 C 925/93, 6 Oct. 1995 (F.R.G.), *at* http://www.cisg.law.pace.edu/cisg/wais/db/cases2/951006g1.html.

Original language: German
Translation: Available

Court (translation):
"The claim for interest is legitimate pursuant to Art. 78 CISG. According to

this provision, the party that fails to pay the price or any other sum in arrears shall pay the other party [at maturity] interest on these amounts. Pursuant to Arts. 58, 59 CISG, the purchase price for the sweaters delivered on 8 December 1992 became due prior to the date from which the [seller] requests interest (9 January 1993). Since Art. 78 CISG does not provide for an interest rate, the matter is to be settled in conformity with the law applicable by virtue of the rules of German private international law (*see* OLG Frankfurt a. M., NJW (1994) 1013 at 1014) ... Therefore, Italian law governs the obligation to pay the purchase price under Art. 28(2) EGBGB, and it also applies to the accompanying claim for interest. Pursuant to Article 1284 Cc, the interest rate is 10% since 16 December 1990 (*see* OLG Frankfurt a. M., NJW (1994) 1013 at 1014)."

58. Landgericht [LG] [District Court] Trier n. 7 HO 78/95, 12 Oct. 1995 (F.R.G.), *at* http://www.cisg.law.pace.edu/cisg/wais/db/cases2/951012g1.html.

    Original language: German
    Translation: Available

59. Landgericht [LG] [District Court] Krefeld n. 12 O 160/93, 19 Dec. 1995 (F.R.G.), *at* http://www.cisg.law.pace.edu/cisg/wais/db/cases2/951219g1.html.

    Original language: German
    Translation: Unavailable

60. Landgericht [LG] [District Court] Bochum n. 13 O 142/95, 24 Jan. 1996 (F.R.G.), *at* http://www.cisg.law.pace.edu/cisg/wais/db/cases2/960124g1.html.

    Original language: German
    Translation: Available

61. Amtsgericht [AG] [Petty District Court] Augsburg n. 11 C 4004/95, 29 Jan. 1996 (F.R.G.), *at* http://www.cisg.law.pace.edu/cisg/wais/db/cases2/960129g1.html.

    Original language: German
    Translation: Available

    Unilex abstract:
    "The Court held that the seller was entitled to interest on the purchase price accruing from the dates on which the different payments were due (Arts. 59 and 78 CISG)... With respect to the interest rate, the Court held that it was to be determined by the domestic law otherwise governing the contract. Thus,

German private international private law rules led to the application of the Swiss statutory interest rate, Swiss law being the law of the seller's place of business."

62. Landgericht [LG] [District Court] Kassel n. 11 O 4185/95, 15 Feb. 1996 (F.R.G.), *at* http://www.cisg.law.pace.edu/cisg/wais/db/cases2/960215g1.html.

Original language: German
Translation: Unavailable

63. Landgericht [LG] [District Court] Kassel n. 11 O 4187/95, 15 Feb. 1996 (F.R.G.), *at* http://www.cisg.law.pace.edu/cisg/wais/db/cases2/960215g2.html.

Original language: German
Translation: Unavailable

64. Landgericht [LG] [District Court] Oldenburg n. 12 O 2943/94, 8 Feb. 1996 (F.R.G.), *at* http://www.cisg.law.pace.edu/cisg/wais/db/cases2/960228g1.html.

Original language: German
Translation: Unavailable

Unilex abstract:
"The Court also stated that the buyer was entitled to interest at the German statutory rate (Art. 78 CISG), being German law applicable by virtue of the German of choice of law rules."

65. Landgericht [LG] [District Court] Düsseldorf n. 36 O 178/95, 5 Mar. 1996 (F.R.G.), *at* http://www.cisg.law.pace.edu/cisg/wais/db/cases2/960305g1.html.

Original language: German
Translation: Unavailable

Unilex database:
"The seller was finally awarded the purchase price and interest according to Art. 78 CISG at the rate of 16.5%, as it had proved it had recourse as its place of business to a bank loan in Italian Lire at this rate of interest."

66. Oberlandesgericht [OLG] [Provincial Court] Frankfurt n. 25 U 187/95, 15 Mar. 1996 (F.R.G.), *at* http://www.cisg.law.pace.edu/cisg/wais/db/cases2/960315g2.html.

Original language: German
Translation: Unavailable

67. Schiedsgericht der Handelskammer [Arbitral Tribunal Hamburg], 21 Mar. 1996 (F.R.G.), *at* http://www.cisg.law.pace.edu/cisg/wais/db/cases2/960321g1.html.

Original language: German
Translation: Available

Arbitral Tribunal (translation):
"The claim to interest arises *ex* Art. 78 CISG. As to the interest rate, national law applies subsidiarly, in the absence of a more specific regulation [page 42] in the CISG, according to its Art 7(2); here, it is the legal rate for bilateral commercial transactions"

68. Landgericht [LG] [District Court] Oldenburg n. 12 O 2541/95, 27 Mar. 1996 (F.R.G.), *at* http://www.cisg.law.pace.edu/cisg/wais/db/cases2/960327g1.html.

Original language: German
Translation: Unavailable

Unilex abstract:
"The seller was thus awarded the contract price (Art. 53 CISG) as well as interest at the Italian statutory rate (Art. 78 CISG), since it had not given evidence of the claimed higher rate of interest."

69. Landgericht [LG] [District Court] Hamburg n. 417 O 165/95, 17 June 1996 (F.R.G.), *at* http://www.cisg.law.pace.edu/cisg/wais/db/cases2/960617g1.html.

Original language: German
Translation: Unavailable

70. Amtsgericht [AG] [Petty District Court] Bottrop n. 12 C 177/96, 25 June 1996 (F.R.G.), *at* http://www.cisg.law.pace.edu/cisg/wais/db/cases2/960625g2.html.

Original language: German
Translation: Unavailable

Unilex (abstract):
"The Court held that the seller was entitled to interest according to Art. 78 CISG, accruing from the date on which the payment was due according to the invoice. Since CISG does not determine the interest rate, the Court applied the Italian statutory interest rate (10%), observing that Italian law was the law

otherwise applicable to the contract. The seller was also granted a higher interest rate of 16,5% as further damages as it had proved a causal connection between its recourse to bank loans and the buyer's late payment."

71. Oberlandesgericht [OLG] [Provincial Court] Düsseldorf n. 6 U 152/95, 15 July 1996 (F.R.G.), *at* http://www.cisg.law.pace.edu/cisg/wais/db/cases2/960711g1.html.

Original language: German
Translation: Unavailable

72. Landgericht [LG] [District Court] Bielefeld n. 12 O 120/95, 2 Aug. 1996 (F.R.G.), *at* http://www.cisg.law.pace.edu/cisg/wais/db/cases2/960802g1.html.

Original language: German
Translation: Available

Court (translation):
"The claim for interest on the purchase price is based on Art. 78 CISG. The interest rate is 5% according to § 352 HGB."

73. Amtsgericht [AG] [Petty District Court] Koblenz n. 16 C 1056/96, 12 Nov. 1996 (F.R.G.), *at* http://www.cisg.law.pace.edu/cisg/wais/db/cases2/961112g1.html.

Original language: German
Translation: Available

Court (translation):
"Contrary to German law, the only prerequisite for a claim for interest under Art. 78 CISG is the maturity of the sum in arrears. Because Article 78 does not define the applicable rate of interest, Article 28 EGBGB leads to the application of Italian law. According to Article 128 of the Italian Civil Code, the statutory interest rate starting from 16 December 1990 is 10%. Nevertheless, the [seller] is entitled to the higher interest rate of 16.5% he requested. Article 78 does not exclude the possibility to demand reimbursement under Art. 74 CISG for losses suffered through a bank credit at a higher rate than the statutory interest rate. In the parallel proceeding before the AG Bottrop [Germany], the [seller] submitted a bank certificate which proves that he is taking credit from his house bank in amounts exceeding the purchase price at an interest rate of at least 16.5%". The [seller] is therefore entitled to interest at the rate of 16.5%."

74. Landgericht [LG] [District Court] München n. 14 HKO 3315/96, 9 Dec. 1996 (F.R.G.), *at* http://www.cisg.law.pace.edu/cisg/wais/db/cases2/961209g1.html.

Original language: German
Translation: Unavailable

75. Landgericht [LG] [District Court] Bielefeld n. 6 O 307/96, 12 Dec. 1996 (F.R.G.), *at* http://www.cisg.law.pace.edu/cisg/wais/db/cases2/961212g1.html.

Original language: German
Translation: Unavailable

76. Oberlandesgericht [OLG] [Provincial Court] Köln n. 27 U 58/96, 8 Jan. 1997 (F.R.G.), *at* http://www.cisg.law.pace.edu/cisg/wais/db/cases2/970108g1.html.

Original language: German
Translation: Available

Court (translation):
"The [buyer] is entitled to interest granted at a rate of 5% since the time the counterclaim was served, independent of the question whether the interest rate is to be determined under German law (§ 352 HGB) or under Dutch law – which provides a higher rate of interest following the [seller]'s own submissions."

77. Oberlandesgericht [OLG] [Provincial Court] Koblenz n. 2 U 31/96, 31 Jan. 1997 (F.R.G.), *at* http://www.cisg.law.pace.edu/cisg/wais/db/cases2/970131g1.html.

Original language: German
Translation: Unavailable

78. Amtsgericht [AG] [Petty District Court] Berlin-Tiergarten n. 2 C 22/97, 13 Mar. 1997 (F.R.G.), *at* http://www.cisg.law.pace.edu/cisg/wais/db/cases2/970313g1.html.

Original language: German
Translation: Unavailable

79. Oberlandesgericht [OLG] [Provincial Court] Düsseldorf n. 6 U 87/96, 24 Apr. 1997 (F.R.G.), *at* http://www.cisg.law.pace.edu/cisg/wais/db/cases2/970424g1.html.

Original language: German
Translation: Unavailable

Unilex database:
"The seller was finally awarded the purchase price and interest according to Art. 78 CISG. Contrary to the Court of first instance, the appellate Court held that the seller had not proved it had taken out on at its place of business a bank loan in Italian Lire at a 16,5% rate of interest. Since CISG does not determine the interest rate, the Court applied Italian law as the law otherwise applicable to the contract. It therefore awarded the statutory rate of 10%."

CLOUT abstract:
"The seller was entitled to interest according to article 78 of the CISG, and, using the rules of private international law, the court applied Italian law to determine the rate of interest."

80. Landgericht [LG] [District Court] München n. 11 HKO 5713/97, 23 June 1997 (F.R.G.), *at* http://www.cisg.law.pace.edu/cisg/wais/db/cases2/970623g1.html.

Original language: German
Translation: Unavailable

81. Oberlandesgericht [OLG] [Provincial Court] München n. 7 U 2070/97, 9 July 1997 (F.R.G.), *at* http://www.cisg.law.pace.edu/cisg/wais/db/cases2/970709g1.html.

Original language: German
Translation: Available

Court (translation):
"The [seller]'s claim of interest follows from Art. 78 CISG in connection with Section 352 HGB"

82. Oberlandesgericht [OLG] [Provincial Court] München n. 7 U 2246/97, 9 July 1997 (F.R.G.), *at* http://www.cisg.law.pace.edu/cisg/wais/db/cases2/970709g2.html.

Original language: German
Translation: Unavailable

83. Landgericht [LG] [District Court] Saarbrücken n. 7 III O 25/96, 18 July 1997 (F.R.G.), *at* http://www.cisg.law.pace.edu/cisg/wais/db/cases2/970718g1.html.

Original language: German
Translation: Unavailable

84. Landgericht [LG] [District Court] Göttingen n. 3 O 198/96, 31 July 1997 (F.R.G.), *at* http://www.cisg.law.pace.edu/cisg/wais/db/cases2/970731g1.html.

Original language: German
Translation: Unavailable

85. Landgericht [LG] [District Court] Hagen n. 22 O 90/97, 15 Oct. 1997 (F.R.G.), *at* http://www.cisg.law.pace.edu/cisg/wais/db/cases2/971015g1.html.

Original language: German
Translation: Available

Court (translation):
"According to Article 78 CISG, interest should be paid from the date of accrual, at an interest rate of 10%, as provided in the applicable Italian law (Articles 28(1) and (2) EGBGB, Article 1284(1) C.C.). [Seller] did not request payment of additional damages (Article 74 CISG)."

86. Oberlandesgericht [OLG] [Provincial Court] Hamm n. 11 U 41/97, 5 Nov. 1997 (F.R.G.), *at* http://www.cisg.law.pace.edu/cisg/wais/db/cases2/971105g1.html.

Original language: German
Translation: Available

Court (translation):
"Seller's claim for the payment of the purchase price is based upon Art. 53 CISG; [seller's] claim for interest is based upon Art. 78 CISG... The CISG does not fix the applicable interest rate. According to unanimous opinion and the case law of this Court (*cf.* IPRax 1996, 197), the interest rate is to be settled in conformity with the law applicable by virtue of the rules of private international law. Therefore, the interest rate is to be determined under Italian law, because the seller's performance is the characteristic performance of a sales contract... Under Italian law, the legal interest rate has been at 10% since 16 December 1990 (*cf.* Piltz, NJW 1996, 2768, 2772; Kindler, IPRax 1996, 16, 21). The [seller] does not seek a higher rate. The [buyer] did not object to the dates from which the [seller] requests interest."

87. Oberlandesgericht [OLG] [Provincial Court] München n. 7 U 3771/97, 28 Jan. 1998 (F.R.G.), *at* http://www.cisg.law.pace.edu/cisg/wais/db/cases2/980128g1.html.

Original language: German
Translation: Available

Court (translation):
"The law governing the contract is the CISG and, on matters not settled by the Convention, Italian law, as the [seller's] performance was to characterize the contract (*cf.* Art. 32(1) no. 4 and Art. 28 no. 2 EGBGB)... The [seller] is entitled to interest on the remainder of the purchase price... The interest rate follows from Art. 1284 cc."

88. Oberlandesgericht [OLG] [Provincial Court] München n. 11 Mar. 1998 (F.R.G.), *at* http://www.cisg.law.pace.edu/cisg/wais/db/cases2/980311g1.html.

Original language: German
Translation: Available

Court (translation):
"The claim for interest is justified only for a rate of 5% according to §§ 352, 353 HGB, because German law is the applicable law supplementing the CISG."

89. Landgericht [LG] [District Court] Berlin n. 102 O 59/97, 24 Mar. 1998 (F.R.G.), *at* http://www.cisg.law.pace.edu/cisg/wais/db/cases2/980324g1.html.

Original language: German
Translation: Unavailable

Unilex database:
"As to the question of interest, since Art. 78 CISG does determine the rate of interest, the Court stated that it was to be determined according to the domestic law otherwise applicable to the contract."

90. Landgericht [LG] [District Court] Erfurt n. 3 HKO 43/98, 29 July 1998 (F.R.G.), *at* http://www.cisg.law.pace.edu/cisg/wais/db/cases2/980729g1.html.

Original language: German
Translation: Available

Court (translation):
"The claim for interest is based on Art. 78 CISG."

91. Landgericht [LG] [District Court] Regensburg n. 6 O 107/98, 24 Sept. 1998 (F.R.G.), *at* http://www.cisg.law.pace.edu/cisg/wais/db/cases2/980924g1.html.

Original language: German
Translation: Available

Court (translation):
"The Court will only allow interest in the amount of 5% under § 352(1) HGB from the time the action was brought, because the [seller] has neither shown that he suffered a higher damage nor proven an earlier culpable delay by the [buyer]."

92. Landgericht [LG] [District Court] Zwickau n. 3 HK O 67/98, 19 Mar. 1999 (F.R.G.), *at* http://www.cisg.law.pace.edu/cisg/wais/db/cases2/990319g1.html.

Original language: German
Translation: Unavailable

93. Landgericht [LG] [District Court] Flensburg n. 2 O 291/98, 24 Mar. 1999 (F.R.G.), *at* http://www.cisg.law.pace.edu/cisg/wais/db/cases2/990324g2.html.

Original language: German
Translation: Available

Court (translation):
"The seller is entitled to interest on the purchase price under Art. 78 CISG in connection with § 352 HGB. Under Art. 78 CISG the [seller] has a right to interest on the purchase price in arrears without sending a request for payment. After the [buyer] had received the goods, she was bound to pay the purchase price at the time stipulated in the invoices (Art. 58 CISG). As the CISG does not settle the rate of interest, national law, that is § 352 HGB, applies (*cf.* v. Caemmerer/Schlechtriem, Art. 78 n. 27 and 32). The [seller's] claim for interest is thus legitimate with respect to 5%, whereas the [seller] did not prove that he suffered a higher damage."

94. Amtsgericht [AG] [Petty District Court] Stendal n. 3 C 1022/98, 19 Oct. 1999 (F.R.G.), *at* http://www.cisg.law.pace.edu/cisg/wais/db/cases2/991012g1.html.

Original language: German
Translation: Unavailable

95. Oberlandesgericht [OLG] [Provincial Court] Koblenz n. 2 U 1556/98, 18 Nov. 1999 (F.R.G.), *at* http://www.cisg.law.pace.edu/cisg/wais/db/cases2/991118g1.html.

Original language: German
Translation: Unavailable

CLOUT abstract:
"The Court granted interest under article 78 CISG and established the interest rate according to French law applicable pursuant to the rules of German private international law."

Unilex abstract:
"Finally, the Court found that the seller was entitled to interests according to Art. 78 CISG. Since CISG does not determine the rate of interest, the Court held that the rate was to be determined in accordance with the domestic law applicable in the seller's country."

96. Oberlandesgericht [OLG] [Provincial Court] Hamburg n. 1 U 31/99, 26 Nov. 1999 (F.R.G.), *at* http://www.cisg.law.pace.edu/cisg/wais/db/cases2/991126g1.html.

Original language: German
Translation: Available

Court (translation):
"The interest claim is justified under article 74 CISG in connection with § 288 BGB (German Civil Code)"

97. Oberlandesgericht [OLG] [Provincial Court] Dresden n. 2 U 2723/99, 27 Dec. 1999 (F.R.G.), *at* http://www.cisg.law.pace.edu/cisg/wais/db/cases2/991227g1.html.

Original language: German
Translation: Available

Court (translation):
"According to Art. 78 CISG, [seller] is entitled to interest on the accounts payable (*cf*. Piltz, NJW 1996, 2768 at 2773 with further references; Piltz, NJW 1994, 1101 at 1105). The applicable interest rate reaches at least 5% per year. Under German law, an interest rate of 5% would be reasonable according to §§ 352, 353 HGB.Under Dutch Law, the statutory interest is 6% (since 1 January 1998) according to Articles 119 and 120 of the 6th book of the Dutch Civil Code in connection with the Ministerial Decree of 18 December 1997."

98. Oberlandesgericht [OLG] [Provincial Court] Stuttgart n. 5 U 118/99, 28 Feb. 2000 (F.R.G.), *at* http://cisgw3.law.pace.edu/cases/000228g1.html.

Original language: German
Translation: Available

Court (translation):
"The [plaintiff] claim for interest on the purchase price is based on Art. 78 CISG, the interest rate follows from Art. 28(2) EGBGB and § 352 HGB."

99. Landgericht [LG] [District Court] München n. 12 HKO 4174/99, 6 Apr. 2000 (F.R.G.), *at* http://www.cisg.law.pace.edu/cisg/wais/db/cases2/000406g1.html.

Original language: German
Translation: Available

Court (translation):
"The rate of interest on the sum in arrears comes to 5% p.a. (Art. 78 CISG, Art. 1284 Cc). A claim for compensation of interest for drawn credit would require that the [seller] conduct his business with an ongoing bank credit which exceeds the sum claimed during the time the payment was in arrears. Furthermore – and this is decisive – the credit has to be repaid by all of the payments received by the [seller] unless such payments must be used immediately for the interest owed on the credit. It is only in such a case that a loss in the meaning of Art. 74 CISG, which exceeds the legal damage for delay, exists. The [seller] did not submit any facts demonstrating such a loss. [Seller] could only claim for payment of an overdraft interest rate if he had established to conduct his business while permanently using an overdraft facility. Further, this overdraft had to extend his claim within these proceedings while [buyer] was in default. And most importantly, this overdraft would have had to be repaid with all incoming cash flow under his trade receivables, unless those cash flows were appropriated to redeem any accrued interest. Only if that were the case, might one establish a claim for compensation of damages beyond the statutory default interest rate pursuant to Art. 74 CISG. [Seller] has not, however, demonstrated any facts as to the aforementioned ingredients to establish such a claim beyond the statutory default interest rate."

100. Amtsgericht [AG] [Petty District Court] Duisburg n. 49 C 502/00, 13 Apr. 2000 (F.R.G.), *at* http://www.cisg.law.pace.edu/cisg/wais/db/cases2/000413g1.html.

Original language: German
Translation: Available

Court (translation):
"The [seller] is also entitled to interest of 5% from 30 November 1998. According to Art. 78 CISG interest accrues from the time the payment is due, in the present case on 29 November 1998. The rate of interest is stipulated in Art. 1284(1) CC. The CISG is silent on this matter. The Court leaves open the question of whether the relevant rate of interest is to be determined under the law of the creditor's place of business (*cf.* LG Stuttgart, RIW 1989, 984) or under the law of the debtor's place of business (*cf.* OLG Frankfurt, NJW 1991, 3102). Both approaches lead to the application of Italian national law, as the [seller] has his place of business in Italy and the rules of German private international law (Art. 28(2) EGBGB) lead to the application of Italian law. With respect to the further requests made by the [seller] the claim is unfounded. The [seller] is not entitled to a higher interest rate. Art. 74 CISG does not lead to a higher rate of interest as the [seller] does not submit that he suffered a respective damage."

101. Landgericht [LG] [District Court] Darmstadt n. 10 O 72/00, 9 May 2000 (F.R.G.), *at* http://www.cisg.law.pace.edu/cisg/wais/db/cases2/000509g1.html.

Original language: German
Translation: Available

Court (translation):
The [seller's] claim for interest results from Art. 78 CISG in connection with § 352 HGB. Under Art. 78 CISG, the [seller] is entitled to interest on any sum that is in arrears. As the CISG does not stipulate the interest rate, the rate is to be determined according to the law applicable by virtue of the rules of private international law (prevailing opinion – *cf.* v.Caemmerer/Schlechtriem, Kommentar zum einheitlichen UN-Kaufrecht, 2nd ed. Art. 78 n. 27). Since the parties did not agree on a choice of law clause (Art. 27(1) EGBGB), the law governing the contract is the law of the [seller's] place of business (Art. 28(2) EGBGB). This law supplements the CISG (*cf.* OLG München, 2 March 1994; OLG Düsseldorf, NJW-RR 1994, 506 (507)). Regardless of how the interest rate is being determined, the re-financing of a businessperson at an interest rate of 5% can be assumed in the Federal Republic of Germany and a return of 5% on an amount of one million DM cannot seriously be questioned. Such a return neither requires specific knowledge nor risky transactions. As the [seller] did not prove a higher loss resulting from bank loans, his claim for interest was reduced by the Court to the 5% stipulated by § 352 HGB, owed from the date of the [buyer's] final payment refusal on 1 February 1999."

102. Landgericht [LG] [District Court] Stendal n. 22 S 234/94, 12 Oct. 2000 (F.R.G.), *at* http://www.cisg.law.pace.edu/cisg/wais/db/cases2/001012g1.html.

Original language: German
Translation: Available

Court (translation):
"According to the prevailing opinion among scholars (*cf.* Staundiger/Magnus, Wiener UN-Kaufrech, Art. 78 n. 12), the rate of interest is to be determined according to he law applicable by virtue of the rules of private international law, as the Convention does not expressly settle this matter. The parties did not agree on a choice of law clause. Art. 28(1) and Art. 28(2) EGBGB lead to the application of Italian law, because [seller], who performed the obligation characteristic of the sale contract (the delivery of goods), is domiciled in Italy. The Court of First Instance granted an interest rate of 5%, which is lower than the rate of 10% provided by Art. 1284 CC (since 16 December 1990, *cf.* Piltz, Internatinales Kaufrecht, § 5 n. 41)."

103. Oberlandesgericht [OLG] [Provincial Court] Köln n. 16 U 45/00, 13 Nov. 2000 (F.R.G.), *at* http://www.cisg.law.pace.edu/cisg/wais/db/cases2/001113g1.html.

Original language: German
Translation: Available

Court (translation):
"Art. 78 CISG forms the basis of the claim for interest. According to prevailing opinion, especially the consistent case law of the courts of appeal, the interest rate is to be determined under supplementary national law (*cf.* Schlechtriem/Bacher, Art. 78 n. 27 *et seq.* with further references). Again, it is of no importance whether German or Italian law is applicable. The 5% requested by the seller can be based both on Art. 1284 CC and on § 352."

104. Landgericht [LG] [District Court] München n. 12 HKO 3804/00, 16 Nov. 2000 (F.R.G.), *at* http://www.cisg.law.pace.edu/cisg/wais/db/cases2/001116g1.html.

Original language: German
Translation: Available

Court (translation):
"The extent of the [seller]'s claim is undisputed; it results from the [seller]'s undisputed pleadings. The claim follows from Art. 78 CISG. The [seller]'s

claim became due with [buyer]'s receipt of the invoice dated 16 April 1999. The interest rate corresponds to Art. 1284 of the Italian Civil Code."

105. Landgericht [LG] [District Court] Flensburg n. 4 O 369/99, 19 Jan. 2001 (F.R.G.), *at* http://www.cisg.law.pace.edu/cisg/wais/db/cases2/010119g1.html.

Original language: German
Translation: Available

Court (translation):
"The [seller] is entitled to claim for payment of interest pursuant to Section 284 et seq. BGB. The [seller] demonstrated coherently and undisputedly that the parties agreed to the obligation of the [buyer] to pay the purchase price within eight days after the actual delivery of the goods. Furthermore, the [seller] stated coherently the level of such damage regarding interest, which the [seller] had to pay for by arranging credit with his bank, and the [buyer] has not denied that statement."

106. Oberlandesgericht [OLG] [Provincial Court] Köln n. 16 U 1/01, 28 May 2001 (F.R.G.), *at* http://www.cisg.law.pace.edu/cisg/wais/db/cases2/010528g1.html.

Original language: German
Translation: Available

Unilex abstract:
"Finally the court stated that the plaintiff was entitled to interest on its claim according to Art. 78 CISG."

107. Landgericht [LG] [District Court] Braunschweig n. 21 O 703/01 (028), 30 July 2001 (F.R.G.), *at* http://www.cisg.law.pace.edu/cisg/wais/db/cases2/010730g1.html.

Original language: German
Translation: Available

Court (translation):
"Under Art. 78 CISG, [buyer] is entitled to interest. The rate of interest was not contested by [seller]."

108. Landgericht [LG] [District Court] München n. 12 HKO 5593/01, 30 Aug. 2001 (F.R.G.), *at* http://www.cisg.law.pace.edu/cisg/wais/db/cases2/010830g1.html.

Original language: German
Translation: Available

Court (translation):
"The [buyer] was in culpable delay with payment of purchase price on 7 February 2001, as the [sellers]' attorneys sent [buyer] a reminder of payment requesting payment to be effected until 6 February 2001. The [buyer] therefore at the latest at this point in time failed to pay the purchase price (Art. 78 CISG). The interest rate for sums in arrears is fixed at 5%. As the CISG does not provide for an interest rate, the interest rate needs to be determined under Italian law. The contract in dispute is governed by Italian law, as the party obliged to effect the characteristic performance, that is the delivery of the goods, has its place of business in Italy (Art. 28(1) and (2) EGBGB). Under Art. 1284(1) of the Italian Civil Code [C.c.] in connection with Art. 2(185) of the Budget Concomitant Act no. 662 of 22 December 1996, the interest rate is 5% per annum (*cf.* Kindler, Jahrbuch des italienischen Recht, vol. 10, p. 149-152). The [buyer] is liable for the pre-judicial expenses shown by the [sellers] under Art. 78 in connection with Art. 74, 61(1)(b) CISG."

109. Oberlandesgericht [OLG] [Provincial Court] Rostock n. 6 U 126/00, 10 Oct. 2001 (F.R.G.), *at* http://www.cisg.law.pace.edu/cisg/wais/db/cases2/011010g1.html.

Original language: German
Translation: Unavailable

110. Landgericht [LG] [District Court] München n. 10 O 5423/01, 20 Feb. 2002 (F.R.G.), *at* http://www.cisg.law.pace.edu/cisg/wais/db/cases2/020220g1.html.

Original language: German
Translation: Available

111. Landgericht [LG] [District Court] München n. 5 HKO 3936/00, 27 Feb. 2002 (F.R.G.), *at* http://www.cisg.law.pace.edu/cisg/wais/db/cases2/020227g1.html.

Original language: German
Translation: Available

Court (translation):
"The purchase price has borne accrued interest since it became due and payable pursuant to Art. 78 CISG. In this case, the purchase price became due and payable 10 days after actual delivery of the Globes due to the agreed discount provision. The applicable interest rate is 5%, which is the statutory

interest rate under Italian law as applicable in this respect. This interest rate is the equivalent to the default interest rate amongst merchants under Sec. 353 S. 1 BGB. Since [buyer 1] and [buyer 2] owed merely a reduced purchase price, the accrued interest as principally claimed by the [seller] for the period up to 7 December 1999 had to be reduced to an amount of *EUR* 1,069.96: viz interest of 5 % on (i) the proportion of the unpaid purchase price for the first delivery in an amount of *Lire* 66,380,000 for a period of 220 days; and (ii) the unpaid remainder of the purchase price for the second delivery in an amount of *Lire* 26,000,000 for a period of 20 days."

112. Amtsgericht [AG] [Lower Court] Viechtach n. 1 C 419/01, 11 Apr. 2002 (F.R.G.), *at* http://www.cisg.law.pace.edu/cisg/wais/db/cases2/020411g1.html.

Original language: German
Translation: Unavailable

Court (translation):
"The [seller] is entitled to interest on the purchase price at a rate of 12% under Art. 78 CISG. According to Art. 58(1) sent. 1 CISG, payment was due when the goods were delivered on 11 July 2001. The [buyer] had to pay the price on that day without the need for another period of time to pass or a reminder of payment (Art. 59 CISG). The Court therefore grants interest from 4 August 2001, as requested. Since the [buyer] did not dispute the interest rate submitted by the [seller], the Court grants the requested rate of 12%."

113. Landgericht [LG] [District Court] Freiburg n. 8 O 75/02, 22 Aug. 2002 (F.R.G.), *at* http://www.cisg.law.pace.edu/cisg/wais/db/cases2/020822g1.html.

Original language: German
Translation: Available

Court (translation):
"The claim for interest on the purchase price is justified under Art. 84(1) CISG; the claim for interest on damages is justified under Art. 78 CISG. As the CISG does not provide for an interest rate, it is appropriate to rely on § 288 I 2 BGB because this is the rule more favorable to the seller in comparison to corresponding regulations in Italian law, which grant higher interest rates."

114. Oberlandesgericht [OLG] [Provincial Court] Schleswig n. 11 U 40/01, 22 Aug. 2002 (F.R.G.), *at* http://www.cisg.law.pace.edu/cisg/wais/db/cases2/020822g2.html.

Original language: German
Translation: Available

Court (translation):
"The [buyer] further pursues with his appeal a challenge of the actual level of the claim for default interest accrued. The Court of First Instance applied Section 284 et. seq. BGB to [seller]'s claim for interest payment and granted the entire claim as pleaded for. The [seller] is of the opinion that this claim for interest payment is justified under relevant Danish law. The [seller]'s claim for interest payment stems from Art. 78 CISG. According to that provision, the defaulting party has to pay interest, provided that payment of the purchase price or any other amount due and payable has been in default. However, the actual level of the interest rate has not been stated within this provision. Henceforth, national law can be applied complementary. In the case of international sales contracts, it is assumed pursuant to Art. 28 Par. 2 EGBGB, that the law of the seat of the [seller] shall be applicable with regards to the payment of the purchase price (v. Caemmerer/Schlechtriem, Art. 78, Note 27). Since the [seller] has not given conclusive evidence that he steadily borrows money at least at an amount equivalent to the purchase price and that he is able to redeem such credit at any time, he is not entitled to claim for a higher interest rate than the statutory interest rate. Consequently, the interest rate as claimed for is limited to 5 % [*p.a.*] pursuant to Section 352 HGB"

115. Landgericht [LG] [District Court] Göttingen n. 7 O 43/01, 20 Sept. 2002 (F.R.G.), *at* http://www.cisg.law.pace.edu/cisg/wais/db/cases2/020920g1.html.

Original language: German
Translation: Available

Court (translation)
"[Seller] is entitled to claim payment from the [buyer] of 5% default interest above the Base Rate [Base Interest Rate, *Basiszinssatz*, Base Interest Rate as set forth in Sec. 1 of the German Act on the Transmission of the Discount Rate]; on the purchase price in an amount of *EUR* 221,221.65 pursuant to Art. 78 CISG in connection with Sec. 288 Par. 1 BGB However, [seller] has not demonstrated that he can claim payment of a higher interest rate. Insofar as [seller] granted and acknowledged credits in an overall amount of *EUR* 7,322.93, he had already reduced his claim within these proceedings accordingly. These credits on [seller]'s claim based on the amount stated in invoice No. 1 were set-off against his own claim. This reduced the amount on which his claim for interest payment had to be calculated. [Seller] has not argued his case, what amounts of which invoices should be reduced by those credits in favor of the [buyer]. He has not particularly adjusted his calculation of

default interest. The Court, moreover, does not have the duty to carry out such an allocation and appropriation. For this reason, the Court reduced the claim for payment of default interest with regard to the most mature claim against the [buyer]. In relation to his claim for damages in an amount of *EUR* 8,250, [seller] can claim payment of interest since the commencement of his legal action pursuant to Sec. 291 BGB. The [seller] only transformed the claim under invoice No. 36 to a claim for damages during the lawsuit, and may therefore not claim interest from the time payment was due under Art. 78 CISG."

116. Oberlandesgericht [OLG] [Provincial Court] Rostock n. 6 U 126/00, 25 Sept. 2002 (F.R.G.), *at* http://www.cisg.law.pace.edu/cisg/wais/db/cases2/020925g1.html.

Original language: German
Translation: Available

Court (translation):
"The [seller]'s claim for interest on the purchase price – beginning with the time of delivery – up to the amount stated above follows from Arts. 59, 78 CISG. The interest rate is determined by §§ 353, 352 HGB, as the sale is a commercial transaction for both parties in the meaning of § 343 HGB. Since Art. 78 CISG does not provide for an interest rate, the rate needs to be determined by the national law which finds supplementary application or by the interest level of the country in whose currency the price is to be paid (cf. v. Caemmerer/Schlechtriem/Bacher, *op. cit.*, Art. 78 n. 27, 33); either way, this leads to the application of German law in the present case."

117. Oberlandesgericht [OLG] [Provincial Court] Köln n. 16 U 77/01, 14 Oct. 2002 (F.R.G.), *at* http://www.cisg.law.pace.edu/cisg/wais/db/cases2/021014g1.html.

Original language: German
Translation: Unavailable

118. Landgericht [LG] [District Court] Saarbrücken n. 8 O 68/02, 25 Nov. 2002 (F.R.G.), *at* http://www.cisg.law.pace.edu/cisg/wais/db/cases2/021125g1.html.

Original language: German
Translation: Available

Court (translation): "Pursuant to Art. 78 CISG, if a party fails to pay the price or any other sum that is in arrears, the other party is entitled to interest on it without any further conditions. The relevant point of time is 4 May 1999 as it was requested and laid down in the default summons; the date 4 May 1998 included in the statement of claim is obviously a clerical error because at that time the goods were neither ordered nor delivered – the latter took place only between 3 September and 11 December 1998. The CISG includes only the grounds for which interest can be ordered but it is silent on the rate of interest. As far as the parties did not agree on the latter, first of all usages referred to in Art. 9 CISG shall be taken into account. Yet, such usages were neither presented by the parties nor could they be otherwise ascertained. Therefore, the rate of interest shall be determined with regard to the statutory law which is applicable, pursuant to the provisions on private international law of the forum, to questions not covered by the CISG. Consequently, based on Art. 28(2) EGBGB, German law is applicable.

The contract has the closest links to Germany because Seller, which has its place of business in Germany, carried out the characteristic service. Since the German EGBGB is silent on the question of the rate of interest, Arts. 352 and 353 HGB shall be applied which provide for a statutory rate of interest at 5 percent. The Seller can enforce its further claims for interest exceeding the statutory rate of interest as part of the damages (Arts. 74, 78 CISG). It is sufficient that the Seller drew on credit of a certain amount during the period of time in question, it is irrelevant that drawing on such credit took place as a direct consequence of the Buyer's delay in paying the purchase price. Conditions set by Arts. 74 and 78 CISG are undisputedly fulfilled because [Seller] drew on a bank credit for which it paid interest at 12 percent, therefore the claim is founded."

119. Landgericht [LG] [District Court] Saarbrücken n. 8 O 68/02, 25 Nov. 2002 (F.R.G.), *at* http://www.cisg.law.pace.edu/cisg/wais/db/cases2/021125g1.html.

Original language: German
Translation: Available

Court (translation):
"Undisputedly, losses in interest have been suffered. The interest rate due is determined by Art. 45(1)(b), Art. 74, Art. 84(1) CISG. A claim for further interest is not substantiated. In particular, § 288 of the German Civil Code (*Bürgerliches Gesetzbuch*, BGB) does not apply. Instead, as the CISG does not provide for rate of interest (Achilles, Art. 84, note 2; Staudinger/Magnus, Art. 84, note 9), § 28(2) of the Introductory Act of the German Civil Code (*Einführungsgesetz zum Bürgerlichen Gesetzbuch*; EGBGB) refers to the Swiss Law of Obligations (*Schweizerisches Obligationenrecht*; OR) as the applicable law). Arts. 73 and 104 of the Swiss Law of Obligations determine an interest

rate of 5%. A claim for further interest is sustainable only to the extent that had already been granted in the judgment of the District Court (*Landgericht*)."

120. Landgericht [LG] [District Court] Mönchengladbach n. 7 O 221/02, 15 July 2003 (F.R.G.), *at* http://www.cisg.law.pace.edu/cisg/wais/db/cases2/030715g1.html.

Original language:	German
Translation:	Unavailable

Summary

Cases involving Article 78: 120

Cases for which an English translation is available: 49

Cases for which only an abstract was available: 29

Cases for which neither translation nor abstract was available: 42

- If a party fails to pay the price or any other sum that is in arrears, the other party is entitled to interest on it without any further conditions.
- The purchase price has borne accrued interest since it became due and payable pursuant to Art. 78 CISG
- The rate of interest is to be determined with regard to the statutory law that is applicable, pursuant to the provisions on private international law of the forum, to questions not covered by the CISG.
- Party can enforce its further claims for interest exceeding the statutory rate of interest as part of the damages (Arts. 74, 78 CISG).
- Party must give evidence of damages not covered by interest.

Appendix 8
Hungary

Courts

Fovárosi Biróság	Metropolitan court

1. Arbitration Court of the Chamber of Commerce and Industry of Budapest, n. Vb 92068, 17 Jan. 1994 (Hung.), *at* http://cisgw3.law.pace.edu/cases/940117h1.html.

   Original language: Hungarian
   Translation: Unavailable

2. Arbitration Court of the Chamber of Commerce and Industry of Budapest, n. Vb 94124, 17 Nov. 1995 (Hung.), *at* http://cisgw3.law.pace.edu/cases/951117h1.html.

   Original language: German
   Translation: Unavailable

   Unilex abstract:
   "The Court found that the seller was entitled to interest on the unpaid price (Art. 78 CISG). After noting that CISG does not specify the interest rate, the Court held that it would be improper to determine it according to the law otherwise applicable to the contract (Hungarian law, as agreed upon by the parties), in particular taking into account the different inflation figures in the two countries involved (Hungary and Austria). Since payment was to be made in Austrian Shillings, the Court disregarded the provisions of the Hungarian Civil Code fixing the interest rate at 20% and granted interest at 5% in accordance with the law of the State in whose currency payment was to be made."

3. Arbitration Court of the Chamber of Commerce and Industry of Budapest, n. Vb 94131, 5 Dec. 1995 (Hung.), *at* http://cisgw3.law.pace.edu/cisg/wais/db/cases2/951205h1.html.

   Original language: German
   Translation: Available

Court (translation):
"CISG Art. 78 provides that, if a party fails to pay the price or any other sum that is in arrears, the other party is entitled to interest on it, since the time the sums were due. CISG Art. 78 is silent on the amount of interest rate (*see* Loewe, p. 95). It is accepted as a problem that it is neither logical nor fair to apply rules of one State on a sum that is expressed in the currency of another State if the currency of one of the States is stable or the influence of inflation is minor and the currency of the other State continuously diminishes in value. In Austria, the inflation rate in 1994 and 1995 was on the average 3%, in Hungary 20%. Commenting on an award of the Court of International Arbitration of the Austrian Federal Economic Chamber in Vienna, *Schlechtriem*, in Recht der Internationalen Wirtschaft 1995 pp. 593/94, proposed three ways of establishing the interest rate:

1. via the application of the *lex contractus*;

2. via the autonomous establishment of the interest rate by the Court or Arbitration Tribunal through comparison of criteria for different bank rates;

3. in conformity to private international law according to Art. 7(2) CISG, preferably taking into consideration the State of the currency.

Schlechtriem advocates the last solution; the arbitrator agrees. Therefore, the interest rate is to be established according to Austrian law; according to § 352 para.1 of the Commercial Code, the rate is 5% for bilateral commercial activities. The [seller] has neither asked nor proved that credits should have been taken into account, which became more expensive since the *Ft* [Hungarian Forint] diminished in value 5% per year compared to the *sA* [Austrian Schilling]."

4. Arbitration Court of the Chamber of Commerce and Industry of Budapest, n. VB 96074, 10 Dec. 1996 (Hung.), *at* http://cisgw3.law.pace.edu/cisg/wais/db/cases2/961210h1.html.

Original language: English

Court:
"The Vienna Convention on the International Sale of Goods (chosen by the parties as applicable law) does not contain relevant provisions on interest for delay. Therefore, the arbitrators have to establish the applicable law by virtue of the relevant Hungarian conflict rules applicable on ground of Article 14(2) of the Rules of Proceedings of this Court of Arbitration. The relevant conflict rule is contained in § 24 of the 1979 Hungarian Act on Private International Law. According to this provision, the applicable law is the substantive law of the Seller – which is in this case Yugoslav law. In Yugoslavia, the relevant norms on

interest on default are contained in the 1978 Act on Obligations (articles 277-279 in particular) as well as in the 1993 Act on the Amount of Interest on Default. The Yugoslav rules referred to above have not made it perfectly clear whether interest on default is only due when delay in payment is attributable to the fault of the debtor, or whether such interest is a simple consequence of the objective fact that payment was not made in time. Article 277 of the Act on Obligations, and Article 1 of the Act on the Amount of Interest on Default simply state that interest on default is owed if the debtor is late with payment. In recent Yugoslav scholarly writings two justices of the Supreme Court of Serbia have taken a position that interest on default is due when the debtor is responsible for the delay. According to Justice Latinovic, "Interest on default is a consequence of breach of contract by the debtor ..." (Z. Latinovic, Zatezna kamatazbog docnje u placanju novcane obaveze, Pravni zivot 9-10/1992, 1426, at p. 1428). In the words of Justice Maljkovic "Interest on default regarding pecuniary claims is due from the moment the debtor is in default." (B. Maljkovic, zatezna kamata na novcano potrazivanje nenovcane stete, Pravni zivot 9-10/1992, 1436, at p. 1438.) Under Yugoslav law, there is no default if lack of performance is not imputable to the debtor. At the same time, according to Article 262 (4) of the 1978 Act on Obligations, the debtor will be responsible even if his performance became impossible, if it became impossible after the debtor fell into default. We shall be guided by these rules."

5. Fovárosi Birósåg Budapest [Metropolitan Court] 12.G.75.715/1996/20, 1 July 1997 (Hung.), *at* http://cisgw3.law.pace.edu/cisg/wais/db/cases2/970701h1.html.

Original language:	Hungarian
Translation:	Unavailable

Summary

Cases involving Article 78: 5

Cases for which an English translation is available: 2

Cases for which only an abstract was available: 1

Cases for which neither translation nor abstract was available: 2

A 1995 decision clearly states it is not fair "to apply rules of one State on a sum that is expressed in the currency of another State if the currency of one of the States is stable or the influence of inflation is minor and the currency of the other State continuously diminishes in value." Instead, the interest rate is to be determined "in accordance with the law of the State in whose currency payment was to be made."

Another 1995 decision, instead, decided the case "in conformity to private international law according to Art. 7(2) CISG, preferably taking into consideration the State of the currency."

A 1996 decision from the same institution, however, reached a quite different solution. As Article 78 does not solve the matter, the gap must be filled by the law determined pursuant to the rules of international private law.

Appendix 9
ICC

COURT OF ARBITRATION OF THE INTERNATIONAL CHAMBER OF COMMERCE (ICC)

1. Int'l Comm. Arb., no. 7153 of 1992, *at* http://cisgw3.law.pace.edu/cases/927153i1.html.

   Original language: German
   Translation: Available (14 J.L. & COM. 217 (1995))

   Court (translation):
   In the absence of an agreement between the parties about the payment of interest accruing from the date of the commencement of this action, the [seller's] claim concerning said interest stems from Article 78 of the Convention, pursuant to which the seller has the right to receive interest if the buyer neglects to pay the price for the goods. Moreover, the rate of said interest is not provided for in the Convention, which is why we need to turn to the national law designated by the rule on conflict of laws. (Cf. Eberstein, in: V. Caemmerer/Schlechtriem, Commentary on the Uniform Law of Sales of the United Nations – CISG – 1990, Article 78, end of line 3.) In this case, the court of arbitration believed the applicable law to be Czech law, *i.e.*, the law applicable at the place of payment. It is true that the contract does not contain any provision as to the place of payment. In the absence of such a provision, Article 57(1) of the Convention nevertheless applies. The latter stipulates that the buyer is required to pay the price at the seller's place of business or, if the payment is to be made against the handing over of the goods, where said handing over takes place. At the hearing, the [seller] alleged that the payment was to be made against the handing over of the goods in Prague. Since the [buyer] did not participate in the proceeding, this position was accepted, given that the contract contains no contrary provision. The New Czech Commercial Code does not explicitly speak to the amount of interest owing. (Cf. Articles 735, 502 of the Commercial Code). Despite intensive efforts undertaken by the arbitrator, it was not possible to gain precise information on this matter. The Czech Embassy in Paris confirmed, however, that, in any case, a claim for interest at a minimum rate of 12% should be customary. In this matter, the research of the [seller] overlaps with that of the arbitration court, such that the court had to allow an accrual rate of 12%."

2. Int'l Comm. Arb., no. 7197 of 1992, *at* http://cisgw3.law.pace.edu/cases/927197i1.html; http://www.unilex.info/case.cfm?pid=1&do=case&id=37&step=Abstract.

Original language: German
Translation: Available (French)

CLOUT abstract no. 104:
"The tribunal awarded the seller interest on the amount due (Article 78 CISG). As the Convention does not specify the interest rate, the tribunal determined the interest rate in accordance with the substantive law applicable to the relationship between creditors and debtors (Article 7(2)). The tribunal held that the interest rate to be awarded may be higher than the legal rate since the entitlement to interest under Article 78 CISG was independent of any claim for damages under Article 74 CISG. In the case in question, the tribunal found that the seller operated on the basis of credit for which it had to pay interest at the rate of 12% and applied that rate since the seller would have to obtain credit in order to replace the funds missing due to the non-payment by the buyer."

Unilex abstract:
"As CISG does not expressly specify the rate of interest payable, the court referred to Austrian law as the law of the creditor's place of business. Although the Austrian statutory rate was 5%, the court awarded additional damages in the form of interest to the seller and the interest finally awarded was 12% being the commercial bank rate in Austria."

3. Int'l Comm. Arb., no. 7585 of 1992, *at* http://cisgw3.law.pace.edu/cases/927585i1.html; http://www.unilex.info/case.cjm?pid=1&do=case&id=134&step=FullText.

Original language: English
Translation: Available (French)

Unilex Abstract:
"Article 78 of Vienna Sales Convention provides that the creditor is entitled to interest 'without prejudice to any claim for damages.' The purpose of this provision is to make a distinction between interest and damages and to give compensation for the financial loss due to the mere fact that delay in payment has a financial cost. The same general idea is at the origin of Article 84 which obliges the seller who is bound to refund the price, to pay interest on it from the date on which he received money. The practical consequence for the present case is that Seller is entitled to claim interest on any sum that was in arrears… Article 78 which declares: 'If a party fails to pay the price or any other sum that is in arrears, the other party is entitled to interest on it' means that any delay in payment entitles the creditor to interest. Contrary to what is sometimes provided in several legal systems, the right to interest doesn't need a formal notice (cf. la mora del articolo 1224 del Codice Civile Italiano; la mise en demeure of Article

1153 of the French Civil Code). For the above reasons, Seller is entitled to interest from the date on which Buyer had to pay (the date of acceptance test and the expected date of installation)... The question of the rate of interest is not solved in the Convention. **The Diplomatic conference did not agree on this issue (See Official Records I p. 138; II p. 223-226, p. 388-392, 415-419, 429-430).** Several solutions are conceivable:

- the rate in force in the state whose law is applicable;
- the rate in force in the place of business of the creditor;
- the rate in force in the place of procedure.

The arbitrator shares another view. In his opinion the rate of interest is linked to a precise currency. It would be rather illogical to base interest for the delayed payment of a price agreed in strong currency on the legal rate in force at a place of business located in a country which has a high inflation figure and consequently, a high rate of interest. The same reasoning would lead to the exclusion of the law applicable to the contract, the lex fori, or that of the place of payment. In the present case, the parties agreed that the price had to be paid in German Marks. The first and the second down payments had been paid in DM. The same currency was used for the payment of the bank guarantee issued by Seller. Clearly, the financial aspects of the sale are linked with the German Mark. The applicable rate of interest is therefore the German one."

4. Int'l Comm. Arb., no. 6653 of 1993, *at* http://cisgw3.law.pace.edu/cases/936653i1.html. (Art. 84)

Original language:	French
Translation:	Available (English)

Court (translation):
"The Convention (Art. 78) generally grants the payment of interest. Article 84 of the Convention prescribes that "If the seller is bound to refund the price, he must also pay interest on it, from the date on which the price was paid." According to this text, interest is due for respondent [seller] to be paid to claimant [buyer] starting from the day of payment. The starting point of the interest is therefore the date of the payment of the item concerned. The question arises whether the interest aspired to by Art. 84 is due even if it had not been formally requested. The Arbitral Tribunal finds that, for two reasons, this question must be answered in the affirmative. First of all, Article 84 of the Convention sets forth that the seller *must* and not "can" pay interest. Furthermore, supposed that one considers Article 84 to be ambiguous in that question, the French Law of Obligations, which has been retained as the subsidiary law, sets forth in Article 1153-1 of the Civil Code that interest is due in

all cases "even in the absence of request." But then the Convention does not regulate the method of determination of the percentage of interest. The Arbitral Tribunal finds that in matters of international commerce, the percentage that must be retained is the one that corresponds to the use which the creditor could have made of the sum to be reimbursed. Consequently, it appears logical to retain a percentage currently applied between merchants and that conforms with the currency in which the settlement was made and in which the payment must be made. This solution, which is in the eyes of the Arbitral Tribunal the most logical one from the economic point of view, leads to retaining the percentage that operators of international commerce apply to settlements made in Eurodollar, i.e., the one-year percentage of LIBOR (London Inter-Bank Offered Rate), published every day in the Wall Street Journal."

5. Int'l Comm. Arb., no. 7331 of 1994, *at* http://cisgw3.law.pace.edu/cases/947331i1.html.

Original language: English
Translation: French

Court:
"It is acknowledged in international law that claimants prevailing on the merits are entitled to receive interest on the principal amount awarded. The Tribunal finds the application of this principle particularly appropriate in this case since [seller] has suffered damages due to delayed payment, which must be compensated by the granting of interest. It is also generally acknowledged that interest does not begin to accrue until proper notice of the claim has been given. In this case, there is no indication that proper notice was given before the filing of the Request for Arbitration. **Regarding the precise rate of interest to be applied, there is no single internationally accepted rate of interest. This is reflected in the Vienna Convention, which only generally provides that parties are entitled to interest without specifying any particular rate of interest.** It is, however, acknowledged in international law that where the parties are silent as to choice of law with respect to the payment of interest, the law of the State applies in which the damage resulting from the delayed payment is suffered. It is furthermore acknowledged in international law that such damage is suffered at the place of the creditor and in the creditor's market [citing ICC arbitration cases 2375 of 1975 and 5460 of 1987]. Therefore, this Tribunal shall apply the rate of interest effective for commercial matter in the country of the creditor, the [seller]."

6. Int'l Comm. Arb., no. 7531 of 1994, *at* http://cisgw3.law.pace.edu/cases/947531i1.html.

Original language: English

CLOUT abstract:
"Citing articles 86 CISG, 87 CISG and 88(1) CISG, the arbitral tribunal allowed as damages costs, expenses and losses related to the buyer's reasonable expenses for preservation of the goods. In addition, under articles 74 CISG and 75 CISG, the arbitral tribunal allowed all damages (except one, the travel costs of the buyer's customer) claimed by the buyer. The buyer's claim of cost of credit was held to be an element of the damages due according to article 74 CISG.

The arbitral tribunal further held that as the CISG was silent on the question of the maturity date of damage claims and taking into account that this element of the claim was undisputed, the buyer was entitled to receive interest from the date it communicated the amount of its claim to the seller by telex."

Editorial remarks by Professor Kritzer: "*Interest (right to, accrual of, rate of)*. In assessing interest under the CISG, support for a creditor's right to interest is encountered under several provisions of the Chapter on Provisions common to the obligations of the seller and the buyer:

- Under Article 74, a provision of the section entitled Damages. This article has to do with damages in general. It provides for recovery of the loss suffered as a consequence of a breach of contract.
- Under Article 78, the provision of the section entitled Interest. This article has to do with the situation in which a party fails to pay a "sum that is in arrears". In this situation, "the other party is entitled to interest on it, without prejudice to any claim for damages recoverable under Article 74."
- Under Article 84(1), a provision of the section on Effects of avoidance. This article has to do with a situation in which "the seller is bound to return the price". In this situation, "he must also pay interest on it, from the date on which the price was paid."

Referring only to Article 74, the tribunal stated: "The damages suffered by [buyer] includes the cost of credit which has been stated by [buyer], undisputedly, at 11% per annum and which should be compensated at that rate as an element of the damages due according to Article 74."

The tribunal also stated: "The Convention is silent on the question of the maturity date of damage claims ... [Buyer] claims interest from the date when it communicated the amount of its claim to [seller] by telex ... [Since] this particular aspect of the claim is ... undisputed, interest should be granted from the date claimed by [buyer]."

7. Int'l Comm. Arb., no. 7565 of 1994, *at* http://cisgw3.law.pace.edu/cases/947565i1.html; http://www.unilex.info/case.cfm?pid=1&do=case&id=141&step=FullText.

Original language: English
Translation: French

Uncitral abstract:
On the claim for interest, Claimant requests Defendant be directed to pay interest on the granted sums 'at a commercial rate compounded monthly from August 14, 1991, through the date of actual payment. As stated above, the Contract is governed by the laws of Switzerland which include the provisions of the Vienna Convention as incorporated therein, but is not limited to such provisions where the Vienna Convention does not expressly settle a particular point of law. **In the Vienna Convention, nothing is said either in Article 74 (damages) nor in Article 78 (interests) about the rates nor the modus of calculation of interests where interests are due to a party in case of breach of contract by another party**. According to Article 7.2 of the Convention, questions not expressly settled by it shall be determined either in accordance with the general principles on which it is grounded or by the law which shall be elected according to private international law. As the general **principles do not settle the matter** [...] and the parties have referred to the laws of Switzerland, it seems justified to refer to Article 73 of the Swiss Code of obligations whereby, in the absence of a determination of the rate of interest by agreement or law or usages, that rate shall be 5% per annum. Interest shall be computed from January 1, 1992, on the assumption that the cargo would normally have been resold to Claimant's customers by the end of December 1991. It shall accrue and be paid until full payment of the awarded amount."

8. Int'l Comm. Arb., no. 7660 of 1994, *at* http://cisgw3.law.pace.edu/cases/947660i1.html; www.unilex.info/case.cfm?pid=1&do=case&id=48&step=Abstract.

Original language: English
Translation: French

Court:
"In assessing the claim for non-delivered spare parts, the tribunal ruled that buyer is entitled to "interest in the amount due under applicable law (Articles 78 and 84 CISG) ... As to the starting date, interest for reimbursement of the purchase price runs from the date of payment (see Article 84(1) CISG) ... [Buyer] is entitled to interest from the maturity of the first promissory notes ... As to the amount of interest, Articles 78 and 84 CISG are silent on the matter ... [U]nder

applicable (see Article 7(2). CISG) Austrian law, the statutory litigation interest applicable to commercial matters is 5% (see Section 352 HGB). "

CLOUT abstract:
"The arbitral tribunal allowed the buyer's claim regarding undelivered spare parts and granted the buyer interest in the amount due under articles 78 and 84 CISG from the maturity of the first promissory notes according to article 84(1) CISG. The arbitral tribunal stated that, as the CISG was silent on the amount of interest (articles 78 CISG and 84 CISG), and, on the basis of article 7(2) CISG, Austrian law had to be applied in order to determine this issue. Given that the contract price, though valued in Lira, was due in DM at an exchange rate agreed by the parties, the arbitral tribunal held that any refund, including interest, should also be due in DM at the same rate."

Unilex abstract:
"The court noted, however, that the questions of prescription and interest rate were governed by substantive domestic Austrian law. The court granted the buyer reimbursement of the price of the non delivered equipment, and the right to interest in compliance with Art. 84 CISG. The court stated that, according to Art. 84(1) CISG, interest for refund of the price paid by the buyer accrues from the date of payment. As to the interest rate, the court applied the Austrian statutory interest rate, since the Convention is silent on this point (Art. 7(2) CISG). With regard to the currency of the reimbursement, the court stated that the buyer was entitled to reimbursement in the same currency agreed upon by the parties for the payment of the price. The amount due was determined with reference to the exchange rate agreed upon by the parties in the contract."

9. Int'l Comm. Arb., no. 7754 of 1995, *at* http://cisgw3.law.pace.edu/cases/957754i1.html.

Original language:	English
Translation:	French

Court:
"Defendant challenged the interest rate put forward by Claimant, claiming that the applicable rate, if any, should be that of Singapore as the currency of the contract or of the creditor's residence. To that end, it relied on two arbitral awards. In ICC case No 5460, the dispute involved an Austrian resident and a South African firm. The single arbitrator awarded the claimant the Austrian interest as a perfectly proper rate, without any particular justification; however, this was the rate claimed by the creditor and the issue does not appear to have been discussed. In ICC case No 6653-1993, the Arbitral Tribunal also applied the rate of the creditor's residence, which it justified as being in relation to the use

which the creditor could have made of the sums and also to the currency of the contract (Journal du droit international, 1993, p. 1046). However, this tribunal was relying primarily on the CISG to adjudicate the dispute and had found that the Convention did not lay down any rule on the matter. In the present case, the parties expressly choose the substantive law of France to rule their relations. This leads the Tribunal to give primary consideration to the French law on the matter. Under French law, the prevailing rule is that the assessment of contractual damages in an international contract is governed by the law of the contract, because the function of damages is to substitute an equivalent to the obligation which was born under that law (Batiffol-Lagarde, Droit international privé, 70 éd., t. 2, No 607, p. 336: la fixation des dommages intérêts obéit à la loi du contrat parce qu'il s'agit de substituer un équivalent àl'obligation créée scion cette loi; see to this effect, Cass. Civ. 15 mai 1935, Journ. dr. mt. 1936.601, Rev. crit. dr. in pr. 1936.463; Cass. com. 20 oct. 1953, Rev. crit. dr. in privé 1954.386). The principle has also been applied by arbitral tribunals (ICC Case No 5428-1988, ICC Case No 5440-1991, quoted by Claimant). A further consideration is in favour of that solution; the choice of French law in this contract between a Polish firm and a Singapore firm obviously stemmed from the desire of each party to avoid the application of the other's national law and therefore to have a neutral law and one with which to get acquainted easily to govern their relations; the rate of interest is an element of that law (see Fr. Civ. C. art. 1907: Interest is legal or contractual. Legal interest is fixed by law. Contractual interest may exceed that fixed by law, whenever this is not prohibited by the law.). The tribunal therefore concludes that the rate of interest to be applied is the legal rate obtaining in France during the relevant period."

10. Int'l Comm. Arb., no. 8128 of 1995, *at* http://cisgw3.law.pace.edu/cases/958128i1.html; http://www.unilex.info/case.cfm?pid=1&do=case&id=207&step=Abstract.

Original language:	French
Translation:	Unavailable

Unilex abstract:
"The buyer was also awarded interest, according to Art. 78 CISG. Interest related to the reimbursement of the cost of the sacks accrued from the time of partial avoidance of the contract, while interest related to the expenses due to the substitute purchase accrued from the time in which the bank of the buyer executed the payment for the replacement goods. Since CISG does not determine the rate of interest, the Arbitral Tribunal applied the average bank short term lending rate to prime borrowers, being the solution adopted either by Art. 7.4.9 of the UNIDROIT Principles of International Commercial Contracts and by Art. 4.507 of the Principles of European Contract Law. The

Arbitral Tribunal considered that such rules were applicable as they must be considered general principles on which CISG is based (Art. 7(2) CISG). In the case at hand, the London International Bank Offered Rate (LIBOR) plus 2% required by the buyer corresponded to the bank short term lending rate to enterprises. The buyer was therefore awarded interest at the required rate."

11. Int'l Comm. Arb., no. 8740 of 1996, *at* http://cisgw3.law.pace.edu/cases/968740i1.html.

Original language:	English
Translation:	Unavailable

Court:
"As the interest rate of 9 percent per annum was not disputed by either party and determined to be reasonable by the Tribunal based on the currency in question, this rate was accepted by the Tribunal."

12. Int'l Comm. Arb., no. 8769 of 1996, *at* http://cisgw3.law.pace.edu/cases/968769i1.html; http://www.unilex.info/case.cfm?pid=1&do=case&id=397&step=FullText.

Original language:	English
Translation:	Unavailable

Court (digest):
"If a party fails to pay the price or any other sum that is in arrears, the other party is entitled to interest on it, without prejudice to any claim for damages recoverable under article 74." CISG Article 78. [Seller] claimed interest at 10.5%. CISG Art. 78 does not specify a particular interest rate. The arbitrator considered it appropriate to apply a commercially reasonable interest rate in accordance with Art. 7.4.9 of the UNIDROIT Principles. Finding that the interest claimed was commercially reasonable, [seller] was awarded interest as claimed."

Unilex excerpt:
"Claimant claims interest at the French statutory rate from [...] Respondent claims interest at 10.5 % on [...] since [...]

Claimant is entitled to interest on the sums awarded pursuant to Art. 78 of the Vienna Convention. Art. 78 Vienna Convention does not specify a particular interest rate. The sole Arbitrator considers it appropriate to apply a commercially reasonable interest rate (see Art. 7.4.9. subs. 2 Unidroit Principles). The interest rate claimed is commercially reasonable for the award currency; Austrian schillings. On […], the date from which Respondent claims interest, the Agreement had been terminated. The sums claimed were due in the sense of Art. 78 Vienna Convention. Accordingly, interest is awarded to Respondent as claimed."

13. Int'l Comm. Arb., no. 8611 of 1997, *at* http://cisgw3.law.pace.edu/cases/978611i1.html.

Original language: German
Translation: Available (English)

Court (translation):
"Art. 78 CISG provides 'If a party fails to pay the price or any other sum that is in arrears, the other party is entitled to interest on it …' … The demand, recognized by the [buyer], for interest on arrears totaling DM 4,128.55 from earlier purchases is excluded from the general payment of interest because this would lead to interest on interest, which is prohibited in Art. 78 CISG, and which, through Art.289 of the German Civil Code and Art.353 of the German Commercial Code, is expressly not provided for… Because Art. 78 CISG does not, for obvious reasons, define the interest rate, the law applicable to this matter, in certain circumstances the monetary law, comes into force. Both are part of German law which, in Art.352 of the Commercial Code concerning trade transactions, fixes the interest rate at 5%."

14. Int'l Comm. Arb., no. 8716 of 1997, *at* http://cisgw3.law.pace.edu/cases/978716i1.html.

Original language: English
Translation: Unavailable

Digest:
"Interest was awarded at a rate of 5%, the rate in force in Italy at the time of the award, running from the time when the [seller] put the [buyer] on notice to fulfill its obligation until payment was made by the [buyer] in full."

15. Int'l Comm. Arb., no. 8962 of 1997, *at* http://cisgw3.law.pace.edu/cases/978962i1.html.

Original language: English
Translation: Unavailable

Court:
"Pursuant to Art. 78 of the United Nations Convention for the International Sale of Goods, if a party is in default with payment of the price of sale or of other amount of money, the other party is entitled to interest on the amount in delay, no rights to compensation for damage being thereby affected pursuant to Art. 74 of the Convention. In the question of the interest the Claimant proposed the Romanian Government's Order Nr. 18 to he applied. With regard to what has already been mentioned about the law applicable to the merits of the dispute, the Arbitrator applies Art. 78 of the mentioned Convention to this question. Since the Claimant has the right for the amount to be paid to him in DEM, the application of Art. 78 of the said Convention implies that a commercially reasonable interest is due to the Claimant. Pursuant to Line (Article) 7 of the Purchasing Contract ... the Defendant had the obligation to pay for the goods which had been delivered within 10 days after the delivery. The delivery was made on January 28th, 1994, which means that the Defendant was obliged to pay by February 7th, 1994; at that time the commercially reasonable interest on German Marks was 5.4% p.a. The Claimant has the entitlement to interest of 5.4% p.a. from February 8th, 1994, until the actual payment. The Defendant has not yet paid the amount of ..., he remains in default, and this default shall expire no sooner than upon payment of the said amount."

16. Int'l Comm. Arb., no. 8908 of 1998, *at* http://cisgw3.law.pace.edu/cases/988908i1.html; http://www.unilex.info/case.cfm?pid=1&do=case&id=401&step=FullText.

Original language:	English
Translation:	Unavailable

Court:
"The Vienna Convention lays down a general rule, in Article 78, that the liability for payment of a sum is subject to interest for late payment, but it does not lay down the criteria for calculating this interest. International case law presents a wide range of possibilities in this respect, but amongst the criteria adopted in various judgments, the more appropriate appears to be that of the rates generally applied in international trade for the contractual currency [...]. In concrete terms, since the contractual currency is the dollar and the parties are European, the applicable rate is the 3-month LIBOR on the dollar, increased by one percentage point, with effect from the due date not respected up until full payment has been made. However, capitalization of interest is excluded, as from Respondent's arbitration answer, since this is not provided for in the Vienna Convention and does not appear to be in keeping with international trade usages. Revaluation is also included in the above mentioned rate."

17. Int'l Comm. Arb., no. 9333 of 1998, *at* http://cisgw3.law.pace.edu/cases/989333i1.html.

Original language:	French
Translation:	Available (English)

Court (translation):
"Claimant has modified its claim attempting to obtain interest on sums in arrears, in that it claims interest that is calculated at the rate of 5 % under the provisions of Article 104 of the Swiss Code of Obligations (and not the legal rate under French law) accruing from the date of filing the arbitration suit … Claimant had already requested the payment of interest when filing the arbitration suit. Had the Claimant persisted on basing its claim on French law, the Tribunal would have been obliged not to declare the claim to be inadmissible, but to apply the Swiss Code of Obligations. Furthermore, one can consider the question whether interest does not after all constitute a part of the principal claim. For example, an author recently wrote:

"From a functional perspective, the interest claim in Art. 78 CISG, just as the one incorporated in Art. 7.4.9 of the UNIDROIT Principles, and any statutory interest claim constitutes the minimum lump sum compensation for damages in areas where the creditor need not prove the actual damage incurred. It is a long-standing practice of international arbitrators, as well as of the Iran-U.S. Claims Tribunal, to consider the interest claim as part of the general claim for damages." (Klaus Peter Berger, *International Arbitral Practice and the UNIDROIT Principles of International Commercial Contracts*, 46, Am. J. Comp. L. 135 (1999).

[…]

Under Article 104 of the Swiss Code of Obligations, to which the contract is subject, every debtor being in delay with a payment of an amount of money owes interest of 5 % per year on the sum in arrears. Nothing in the contract suggested that the parties had intended to exclude the right to the payment of interest for delayed payment. Such an exclusion would have been difficult to reconcile with the usages of international trade which are echoed by, among others, the United Nations Convention on Contracts for the International Sale of Goods (CISG) and also the UNIDROIT Principles of International Commercial Contracts, referred to by the author mentioned above. In the light of Article 104 of the Swiss Code and the claim of Claimant, it is adequate to combine ordering the Respondent to make payment to Claimant for the commission with an order for the payment of interest at a rate of 5% since the date of filing the arbitration suit."

18. Int'l Comm. Arb., no. 9574 of 1998, *at* http://cisgw3.law.pace.edu/cases/989574i1.html; http://www.unilex.info/case.cfm?pid=1&do=case&id=527&step=FullText.

Original language:	English
Translation:	Unavailable

Court:
"In case of transactions subject to the Austrian Commercial Code, for defaults in making money payments the debtor must pay interest at the rate of 5% p.a. (section 352 Austrian Commercial Code; Article 78 UN Sales Convention). Since the parties are both businessmen and the present contract is thus subject to the Austrian Commercial Code, the Plaintiff is, in principle, also entitled to claim interest on the remaining purchase price."

19. Int'l Comm. Arb., no. 9187 of 1999, *at* http://cisgw3.law.pace.edu/cases/999187i1.html.

Original language:	English
Translation:	Unavailable

Court:
"According to Art. 78 CISG, interest is owed if a party fails to pay the price or for any other sum that the party is in arrears with. Neither the CISG not the CO indicates whether interest is owed on **damages**. Legal writers are controversial, but the majority of writers answer in the affirmative and would grant the creditor of damages interest calculated from the date of occurrence of the damage (Stoll in V Caemmerer/Schlechtriem, op. cit. N 15 to Art. 78 CISG). Damage arose when the respective payments were actually made. In principle, from those points in time (and not from the date of the payment of the purchase price as contended by Claimant) interest began to accrue. However, since Claimant fails to submit a detailed interest calculation based on the respective dates, the Arbitral Tribunal deems it appropriate to award interest as of the date when Claimant filed its Request ... This takes into consideration that, while some parts of the losses ... occurred prior to that date, other relevant payments ... had to be effected only at a later stage. As to the rate of interest, Art. 78 CISG is silent. Therefore, national law is supplementarily applicable (Stoll in V Caemmerer/Schlechtriem, op. cit., N 21, 26 to Art. 78 CISG). Swiss law provides that if and as long as the customary bank discount exceeds 5% at the place of payment, the interest rate between business people may be charged at such higher rate (Art.104/3 CO). The burden of proof for such higher rate during the entire period for which interest is claimed lies with the claiming party. Claimant has made no argument for a higher rate short of a reference to

exhibits. This reference is not sufficient since the documents submitted fail to prove that the customary discount for USD exceeded 5% between ... and today. As a consequence, the Arbitral Tribunal applies the legal rate of 5%."

20. Int'l Comm. Arb., no. 9448 of 1999, *at* http://cisgw3.law.pace.edu/cases/99 9448i1.html.

Original language:	English
Translation:	Unavailable

Court:
"According to art. 78 CISG, if a party fails to pay the price or any other sum that is in arrears, the other party is entitled to interest on it. The rate to be applied is, however, a matter, in the first place, for the domestic law (Farnsworth, in Bianca-Bonell, Commentary an the International Sales Law, The 1980 Vienna Sales Convention, page 570). Therefore, the Swiss Code of Obligations (CO) is applicable, According to art. 104 (1) C0, if an obligor is in default as to the payment of a financial debt, he shall pay penalty interest at five percent per annum. Between merchants, penalty interest may be calculated at a higher rate, when the usual bank discount at the place of payment is higher than five percent (art. 104 (3) CO). As Claimants did not offer any proof for this usual bank discount (which according to the Swiss Federal Supreme Court Decision BGE 116 II 141 is not the same as the interest rate on a bank loan), the penalty interest to be awarded to Respondent is five percent according to art. 104 (1) CO. Pursuant to Art.106 (1) CO, "if the obligee has incurred greater damage than that compensated by the penalty interest (arts. 104, 105), the obligor will be obligated to also compensate such damage unless he proves that no fault is attributable to him". An example of such damage is the borrowing of third-party funds an which a higher interest than covered by the penalty interest has to be paid (Zürcher Kommentar zum Schweizerischen Privatrecht, N 2 at art. 106). Claimants submitted a table showing payments to... (an importer of Claimants) for which allegedly a credit loan was engaged... Furthermore, Claimants submitted bank statements showing that Claimants were charged a certain interest rate an their loan from the bank. This interest rate ranged between 9.0625% and 9.375% in the period of time between September 24, 1996 (the date of the earliest submitted bank statement) and June 12, 1997 (this being the maturity date for the loan as of the bank statement of February 20, 1997). Claimants' submitted bank statements provide evidence that Claimants had, in fact, taken up credit, even though these did not show the entire claimed amount for the entire time. As Claimants have not provided strict evidence for their claim – they request 9.5%, but prove at the most a rate of 9.375% for a limited period of time and a limited amount – the Arbitral Tribunal will not apply the percentage rate most favorable to

Claimants, but rather an average rate of 9%. Within the Arbitral Tribunal's scope of free evaluation of the evidence, and considering that taking up a credit in a situation in which an obligor is in default is common nowadays, it accepts that for the period of time Claimants have submitted evidence, they have shown that they have suffered damages higher than the penalty interest of five percent. The Arbitral Tribunal therefore awards interest at a rate of 9% on the unpaid invoices for the time between September 24, 1996 and June 12, 1997. For the rest of the time interest is claimed, Claimants have not submitted any evidence in regard to having incurred greater damage than 5%. The burden of proof, however, lies on Claimants for the amount of the interest owed (Swiss Federal Supreme Court Decision BGE 116 II 141). Therefore, for the remainder of the time, an interest rate of 5% is to be applied as penalty interest, as no proof for a greater damage has been submitted for this period of time."

Summary

Cases involving Article 78: 20

Cases for which an English translation/text is available: 17

Cases for which only an abstract was available: 3

Cases for which neither translation nor abstract was available: 0

- Contrary to what is sometimes provided in several legal systems, the right to interest doesn't need a formal notice
- Neither the CISG not the CO indicates whether interest is owed on **damages**. Legal writers do not agree, but the majority of them answer in the affirmative and would grant the creditor of damages interest calculated from the date of occurrence of the damage.
- Rate interest fixed by according to *lex fori*. Out of 12 cases resorting to domestic law to fix rate, at least 6 made direct reference to domestic international private law.
- At least 3 cases made reference to LIBOR/UNIDROIT/PECL principles for determining interest rate.
- At least 2 cases made reference to *lex monetae*.

Appendix 10
Italy

Courts

Pretura circondariale	Court of First Instance
Pretura	District Court
Tribunale	District Court
Coste di Apello	Court of Appeals

1. Pretura circondariale [Court of First Instance] di Parma, sez. di Fidenza n. 77/89, 24. Nov. 1989 (Italy), *at.* http://cisgw3.law.pace.edu/cases/891124i3.html.

   Original language: Italian
   Translation: Available

   Court (translation):
   "The Court directs the [seller] to return to the [buyer] the sum of IT£ [...] plus legal interest and devaluation from [date of avoidance] until the date of the payment. The Court, however, rejects the [buyer's] request for damages and for immediate enforceability because [buyer] did not prove any of the material elements of these claims."

2. Pretura di Torino [District Court] (docket: unavail), 30 Jan. 1997 (Italy), *at* http://cisgw3.law.pace.edu/cases/970130i3.html.

   Original language: Italian
   Translation: Available

   Court (translation):
   "The [seller's] demand for payment of greater damage under art. 1224 c.c. [Italian Civil Code] may be further granted, seeing that, should it be proven that the [seller] suffered damages greater than that returned with lawful interest (*cf.* the interest liquidation tables produced sub 11 by [seller]); the aggregate interest is to be fixed in the measure of 12% and is to run from 13 October 1994 (the [buyer] has not challenged that the parties agreed upon payment thirty days from receipt of the goods)."

3. Corte di Appello di Milano [Court of Appeals] (docket: unavail), 11 Dec. 1998 (Italy), *at* http://cisgw3.law.pace.edu/cases/981211i3.html.

Original language: Italian
Translation: Available

Court (translation):
"The amount to which the [seller] would be entitled to should be increased by the accrued interest at the Italian legal rate, from the date of the breach."

4. Tribunale di Pavia [District Court] (docket: unavail), 29 Dec. 1999, *at* http://cisgw3.law.pace.edu/cases/991229i3.html.

Original language: Italian
Translation: Available

Court (translation): "As far as interest on the sums not paid, it will be observed that the United Nations Convention provides only a general right to interest, without specifying which rate is to be applied. In light of the fact that the drafters of the Convention have intentionally left the problem of the applicable rate unresolved, as one evinces from the *travaux préparatoires*, it cannot be maintained that this is an issue dealing with one of the areas which, by virtue of Article 7(2) of the Convention, should be governed by the general principles upon which the Convention is based. Instead, it is a question not at all addressed by the Convention and which hence is to be resolved in light of the applicable law, that is to say, in light of [internal] Italian law – such being the law of the seller, which Art. 3(1) of the Hague Convention of 1955 beckons to. This solution corresponds besides to that adopted by foreign case law (see, for example, *Pretore della giurisdizione Locarno-Campagna* 16 December 1991 [of Switzerland] which, although not binding, is however to be taken into consideration as required by Art. 7(1) of the CISG. Consequently, interest is determined according to the measure of the legal rate in force in Italy. With respect to the life of the interest, it will be noted that being in default is not required; interest is therefore due from the due date of the invoice to settlement of the debt. Nothing is due by right of greater damages from monetary devaluation because, in the period of time involved here, the legal annual interest rates have always been greater than the rate of inflation. On the other hand, the plaintiff [seller] which has the burden of proving damages (Art. 7(2), Art. 79 CISG), has not proved damages incurred because of the missing payment and the Convention clearly distinguishes between interest and damages (see Art. 78)."

5. Tribunale di Padova [District Court] n.40466, 31 Mar. 2004, *at* http://cisgw3.law.pace.edu/cases/040331i3.html.

Original language: Italian
Translation: Available

Court (translation): "The right to interest on the unpaid sum is expressly provided by Article 78 of the Convention, which hereby states: "*If a party fails to pay the price or any other sum that is in arrears, the other party is entitled to interest on it, without prejudice to any claim for damages recoverable under article 74.*" From the reading of this provision it is easily ascertained that it does not resolve all the problems related to the interest on the sums not paid. In fact, as is often emphasized from doctrine and judicial decisions, the foretold article only forecasts a "general right to interest" (see the arbitral award of the ICC arbitral tribunal, no. [7585 of 1992], in *Journal du droit international*, 1995, 1015 et seq.; OLG [Provincial Court of Appeal] Koblenz [Germany], 17 September 1993, in *Recht der internationalen Wirtschaft*, 1993, 938); other issues were not addressed by the drafters of the United Nations Convention, among those the applicable rate of interest (an important issue relative to the decision in this controversy).

[16] The missing criteria on the base of which the rate of interest is to be determined has generated a dispute in doctrine among those who sustain that the question is dealt with by the Convention, even if not expressly (internal gap), and those who, on the other hand, believe that the determination of the rate of interest is a subject excluded from the scope of application of the Convention (external gap). In the first hypothesis, it is possible to make reference to the general principles of the Convention; meanwhile, in the second, it is necessary to make reference to the rules of private international law, in order to identify the applicable substantive law. This Tribunal is inclined, as are the prevailing doctrine and court decisions, toward the second thesis. The measure of interest must be considered a subject excluded from the Convention, since the [Convention's drafters] were not able to come to any agreement on that point, and therefore intentionally excluded addressing that problem (see also Tribunale di Pavia, [cited above]). It follows that it is not justified, as per Article 7(2), to turn to the general principles on which the Convention is based – as, on the contrary, some courts have held (see for example RB Koophandel [District Court] Ieper [Belgium], 29 January 2001, published on the Internet at the following site: [...]; Juzgado Nacional de Primiera Instancia en lo Comercial n. 10 [National Commercial Court of First Instance], Buenos Aires [Argentina], 6 October 1994, published on the Internet at the following site: [...]; arbitral decisions of the Arbitral Court of the Vienna [Austria] Federal Chamber of Commerce, nos. 4366 and 4318, in *Recht der internationalen Wirtschaft*, 1995, 590 et seq.) –, the employment of which would give to this question wide discretionary if not even arbitrary solutions, and therefore solutions contrary to that requirement of the certainty of law that is an indispensable condition for the development of international commerce.

In order determine the interest rate, one must then make reference to the law applicable by virtue of the norms of the private international law of the forum (in this sense, *see* LG [District Court] Saarbrücken [Germany], 25 November 2002, in

Internationales Handelsrecht, 2003, 70-71; LG [District Court] Stendal [Germany], [12 October] 2000, in *Internationales Handelsrecht*, 2001, 30 et seq.; LG [District Court] Darmstadt [Germany], 9 May 2000, in *Internationales Handelsrecht*, 2001, 27 et seq.; OLG [Appellate Court] Stuttgart [Germany], 28 February 2000, in *OLG Report-Stuttgart*, 2000, 407 et seq.; Trib. Pavia, [cited above]; OLG [Appellate Court] Koblenz [Germany], 18 November 1999, published on the Internet at the following site: [...]; KA [District Court] Zug [Switzerland], 21 October 1999, published on the Internet at the following site: [...] KG [District Court] Kanton Zug [Switzerland], 16 October 1997, published on the Internet at the following site: [...]. In this case it is necessary therefore to make reference to the already mentioned norms of the Hague Convention of 1955, that refer back to Italian law as the law of the seller (see Article 3(1) of the Hague Convention of 1955). Consequently, it is necessary to apply the legal rate as per Article 1284 of the Italian Civil Code considering obviously the variations that this has undergone over time."

Summary

Cases involving Article 78: 5

Cases for which an English translation is available: 5

Cases for which only an abstract was available: 0

Cases for which neither translation nor abstract was available: 0

- The CISG provides only a general right to interest, without specifying which rate is to be applied. In light of the fact that the drafters of the Convention have intentionally left the problem of the applicable rate unresolved (see the *travaux préparatoire*), it cannot be maintained that this is an issue dealing with one of the areas which, by virtue of Article 7(2) of the Convention, should be governed by the general principles upon which the Convention is based.
- Instead, it is a question not at all addressed by the Convention and which hence is to be resolved in light of the otherwise applicable law. This solution matches foreign case law (see, for example, *Pretore della giurisdizione Locarno-Campagna* 16 December 1991, Switzerland] which, although not binding, is however to be taken into consideration as required by Art. 7(1) of the CISG.
- As to when interest start running, although the first Italian case stated otherwise, given that a formal request is not required, interest is, therefore, due from the due date.
- Greater damages may be awarded. However, they must be proved.
- The Convention clearly distinguishes between interest and damages.

Appendix 11
Netherlands

Courts

Arrondissementsrechtbank	District Court
Gerechshof	District Court of Appeals
Hoge Raad	Supreme Court

1. Hoge Raad [Supreme Court] n.14422, 13 Sept. 1991 (Neth.), *at* http://cisgw3.law.pace.edu/cases/910913n1.html.

   Original language: Dutch
   Translation: Unavailable

2. Arrondissementsrechtbank Arnhem [District Court] n.1992/182, 25 Feb. 1993 (Neth.), *at* http://cisgw3.law.pace.edu/cases/930225n1.html.

   Original language: Dutch
   Translation: Unavailable

   Unilex abstract:
   "The seller was entitled to payment of the purchase price plus interests under Art. 78 CISG."

3. Arrondissementsrechtbank Roermond [District Court] n.920159, 6 May 1993 (Neth.), *at* http://cisgw3.law.pace.edu/cases/930506n1.html.

   Original language: Dutch
   Translation: Unavailable

   Unilex abstract:
   "The seller was entitled to interest under Art. 78 CISG, accruing from the date when payment was due which, in the absence of an agreement between the parties, was the date of delivery of the goods (Art. 58 CISG). As Art. 78 CISG does not determine the rate of interest, the Court applied the Dutch private international law rules which led to the law of Italy and as such to the Italian statutory interest rate."

4. Arrondissementsrechtbank Arnhem [District Court] n.1992/1257, 30 Dec. 1993 (Neth.), *at* http://cisgw3.law.pace.edu/cases/931230n1.html.

   Original language: Dutch
   Translation: Unavailable

   Unilex abstract:
   "The buyer was condemned to pay the purchase price plus a contractual penalty for late payment, as well as interest under Art. 78 CISG. The Court held that it was reasonable to apply German law in order to determine the rate of interest since the price was to be paid in German currency and the law applicable to the contract in the absence of CISG was German law."

5. Arrondissementsrechtbank Hertogenbosch [District Court] n.1369/92, 4 Feb. 1994 (Neth.), *at* http://cisgw3.law.pace.edu/cases/940204n1.html.

   Original language: Dutch
   Translation: Unavailable

6. Arrondissementsrechtbank Amsterdam [District Court] n.H 92.3572, 15 June 1994 (Neth.), *at* http://cisgw3.law.pace.edu/cases/940615n1.html.

   Original language: Dutch
   Translation: Unavailable

   Unilex abstract:
   "Furthermore the seller was entitled to interest since the buyer had failed to pay the price (Art. 78 CISG). As Art. 78 CISG does not determine the rate of interest the Court, on the basis of Art. 7(2) CISG, applied the Dutch private international law rules which led to the law of Denmark."

7. Arrondissementsrechtbank Zutphen [District Court] n.206h/94, 27 Apr. 1995 (Neth.), *at* http://cisgw3.law.pace.edu/cases/950427n1.html.

   Original language: Dutch
   Translation: Unavailable

8. Arrondissementsrechtbank Almelo [District Court] n.4367, 9 Aug. 1995 (Neth.), *at* http://cisgw3.law.pace.edu/cases/950809n1.html.

   Original language: Dutch
   Translation: Unavailable

Unilex abstract:
"As to the question of interest, since CISG does not determine the rate of interest, the Court stated that the rate was to be determined according to the law of the country where the price was to be paid (in this case German law as the law of the country where the seller had its place of business) (Art. 57(1)(a) CISG)."

9. Gerechtshof Arnhem [District Court of Appeals] n. 94/305, 22 Aug. 1995 (Neth.), *at* http://cisgw3.law.pace.edu/cases/950822n1.html.

Original language:	Dutch
Translation:	Unavailable

Editorial remarks:
"The Appellate Court upheld the following ruling of the District Court. "[Seller] also claimed interest is due according to CISG Article 78. Because the rate of interest has not been arranged in the CISG, a rate of interest should be paid in a reasonable amount according to German law, Section 288 BGB (4%)". The basis of this conclusion is said to be "because the payment has been agreed in Germany currency and moreover, besides the CISG, German law is applicable."

10. Gerechtshof Hertogenbosch [District Court of Appeals] n.456/95/H, 24 Apr. 1996 (Neth.), *at* http://cisgw3.law.pace.edu/cases/960424n1.html.

Original language:	Dutch
Translation:	Unavailable

Unilex abstract:
"The seller was thus awarded the purchase price and interest at the rate fixed by the standard terms."

11. Arrondissementsrechtbank Amsterdam [District Court] n.H 94.1364, 15 May 1996 (Neth.), *at* http://cisgw3.law.pace.edu/cases/960515n1.html.

Original language:	Dutch
Translation:	Unavailable

12. Hof Arnhem [District Court of Appeals] n.95/570, 15 Apr. 1997 (Neth.), *at* http://cisgw3.law.pace.edu/cases/970415n1.html.

Original language:	Dutch
Translation:	Unavailable

Unilex abstract:
"The seller was also awarded interest according to Art. 78 CISG. As CISG does not determine the interest rate, the Court stated that it was to be determined in accordance with the domestic law otherwise applicable to the contract (Italian Law)."

13. Hof Hertogenbosch [District Court of Appeals] n.1034/95/BR, 2 Oct. 1997 (Neth.), *at* http://cisgw3.law.pace.edu/cases/971002n1.html.

Original language:	Dutch
Translation:	Unavailable

Unilex abstract:
"The Court awarded the seller payment of the price plus additional interest as damages (Arts. 74 and 78 CISG), as well as reimbursement of extra-judicial collecting charges."

14. Hoge Raad [Supreme Court] n.16.442, 20 Feb. 1998 (Neth.), *at* http://cisgw3.law.pace.edu/cases/980220n1.html.

Original language:	Dutch
Translation:	Unavailable

Unilex abstract:
"The seller was awarded interest on the sums due at the Italian statutory rate, accruing from the date in which payment had to be made, without the need of a formal request by the seller (Arts. 78 and 59 CISG)."

15. Netherlands Arbitration Institute n.2319, 15 Oct. 2002 (Neth.), *at* http://cisgw3.law.pace.edu/cases/021015n1.html.

Original language: English

Court:
"Finally, parties have come to an agreement that the Dutch statutory interest rate is applicable and, thus, damages as determined in this award will be increased with the applicable Dutch statutory interest rate."

Summary

Cases involving Article 78: 15

Cases for which an English (translation/text) is available: 1

Cases for which only an abstract was available: 10

Cases for which neither translation nor abstract was available: 4

- Courts apply domestic law to determine the proper interest rate. The applicable domestic law is determined by the forum international private law. Currency may play a role in determining the rate.
- No need for formal request.
- Damages under Article 74 are available in addition to interest under Article 78.

Appendix 12
Russia

1. Tribunal of International Commercial Arbitration at the Russian Federation Chamber of Commerce and Industry n.1/1993, 15 Apr. 1994 (Russ.), *at* http://cisgw3.law.pace.edu/cases/940415r1.html.

   Original language: Russian
   Translation: Unavailable

   Unilex abstract:
   "The buyer, with reference to Art. 81(2) CISG, had also claimed restitution of the sum paid as the price of the goods under the contract. With reference to Art. 78 and Art. 84(1) CISG the buyer had claimed interest on the price to be refunded.

   The Tribunal decided in favor of the buyer and ordered the seller to refund the price paid for the goods and to pay interest on this sum at the rate established by the law of the buyer's country. The time period within which interest was to be paid was determined as starting from the date of the payment of the price of the goods until the actual date payment of the debt."

2. Tribunal of International Commercial Arbitration at the Russian Federation Chamber of Commerce and Industry n.375/1993, 9 Sept. 1994 (Russ.), *at* http://cisgw3.law.pace.edu/cases/940909r1.html.

   Original language: Russian
   Translation: Unavailable

   Unilex abstract:
   "The Tribunal also awarded, on the basis of Art. 78 CISG, interest on all the sums the seller owed at the rate provided for by the law of the seller's country."

3. Tribunal of International Commercial Arbitration at the Russian Federation Chamber of Commerce and Industry n.493/1993, 17 Nov. 1994 (Russ.), *at* http://cisgw3.law.pace.edu/cases/941117r1.html.

   Original language: Russian
   Translation: Unavailable

4. Tribunal of International Commercial Arbitration at the Russian Federation Chamber of Commerce and Industry n.80/1994, 24 Apr. 1995 (Russ.), *at* http://cisgw3.law.pace.edu/cases/950424r1.html.

   Original language: Russian
   Translation: Unavailable

5. Tribunal of International Commercial Arbitration at the Russian Federation Chamber of Commerce and Industry n.400/1993, 28 Apr. 1995 (Russ.), *at* http://cisgw3.law.pace.edu/cases/950428r1.html.

   Original language: Russian
   Translation: Unavailable

6. Tribunal of International Commercial Arbitration at the Russian Federation Chamber of Commerce and Industry n.321/1994, 15 May 1995 (Russ.), *at* http://cisgw3.law.pace.edu/cases/950515r1.html.

   Original language: Russian
   Translation: Available

   Court (translation):
   "As for the claimant [seller]'s demand for interest on the debt at an annual rate of 10 percent, the Tribunal found this claim justified and based on para. 9 of the contract. In the course of the arbitration proceedings, the claimant [seller] specified the date of the beginning of the period of the delay in payment and, therefore, the date from which the interest on the sum of the debt shall be reckoned. This date is understood as the date of rendering the invoice in the bank of the [respondent] buyer.

   The Tribunal awarded interest at an annual rate of 10 percent starting from 8 June 1992 till the execution of the payment."

7. Tribunal of International Commercial Arbitration at the Russian Federation Chamber of Commerce and Industry n.369/1994, 1 Dec. 1995 (Russ.), *at* http://cisgw3.law.pace.edu/cases/951201r1.html.

   Original language: Russian
   Translation: Available

8. Tribunal of International Commercial Arbitration at the Russian Federation Chamber of Commerce and Industry n.364/1994, 13 Dec. 1995 (Russ.), *at* http://cisgw3.law.pace.edu/cases/951213r1.html.

Original language: Russian
Translation: Unavailable

9. Tribunal of International Commercial Arbitration at the Russian Federation Chamber of Commerce and Industry n.133/1994, 19 Dec. 1995 (Russ.), *at* http://cisgw3.law.pace.edu/cases/951219r1.html.

Original language: Russian
Translation: Available

10. Tribunal of International Commercial Arbitration at the Russian Federation Chamber of Commerce and Industry n.228/1995, 31 Jan. 1996 (Russ.), *at* http://cisgw3.law.pace.edu/cases/960131r1.html.

Original language: Russian
Translation: Available

11. Tribunal of International Commercial Arbitration at the Russian Federation Chamber of Commerce and Industry n.328/1994, 10 Feb. 1996 (Russ.), *at* http://cisgw3.law.pace.edu/cases/960210r1.html.

Original language: Russian
Translation: Available

Court (translation):
"The [buyer] claims annual interest at the rate of LIBOR + 2% from the date of filing the counteraction. Since the counteraction was filed after the first part of the Civil Code of the Russian Federation had come into force, the Tribunal is guided by the Article 395 of this Code when resolving this issue. The Tribunal believes that the annual interest shall be awarded at the rate of LIBOR on the date of this judgment, without the extra 2% charge from the date of filing of the counteraction ... to the date of payment, because the [buyer] has not presented any evidence which can serve as a ground for such extra charge."

12. Tribunal of International Commercial Arbitration at the Russian Federation Chamber of Commerce and Industry n.166/1995, 12 Mar. 1996 (Russ.), *at* http://cisgw3.law.pace.edu/cases/960312r1.html.

Original language: Russian
Translation: Available

Court (translation):
"Taking into account the aforesaid, as well as the calculations provided by the [buyer] on separate sums of [buyer]'s claims and proof of their amounts, contained in the case materials, the Tribunal considered it possible to grant the following claims of the [buyer]:

[...]

- annual interest for the period until 31 December 1994 (inclusive) on the basis of Article 66(3) of the Fundamentals of Civil Legislation of the USSR 1991."

13. Tribunal of International Commercial Arbitration at the Russian Federation Chamber of Commerce and Industry n.218/1995, 12 Mar. 1996 (Russ.), *at* http://cisgw3.law.pace.edu/cases/960312r2.html.

Original language:	Russian
Translation:	Available

14. Tribunal of International Commercial Arbitration at the Russian Federation Chamber of Commerce and Industry n.72/1995, 25 Apr. 1996 (Russ.), *at* http://cisgw3.law.pace.edu/cases/960425r1.html.

Original language:	Russian
Translation:	Available

15. Tribunal of International Commercial Arbitration at the Russian Federation Chamber of Commerce and Industry n.448/1995, 18 Sept. 1996 (Russ.), *at* http://cisgw3.law.pace.edu/cases/960918r1.html.

Original language:	Russian
Translation:	Available

16. Tribunal of International Commercial Arbitration at the Russian Federation Chamber of Commerce and Industry n.433/1994, 26 Sept. 1996 (Russ.), *at* http://cisgw3.law.pace.edu/cases/960926r1.html.

Original language:	Russian
Translation:	Available

Court (translation):

"3.3.3 [Recovery of the interest for bank loan paid by the buyer]

The [buyer] proved that it had used the loan from the Danish bank and paid in average 12% of the annual interest for the loan. The Tribunal held that the sum paid by the [buyer] to the bank constituted losses of the [buyer], thus, under Article 74 CISG, [buyer] had to be compensated by the [seller] in the amount of 12%, of the granted principal sum of the debt.

3.3.4 [Recovery of the annual interest for delay in shipment]

The Tribunal denied the [buyer]'s claim as to recovery of annual interest for delay in the payment of a monetary obligation under Article 78 CISG and rules of Russian civil law, since the seller was not a debtor in connection with the monetary obligations set forth in the contract; but annual interest was to be calculated for the delay or failure to pay a monetary debt."

17. Tribunal of International Commercial Arbitration at the Russian Federation Chamber of Commerce and Industry n.407/1995, 8 Oct. 1996 (Russ.), *at* http://cisgw3.law.pace.edu/cases/961008r1.html.

Original language:	Russian
Translation:	Available

18. Tribunal of International Commercial Arbitration at the Russian Federation Chamber of Commerce and Industry n.430/1995, 25 Feb. 1997 (Russ.), *at* http://cisgw3.law.pace.edu/cases/970225r1.html.

Original language:	Russian
Translation:	Available

19. Tribunal of International Commercial Arbitration at the Russian Federation Chamber of Commerce and Industry n.38/1996, 28 Mar. 1997 (Russ.), *at* http://cisgw3.law.pace.edu/cases/970328r1.html.

Original language:	Russian
Translation:	Available

Court (translation):
"The Tribunal finds it possible to grant the [seller]'s claim of 12% annual interest for the delay in payment for the goods. Since prior to institution of the action, the [seller] did not claim annual interest from the [buyer], the Tribunal has reached the conclusion that annual interest shall be paid on the principal sum of debt under the contract starting on the date of filing the action. As to the other amounts claimed for recovery from the [buyer], annual interest on them shall be awarded starting from the date of rendering of the present

decision. In holding that the [buyer] shall pay 12% annual interest, the Tribunal took into account the following. The party's obligation to pay interest in case of delay in payment of the price is directly stated in Article 78 CISG. Since the interest rate is not set forth in the Convention and since it cannot be determined in conformity with general principles pursuant to Article 7(2) CISG, the provisions of the Russian laws shall apply. Under Article 395 of the Civil Code of the Russian Federation, in case of delay of performance of money obligations, annual interest shall be recovered in the amount of the bank discount interest rate at the place of creditor's location. The [seller]'s claim of 12% annual interest does not exceed the interest rate used for short-term hard currency loans in Russia."

20. Tribunal of International Commercial Arbitration at the Russian Federation Chamber of Commerce and Industry n.220/1996, 11 Apr. 1997 (Russ.), *at* http://cisgw3.law.pace.edu/cases/970411r1.html.

Original language: Russian
Translation: Available

Court (translation):
"The Tribunal decided to grant the [seller]'s claims as to recovery from the [buyer] of the annual interest for using [seller]'s money calculated over the sums of delayed payments according to the calculation presented in the statement of action for the whole period of delay until the date of institution of the action.

The reasonableness of this calculation of annual interest is proved by the article in the official reporter on the average banking rate for given loans on the day of institution of the action of one of the leading UK banks that serves the [seller].

The Tribunal did not grant the [seller]'s motion to employ the interest rate on the day of rendering of the judgment rather than on the day of institution of the action. By so deciding, [the Tribunal] took into attention that the question as to which rate should be employed in case of judicial recovering of the debt on the grounds of Article 395 of the Russian Federation Civil Code is left for the court's discretion."

21. Tribunal of International Commercial Arbitration at the Russian Federation Chamber of Commerce and Industry n.439/1995, 29 May 1997 (Russ.), *at* http://cisgw3.law.pace.edu/cases/970529r1.html.

Original language: Russian
Translation: Available

22. Tribunal of International Commercial Arbitration at the Russian Federation Chamber of Commerce and Industry n.256/1996, 4 June 1997 (Russ.), *at* http://cisgw3.law.pace.edu/cases/970604r1.html.

Original language:	Russian
Translation:	Available

23. Tribunal of International Commercial Arbitration at the Russian Federation Chamber of Commerce and Industry n.451/1996, 6 Nov. 1997 (Russ.), *at* http://cisgw3.law.pace.edu/cases/971106r1.html.

Original language:	Russian
Translation:	Available

24. Tribunal of International Commercial Arbitration at the Russian Federation Chamber of Commerce and Industry n.309/1996, 16 Jan. 1998 (Russ.), *at* http://cisgw3.law.pace.edu/cases/980116r1.html.

Original language:	Russian
Translation:	Available

25. Tribunal of International Commercial Arbitration at the Russian Federation Chamber of Commerce and Industry n.102/1997, 22 Jan. 1998 (Russ.), *at* http://cisgw3.law.pace.edu/cases/980122r1.html.

Original language:	Russian
Translation:	Available

26. Tribunal of International Commercial Arbitration at the Russian Federation Chamber of Commerce and Industry n.243/1996, 18 Feb. 1998 (Russ.), *at* http://cisgw3.law.pace.edu/cases/980218r1.html.

Original language:	Russian
Translation:	Available

Court (translation):
"Having discussed the [seller]'s claim concerning recovery from the [buyer] of the annual interest for use of the [seller]'s money, the Tribunal held that this claim should be granted on the basis of Article 78 CISG. The interest rate should be determined in accordance with Article 395 of the Civil Code of the Russian Federation. However, since the [seller] did not present evidence that the [buyer] had received his invoices, these invoices are deemed to be received by the [buyer] on 27 January 1997 (according to the notice of the ELSI postal

service on the acknowledgement of receipt), i.e., on the day of serving on the [buyer] the [seller]'s statement of action with all the attachments which it included, *inter alia*, the invoices mentioned above. Whereas in accordance with clause 2 of the contract the payment must be made five days after the receipt of the invoice by the buyer, thus the date from which the [buyer]'s obligation to pay the price arose, should be considered 2 February 1997. Therefore, the [buyer] should pay annual interest for use of [seller]'s money from 2 February 1997 up to the date of factual payment, according to the loan rate specified in the report of one of the leading banks at the place of whereabouts of the [seller] on the day the Tribunal's ruling is rendered."

27. Tribunal of International Commercial Arbitration at the Russian Federation Chamber of Commerce and Industry n.160/1997, 5 Mar. 1998 (Russ.), *at* http://cisgw3.law.pace.edu/cases/980305r2.html.

Original language: Russian
Translation: Available

Court (translation):
"Based on Art. 78 of the CISG, [buyer] demanded recovery of the annual interest on the sum of the principal debt and on the sum of the damages suffered, however the [buyer] failed to calculate the sum of the interest to be recovered from [seller], as required by para. 16 of the Rules of the Tribunal, and failed to pay the appropriate arbitration fee relating to the interest. For this reason, the Tribunal left this claim without consideration."

28. Tribunal of International Commercial Arbitration at the Russian Federation Chamber of Commerce and Industry n.487/1996, 11 Mar. 1998 (Russ.), *at* http://cisgw3.law.pace.edu/cases/980311r1.html.

Original language: Russian
Translation: Available

Court (translation):
"Since the contract provided for the application of the law of the seller, the relations between the parties not covered by the contract must be regulated by Russian law and the Vienna Convention 1980 as the part of the Russian Federation's legal system because the Russian Federation is a party to the Vienna Convention and, according to Article 1(1)(b), its provisions are applicable to the above mentioned sales contract.

[...]

According to Article 78 of the Vienna Convention 1980, the [seller] is entitled to interest on sums in arrears. In accordance with Article 395 of the Russian Federation Civil Code, the interest rate is determined on the basis of the place of the [seller]-creditor's banking rate on the date of the fulfillment of the pecuniary obligation; also the creditor's claim may be satisfied on the basis of the banking rate on the date of bringing of the claim or of delivering of the judgment.

The case materials contained a report issued by one of the leading Russian banks on 14 November 1996 in which the bank reports the average rates for credits in foreign currency.

Bearing in mind that the [seller] based his calculation on the minimal rate and that he had the right to claim the recovery of the interest till the moment of the actual payment of the sum in question but limited himself to the sum determined on the date preceding the date of bringing of the claim and that the calculation was supported by case materials, [seller]'s claim for the recovery of the interest must be satisfied."

29. Tribunal of International Commercial Arbitration at the Russian Federation Chamber of Commerce and Industry n.491/1996, 25 Mar. 1998 (Russ.), *at* http://cisgw3.law.pace.edu/cases/980325r1.html.

Original language:	Russian
Translation:	Available

Court (translation):
"The Vienna Convention 1980 is applicable to the relations between the parties (Article 1(1)(a)). The issues not covered by the Convention are regulated by the law determined on the basis of the rules of international private law (Article 7). Since the parties did not determine which law must be applied to their relations the Tribunal pursuant to Article 28 of the Law of the Russian Federation on the Tribunal of International Commercial Arbitration when choosing the applicable law, based [its decision] on Article 166 of the Fundamentals of Civil Law [USSR] of 1991. According to this rule, the law that must be applied is the law of the country of seller, where the seller to the sales contract is established or has the main place of business, *i.e.*, Bulgarian law in this case.

[...]

According to Article 78 of the Vienna Convention 1980, if a party fails to pay the price in time, the other party is entitled to recover interest on the sum in arrears. The [seller] claims the sum which constitutes the annual rate of 5% of the sum of principal debt from 1 January 1995 till 31 December 1996. In his letter of 10 February 1998, the [seller] bound himself to justify the interest rate that he claims in the Tribunal hearing. But during the hearing his representative was absent. No written explanations on the interest rate calculated according to Bulgarian legislation were produced [by the seller].

Taking into account the fact that the annual rate of 5% which the [seller] claims does not exceed the LIBOR rate usually applicable in international trade relations, the Tribunal found it possible to grant the [seller]'s claim.

[...]

The Tribunal granted the claim concerning recovery of the annual interest until the complete recovery of the principal debt from the date of delivery of the judgment till the date of payment of the sum of principal debt at the annual rate of 5%."

30. Tribunal of International Commercial Arbitration at the Russian Federation Chamber of Commerce and Industry n.387/1995, 4 Apr. 1998 (Russ.), *at* http://unilex.info/dynasite.cfm?dssid=2376&dsmid=13354&x=1.

Original language:	Russian
Translation:	Unavailable

Unilex abstract:
"The arbitration tribunal held the right of the seller to interest on the overdue sum on the ground that interest could not be regarded neither as penalties nor like damages according to Art. 78 CISG under which the creditor is entitled to interest, without prejudice to any claim for damages recoverable under Art. 74 CISG."

31. Tribunal of International Commercial Arbitration at the Russian Federation Chamber of Commerce and Industry n.104/1997, 25 May 1998 (Russ.), *at* http://cisgw3.law.pace.edu/cases/980525r1.html.

Original language:	Russian
Translation:	Available

32. Tribunal of International Commercial Arbitration at the Russian Federation Chamber of Commerce and Industry n.83/1997, 10 June 10 1998 (Russ.), *at* http://cisgw3.law.pace.edu/cases/980610r1.html.

Original language: Russian
Translation: Available

Court (translation):
"Since there is no agreement on the applicable law between the parties, the Tribunal pursuant to Article 28 of the Federal Law "On international commercial arbitration" determines the applicable law in accordance with Russian rules of private international law. At the time of the conclusion of the contract, Article 566 of the Civil Code of the Russian Soviet Federal Socialist Republic 1964, which was in force at that time, provided that the rights and obligations of the parties to foreign economic contract are determined under the laws of the place of its conclusion if the parties did not agree otherwise. Since the contract out of which the dispute arose was concluded in Moscow, the relations of the parties are governed by Russian material law. That is why pursuant to Article 1(1)(b) of the Vienna Convention 1980, the relations between of the parties are also governed by the provisions of this Convention which under Article 15 of the Constitution of the Russian Federation prevail over the corresponding provisions of Russian law.

[...]

Under Article 78 of the Vienna Convention 1980, if a party fails to pay the price, the other party is entitled the interest on it. Since the Convention does not fix the interest rate, it is to be determined in conformity with the law applicable by virtue of the rules on of private international law. Referring to Article 395 of the Civil Code of the Russian Federation the [seller] claims to exact the interest for the years 1994, 1995, 1996 and for the first quarter of the year 1997.

But the sum of the interest claimed by the [seller] is not in conformity with the applicable rules or Russian law. First, the Civil Code of the Russian Federation was not in force in 1994 since it came into force only on 1 January 1995. That is why during the year 1994 must be applied the 5% rate fixed by Article 66(3) of the Fundamentals of Civil Law 1991 which were in force at that time in Russia. Second, under Article 395 of the Civil Code of the Russian Federation for the delay in subsequent years, the interest rate is determined on the basis of the bank discount rate at the creditor's place of residence. However, the [seller] applied the rate existing on 11 March 1997 and at the debtor's (not the creditor's) place of residence. Afterwards the [seller], in response to the panel's proposal to submit the evidence proving the rate applicable to the sums in arrears fixed in USD, produced a certificate of 18 April 1998 signed by the manager of a Pakistani bank and stating that under the rules of the State Bank of Pakistan short-term credits are not granted in USD and that the Government of Pakistan permits short-term financing in Pakistani rupees.

In this situation, the Tribunal considered it possible to apply the LIBOR rate, habitually applied in international trade, on the date of the hearing. Under the contract, this sum must be converted into Pakistani rupees. Article 8 of the contract provides that payments for the delivered goods are effected in Pakistani rupees by means of submitting account numbers for collection in National Bank of Pakistan with the conversion at the rate on the date of submission of the papers to the bank. Taking into account the fact that there is no indication in the case concerning this date and that the Tribunal's decision will serve as a ground for exaction of this sum, the Tribunal, applying Article 317 of the Civil Code of the Russian Federation by analogy, considers that the sum to be paid in Pakistani rupees must be determined at the official rate of USD on the date of the actual payment."

33. Tribunal of International Commercial Arbitration at the Russian Federation Chamber of Commerce and Industry n.113/1997, 2 Oct. 1998 (Russ.), *at* http://cisgw3.law.pace.edu/cases/981002r1.html.

Original language:	Russian
Translation:	Available

Court (translation):
"The Tribunal has found that in case of delay of payment, § 55 of GTD [General Terms of Delivery USSR – People's Republic of China] provides for the payment of interest at the annual rate of 6%. Since the [seller] claimed the recovery of interest at the LIBOR annual rate of 5.4207%, which was less than 6% per annum, the Tribunal concluded that [seller]'s claim was reasonable.

According to clause 4 of the contract, the [buyer] should make payment for the goods within 90 days from the date of receipt. The [buyer] with the fax of 6 June 1996 has confirmed the receipt of the last deliveries of goods on 15 February 1996. Therefore, the initial date for the calculation of annual interest is 15 May 1996. Thus, the [seller]'s claim to recover interest at the rate of 5.4207% per annum charged on the principal amount of the claim since 15 May 1996 till the day of payment is granted."

34. Tribunal of International Commercial Arbitration at the Russian Federation Chamber of Commerce and Industry n.196/1997, 22 Oct. 1998 (Russ.), *at* http://cisgw3.law.pace.edu/cases/981022r1.html.

Original language: Russian
Translation: Available

Court (translation):
"According to Art. 78 CISG, the [seller] is entitled to interest on the sum to be paid by the [buyer]. The interest, though not specified in the CISG, is to be calculated in conformity with subsidiary applicable law, that is the Russian Federation Civil Code Article 395, which provides that the interest for the use by the [buyer] of the unlawfully kept money is to be calculated on the basis of the bank interest rate at the [seller]'s place of business. The Tribunal, thus, admits the Certificate of 21 November 1997, issued by the Cypriot Central Bank, presented by the [seller], which certifies that on the day of bringing the action before the Tribunal the interest rate amounted to 8%. The [buyer] did not contest this certificate.

The Tribunal rules that this interest shall be applied at least from 1 August 1996, as the contractually fixed payment time, to 19 June 1997, i.e., when the action was brought before the Tribunal, and the [seller] duly paid the arbitration fees for his claim for recovery of interest."

35. Tribunal of International Commercial Arbitration at the Russian Federation Chamber of Commerce and Industry n.302/1996, 27 July 1999 (Russ.), *at* http://cisgw3.law.pace.edu/cases/990727r1.html.

Original language: Russian
Translation: Available

Court (translation):
"The Tribunal granted the claim of the [buyer] to recover annual interest on the granted sum of lost profit at the LIBOR rate plus 2% per annum, on the basis of Article 78 CISG and Article 395 of the Russian Federation Civil Code that refers to the rate of bank loan at the place of creditor. The Tribunal found that the mentioned rate of interest accorded to the rate which prevailed in Switzerland (place of [buyer]'s company) respectively. The Tribunal has also taken into account that [seller] raised no objections regarding the issue of rate of interest."

36. Tribunal of International Commercial Arbitration at the Russian Federation Chamber of Commerce and Industry n.55/1998, 10 June 1998 (Russ.), *at* http://cisgw3.law.pace.edu/cases/991006r1.html.

Original language: Russian
Translation: Available

Some references, but nothing interesting.

37. Tribunal of International Commercial Arbitration at the Russian Federation Chamber of Commerce and Industry n.88/2000, 25 Jan. 2001 (Russ.), *at* http://cisgw3.law.pace.edu/cases/010125r1.html.

Original language: Russian
Translation: Available

Court (translation):
"As to the [Seller]'s claims to recover from the [Buyer] penalties for the delay in payment as well as annual interest for the use of another's funds, the Tribunal found that the [Buyer] committed a breach which gives the [Seller] a right to claim such recovery in accordance with the contract. At the same time, when resolving this issue, the Tribunal took into consideration the following.

- First, the contract of the parties sets forth two penalties imposed on the buyer for one breach of contract (the delay in payment).
- Second, the [Seller]'s claim to recover annual interest is based on Article 78 CISG. The rate of annual interest corresponds with the LIBOR rate for the short-term loans in hard currency in US dollars. [The LIBOR rate] represents a median rate applied by the leading U.K. banks (i.e., the banks in the place of the creditor).
- Third, pursuant to Article 333 of the Russian Federation Civil Code, if the penalty is clearly disproportionate to the consequences of a breach, the court has discretion to reduce such penalty. The UNIDROIT Principles of International Commercial Contracts follow the same rule. Pursuant to Clause 2 of Article 7.4.13 of the UNIDROIT Principles, notwithstanding any agreement to the contrary, the set amount of the penalties in case of a breach can be reduced to a reasonable amount, if it is substantially greater than the damages resulted from the breach or from other circumstances.
- Fourth, Clause 6 of Resolution No. 13/14 of 8 October 1998 "On the case law applying the provisions of the Russian Federation Civil Code regarding annual interest for the use of another's funds" issued by the Plenum of the Russian Federation Supreme Court and the Russian Federation Higher Arbitration Court states that in cases, in which a creditor has a right to recover damages and interest for a breach of a monetary obligation, the creditor can use only one of these remedies.

Taking the above into consideration, the Tribunal came to the conclusion that the [Seller] could recover only annual interest provided for in the contract. [Such annual interest can be recovered] in the amount stated in the claim."

38. Tribunal of International Commercial Arbitration at the Russian Federation Chamber of Commerce and Industry n.406/1998, 6 June 2000 (Russ.), *at* http://cisgw3.law.pace.edu/cases/000606r1.html.

Original language:	Russian
Translation:	Available

Court (translation):
"Concerning the [buyer]'s claim for annual interest based on Article 395 of the Russian Federation Civil Code, the Tribunal holds that the [buyer] did not satisfy the requirements of that Article, *inter alia*, the [buyer] did not provide to the Tribunal the rates of annual interest at the creditor's place of business and the period for which the interest should be calculated that would have allowed the Tribunal to evaluate the [buyer]'s claim. Accordingly, the [buyer]'s claim for interest has to be denied."

39. Tribunal of International Commercial Arbitration at the Russian Federation Chamber of Commerce and Industry n.198/2000, 30 July 2001 (Russ.), *at* http://cisgw3.law.pace.edu/cases/010730r1.html.

Original language:	Russian
Translation:	Available

Court (translation):
"When reviewing the [Seller]'s claim to recover annual interest, the Tribunal considered the following circumstances. Pursuant to Article 78 CISG, if a party fails to pay the purchase price or any other sum, the other party is entitled to interest on it. Since Article 78 does not set forth the exact interest rate, then, as stated above, the law of Italy should apply.

The [Seller] presented an affidavit of 2 May 2001 certified by A.M., a notary public from the city of Milan. It follows from the affidavit that, in accordance with Article 1224 of the Civil Code of Italy, interest on the sum in arrears should be determined based on the parties' agreement. In the absence of such agreement, the rate set forth in the law should apply. From 30 September to 31 December 1998 the annual interest rate in Italy was 5%. From 1 January 1999 to 31 December 2000 the annual interest rate was 2.5%. From 1 January 2001 the annual interest rate has been 3.5%.

Thus, annual interest should be recovered for the period from 30 September 1998 to 25 May 2001. In addition, annual interest at the rate of 3.5% should be paid on the sum in arrears from 26 May 2001 to the date of factual payment.

When calculating the amount of interest, the Tribunal took into consideration that the [Buyer] made no objections in connection with the periods of time for which interest was calculated as well as in connection with the interest rate.

Taking into consideration the partially sustained claim of the [Seller] reduced by the amount of interest incorrectly calculated, in accordance with Article 6(2) of the Regulations on Arbitration Expenses and Fees, the [Buyer] should pay the [Seller]'s arbitration expenses in the amount proportionate to the sustained claims."

40. Tribunal of International Commercial Arbitration at the Russian Federation Chamber of Commerce and Industry n.108/2001, 28 Nov. 2001 (Russ.), *at* http://cisgw3.law.pace.edu/cases/011128r1.html.

Original language: Russian
Translation: Available

Court (translation):
"The Tribunal found reasonable the claim of [Seller] to compensate him for losses arisen in connection with payment of interest for credit to the bank due to delay of payment by [Buyer] since it is confirmed by relevant banking documents and should be granted on the basis of Art. 74 CISG.

The Tribunal also found reasonable the claim of [Seller] to recover interest according to Art. 78 CISG and para. 352 of the German Commerce Code since it is proved by relevant calculations and thus should be granted.

The Tribunal left without consideration the claims to recover annual interest in the amount of 9 percent of the principal debt from 1 June 2001 to the day of payment, and also 5 percent of the principal debt from 1 June 2001 to the day of payment since they were not covered by the arbitration fees as is required by para. 18 of the Rules of Tribunal."

Summary

Cases involving Article 78: 40

Cases for which an English translation/text is available: 19

Cases for which only an abstract was available: 3

Cases for which neither translation nor abstract was available: 18

Appendix 13
Switzerland

Courts

BG	Bezirksgericht	District Court
KG	Kantonsgericht	District Court
RA	*Richteramt*	District Court
HG	*Handelsgericht*	Commercial Court
	Pretore	District Court
	Tribunal Cantonal	Canton Appellate Court
OG	*Obergericht*	Appellate Court
ZG	*Zivilgericht*	Civil Court
BGer	Bundesgericht	Supreme Court

Codes

CCP		Swiss Code of Civil Procedure
IPRG	*Bundesgesetz über das Internationale Privatrecht*	Swiss Federal Act on International Private Law
LPIL		Swiss Federal Law on Private International Law
BGE	*Entscheidungen des Bundesgerichts*	Official Reporter of the Federal Court
ZPO	*Zivilprozessordnung*	Swiss Code of Civil Procedure
CC	Codice Civile	Italian civil code

1. Pretore della giurisidizione di Locarno Campagna [District Court] n. 15/91, 16 Dec. 1991 (Switz.), *at* http://cisgw3.law.pace.edu/cases/911216s1.html.

 Original language: Italian
 Translation: Available

 Court (translation):
 "The Vienna Convention regulates the problem of interest very briefly in Art. 78, which states: '*If a party fails to pay the price or any other sum that is in*

arrears, the other party is entitled to interest on it, without prejudice to any claim for damages recoverable under article 74.' This Article sanctions the principle that the run of interest does not depend on arrearage, but rather simply on the lack of payment of the price on time (*cf* Berner Tage für die Juristische Praxis 1990, Wiener Kaufrecht, page 208)... Art. 78 of the Vienna Convention is the result of compromise which the Contracting States reached after long discussions. However, it was not possible to reach an agreement on the interest rate (*cf.* Berner Tage für Juristische Praxis 1990, Wiener Kaufrecht, p. 208). In consequence, the interest rate to be applied is the rate prescribed by the law which would be applicable if the Vienna Convention were not applied."

2. Zivilgericht [ZG] [Civil Court] Basel n. P4 1991/238, 21 Dec. 1992 (Switz.), *at* http://cisgw3.law.pace.edu/cases/921221s1.html.

   Original language: German
   Translation: Available

   Court (translation):
   "Under Article 78 CISG, a claim for interest may be raised if a party fails to pay the sales price or another due sum ... The rate of interest is not provided for in the CISG. The CISG refers to the national law which the previously considered conflict of laws provisions refer to (*cf.* 2.) [Austrian Law]. Under Para 352 of the Austrian Commercial Code, the rate of interest laid down amounts to 5%. However, this rate of interest only applies if no rate of interest was agreed between the parties (*cf.* Straube, Commentary to the Commercial Code, N 1 ff. to para. 352). The general terms and conditions of trade of the [seller] which are printed on the back of the carbon copies of the letters of confirmation of 24 February 1989 submitted by the [buyer] to the court ... provide, in Number 4.6, for a rate of interest which exceeds the bank rate of the Austrian National Bank by at least 3.5%. According to the prevailing legal theory in Austria, the general terms and conditions of trade are also valid if reference is first made to these in a confirmation (*cf.* Code of Commercial Law, edited by Fritz Schoenherr and Gunter Nitsche, Vienna 1981, page 288, E. 1b). The defendant does not in general contend that the General Terms and Conditions of Trade of the [seller] had not become contractual content. That the bank rate of the Austrian National Bank 1989 was 5.5% or more according to the General Terms and Conditions of Trade of the [seller] can, given the interest situation in Austria, be regarded as established. Therefore, it is to be established that the 9% interest claimed by the [seller] was agreed upon. Thus the interest claim of the [seller] can also be awarded in full."

3. Richteramt [RA] [District Court] Laufen des Kantons Bern, 7 May 1993 (Switz.), *at* http://cisgw3.law.pace.edu/cases/930507s1.html.

   Original language: German
   Translation: Available

   Court (translation):
   "Only in regard to the determination of the interest in arrears does the national law gain significance, since Art. 78 CISG only constitutes the obligation to pay interest, however, without determining the rate of interest. It is especially controversial in German doctrine, what national law should be applicable to that matter. Following Schlechtriem/Eberstein (Art. 78, para. 3), the law determined by the conflict of laws provisions shall be applicable, whereas following a dissenting and significant opinion, the rate of interest should be determined by the law of the interest-creditor (*cf.* the references in Schlechtriem/Eberstein, Art. 78, para. 9). However, this controversy is only of significance when the seller is in arrears with his obligation to pay the price, *e.g.*, with the liability for damages for defective goods under Art. 74 CISG *et seq.*; here, applying the conflict of laws provisions, the rate of interest is determined by the statute of the seller, whereas the rate of interest is determined by the statute of the buyer when applying the law of the interest-creditor. In cases where, as brought forward by the [seller], the buyer is in arrears with his obligation to pay the price, which should be the majority of all cases, the rate of interest is – under both approaches – to be determined by the law of the seller, which in the case at issue is Finnish law. Nevertheless, it is all in all clear that the present case, regarding the matters disputed, is solely governed by the scope of application of the CISG; in other words, on the merits of the case, the CISG is relevant and has to be referred to for the solution of the matter of dispute, and not any pure national Finnish law. Finnish law is presently significant only for the determination of the rate of interest, as far as the [buyer] owes interest at all and this is disputed …"

4. Handelsgericht [HG] [Commercial Court] Zürich HG 92493 U/HG 92, 1 Sept. 1993 (Switz.), *at* http://cisgw3.law.pace.edu/cases/930901s1.html.

   Original language: German
   Translation: Unavailable

5. Handelsgericht [HG] [Commercial Court] Zürich HG 930138. U/HG93, 9 Sept. 1993 (Switz.), *at* http://cisgw3.law.pace.edu/cisg/wais/db/cases2/930909s1.html; http://www.unilex.info/case.cfm?pid=1&do=case&id=136&step=Abstract.

   Original language: German
   Translation: Unavailable

CLOUT abstract:
"The court ordered the buyer to pay the purchase price with interest at the statutory interest rate of the applicable Italian law (Article 78 CISG)."

Unilex abstract:
"The Court awarded the seller the full purchase price plus interest (Art. 78 CISG), at the statutory rate provided for by the law otherwise applicable to the contract (Italian law)."

6. Tribunal Cantonal Vaud [Canton Appellate Court], 6 Dec. 1993 (Switz.), at http://www.unilex.info/case.cfm?pid=1&do=case&id=173&step=Abstract.

Original language:	French
Translation:	Unavailable

Unilex abstract:
"The Court further held that the seller was entitled to interest on the price (Art 78 CISG). As CISG does not determine either the time of interest accrual or the interest rate, the Court stated that both questions had to be determined by the law otherwise applicable to the contract (in this case French law). Therefore, interest accrued from the date the seller requested buyer to pay the price. French law was also applicable to determine the rate of interest. However, as the seller failed to prove the relevant rate in France, the Court referred to Swiss law to ascertain the applicable rate."

7. Tribunal Cantonal Valais [Canton Appellate Court] n. C 118/94, 29 June 1994 (Switz.), *at* http://cisgw3.law.pace.edu/cases/940629s1.html.

Original language:	German
Translation:	Available

Journal of Law and Commerce abstract:
"Article 78 CISG does not fix the rate of interest. Thus this rate is fixed by the law applicable by virtue of private international law. According to Article 117 IPRG (Swiss private international law), if there is no choice of law, a contract is governed by the law with which it is most closely connected. There is a presumption that the country with the most close connection is the country in which the party obliged to the characteristic performance has her residence. In contracts for the sale of goods the performance of the seller is the characteristic performance. According to these rules of private international law, Italian law is applicable as to the rate of interest. Characteristic performance is the performance of delivering furniture, performance of the plaintiff having her place of business in Italy. According to Article 1284 of the Italian Codice Civile

the rate of legal interest is 10%. Interest over and above this rate must be contracted to in writing. A contract of this kind is not presented; thus the rate of interest is 10%."

8. Kantonsgericht [KG] [District Court] Zug n. A3 1993 84, 1 Sept. 1994 (Switz.), *at* http://www.unilex.info/case.cfm?pid=1&do=case&id=237&step=Abstract.

   Original language: German
   Translation: Unavailable

   Unilex abstract:
   "The seller was awarded interest on the unpaid price. As CISG does not determine the interest rate the Court applied the law otherwise applicable to the contract (in the case at hand, German law) and, as the seller had given evidence of having had recourse to bank loans, granted the higher interest rate of 12%."

9. Bezirksgericht [BG] [District Court] Arbon BG 341/1994, 9 Dec. 1994 (Switz.), *at* http://www.unilex.info/case.cfm?pid=1&do=case&id=172&step=Abstract.

   Original language: German
   Translation: Unavailable

   Unilex abstract:
   "The Court held that interest was payable on the sums due to the claimant. As CISG does not determine the interest rate (Art. 78 CISG), the Court stated that it was to be determined in accordance with the domestic law of the creditor's country (Austria)."

10. Kantonsgericht [KG] [District Court] Zug A3 1994 85, 15 Dec. 1994 (Switz.), *at* http://www.unilex.info/case.cfm?pid=1&do=case&id=235&step=Abstract.

    Original language: German
    Translation: Unavailable

    Unilex abstract:
    "The Court further held that the seller was entitled to interest on the price (Art. 78 CISG). In the absence of an express provision in CISG, the Court held that the interest rate was to be determined in accordance with the law otherwise applicable to the contract."

11. Tribunal Cantonal Valais [Canton Appellate Court] n. 323/94, 20 Dec. 1994 (Switz.), *at* http://cisgw3.law.pace.edu/cases/941220s1.html.

Original language: French
Translation: Available

Court (translation):
"Art. 78 CISG provides for the payment of default interest without stating the interest rate. The interest rate must be determined in conformity with the law applicable by virtue of the rules of private international law (art. 7(2) CISG). According to art. 117 LPIL ' in case of a failure to choose the governing law, the contract is governed by the law of the State to which the contract is mostly related (art. 117(1) LPIL); the contract is deemed to be related to the State in which the party which has to fulfill the principal obligation under the contract has its place of residence, or – if the contract forms part of professional or commercial activities – its place of business (art. 117(2) LPIL); in contracts for the transfer of property, the duty of the owner is crucial for the determination of the governing law (art. 117(3) LPIL).

According to art. 118 LPIL, sales of goods are governed by the Convention on the Law Applicable to International Sales of Goods, adopted in The Hague on 15 June 1955. Rules of conflict of laws stated in that Convention are applicable even if the law governing the contract is the law of a non-Contracting State (Schwander, Internationales Vertragsschuldrecht – Direkte Zuständigkeit und Objektive Anknüpfung, in Beiträge zum neuen IPR des Sachen-Schuld-und Gesellschaftsrecht, in Festschrift für Rudolf Moser, p. 89; Knoepfler, Le contrat dans le nouveau droit international privé suisse, in Le Nouveau Droit international privé suisse, CEDIDAC, p. 93; Schnyder, Das neue IPR-Gesetz, 2e éd., p. 109).

Art. 3(1) of the 1955 Hague Convention states that sales of goods are governed by the law of the State where the seller has its place of residence at the moment of the receipt of the offer, unless otherwise agreed by the parties.

In the present case, application of those rules of conflict of laws leads to the application of Italian law. This conclusion is also the result of the application of art. 117 LPIL; the principal obligation under the present contract (delivery of blocks of stone) is the [seller's] responsibility, whose place of business is in Italy. According to art. 1284 of the Civil Code of Italy, the rate of default interest is 10%, unless a higher rate is fixed by the parties. The [seller] in the present case claims the default interest at the rate of 8%. Therefore, it is possible to award a higher rate of default interest only if the Court rules *ultra petita*."

12. Handelsgericht [HG] [Commercial Court] Zürich n. HG 930476, 21 Sept. 1995 (Switz.), *at* http://cisgw3.law.pace.edu/cases/950921s1.html; http://www.unilex.info/case.cfm?pid=1&do=case&id=159&step=Abstract.

Original language: German
Translation: Unavailable

CLOUT abstract:
"The court ruled in favour of the [Austrian seller]. With respect to damages, the court explained that the [seller] could ask for higher damages than those under the applicable law by proving that it was paying a higher rate of interest (article 74 CISG). As regards interest, the court found that article 78 CISG was applicable. However, as article 78 CISG does not address the question of the applicable rate of interest, the court applied Austrian law in determining the rate of interest."

Unilex abstract:
"The Court stated that the buyer had to pay the purchase price and furthermore that interest was payable in compliance with Art. 78 CISG; according to the Court, the interest rate had to be determined, absent an express provision in CISG, by applying the private international law rules of the forum, which, in the case at hand, led to the application of Austrian law. Although Austrian statutory interest rate amounted to 5%, the Court held that the seller was entitled to the higher interest rate of 9,75% as further damages (Arts. 78 and 74 CISG). In this respect, the Court observed that the seller had only to prove the recourse to bank loans since it can be assumed that companies normally resort to external sources of credit to finance their activities."

13. Handelsgericht [HG] [Commercial Court] St. Gallen n. HG 45/1994, 5 Dec. 1995 (Switz.), *at* http://cisgw3.law.pace.edu/cases/951205s1.html; http://www.unilex.info/case.cfm?pid=1&do=case&id=190&step=Abstract.

Original language: German
Translation: Unavailable

Unilex abstract:
"The Court held that the seller was entitled to recover the full contract price. In addition, the seller was awarded interest according to Art. 78 CISG. With respect to the interest rate, the Court applied Swiss private international law rules which led to the German statutory interest rate. The seller was then awarded a higher interest rate as further damages since it provided a bank certificate proving that it had paid interest on bank loans during a specific time period."

14. Kantonsgericht [KG] [District Court] Zug, 30 Nov. 1995 (Switz.), *at* http://cisgw3.law.pace.edu/cases/951130s1.html. [Second instance: see infra No. 21; Third instance: see infra No. 36].

Original language: German
Translation: Unavailable

15. Tribunale d'Appello di Lugano [Appellate Court] n. 12.95.00300, 12 Feb. 1996 (Switz.), *at* http://cisgw3.law.pace.edu/cases/960212s1.html. [First instance: Pretura Lugano, No. 1315, October 16, 1995]

Original language: Italian
Translation: Available

Court (translation):
"Article 78 of the CISG provides that the buyer, if he fails to pay the price, must pay interest accrued on it. Interest is due since the price is due and not only when a demand for payment has been made (Weber, Vertragsverletzungsfolgen, in: Wiener Kaufrecht, Berna, 1991, page 208). The CISG is silent on the issue of default interest, which results in the application of the law that would otherwise apply absent the Convention (Weber, *id.*). In the present case, since the parties did not choose the applicable law, the connection criterion must be applied, which leads to the application of the law of the seller (article 117, cpv. lit a LDIP), that is, the Italian law."

16. Tribunal Cantonal Vaud [Canton Appellate Court] n. 01 93 0661, 11 Mar. 1996 (Switz.), *at* http://www.unilex.info/case.cfm?pid=1&do=case&id=320&step=Abstract.

Original language: French
Translation: Unavailable

CLOUT abstract:
"The case related to the CISG only insofar as the court had to determine the interest rate (article 78 CISG). Notwithstanding the prevailing case law, the court applied the law at the debtor's (i.e. buyer's) place of business because only the buyer's obligation was in dispute and the parties did not rely on Hungarian or Austrian law, which would have been applicable pursuant to the Swiss rules of private international law."

Unilex abstract:
"The seller was also awarded the interest (Art. 78 CISG) accruing from the expiration of the period of time for payment of the price agreed by the parties. The court observed that according to Art. 78 CISG, the obligation to pay interest for the delay in payment of the price is not subject to a formal request by the seller. Since CISG does not determine the interest rate, the court held that the rate was to be determined in accordance with the domestic law of the

buyer's country (Switzerland) as the buyer's obligation was the only disputed performance in the case at hand."

17. Tribunal Cantonal Vaud [Canton Appellate Court] n. 01 93 1061 [163/96/BA and 164/96/BA], 11 Mar. 1996 (Switz.), *at* http://cisgw3.law.pace.edu/cases/960311s2.html.

    Original language: French
    Translation: Available

    Court (translation):
    "Article 78 CISG provides the principle for the payment of interest on any sums that are in arrears if the buyer delays the payment of the purchase price. The Convention, however, provides neither the rate nor the date for calculation of the interest, their determination being left to the applicable national law (Stoffel, Le droit applicable aux contrats de vente internationale de marchandises, in Les contrats de vente internationale de marchandises, CEDIDAC 20, Lausanne 1991, pp. 39-40; Neumayer/Ming, op cit., pp. 511 et seq.). The only disputable obligation in the present case is that of the buyer which is established in Switzerland. It is appropriate to refer to the rate applied in the place of establishment of the debtor (Neumayer/Ming, op. cit., p. 514). In these conditions and without Hungarian law being invoked, there are grounds to apply Swiss law. Interest rate, thus, must be fixed according to the Swiss legal rate of 5 percent per annum (Art.104 para. 1 of the CO [*Code des Obligations*]).

    Regarding the date for the calculation of interest in arrears, the Plaintiff [seller] fixes it thirty days after the date of the last invoice which, like the previous ones, is payable within thirty days. The Vienna Convention contains a rule concerning the principle of interest and damages in case of breach of contract (arts. 74 and 78). Pursuant to this rule, compensation is due as from the moment of occurrence of the damage or of the breach of contract. Therefore, the obligation to pay the interest does not depend on the fact that the defaulting party was put into arrears; it is sufficient that the sum due was not paid within the term of payment (Weber, Vertragsverletzungsfolgen, in Wiener Kaufrecht, Berne 1991, p. 208). Other scholars are of the same opinion (Wiegand, Die Pflichten des Käufers und die Folgen ihrer Verletzung, in Wiener Kaufrecht, op. cit., p. 156; Tercier, Les contrats spéciaux, 2ème éd., 1995, p. 161, n. 1286)."

18. Tribunal civil de la Glâne [District Court], 20 May 1996 (Switz.), *at* http://www.unilex.info/case.cfm?pid=1&do=case&id=239&step=Abstract.

Original language: French
Translation: Unavailable

Unilex abstract:
"The Court held CISG applicable to the contract and found the seller entitled to payment of the price plus interest. As CISG does not determine the interest rate (Art. 78 CISG), the Court held that it had to be determined according to the domestic law otherwise applicable to the contract."

19. Zürich Chamber of Commerce n. ZHK 273/95, 31 May 1996 (Switz.), *at* http://cisgw3.law.pace.edu/cases/960531s1.html.

Original language: English

20. Handelsgericht [HG] [Commercial Court] Zürich n. HG 940513, 10 July 1996 (Switz.), *at* http://cisgw3.law.pace.edu/cases/960710s1.html; http://www.unilex.info/case.cfm?pid=1&do=case&id=381&step=Abstract.

Original language: German
Translation: Unavailable

CLOUT abstract:
"As regards interest, the court determined the interest rate under the law designated by the relevant choice-of-law rule (articles 74 and 78 CISG). Accordingly, the court applied the German law at the seller's place of business (Section 352(1) of the *Handelsgesetzbuch*). Inasmuch as the seller had to obtain a loan owing to the buyer's refusal to pay the purchase price, the seller was awarded the higher interest rate of 9 percent, which had to be paid on the loan."

Unilex abstract:
"The seller was finally entitled to recover interests. Since CISG does not determine the interest rate, the Court applied the statutory interest rate provided by German law, as the law otherwise applicable to the contract (Art. 78 CISG). The seller was also a higher interest rate as further damages according to Art. 74 CISG, at the rate it was actually charged for a bank loan obtained after the buyer's refusal to pay the purchase price. "

21. Handelsgericht [HG] [Commercial Court] Aargau n. OR.96.00057, 19 Dec. 1996 (Switz.), *at* http://cisgw3.law.pace.edu/cases/961219s1.html.

Original language: German
Translation: Unavailable

22. Handelsgericht [HG] [Commercial Court] Zürich n. HG 95 0347, 5 Feb. 1997 (Switz.), *at* http://cisgw3.law.pace.edu/cases/970205s1.html; http://www.unilex.info/case.cfm?pid=1&do=case&id=305&step=Abstract.

Original language: German
Translation: Unavailable

Unilex abstract:
"The court stated that, although in principle the buyer would have been entitled also to interest on the loss of profit according to Art. 74 of CISG, in the case at hand the buyer lost its right to interest as it did not give sufficient evidence as to the time in which the profits would have been made. The court awarded the buyer the restitution of the advance payment plus interest (Art. 78 CISG). As to the applicable rate of interest, the court applied the interest rate of the sellers' place of business, that being the place in which the sellers usually invest their money."

23. Bezirksgericht [BG] [District Court] Unterrheintal 2 BZ/96-70, 11 Apr. 1997 (Switz.), *at* http://cisgw3.law.pace.edu/cases/970411s1.html.

Original language: German
Translation: Unavailable

24. Bezirksgericht [BG] [District Court] St. Gallen n. 3 PZ 97/18, 3 July 1997 (Switz.), *at* http://cisgw3.law.pace.edu/cases/970703s1.html; http://www.unilex.info/case.cfm?pid=1&do=case&id=306&step=Abstract.

Original language: German
Translation: Unavailable

CLOUT abstract:
"The interest rate was fixed based on the law applicable pursuant to the forum's rules of private international law, which led to Dutch law. However, the court mentioned the possibility of determining the rate of interest in application of the law at the debtor's place of business, pointing out that it was the debtor who could profit from the fact that the purchase price had not been paid."

Unilex abstract:
"The court awarded the seller the price indicated on the corrected invoice plus interest (Art. 78 CISG). With respect to the interest rate, although the court pointed out the two leading theories on the determination of the interest rate under CISG (interest rate to be determined according to the domestic law

governing the contract in the absence of CISG or according to the domestic law of the debtor's place), it awarded the Swiss rate of interest, as that was the rate requested by the seller in the judicial complaint to which the buyer did not raise an objection during the court proceeding."

25. Handelsgericht [HG] [Commercial Court] Aargau n. OR.96.0-0013, 26 Sept. 1997 (Switz.), *at* http://cisgw3.law.pace.edu/cases/970926s1.html; http://www.unilex.info/case.cfm?pid=1&do=case&id=404&step=Abstract.

    Original language: German
    Translation: Unavailable

    CLOUT abstract:
    "The interest rate was determined based on the German law as the seller's place of business (352 Handelsgesetzbuch), applicable pursuant the forum's rules of private international law."

    Unilex abstract:
    "Finally, the court awarded the seller interest on the price of the unsold goods and the accrued damages. As to the applicable interest rate, in the absence of CISG the court held that the interest rate had to be determined according to the 1955 Hague Convention on the international sales of goods, which led to German law, being Germany the country where the Seller has its principal place of business."

26. Kantonsgericht [KG] [District Court] Zug n. A3 1997/39, 16 Oct. 1997 (Switz.), *at* http://cisgw3.law.pace.edu/cases/971016s1.html; http://www.unilex.info/case.cfm?pid=1&do=case&id=405&step=Abstract.

    Original language: German
    Translation: Unavailable

    CLOUT abstract:
    "The interest rate was determined based on the law applicable pursuant to the forum's rules of private international law, which led to German law (352 Handelsgesetzbuch)."

    Unilex abstract:
    "The seller was entitled to interest since the buyer had failed to pay the purchase price (Art. 78 CISG). The interest rate was determined by German law which was applicable in accordance to the Swiss private international law."

27. Tribunal Cantonal Valais [Canton Appellate Court] n. C1 97 167, 28 Oct. 1997 (Switz.), *at* http://cisgw3.law.pace.edu/cases/971028s1.html; http://www.unilex.info/case.cfm?pid=1&do=case&id=311&step=Abstract.

Original language:	French
Translation:	Unavailable

CLOUT abstract:
"The interest rate was determined in application of the forum's rules of private international law, which led to Italian law."

Unilex abstract:
"The seller was entitled to payment of the full purchase price, plus interest (Art. 78 CISG) accruing from the due date of payment fixed by the contract. With regard to the interest rate, the Court considered this to be a matter governed but not expressly settled by CISG (Art. 7(2) CISG) and applied the statutory rate of the State whose law would have been the governing law of the contract in the absence of CISG (Italy). However, the Court awarded interest at the rate expressly referred to in the seller's counterclaim (5%) which was lower than the Italian statutory rate (10%)."

28. Kantonsgericht [KG] [District Court] Nidwalden n. 15/96 Z, 3 Dec. 1997, *at* http://cisgw3.law.pace.edu/cases/971203s1.html; http://www.unilex.info/case.cfm?pid=1&do=case&id=312&step=Abstract.

Original language:	German
Translation:	Unavailable

CLOUT abstract:
"The interest rate was determined on the basis of Italian law. The court also determined the period for which the buyer had to pay interest based on Swiss law, which provides that a debt only becomes due and interest starts to accrue after a reminder by the seller (article 102(1) Swiss Code of Obligation)."

Unilex abstract:
"The Court decided in favor of the seller and awarded the seller the contract price plus interest according to Art. 78 CISG. Since CISG does not determine the interest rate, the Court applied the Swiss law as the law otherwise applicable to the contract and applied the statutory interest rate of Switzerland."

29. Handelsgericht [HG] [Commercial Court] Aargau n. OR.97.00056, 19 Dec. 1997, *at* http://cisgw3.law.pace.edu/cases/971219s1.html.

Original language: German
Translation: Available

Court (translation):
"If a debtor does not pay an amount due, he, without a further demand being necessary, becomes obligated to pay interest according to Art. 78 CISG in connection with Art. 59 CISG (v.Caemmerer/Schlechtriem, "Kommentar zum Einheitlichen UN-Kaufrecht" [Commentary on the Uniform UN Sales Law], Munich 1990, Art. 59 at 2; Reinhart, "Einheitliches UN-Kaufrecht" [UN Sales Law], Heidelberg 1991, Art. 59 at 2). Thus, the "*Fashion House* ..." company was in arrears as regards the sales price 60 days after the dates of the invoices. The [CISG] stipulates in Art. 78, that a buyer, who is in arrears in payment of the purchase price, must pay interest, but without stating the interest rate.

According to Condition V.4 of the [seller's] sales conditions, [seller] is entitled to demand interest of 5% above the discount interest rate determined by the *Deutsche Bundesbank* [German Federal Reserve]. The seller has reserved the right to offer proof for the interest rate, but has not furnished it. Under these circumstances, the interest rate must be determined according to the German law applicable to the contract by the parties (choice of law in Condition XI.2 of the general conditions of sale of the [seller] according to Art.116(1) IPRG [German Code of Private International Law]. According to § 352 of the German HGB [Commercial Code] the legal interest rate among merchants is 5% ... In addition to the right to interest, a seller is also entitled to further damages according to Art. 74 CISG (Art. 78 [CISG])."

30. Tribunale d'Appello di Lugano [Appellate Court] n. 12.97.00193, 15 Jan. 1998 (Switz.), *at* http://cisgw3.law.pace.edu/cases/980115s1.html. [First instance: Pretore di Lugano, June 12, 1997, reversed]

Original language: Italian
Translation: Available

Court (translation):
"On these amounts are due interest counted from the day of payment (Art. 84(1) CISG), that is to say, from 8 June 1994 for the sale price; the same date has also to be employed for the expenses previously incurred as far as thus requested by [buyer]. The rate of the interest is not governed by the Convention, and must therefore be determined by internal law resulting from the application of the pertinent rules of conflict of laws (Honsell, op. cit., n. 10 to Art. 84 CISG), that is, according to Art.188(1) LDIP, from the law of the country where the seller has his habitual residence, and therefore from Swiss law. The interest is consequently to be set at the rate of 5% (Art. 93(1)

CO; Giger, Commentario Bernese, n. 25 to art. 208), there being no sufficient proof of the fact that [buyer] had for the whole depended upon a bank credit at 9.25% (cf. the undecipherable indication at the bottom of doc. L), and not even of the fact that, the relationship being between merchants, the discount rate in Switzerland was at the moment greater than 5% (Art.104(3) CO)."

31. Obergericht [OG] [Appelate Court] Zug n. OG 1996/2, 24 Mar. 1998 (Switz.), *at* http://cisgw3.law.pace.edu/cases/980324s1.html. [First instance: KG Zug, November 30, 1995, supra No. 14; third instance: BGer, October 28, 1998, infra No. 36]

Original language:	German
Translation:	Unavailable

32. Tribunal Cantonal du Valais [Canton Appellate Court] n. CI 97 288, 29 June 1998 (Switz.), *at* http://cisgw3.law.pace.edu/cases/980629s1.html; http://www.unilex.info/case.cfm?pid=1&do=case&id=366&step=Abstract.

Original language:	French
Translation:	Unavailable

CLOUT abstract:
"The interest rate on the purchase price was determined by application of the law governing the contract, which in this case was Italian law (article 7(2) CISG)."

Unilex abstract:
"The Court awarded the Italian seller interest on the sum in arrears, in accordance with Art. 78 CISG. The Court observed that, pursuant to Art. 7(2) CISG, the interest rate should be determined in accordance with the law otherwise applicable to the contract. As the Swiss rules of private international law led to the application of Italian law, the Court applied the Italian statutory interest rate."

33. Tribunal Cantonal du Valais/Kantonsgericht Wallis [Canton Appellate Court] CI-98-9, 30 June 1998 (Switz.), *at* http://cisgw3.law.pace.edu/cases/980630s1.html; http://www.unilex.info/case.cfm?pid=1&do=case&id=369&step=Abstract.

Original language:	German
Translation:	Unavailable

Unilex abstract:
"The Court finally found that the seller was entitled to interest on the unpaid price (Art. 78 CISG). With respect to the interest rate, as CISG does not determine the interest rate, the Court applied the law otherwise applicable to the contract (in the case at hand: the law of Italy) and awarded interest at the Italian statutory rate."

34. Bezirksgericht [BG] [District Court] Unterrheintal EV.1998.2 (1KZ.1998.7), 16 Sept. 1998 (Switz.), *at* http://cisgw3.law.pace.edu/cases/980916s1.html; http://www.unilex.info/case.cfm?pid=1&do=case&id=486&step=Abstract.

Original language:	German
Translation:	Unavailable

Unilex abstract:
"Finally, the buyer had to pay interest according to Art. 78 CISG, which was calculated according to the applicable German domestic law."

35. Handelsgericht [HG] [Commercial Court] Zürich n. HG 960527/O, 21 Sept. 1998 (Switz.), *at* http://cisgw3.law.pace.edu/cases/980921s1.html; http://www.unilex.info/case.cfm?pid=1&do=case&id=408&step=Abstract.

Original language:	German
Translation:	Unavailable

CLOUT abstract:
"[The court also ordered interest paid with the rate determined by the otherwise applicable law]."

Unilex abstract:
"The seller was thus granted payment and interest on it under Art. 78 CISG. Absent an express provision in CISG, the Court held that the interest rate was to be determined in accordance with the law otherwise applicable to the contract, that is Italian law."

36. Bundesgericht [BGer] [Supreme Court] Schweizerisches 4C.179/1998/odi, 28 Oct. 1998 (Switz.), *at* http://cisgw3.law.pace.edu/cases/981028s1.html; http://www.unilex.info/case.cfm?pid=1&do=case&id=382&step=Abstract. [First instance: supra No. 14; Second instance: supra No. 31]

Original language:	German
Translation:	Unavailable

Unilex abstract:
"The Court finally held that the sellers were entitled to recover interests. Since CISG does not determine the interest rate (Art. 78 CISG), the Court applied the statutory interest rate provided by German law, as the law otherwise applicable to the contract. The sellers were also awarded a higher interest rate as further damages pursuant to Arts. 78 and 74 CISG, since they provided sufficient evidence of recourse to bank loans."

37. Handelsgericht [HG] [Commercial Court] Zürich n. HG 930634/O, 30 Nov. 1998 (Switz.), *at* http://cisgw3.law.pace.edu/cases/981130s1.html; http://www.unilex.info/case.cfm?pid=1&do=case&id=409&step=Abstract.

Original language:	German
Translation:	Unavailable

Unilex abstract:
"The seller was further awarded interest on the price (Art. 78 CISG), without the need of a formal request by the seller, accruing from the date the price was due (Arts. 58 and 59 CISG) and at the rate determined by the domestic law otherwise applicable in the absence on CISG (in the case at hand, Swiss law)."

38. Handelsgericht [HG] [Commercial Court] Zürich n. HG 970238.1, 10 Feb. 1999 (Switz.), *at* http://cisgw3.law.pace.edu/cases/990210s1.html.

Original language:	German
Translation:	Available

Court (translation):
"Under Art. 78 CISG, interest is due on any sum in arrears based on a sales contract governed by the Convention ... Following established opinion, the interest rate is determined by the applicable national law, in the present case by Italian law (Honsell, *op. cit.*, Art. 78 n. 12). Under Art. 1284(1) C.c the legal interest rate in Italy is 10%. Contractual interest is calculated at the same rate, unless the parties have agreed upon a different interest rate, which has not submitted by either party to the present dispute (Art. 1284(2) C.c.; see also v. Caemmerer/Schlechtriem, *op. cit.*, p. 672 *et seq.*)."

39. Kantonsgericht [KG] [District Court] Zug A3 1998 153, 25 Feb. 1999 (Switz.), *at* http://cisgw3.law.pace.edu/cisg/wais/db/cases2/990225s1.html; http://www.unilex.info/case.cfm?pid=1&do=case&id=411&step=Abstract.

Original language:	German
Translation:	Unavailable

CLOUT abstract:
"The court held that the seller was entitled to default interest according to article 78 CISG, the amount of which had to be determined by German domestic law as applicable under private international law provisions."

Unilex abstract:
"The seller was awarded payment of the price plus interest according to Art. 78 CISG, accruing from the time indicated in the seller's pleadings. The interest rate was determined by the domestic law otherwise applicable to the contract, absent an express provision in CISG."

40. Kantonsgericht [KG] [District Court] Zug n. A3 1997 61, 21 Oct. 1999 (Switz.), *at* http://cisgw3.law.pace.edu/cases/991021s1.html.

Original language:	German
Translation:	Available

Court (translation):
"According to Art. 78 CISG, if a party fails to pay the price or any other sum that is in arrears, the other party is entitled to interest on it, from the due date. Interest accrues from the due date for claims of damages as well, i.e., from the original date of breach. It is a uniform opinion that the interest rate is governed by the law of the country which the rules of conflict of laws refer to as law of the contract (Magnus, in: Honsell, *op. cit.*, at n.5, 9 and 12 on Art. 78 CISG). Under Art.117(1) IPRG, in the absence of a choice of law, the contract is governed by the law of the country to which the contract has the closest connection. Under Art.117(2) and (3) IPRG, this country is Germany in the present case; therefore the interest rate is to be determined under German law. As both parties are undoubtedly businesspeople, as provided in Art. 1 of the German Commercial Code (hereinafter HGB), the interest rate is to be adjusted by this source of law. According to Art.352(1) HGB, the rate of interest in bilateral commercial transactions is 5% per annum.

[...]

As mentioned above, under Art. 78 CISG the obligation to pay interest arises at the due date of any payment; payment for a claim of damages for breach of contract is due from the date of the breach. [Buyer] claims interest only since 29 November 1994 (Appendix 18, p. 1), therefore, [buyer] is entitled to 5% interest on the amount of US $50,000 (Art. 54 ZPO)."

41. Kantonsgericht [KG] [District Court] Schaffhausen n. 11/1999/35, 23 Apr. 2002 (Switz.), *at* http://cisgw3.law.pace.edu/cases/020423s1.html.

Original language: German
Translation: Available

Court (translation):
"The [buyer] never made any submissions regarding the point in time from which interest is claimed; the rate of interest claimed is within the usual frame."

42. Obergericht [OG] [Appelate Court] Luzern n. 11 01 125, 29 July 2002 (Switz.), *at* http://cisgw3.law.pace.edu/cases/020729s1.html.

Original language: German
Translation: Available

Court (translation):
"The [seller]'s pleadings (including the basis and the calculation) regarding interest on arrears and damages for default in the form of interest on debts were also not disputed by the [buyer]. In the absence of a substantiated denial by the [buyer], the interest on arrears and the additional damages for interest on debts was granted to the [seller] as requested."

43. Handelsgericht [HG] [Commercial Court] Aargau n. OR.2001.00029, 5 Nov. 2002 (Switz.), *at* http://cisgw3.law.pace.edu/cases/021105s1.html.

Original language: German
Translation: Available

Court (translation):
"If the buyer fails to pay the purchase price when due, the seller is entitled to interest on it "without prejudice to any claim for damages recoverable under Art. 74." (Art. 78 CISG). The amount of interest is not laid down in the UN Sales Law. It is controversial, whether one must aim for automous contract gap-filling and a uniform solution or if recourse must be made to national law. In regard to national law, the mainly recommended recourse, it is again uncertain how the determination of that law within the scope of the conflicts of law is supposed to take place (Schlechtriem/Bacher, *op. cit.*, note 27 and 32 to art. 78 CISG). The doctrine convincingly postulates that to determine the relevant national law, it is the connection to the currency that is decisive for the primary claim. (Schlechtriem/Bacher, id., note 33 to Art. 78 CISG). Decisive in this connection is the rule of the amount of the interest on arrears that is reached by the concerned system of laws (Bacher, id., note 34 to Art. 78 CISG).

In the present case, the primary claim is owed in Swiss francs. Thus, Swiss law is the applicable law for the determination of the amount of interest owed on arrears. Since the [seller] did not prove or demand a discount rate that would exceed the usual 5% percent (Art.194 para. 3 OR), the statutory interest on arrears of 5% is owed (Art.104 para. 1 OR).

In the CISG's sphere of application, even the default of payment on the date of maturity creates a dereliction of duty, so that the need of payment of interest sets in immediately with the maturity (Schlechtriem, *op. cit.*, note 319). As the maturity started off on 20 June 2000 (see 6a, *supra*), the [seller] is entitled to interest to the amount of 5% from this date on.

Proceeding on that assumption, the [buyer] is fully liable to pay the cost (§ 112 para.1 ZPO."

44. Kantonsgericht [KG] [District Court] Zug n. A3 2001 34, 12 Dec. 2002 (Switz.), *at* http://cisgw3.law.pace.edu/cases/021212s1.html.

Original language:	German
Translation:	Available

Court (translation):
"The [seller] furthermore claims interest at a rate of 10.5% from 23 January 2001. During the main proceedings, the [seller] argued that the interest on arrears of 10.5% corresponded to the interest on debts which the [seller] had to pay at the time concerned for [seller]'s US Dollar account with the UBS bank in Geneva. If a party fails to pay the price or any other sum that is in arrears, the other party is entitled to interest on it, without prejudice to any claim for damages recoverable under Art. 74 (Art. 78 CISG). Consequently, the fact that a sum *is* in arrears is the only requirement for interest on arrears; a culpable delay in the meaning of Swiss law with all its prerequisites is not necessary (*cf.* v. Caemmerer/Schlechtriem, Kommentar zum Einheitlichen UN-Kaufrecht, 3rd ed., Munich 2000, Art. 78 n. 7 *et seq.*). The [seller]'s claim was due by the latest on 23 January 2001. The [seller] claimed interest from 23 January 2001, which is why the interest is to be granted from this point in time onwards. The "Vienna Sales Law" does not provide for the applicable interest rate. Therefore, the interested rate determined by the respective national law is owed (*cf.* v. Caemmerer/Schlechtriem, *op. cit.*, Art. 78 n. 26 *et seq.*). The interest rate in the present case is determined by German law (Art.117(1) and (3)(a) IPRG). Under § 352(1) HGB, the interest on arrears for commercial transactions is 5%. A higher interest is only owed if the creditor proves that he was in fact – due to the debtor's delay – obliged to pay interest on debts at this rate, or that he lost this amount in interest on investments (*cf.* Baumbach/Hopt, Handelsgesetzbuch, 29th ed., Munich 1995, § 352 HGB n. 5). The [seller] asserts that the interest on arrears claimed at the rate of 10.5% corresponds to the interest on

debts payable at the time for [seller]'s US Dollar account with the UBS bank in Geneva. The [buyer] did not dispute this submission. Therefore, the interest rate payable on the [seller]'s claim from 23 January 2001 lies at 10.5%."

Summary

Cases involving Article 78: 44

Cases for which an English translation is available: 16

Cases for which only an abstract was available: 23

Cases for which neither translation nor abstract was available: 5

Appendix 14
UNITED STATES OF AMERICA

1. Delchi Carrier, S.p.A. v. Rotorex Corp., 1994 WL 495787 (N.D.N.Y 1994) [U.S. District Court], *at* http://cisgw3.law.pace.edu/cases/940909u1.html.

   Original language: English

   Court:
   "[Buyer] is entitled to prejudgment interest pursuant to UNCCISG Article 78. Because Article 78 does not specify the rate of interest to be applied, the court in its discretion awards [Buyer] prejudgment interest at the United States Treasury Bill rate as set forth in 28 U.S.C. § 1961(a)."

2. Zapata Hermanos Sucesores, S.A. v. Hearthside Baking Co., 2001 WL 1000927 (N.D. Ill. 2001) [U.S. District Court], *at* http://cisgw3.law.pace.edu/cases/010828u1.html.

   Original language: English

   UNCITRAL abstract:
   "The plaintiff argued that express provisions in its invoices called for the payment of interest and proposed a calculation of the amount of interest owed. The defendant denied that it was liable for interest because the parties' course of conduct demonstrated that the defendant was never in arrears. It did not present to the jury a proposed calculation of interest. The jury resolved the dispute in favor of the plaintiff. The defendant then objected to the amount of interest awarded and asked the court to take judicial notice of the Illinois statutory rate and the U.S. treasury bill rate … [T]he court turned down the defendant's request. Purporting to apply article 78 CISG, the court stated that the amount of interest should reflect a reasonable commercial rate as between merchants. It reduced the jury award of interest to reflect the amount of principal shown to be owed to the plaintiff."

   To this end, Jury Instruction No. 28 (the instruction that spoke to the damages recoverable by [seller] if the jury found a breach of contract on [buyer's] part) reads in relevant part:

   "Unless you find that the parties agreed otherwise, either expressly or through a course of conduct, [seller] is also entitled to recover interest on the amounts past due. If interest is recoverable, the rate of interest is that rate, if any, to which the parties agreed. If you find that no rate was agreed to by the parties, then the rate is that which you determine to be reasonable."

3. Chicago Prime Packers, Inc. v. Northam Food Trading Co., et al., 2004 WL 11666628 (N.D. Ill. 2004) [U.S. District Court], *at* http://cisgw3.law.pace.edu/cases/040524u1.html.

Original language: English

"Damages

The final matter before court is the award of damages. In its Amended Complaint, Chicago Prime seeks judgment "in the amount of $178,200 plus interest, attorney's fees, costs, and other and further relief as this Court shall deem just and appropriate." (Am. Compl., Count I.)

The CISG provides:

"Damages for breach of contract by one party consist of a sum equal to the loss, including loss of profit, suffered by the other party as a consequence of the breach. Such damages may not exceed the loss which the party in breach foresaw or ought to have foreseen at the time of the conclusion of the contract, in the light of the facts and matters of which he then knew or ought to have known, as a possible consequence of the breach of contract." CISG, Art. 74.

This provision is "designed to place the aggrieved party in as good a position as if the other party had properly performed the contract." *Delchi Carrier SpA*, 71 F.3d at 1029 (quotation omitted). It is undisputed that Chicago Prime's loss is $178,200.00.

The CISG further provides that "[i]f a party fails to pay the price or any other sum that is in arrears, the other party is entitled to interest on it, without prejudice to any claim for damages recoverable under article 74." CISG, Art. 78. Thus, Chicago Prime is clearly entitled to prejudgment interest. However, Article 78 does not specify the rate of interest to be applied or how the rate should be determined; and the parties have not addressed the issue. The court's research has revealed that the interest issue under the CISG has been the subject of great controversy. In fact, "[t]he interest issue, while relatively mundane-sounding, has been the subject of up to 30 percent of total CISG cases worldwide." Tom McNamara, *U.N. Sale of Goods Convention: Finally Coming of Age?*, 32 COLO. LAW. II, 19 (2003). (citation omitted); *see also* Louis F. Del Duca & Patrick Del Duca, *Practice Under the Convention on International Sale of Goods (CISG): A*

Primer for Attorneys and International Traders (Part II), 29 UCC L.J. 99, 157 (1996) (stating that "[42] of the 142 cases reported thus far involve issues as to what interest rate should be applicable to overdue payments or refunds"). One author outlined nine different approaches that courts have used (or authors have suggested) in determining the rate of interest under the CISG, including using the law applicable to the contract in the absence of the CISG, the law of the creditor's place of business, the law of payment currency, trade usages observed in international sale, general principles of full compensation and the law of the forum. See Christian Thiele, Interest on Damages and Rate of Interest Under Article 78 of the U.N. Convention on Contracts for the International Sale of Goods, http://www.cisg.law.pace.edu/cisg/biblio/thiele.html (updated July 5, 2001). Another author, finding that the current approaches do not fully satisfy the objectives of a default rule (such as international uniformity), suggests that adjudicators should "customize" the rate by awarding the actual borrowing or savings rate or the lending rate in the absence of evidence of borrowing costs. Karin L. Kizer, *Minding the Gap: Determining Interest Rates Under the U.N. Convention for the International Sale of Goods*, 65 U. Chi. L. Rev. 1279, 1302- 05 (Fall 1998).

However, because there is no single approach used by all courts and the parties have failed to address the interest issue or provide information necessary to "customize" a rate, this court will award interest according to the principles used by federal courts in determining choice of law issues. It is well-settled that "[a] federal court sitting in diversity jurisdiction must apply the substantive law of the state in which it sits," including its choice of law. Land v. Yamaha Motor Corp., U.S.A., 272 F.3d 514, 516 (7th Cir. 2001) (citing Erie R.R. Co. v. Tompkins, 304 U.S. 64, 58 S.Ct. 817, 82 L.Ed. 1188 (1938)). See also Allen & O'Hara, Inc. v. Barrett Wrecking, Inc., 964 F.2d 694, 695 n.3 (7th Cir. 1992) ("In diversity cases, federal courts look to state law to determine the availability of and rules for computing prejudgment interest.").

In contract disputes, Illinois follows the Restatement (Second) of Conflict of Laws, which refers courts either to a choice of law provision in the contract at issue, or to the place of performance. Midwest Grain Prods. of Illinois, Inc. v. Productization, Inc., 228 F.3d 784, 787 (7th Cir. 2000) (citing Esser v. McIntyre, 169 Ill.2d 292, 214 Ill.Dec. 693, 661 N.E.2d 1138, 1141 (Ill. 1996)). In this case, there is no choice of law provision found in the contract but performance undoubtedly took place in Illinois. The contract was one for the purchase of ribs and the ribs were delivered to Northam's agent in Illinois. "In Illinois, prejudgment interest, whether grounded in a statute or equity, is based on the concept of fairness and is awarded to make the plaintiff whole for the loss of use of money wrongfully withheld ." Platinum Tech., Inc. v. Federal Ins. Co., 282 F.3d 927, 933 (7th Cir. 2002) (citing In re Estate of Wernick, 127 Ill.2d 61, 129 Ill.Dec. 111, 535 N.E.2d 876, 888 (Ill. 1989)). The Illinois Interest Act, 815 ILCS

§ 205, provides a statutory rate of 5% per annum, calculated from the time the money was due under the contract:

"Creditors shall be allowed to receive at the rate of a five (5) per centum per annum for all moneys after they become due on any bond, bill, promissory note, or other instrument of writing; on money lent or advanced for the use of another; on money due on the settlement of account from the day of liquidating accounts between the parties and ascertaining the balance ..." *Id.* § 205/2.

Coincidently, the result of applying Illinois choice of law rules in this case is to apply the law of Illinois, the forum state. Using the forum's interest rate is a common choice in CISG cases, notwithstanding its tension with the CISG's goal of promoting international uniformity. *See* McNamara, *supra*, 32 COLO. LAW. at 19 ("In the absence of direction, courts have often awarded interest according to the applicable law of the forum jurisdiction.").

The undisputed contract price for the ribs was $178,200.00, which is evidenced in the Confirmation and the Invoice. Based on the statutory rate of 5% and the finding that $178,200.00 was due under the contract on May 1, 2001, simple prejudgment interest is $27,242.63. Therefore, Chicago Prime is entitled to damages in the amount of $178,200.00 plus prejudgment interest in the amount of $27,242.63.

A claim for attorney's fees is a procedural matter governed by the law of the forum. Ajax Tool Works, Inc., 2003 WL 223187 at 7. The Seventh Circuit recently decided that the term "loss" in Article 74 of the CISG does not include attorney's fees incurred in the litigation of a suit for breach of contract. Zapata Hermanos Sucesores, S.A. v. Hearthside Baking Co., Inc., 313 F.3d 385, 389 (7th Cir. 2002). Accordingly, Chicago Prime's claim for attorney's fees is denied.

Conclusion

In accordance with the foregoing Findings of Fact and Conclusions of Law, the Clerk of the Court is directed to enter judgment in favor of the plaintiff Chicago Prime Packers, Inc. and against the defendant Northam Food Trading Co. in the sum of $178,200.00 plus $27,242.63, representing prejudgment interest calculated at a rate of 5% from May 1, 2001, for a total payment of $205,442.63."

Summary

Cases involving Article 78: 3

Cases for which an English translation/text is available: 3

Cases for which only an abstract was available: 0

Cases for which neither translation nor abstract was available: 0

Case text (English translation)
Queen Mary Case Translation Programme

Swiss Federal Supreme Court *(Bundesgericht)*
13 November 2003 [4C.198/2003/grl]

Translation by Mariel Dimsey***

A. Company *A-GmbH*, situated in Germany, sold to Company *B & Co.*, situated in Switzerland, a used laundry machine of the brand Seco SS 240. This was adapted to use KWL as a substance, which, in addition to the laundry machine, also made a distillation plant and a nitrogen generator necessary. The purchase price was fixed at Deutsche Mark [DM] 55,600. The machine was delivered to the Buyer on 29 July 1996. By letter dated 26 August 1996, the Buyer notified that the distillation of the machine was defective and that the stainless steel (*Nieroster*) container leaked and urgently needed to be replaced.

On 29 August 1996, a representative of the Seller examined the machine in order to compile a "findings report". By letter dated 5 September 1996, under the heading "UNUSABLE MACHINE DELIVERY", the Buyer communicated the following to the Seller:

> "As you are aware from the letter dated 28 [sic – correct: 26] August 1996 and from various telephone conversations, the machine delivered is not usable. Your visit on 29 August 1996 with our Ms. D., together with information provided over the telephone between you and Mr. D., has shown that the machine distillation system does not work. You have confirmed that several things were forgotten when making delivery and that you are under an obligation to complete this. We are happy to list the defects for you again.
>
> a. The distillation control unit (floating head) is defective and the consequences of this are: the distillation does not automatically turn off and pulls air into the system, [which] in turn leads to further consequential damages.

* For purpose of this translation, Plaintiff-Appellee, the assignee of the German company that sold the goods is referred to as [Seller's assignee] and the Defendant-Appellant of Switzerland is referred to as [Buyer].

** Mariel Dimsey is a Research Assistant and Teaching Assistant at the University of Basel, Switzerland

b. The stainless steel (*Nieroster*) container for the light ends is leaking (The consequences: flooding the ground with KWL).
c. The condensed water is not being separated.
d. The booster pump for the cleaner was not connected and adjusted.
e. The impregnating pump was not delivered [...].

[...]

"To this day, we have still not received the pump.

[...]

"Our advice from legal services has shown that we can immediately avoid the contract if these guarantee obligations are not performed within 10 days.

"We will exercise this right if there is no other way to solve the problem. We will offset the entire invoice, since the delivered machine components do not work.

[...]

"We give you 10 days in which to remedy all grievances; otherwise we shall be forced to institute legal proceedings."

On 6 September 1996, the Seller assigned its claim for the purchase price to C, situated in Germany. On 9 September 1996, the Seller was declared insolvent.

In its letter dated 18 September 1996, the Buyer basically communicated to the Seller that it would assert a claim for damages in the amount of DM 59,600 based on the failure to repair the machine, which was to be settled within 30 days. In addition, the Buyer indicated that it would have the machines disposed of if no repairs were carried out by 30 September 1996.

With its letter dated 27 September 1996, [Seller's assignee] C requested the Buyer to pay the purchase price that had been assigned to him by 4 October 1996.

With its letter dated 19 October 1996, the Buyer sent a reminder to the Seller regarding the claim for damages and set a final 10-day payment deadline. In addition, the Buyer basically stated that, as the Seller had shown no interest in resuming possession of the machine, it would dispose of it as indicated.

On 16 April 1998, [Seller's assignee] C brought a claim against D at the Lucerne-Land Local District Court (*Amtsgericht*) for payment of the purchase price. The claim was dismissed with costs on 21 January 1999 due to D's lack of capacity to be made a Defendant (*Passivlegitimation*).

B. On 2 August 1999, [Seller's assignee] brought a claim against the Buyer at the Lucerne-City Local District Court (*Amtsgericht*) for payment of the purchase price of DM 55,600 plus interest at a rate of 4% since 30 July 1996. In addition, the [Seller's assignee] claimed damages in the amount of Swiss Francs [CHF] 12,902 plus interest at a rate of 5% since 21 January 1999. As basis for this claim, the [Seller's assignee] stated that it had had to pay procedural costs in this amount, as it had initially brought a claim against D, which could be attributed to the [Buyer]'s breach of the obligation to correctly denote the name of the company (*Firmengebrauchspflicht*). The Buyer requested dismissal of the claim, particularly claiming that it had avoided the sales contract due to the defectiveness of the machine delivered.

The [Buyer] was liquidated with effect as of 31 December 2000 and was deleted from the commercial register. The deletion was published in the Official Swiss Trade Gazette (*Schweizerischen Handelsamtsblatt*) on 25 April 2001.

The Local District Court (*Amtsgericht*) dismissed the claim in a judgment dated 6 April 2001. The [Seller's assignee] appealed against this decision at the Court of Appeal (*Obergericht*) of the Canton of Lucerne. This court accepted that the [Buyer] could not be deemed to have been liquidated on account of the claim raised against it. Consequently, regardless of the fact that the [Buyer] had been deleted from the commercial register, it still continued to exist and thereby was capable of being a party to the action. With an order dated 30 November 2001, the Court of Appeal (*Obergericht*) ordered the compilation of an expert report for the purpose of clarifying the defects in the delivered machine, which was submitted to the court on 27 August 2002. On 12 May 2003, the Court of Appeal (*Obergericht*) reversed the judgment of the Local District Court (*Amtsgericht*) and allowed the claim in the amount of DM 55,600 plus 4% interest since 14 April 1999 and dismissed the claim for damages.

C. The [Buyer] lodged a federal appeal with the applications that the judgment of the Court of Appeal (*Obergericht*) dated 12 May 2003 should be annulled and the claim dismissed. In addition, the [Seller's assignee] should be ordered to collect the delivered machine from the [Buyer]. Alternatively, the purchase price should be reasonably reduced or this matter should be referred to the previous instance for the purpose of clarifying the price reduction claim. The [Seller's assignee] asks for the appeal to be dismissed.

In the opinion of the Federal Court *(Bundesgericht)*:

1. The [Seller's assignee] did not cross-appeal the dismissal of its claim for damages, with the consequence that, to this extent, the judgment appealed against becomes legally effective.

2.

2.1. An argument must generally be made with respect to the extent that the appeal complied with time limits and requirements as to form, as the final decision appealed against concerns a civil law dispute and cannot be appealed against by proper cantonal legal proceedings (Art. 48(1) OG [*]). In addition, the necessary value of the dispute of CHF 8,000 has been reached (Art. 46 OG).

2.2 It can be asserted in the appeal that the final decision appealed against concerned an infringement of federal law, including international agreements concluded by the federal state (Art. 43(1) OG). One such agreement is the United Nations Convention on Contracts for the International Sale of Goods (CISG or UN Sales Law, SR 0.221.211.1). This is applicable in the present case as the sales contract in dispute was concluded between two parties whose place of business lies in different Contracting States (Art. 1(1)(a) CISG).

2.3 According to Art. 55(1)(c) OG [*], which provisions of federal law and to which extent the final decision appealed against has infringed these provisions must be contained in the request for appeal. In contrast, objections to the actual determinations and to the weight given to the evidence in the previous instance are not admissible, unless an obvious mistake or an infringement of federal evidentiary law provisions (Art. 63(2) OG) or incomplete determination of the facts is being alleged (Art. 64 OG; BGE [*] 120 II 97 Reason 2b p 99; 119 II 84 Reason 3; 116 II 93 Reason 2, 489 Reason d, 749, with references).

The [Buyer] infringes these provisions if it attempts to call the findings of the Court of Appeal regarding the defects into doubt without asserting one of the named exceptions.

To this extent, no argument is to be made on appeal.

2.4 The request of the [Buyer] to order the [Seller's assignee] to collect the machine is new and therefore inadmissible (Art. 55(1)(b) OG).

3.

3.1 Under the UN Sales Law, the buyer must examine the goods, or cause them to be examined, within a short a period as is practicable in the circumstances (Art. 38(1) CISG). It loses the right to rely on a lack of conformity of the goods if it does not give notice to the seller specifying [in the German version: precisely] the nature of the lack of conformity within a reasonable time after it has discovered it or ought to have discovered it (Art. 39(2) [sic – correct: Art. 39(1)] CISG). Whether these time periods have been complied with is for the court to decide in its own discretion. The Federal Supreme Court (*Bundesgericht*) is generally free to examine discretionary decisions in appellate proceedings. However, it thereby exercises restraint and only intervenes if the previous instance has deviated from the principles recognized in academic opinion and jurisprudence without reason, if it has taken account of facts that should not have played any role in the decision in the case at hand, or if it, conversely, has failed to consider circumstances that it would have been obliged to consider. The Federal Supreme Court (*Bundesgericht*) will also intervene in discretionary decisions if they prove to be obviously inequitable or manifestly unjust (BGE [*] 127 III 351 Reason 4a p 354, with further references).

3.2 Upon a consideration of academic opinion and jurisprudence, the Court of Appeal (*Obergericht*) assumed in the present case that a period of examination of one week and a period of notification of one month could be accepted, in which case the notification dated 26 August 1996 took place in good time. In addition, on 5 September 1996, the [Buyer] gave a new, more detailed notification of defects, which was, in any case, one month after it would have had to have been assumed that it had discovered the defects notified. Upon a consideration of the circumstance that a representative of the Seller examined the machine again on 29 August 1996, the second and more detailed notification of the defects dated 5 September 1996 would also in no way appear to have been made too late. In respect of this finding, the Court of Appeal (*Obergericht*) does not appear to have exceeded its discretion. This has also not been asserted by the [Seller's assignee].

4.

4.1 The Court of Appeal (*Obergericht*) accepted that, with the notification of defects dated 5 September 1996, the [Buyer] had notified that the distillation regulator was defective, that the stainless steel (*Nieroster*) container leaked, that the condensed water was not being separated off, that the booster pump for the cleaner was not connected and adjusted and that the impregnating pump was not delivered. In addition, the Court of Appeal (*Obergericht*) indicated that although the experts stated that the functionality of the machine was not guaranteed, as it did not meet the requirements of a standard prototype, the [Buyer] nevertheless failed to notify the [Seller's assignee] of this defect. Similarly, the [Buyer] also failed to notify the [Seller's assignee] that the measuring cells on the nitrogen generator were defective and that the nitrogen generator itself was dirty and had been poorly maintained. Therefore, contrary to the view of the Local District Court (*Amtsgericht*), the [Buyer] could not derive any rights from this defect.

4.2 The [Buyer] alleges that the Court of Appeal (*Obergericht*) incorrectly only examined the defects that were individually mentioned in its letter dated 5 September 1996. The court failed to consider that, in this letter, the [Buyer] had generally notified of an "unusable machine delivery" and that the individual defects were only to be understood as referring to the problem areas, to which, in the opinion of the [Buyer], the lack of functionability could be attributed. Thereby, the [Buyer] gave sufficient notice that the machine was unusable.

4.3 The UN Sales Law was drafted in Arabic, English, French, Spanish, Russian and Chinese. It was also translated into German, among other languages. In the case of ambiguity in the wording, reference is to be had to the original versions, whereby the English version, and, secondarily, the French version are given a higher significance as English and French were the official languages of the Conference and the negotiations were predominantly conducted in English (Witz, in *International Einheitliches Kaufrecht, Praktiker-Kommentar und Vertragsgestaltung zum CISG* by Witz/Salger/Lorenz, Art. 7 CISG, para. 20; Achilles, *Kommentar zum UN-Kaufrechtsübereinkommen (CISG)*, Art. 7 CISG, para 4; cf. also Siehr, in Honsell (ed), *Kommentar zum UN-Kaufrecht*, Präambel, para. 6; Ferrari, in Schlechtriem (ed), *Kommentar zum Einheitlichen UN-Kaufrecht*, 3rd ed, Art. 7 CISG, para. 35). According to the German translation of Art. 39(1) CISG, the buyer must precisely specify the nature of the lack of conformity in the notice to the seller. The English and French texts of the Convention talk about "specifying the nature of the lack of conformity" and "*en précisant la nature de ce défaut*", respectively. Thereby, the notice must specify the nature, type or character of the lack of conformity (cf. Merriam-Webmaster Dictionary, which defines "nature", being a synonym for "essence", as "the inherent character or basic constitution of a person or thing", cf. also Le Grand Robert de la langue française, which equates "nature" with "essence"). What must be considered is that the verbs "specify" and "*préciser*" can not only be translated as "*genau bezeichnen*" (precisely describe), but also with "*bezeichnen*" (describe) or with "*angeben*" (indicate). Consequently, the original versions do not require the description to be as precise as could be expected from the German translation (Schwenzer, in Schlechtriem (ed), *Kommentar zum Einheitlichen UN-Kaufrecht*, 3rd ed, Art. 39 CISG, para. 6; Michael G. Gerny, *Untersuchungs- und Rügepflichten beim Kauf nach schweizerischem, französischem und US-amerikanischem Recht sowie nach CISG*, Diss. Basle 1999, p 196). According to those texts, a notification of defects that (precisely) indicates the nature or the character of the lack of conformity is sufficient. The wording of Art. 39(1) CISG does not require a more precise circumscription. This is also not necessary, as in this day and age of electronic communication, the seller can be expected to ask questions in any case if he desires more precise instructions from the buyer (cf. Schwenzer, *ibid*, Art. 39 CISG, para. 8; David Rüetschi, Substanziierung der Mängelrüge, *recht* 2003, p 115 et seq, p 121; Gerny, *ibid*, p 199). In order to circumscribe the nature or type of the lack of conformity, it is sufficient if the buyer communicates that a machine or parts thereof are not functioning and indicates the appropriate symptoms. It is not necessary that he also elaborate the causes of the functional faults (Schwenzer, *ibid*, Art. 39 CISG, para. 7; Lüderitz/Schüssler-Langeheine, in Soergel (ed), *Kommentar zum Bürgerlichen Gesetzbuch*, 13th ed, vol 13 CISG, Art. 39 CISG, para. 8; Hans-Josef Vogel, *Die Untersuchungs- und Rügepflicht im UN-Kaufrecht*, Diss. Bonn 2000, p 98 et seq). To the extent that the seller is not aware of the intention of the buyer's declaration, its notification of defects and other behavior is to be interpreted in the way a reasonable person in the same position as that of the seller under the same circumstances would have understood it (Art. 8(2) CISG).

4.4 The [Buyer] indicated in its letter dated 5 September 1996 that the delivered machine was not usable. This statement is to be appreciated in its context. Additionally, the [Buyer] then stated the individual functional faults or missing parts, respectively, and demanded the removal of the problems. It is evident from the request to make repair and the faults listed individually that the [Buyer] was not notifying the [Seller's assignee] of the general lack of functionability based on its construction, but rather regarded the machine as defective but generally functional. Therefore, the Court of Appeal (*Obergericht*) correctly accepted that the lack of functionality of the machine owing to the failure to meet a prototype standard, which was determined by the experts, was not notified by the [Buyer]. The fact that the [Buyer] indicated the defects again, shows that the list of defects was to be understood as exhaustive. As the nitrogen generator was not included in this list, the [Seller's assignee] could have assumed that there was no objection in this regard. Thereby, the Court of Appeal (*Obergericht*) correctly found that to this extent, a notification of defects was lacking, and that the Buyer, therefore, could not derive any rights from the defectiveness of the nitrogen generator and the insufficient technical standard of the machine.

5.

5.1 The Court of Appeal (*Obergericht*) then stated that the expert report obtained basically concluded that, in relation to the defects notified in the letter dated 5 September 1996, with the exception of the missing impregnating pump, there was neither evidence indicating the existence or non-existence of such. As these defects were notified within the period under Art 39 CISG, the seller must generally prove that these lacks of conformity did not exist at the point in time in question.

However, in the present case, the [Buyer] disassembled the apparatus, which led to the expert being unable to make any statement with respect to the defects notified, with the exception of the missing impregnating pump. In accordance therewith, the evidentiary difficulties were allegedly caused by the [Buyer], in which case it seems justified that it bear the consequences of the lack of evidence. Thereby, the [Buyer] can only derive rights from the missing impregnating pump, as the remaining defects notified could not have been proved.

5.2 The [Buyer] states that the Court of Appeal (*Obergericht*) incorrectly found that it had to prove that the defects were notified on time. The court allegedly failed to consider that the impossibility of providing evidence was to be borne by the Seller, as it did not deliver any connection diagram and therefore made the re-commencement of operation of the three machine components stored at various places impossible.

5.3 According to the prevailing academic opinion, the allocation of the burden of proof forms part of the matters regulated in the UN Sales Law (Siehr, in Honsell (ed), *Kommentar zum UN-Kaufrecht*, Art. 4 CISG, para. 10; Magnus, in *J. von Staudingers Kommentar zum Bürgerlichen Gesetzbuch, Wiener UN-Kaufrecht (CISG)*, 13th revision, Art. 4 CISG, para. 63; Ferrari, *ibid*, Art. 4 CISG, para. 49, with further references). If the UN Sales Law is lacking an express rule on the burden of proof, then this gap is to be filled in accordance with the general principles upon which this Convention is based (Art. 7(2) CISG; Schnyder/Straub, in Honsell (ed), *Kommentar zum UN-Kaufrecht*, Art. 45 CISG, para 68). That, generally, each party is obliged to prove the actual elements of the provision acting in its respective favor is recognized as such a principle (Magnus, *ibid*, Art. 4 CISG, para. 67; Ferrari, *ibid*, Art. 4 CISG, para. 52; Achilles, *Kommentar zum UN Kaufrechtsübereinkommen (CISG)*, Art. 4 CISG, para. 15; Witz, *ibid*, Art. 7 CISG, para. 93). Furthermore, a party who is relying on an exception generally has to prove the actual elements of such exception (Magnus, *ibid*, Art. 4 CISG, para. 68; Ferrari, *ibid*, Art. 4 CISG, para. 50, with further references; cf. also Schnyder/Straub, *ibid*, Art. 45 CISG, para. 68, who differentiate between the existence of the general and the opposing facts). Finally, that facts from an area that is clearly better known to one party than to the other are to be proven by the party that has the control over this area is also recognized as a principle (Magnus, *ibid*, Art. 4 CISG, para. 69; Ferrari, *ibid*, Art. 4 CISG, para. 51; Schnyder/Straub, *ibid*, Art. 45 CISG, para. 68; Clemens Antweiler, *Beweislastverteilung im UN-Kaufrecht*, Diss, Mainz 1994, p 96 *et seq*). If the proximity to the evidence and a party's possibility to prove facts are observed, then evidentiary problems should be avoided.

According to the principle that a party has to prove the elements of a provision acting in its favor, a seller who demands the purchase price must prove that delivery was made in conformity with the contract and a buyer who bases a defense (e.g., for rescission of the contract or for a reduction of the price) on the lack of conformity of the goods must prove the lack of conformity. Thereby, according to the principle mentioned, both parties bear the burden of proving conformity with the contract, to the extent that they derive rights from the presence or lack of such conformity. Consequently, as there is no exception in the present case, the allocation of the burden of proof regarding the lack of conformity of the goods is to be ascertained by reference to proximity to the evidence. Following this principle, the transfer of the goods to the buyer's sphere of control is decisive. This is in accordance with the jurisprudence of the German Federal Supreme Court (*BGH*), whereby a buyer who has accepted the goods without objection has then to prove their lack of conformity. Acceptance under Art. 60(d) [sic – correct: Art. 60(b)] CISG means the physical assumption of the goods (Judgment of the BGH dated 8 March 1995, BGHZ 129 p 75 *et seq*, p 81; CISG-online No 144, Reasons 1b/aa; cf. also the judgment of the Frankfurt am Main Court of Appeal (*Oberlandesgericht*) dated 13 June 1991, NJW 1991, p 3102, CISG-online No 23; coming to the same result: Judgment of the Cour d'appel, Mons (Belgium) dated 8 March 2001 [R.G. 1999/242]; concurring: Achilles, *ibid*, Art. 4 CISG, para. 15; Ferrari, *ibid*, Art. 4 CISG, para. 52; Burghard Piltz, *Neue Entwicklungen im UN-Kaufrecht*, NJW 2003, p 2056 *et seq*, p 2061; coming to the same result: Schnyder/Straub, *ibid*, Art. 50 CISG, para 58; Bianca, in: *Commentary on the International Sales Law, the 1980 Vienna Sales Convention*, Bianca/Bonell (eds), Art. 36 CISG, para. 3.1.). In contrast thereto, the view has been supported that an acceptance of the goods without notification of lack of conformity can only be assumed after the period for examining the goods and notifying the lack of conformity has expired without having being made use of. If defects were to have been notified within this period, then the seller would be obliged to prove that these defects were not in existence at the time of the passing of the risk (Huber, in: Schlechtriem (ed), *Kommentar zum Einheitlichen UN-Kaufrecht*, 3rd ed, Art. 45 CISG, para. 13; Schwenzer, *ibid*, Art. 35 CISG, para. 49; Antweiler, *ibid*, p 169; cf. also the judgment of the Zurich Commercial Court (*Handelsgericht*) dated 30 November 1998, SZIER 1999, p 185 *et seq*, p 188). However, this view does not take account of the situation that, after being accepted by the buyer, the goods are solely within his sphere of control and he is therefore in a better position to prove the existence of a lack of conformity than the seller is to prove the absence of such. Particularly during the reasonable period of time in which the buyer is to notify defects under Art. 39 CISG, the seller then has no possibility to secure evidence. According thereto, it is justified that the buyer, who has accepted the goods and has obtained control over them, be required to prove the lack of conformity of the delivered goods, to the extent that he is asserts rights on this basis.

5.4 It follows from the above that the [Buyer] who has accepted and taken possession of the delivered machine, must also be required to prove its lack of conformity, to the extent that he based his right to avoid the contract or reduce the purchase price on this. Therefore, in the end result, the Court of Appeal

(*Obergericht*) has allocated the burden of proof in conformity with federal law. However, it is insignificant that the machine was disassembled by the [Buyer], as this act only made its own submission of evidence more difficult, and not that of the [Seller's assignee] (cf. judgment of the BGH dated 25 June 1997, NJW 1997, 3311 *et seq*, CISG-online No.277, Reason 2). It is also irrelevant whether the Seller delivered diagrams, as the [Buyer] did not give timely notice of the absence of these plans and cannot, therefore, derive any rights from this from an evidentiary law perspective.

6.

6.1 The [Buyer] bases a claim of avoidance of the contract primarily on the contractual lacks of conformity it asserts. In its appeal, the [Buyer] indicates the foundation for this claim, in summary, as being that the machine was not able to be used for professional cleaning of laundry due to the insufficient technical standard and was thereby obviously unsuitable for the use as set out in the contract. Therein lay a fundamental breach of contract, which could justify the avoidance of the contract in accordance with Art 49(1)(a) CISG. This reasoning cannot be upheld, as the [Buyer], contrary to its assumption, did not notify of the insufficient technical standard and cannot, therefore, derive any rights from this (cf. Reason 4 above). The lack of conformity notified by the [Buyer], with the exception of the missing impregnating pump, could not be proven by it. The [Buyer] did not assert, and it is also not apparent, that this lack of conformity amounted to a fundamental breach; therefore, the [Buyer]'s claim for avoidance of the contract should be denied. It is thereby insignificant whether the [Buyer] timely declared the contract avoided, which was denied by the Court of Appeal (*Obergericht*). Therefore, owing to the lack of sufficient interest warranting legal protection (*Rechtsschutzinteresse*), the criticism the [Buyer] directed against this is not to be argued (cf. BGE [*] 122 III 279, Reason 3a, p 282).

6.2 The alternative claim for reduction of the purchase price was dismissed by the Court of Appeal (*Obergericht*) with the reasoning that a decrease in value of the machine owing to the missing impregnating pump could not be determined, as, due to the failure to meet prototype standard, the machine would be worthless anyway. In what way this reasoning is supposed to infringe federal civil law was not set out by the [Buyer] and is also not apparent. Thereby, the ultimate application for return of the matter in dispute for a new determination of the reduction in value is to be dismissed.

7. Owing to the above, the appeal is dismissed. On this result of the proceedings, the [Buyer] must bear the costs and the amount of reimbursement (Art.156(1) and Art.159(2) OG).

Holding

Therefore, the Federal Court (*Bundesgericht*) holds that:

1. The appeal is dismissed.
2. The court fees of CHF 2,000 are to be borne by the [Buyer].
3. The [Buyer] must reimburse the [Seller's assignee] with CHF 2,500 for the federal court proceedings.

Translator's note on abbreviations:

BGB *Bürgerliches Gesetzbuch* [German Civil Code];

BGE *Entscheidungen des Bundesgerichts* [Official Collection of Decisions of the Swiss Federal Court];

CHF Swiss Francs;

DM German Marks (no longer in circulation);

OG *Bundesgesetz vom 16. Dezember 1943 über die Organisation der Bundesrechtspflege* [Swiss Federal Rules of (Civil) Procedure];

SR *Systematische Sammlung des Bundesrechts* [Systematic Collection of Swiss Federal Law].

Case commentary
Switzerland Federal Supreme Court *(Bundesgericht)*, 13 November 2003

*Commentary by Florian Mohs**

*Translation by Mariel Dimsey**

The judgment to be discussed raises two questions on the application of the CISG. Firstly, it concerns the requirements as to content of a notification of defects under Art. 39(1) CISG [1.]. Secondly, the Federal Court (*Bundesgericht*) takes a position on the issue of the allocation of the burden of proof in the event of delivery of goods lacking conformity with the contract [2.].

1. With respect to the abstract explanation of the legal position under the CISG, the Federal Supreme Court (*Bundesgericht*) finds absolute approval.[1] It clarifies that the decisive original texts, particularly the English and French version, formulate Art. 39(1) CISG more generously than the German translation and require a general, but not "precise" description of the lack of conformity.[2] In the case of delivery of a machine, only the symptoms, but not the causes of the lack of conformity must be mentioned.[3] In the age of electronic communication, an exact clarification of the situation could be left to questions of the Seller.[4]

However, the Federal Supreme Court (*Bundesgericht*) must be clearly contradicted in the application of this legal position to the case at hand. In its notification, the Buyer had used the heading "Unusable Machine Delivery" and had stated in this letter that the "machine was unusable", the "machine distillation system did not function" and "the delivered machine components did not function".[5] However, the Federal Supreme Court (*Bundesgericht*) still manages to come to the conclusion that the Buyer viewed the machine as "defective but generally functional".[6] To the

---

* Florian Mohs and Mariel Dimsey are Research and Teaching Assistants at the University of Basel, Switzerland.

1 BGE 130 III 258, 262, Reason 4.3.

2 Cf. Schwenzer, in: Schlechtriem/Schwenzer, *Kommentar zum Einheitlichen UN-Kaufrecht – CISG -*, 4th ed 2004, Art. 39 para. 6.

3 Cf. Schwenzer, *ibid*, Art. 39. para. 8.

4 Cf. Schwenzer, *ibid*, Art. 39 para. 7.

5 BGE 130 III 258, 259, Facts under A.

6 BGE 130 III 258, 263, Reason 4.4.; this argument is also decisively rejected by Stalder, *Die Beweislast und wichtige Rügemodalitäten bei vertragswidriger Warenlieferung nach UN-Kaufrecht (CISG)*, AJP 2004, under IV.A.

extent that the Federal Supreme Court (*Bundesgericht*) focuses on the fact that the Buyer did not state individual defects, it should be admitted that a Buyer generally has to indicate each various defect individually.[7] However, in the case at hand, the Buyer listed five defects, but forgot two others. This was sufficient for it to lose the proceedings, as the Federal Supreme Court (*Bundesgericht*) assessed its incomplete list as "exhaustive".[8] In my opinion, the context of the list together with the general assessment of the performance of the machine was totally misconstrued. However, the Federal Supreme Court's (*Bundesgericht's*) assessment of the two "forgotten" defects cannot be upheld by a substantial examination either. That the Buyer did not notify the "insufficient technical standard of the machine" cannot be substantiated by the excerpts from the letter of notification cited above. The fact that the Federal Supreme Court (*Bundesgericht*) was lacking details regarding the nitrogen generator is to be held against the result that, by entering into this argument, the step would be taken in the area of stating causes, which the Federal Supreme Court (*Bundesgericht*) itself, in its abstract portrayal of the legal position, does not require. Finally, it can be ascertained that the notification, which was objected to on account of its content, resulted from a joint examination by the Buyer and the representatives of the Seller. The purpose of the requirements of certainty in a notification, namely to give knowledge to the contractual partner to the greatest extent possible,[9] was not achievable with this notification right from the very start, as the Seller itself had already obtained knowledge through its representatives.[10] The statements of the Federal Supreme Court (*Bundesgericht*) appear unnecessary on these facts, as well as being incorrect *obiter dicta*.

2. The question of the (objective) allocation of the burden of proof, which is not expressly dealt with in the CISG, can be decided in accordance with the general principles of the Convention, Art. 7(2) CISG.[11] Each party must prove the facts that fulfill the elements of a provision that is favorable to it.[12] From this, the Federal Supreme Court (*Bundesgericht*) concludes that the lack of conformity of the goods at the time of the passing of risk in the case of a claim for the purchase price is to be proven by the seller, in the case of a remedy claim (cure, damages or (partial) repayment of the purchase price after avoidance or a reduction of the price), by the

---

7 Cf. Schwenzer, *ibid*, Art 39. para. 10.

8 BGE 130 III 258, 263, Reason 4.4.

9 Cf. Schwenzer, *ibid*, Art. 39 para. 6.

10 BGE 130 III 258, Facts under A.

11 Cf. Schwenzer, *ibid*, Art. 35 para. 49. On the application of the CISG on this issue in detail, Ferrari, CISG and Private International Law, in: Ferrari (ed), *The 1980 Uniform Sales Law, Old Issues Revisited in the Light of Recent Experiences*, Sellier.ELP/Giuffrè: Munich/Milan (2003), pp 19, 40 et seq, with further references.

12 Cf. Ferrari, in: Schlechtriem/Schwenzer, *Kommentar zum Einheitlichen UN-Kaufrecht – CISG –*, 4th ed 2004, Art. 7 para. 56.

buyer.[13] The Federal Supreme Court (*Bundesgericht*) thereby overlooks that the conformity of the goods is not a requirement of a claim for the purchase price. Rather, the case of lack of conformity is concerned with a defense of the buyer (right of retention, reduction of the price or avoidance of the contract), the presence of which, on its elements, is consequentially to be proven by the buyer.[14] A widely held opinion in the German literature that a principle of the Convention derived from Art. 79(1) CISG generally attributes the promisor with the burden of proof for the performance of its obligation, here namely the Seller for the burden of proof for the conformity of the goods at the time of delivery, is similarly unpersuasive. Here, a far too obvious attempt is being made to transcribe the German doctrine of performance (*Erfüllungslehre*) (§ 363 BGB) into the uniform sales law. According to a correct reading, under Art. 79(1) CISG, the Seller can attempt to prove that the determined (!) lack of conformity is based on an impediment beyond its control that was neither foreseeable nor able to be overcome. The opinion advocated here is supported by the principle of the proximity of evidence, which has been regarded as a general principle of the CISG by the Federal Supreme Court (*Bundesgericht*).[15] Owing to its control over the goods, the buyer is in a better position to collect and secure evidence. The importation of Argentinean citrus fruits into Germany may serve as an example: the Argentina-based seller has practically no possibility to rebuke the claim of the German-based buyer that the fruit was already rotten at the time of the passing of the risk. However, support for the claim of the buyer is found in the circumstantial evidence that the rottenness of the fruit was already inherent in the core, or that the goods were not properly packed or chilled. However, even in the case of a complex machine, the buyer can usually more easily demonstrate that a lack of conformity is not to be attributed to incorrect use by its people, but rather to a fault in the machine.[16] Therefore, it can be ascertained as a preliminary result that generally the buyer has to prove the lack of conformity of the goods at the time of the passing of the risk.[17]

---

13 BGE 130 III 258, 265, Reason 5.3.

14 Probably also incorrect: Hager, in: Schlechtriem/Schwenzer, *ibid*, Art. 67 para. 11. In contrast, correct: Kruisinga, *(Non-)conformity in the 1980 UN Convention on Contracts for the International Sale of Goods: a uniform concept?*, 2004, p 170.

15 BGE 130 III 258, 264, 265, Reason 5.3.

16 Cf. in this regard BGH, 3 November 1999, CISG-online 475.

17 Also reaching the same result: *Chicago Prime Packers, Inc. v. Northam Food Trading Co.*, U.S. Dist. Ct. (N. D. Ill.), 24 May 2004, CISG-online 851, IHR 2004, 156, 159; Kruisinga, *ibid*, pp 168-177; Ferrari, *ibid* (Fn. 12), Art 4 para 52. Differentiating: Staudinger/Magnus, *Wiener UN-Kaufrecht (CISG)*, Art. 35 para. 55, Art 36. para. 25, according to whom the buyer must prove the lack of conformity at the time of the actual handing over of the goods; however, the seller is responsible for giving contrary evidence of the conformity at the time of the passing of the risk. That, firstly, giving contrary evidence is (procedurally) always possible,

Every reversal of the burden of proof that affects the seller is to be established based on this approach.[18] The rule established in the literature and case law, that where the goods are accepted without notifying of defects, the buyer bears the burden of proof,[19] is, in the author's opinion, to be so understood that the seller bears the burden of proof if the buyer gives notice of defects immediately, i.e., when it physically takes over the goods.[20] This must also apply when the buyer notifies after a short period of examination within the meaning of Art 58(3) CISG.[21] It is only right that the seller bear the burden of proof if the buyer rejects the goods; technically speaking, if it asserts a right of retention with respect to the obligation to take over the goods.[22] The much more further-reaching opinion that, where substantiated notice is given within a reasonable period of time, the burden of proof is also transferred to the seller,[23] is to be rejected. According thereto, the buyer would only bear the burden of proof in cases where it had not made proper or timely notice, namely in cases in which, under Art. 39(1) CISG, it is usually precluded; in such cases the allocation of the burden of proof is no longer relevant. In practice, the burden of proof would only affect the buyer in cases of Art. 40 and Art. 44 CISG; according to *Antweiler*, also in cases of hidden defects.[24] In that way, a far-reaching mechanism of loss of legal rights owing to failure to notify and reversal of the burden of proof would be put in motion, which would detract from the independence of the

---

and, secondly, the risk of *non liquet* ("at the passing of risk") is not clearly attributable to one party, is to be held against this opinion.

18 Cf. BGH, 9 January 2002, IHR 2002, 16-21; commented on by Perales Viscasillas, *VJ* 2002, 217-228. In this judgment, a reversal of the burden of proof based on national law was affirmed, as the seller had recognized the lack of conformity.

19 Cf. BGH, 8 March 1995, CISG-online 144; Schwenzer, *ibid*, Art. 35 para. 49, with further references; also Staudinger/Magnus, *ibid*, Art. 36 para. 26.

20 Differing Kruisinga, *ibid*, p 174.

21 This period is not to be confused with that under Art. 38 CISG.

22 There are insubstantial differences in between the German version, cf. Germany: Abnahmepflicht; Switzerland, Austria: Annahmepflicht.

23 But see Stalder, *ibid*, III.E. Obergericht des Kantons Luzern, 12 May 2003, CISG-online 846, thereto the summary of the Federal Justicial Office (*Bundesamt für Justiz*) in SZIER 2004, 103, 104, 105; cf. also Antweiler, *Beweislastverteilung im UN-Kaufrecht insbesondere bei Vertragsverletzungen des Verkäufers*, Diss Mainz 1994, pp 162-171; Henninger, *Die Frage der Beweislast im Rahmen des UN-Kaufrechts – zugleich eine rechtsvergleichende Grundlagenstudie zur Beweislast*, Diss Munich 1994, p 222; Baumgärtel/Laumen, *Handbuch der Beweislast im Privatrecht*, Vol 2, 2nd ed 1999, Art. 35 WKR para. 1, Art. 36 WKR para 11 *et seq.*

24 The circumstance that, in cases of hidden defects, the period under Art. 39(1) CISG begins to run anew from the time of discovery (cf. Schwenzer, *ibid*, Art. 39 para. 20, with further references), is held by Antweiler against the fact that Art. 39 CISG, independent, reasonable time period is concerned, cf. Antweiler, *ibid*, p 168, 169. This construction creates an important case of application for this opinion, but is to be rejected as non-practical.

allocation of the burden of proof. In addition, the opinion that the calculation of a reasonable period is, above all, dependent on the circumstances of the individual case, usually resulting, however, in a period of (at least) one month, has received support at an international level.[25] The period begins to run upon expiry of the period of examination, with the consequence that a total of several months could go by without the buyer ever having to bear the burden of proof. Under this opinion, one could easily establish a notion of protection for the buyer, which is only present in this way under national consumer protection law.[26] The CISG would become unattractive for trade transaction, which is why this opinion is to be rejected.

With respect to the case at hand, the issue is raised as to whether the Seller would have had to have been assigned the burden of proof. The Seller, through its representatives, had the machine and its components examined in order to compile a "report of findings". In such a situation, the argument of physical proximity can no longer be upheld. Rather, the Seller's (usually) greater knowledge of the goods must be taken into account. This is all the more so as, in the present case, a complex machine was being dealt with. As a result, in the case of delivery of a machine and the mutual possibility of being able to secure evidence, the Seller must bear the burden of proof. Based on this result, the considerations of the Court of Appeal (*Obergericht*) that the Buyer knowingly disassembled the machine and kept the parts thereof at different locations in order to create evidentiary difficulties, are to be given due regard. As the Seller bears the burden of proof, a frustration of evidence, to be judged under national procedural law,[27] could be present here, as was held by the Court of Appeal (*Obergericht*).[28]

By and large, an assessment of the Federal Supreme Court (*Bundesgericht*) judgment discussed turns out to be inconsistent. The Federal Supreme Court's (*Bundesgericht*) application of the notification of defects under the requirements of the CISG gives rise to a variety of criticism and is consequently not persuasive. With respect to the allocation of the burden of proof in the event of delivery of non-conforming goods,

---

25 Cf. instead of all these, Schwenzer, *ibid*, Art. 39 para. 17 and CISG-AC, Op. No. 2 (Bergsten), *Examination of the Goods and Notice of Non-Conformity – Articles 38 and 39*, IHR 2004, 163, available at: http://www.cisg-online.ch/cisg/docs/CISG-AC_Op_no_2.pdf. However, the supporters of the opinion that the burden of proof is connected to the expiry of the period of examination still assumed a short period closely resembling that under ULIS, cf. Antweiler, *ibid*, pp 164, 165; differing Stalder, *ibid*, IV.B.

26 Cf. § 476 BGB.

27 Even if the frustration of evidence is sanctioned by a reversal of the burden of proof, the effects of this are determined under the procedural law of the lex fori.

28 BGE 130 III 258, 266, Reason 5.4. See also BGH, 25 June 1997, CISG-online 277, Reason II.2.

the Federal Supreme Court (*Bundesgericht*) resolved a difficult issue of valuation at the highest judicial level. The direction adopted, that the buyer generally bears the burden of proof for the lack of conformity at the time of the passing of the risk, is to be affirmed; it is now the task of scholarly opinion and case law to develop exceptions in which a reversal of the burden of proof in favor of the buyer is indicated.